# FROM EARLY WARNING TO EARLY ACTION?

## The debate on the enhancement of the EU's Crisis Response capability continues

EUROPEAN COMMISSION

EXTERNAL RELATIONS DIRECTORATE-GENERAL

DIRECTORATE Crisis Platform and Policy Coordination in CFSP

Manuscript completed in 2008

The contents of this publication do not necessarily reflect the opinion or position
of the European Commission's Directorate-General for External Relations.

For weekly news by e-mail from the Directorate-General for External Relations, please visit this site:
http://ec.europa.eu/comm/external_relations/feedback/weekly.htm

Editor - Andrea Ricci, DG RELEX
Editorial, production and art work – GOPA-Cartermill
Cover photo credits: © David Sauveur / Agence VU
Cover design: © Gregorie Desmons, Art Director, GOPA-Cartermill

A great deal of additional information on the European Union is available on the Internet.
It can be accessed through the Europa server (http://europa.eu).

Cataloguing data can be found at the end of this publication.

Luxembourg: Office for Official Publications of the European Communities, 2008

ISBN 978-92-79-07028-0

Printed in Belgium

PRINTED ON WHITE CHLORINE-FREE PAPER

# Table of Contents

# FOREWORD

In the two years since the first major conference organized by the European Commission on Crisis Response in Europe, in 2006, the European Union has enhanced its capacity to deal with international crises and natural disasters.

First, financial resources for crisis response interventions have grown substantially, reaching into the budget for CFSP/ESDP operations and the new Instrument for Stability. The year 2008 began with major EU operations in Chad and Kosovo as well as 20 ongoing and planned crisis response projects under the Stability Instrument, around the world. In addition, European institutions have strengthened their operational cooperation.

Second, EU resources are being integrated with those of Member States, NGOs and the think-tank community in Europe and beyond. We are developing a new Peace-building Partnership to promote closer co-operation between NGOs, EU institutions and Member States.

Third, we have been focusing on reacting faster to reliable early warning information, a key challenge for the European Union in the field of Crisis Response and Peace-building.

This new book illustrates the progress made in these three areas and emphasizes the nexus between early warning and early action. It is based on contributions to the Conference "From Early Warning to Early Action" of November 2007, which brought together practitioners in the field and drew on the wealth of civilian expertise on peace-building issues, identifying ways of responding to crises faster and more coherently.

Much remains to be done, but I believe that the ideas expressed in this book show what it takes for peace-building to be carried out successfully; that freedom from fear and want, freedom to take action on one's own behalf and freedom from effects of natural disasters are not utopian ideals. I commend this book, thank the contributors and look forward to further developing and implementing its ideas in the months and years to come.

BENITA FERRERO-WALDNER

# Acknowledgements

European Commission's Directorate-General for External Relations and the editor Andrea Ricci wish to thank all those without whom this work would not have been possible: first and foremost all the authors (writers, interviewees and photojournalists) who contributed to making this book special. Thanks to Christian Berger, Head of the Crisis Response and Peacebuilding Unit in DG RELEX, and to Annie Niemela and Pascal Havelange from DG Relex Crisis Room.

Thanks to the devoted team from GOPA-Cartermill for their professional work conceiving this book; Olaf Deussen (Project Manager), Gregorie Desmons (Art Director), the whole editorial team of GOPA-Cartermill and the journalists; Chris Coakley, Amy Shifflette, Gareth Harding, Daniela Schröder and Cillian Donnelly.

Thanks to Antje Herrberg, Nicolas Beger, Philippe Bartholomé from EPLO and Kristiina Rintakoski from CMI for their tremendous support before and after the "From Early Warning to Early Action" Conference (2007).

Finally thanks to Agence VU for its tremendous role in the development of the European photographic and photojournalistic culture, realised through this book.

# INTRODUCTION

Three contradictory conceptions of security clash in the contemporary public discourse: one equates security with (pre-emptive) attack, the other relates security to defence; the third connects security to peace and freedom from fear. In all three cases — the latter being the most representative of the European institutions' doctrine — the link between early warning and early action is critical to prevent the loss of human lives.

A search through open sources quickly reveals hundreds of documents describing recent systemic failures to connect warnings to action: the 2000 floods in Mozambique[1], the 2001 food security crisis in Sudan[2], the 2003 floods in the Philippines[3], the 2004 Sahel locust invasion and Niger food crisis[4], the 2006 landslide in the Philippines[5], the 2006 Tsunami in Java[6], the 2007 earthquake in Sumatra[7], the 2008 dengue fever epidemics in Paraguay[8] and bird flu in West Bengal[9]. To this, we should add *the ex* post analysis on the intelligence failures that led to the Rwandan genocide[10], to 9/11, to the War in Iraq[11], to the crisis with North Korea in 2006[12], to the "unexpected" victory of Hamas in the same year[13], to the 7/7 attacks in London[14], to the wave of terrorist attacks that shook India in 2007[15], to the Ejercito Popular Revolucionario attacks in Mexico in 2007[16], to the Red Mosque crisis in Pakistan[17], to Darfur[18], and lately, to the crisis in Kenya[19].

A warning is defined as an "intimation", a "threat", a "sign of impending danger or evil". We are surrounded by these signs. Wars have always been around us, and complete freedom from fear is a state of grace that few countries can claim to enjoy. So there is little in these areas that comes as totally "unexpected". Asia is the region of the world that, statistically, is the most exposed to deadly natural disasters. There are more than a hundred political conflicts around the world (130 according to the HIIK report for 2007), the great majority of which have deep roots going back over time. The geo-strategic implications of fossil fuel reserves have certainly not been discovered in the last decade. The spillover effect of the Middle East conflict has been with us for the last 50 years. When can policymakers really afford to claim that they have been taken by surprise?

What does explain the failures of the world's intelligence superpowers? What can justify the fact that — almost on a yearly basis — natural catastrophes continue to claim lives all over the world, regardless of the Internet, the mathematical models available, the super computers, the ground detection technologies, and the earth observation facilities? Scholars and policy-makers say we are living in an "information society": is this really the context in which strategic decisions in the field of international relations are taken?

*Andrea Ricci designed and runs the Crisis Room of the Directorate-General for External Relations of the European Commission. He conceived both Tariqa and the Directorate-General for External Relations' internal training programme for Open Source Intelligence. He represents the Commission in the working group that defines the EU watchlist. Previously he was responsible for the EuroMediterranean Information Society Initiative (EUMEDIS). Mr Ricci holds a Master's degree in European Studies from the College of Europe (Bruges). He is currently working on his PhD on "Digital Propaganda" with the Catholic University of Brussels and the Université Libre de Bruxelles.*

Joseph Stiglitz was awarded the Nobel Prize for Economics in October 2001 for his contribution to the study of imperfect information. He received the prestigious award for having criticised a key assumption of traditional economic analysis. Stieglitz's works have largely been devoted to prove and elaborate the idea that competitive markets are not *efficient*, as the classic competitive model suggests. Individuals and companies do not possess perfect information: individuals do not necessarily buy at the lowest price, while companies do not necessarily produce at the lowest costs. One of the ways we can explain the recent failures in intelligence and early warning is that we cannot rely on the assumption that "perfect information" exists in the context of diplomacy, humanitarian relief and intelligence. Policy making is often carried out on the basis of imperfect information; it's inefficient. The use of available knowledge is often not adequate to the challenges we face.

One of the causes of imperfect information is its asymmetry: if one counts the number of articles on any given country in the world as delivered daily by Google News[20] one can easily discover a set of *hypertrophic* signals (Iraq with an average of 448 articles, followed by Iran with 307 articles daily on average, and Afghanistan with 265.5) and many *hypotrophic* signals such as Venezuela (149.6), Somalia (79.6), Kenya (76.4) and Zimbabwe (64.48). Regardless of the gravity of the situation, the humanitarian implications or the losses of human lives, a strong signal "blocks out" a weak one. Iraq blocks out Iran, which blocks out Afghanistan, which blocks out Venezuela, which blocks out Somalia, Kenya and Zimbabwe. It would be totally unrealistic to assume that these asymmetries are *not* matched by equally asymmetric political attention, intelligence monitoring, project responses, public compassion etc. The attention economy and the compassion economy are inefficient, in the same way as economic behaviour in general. The shares of attention given to each conflict in the world are not all equal. Too many wars; not enough *digestible* knowledge on the vast majority of them.

Politicians, diplomats, humanitarian workers, mediators, intelligence operatives are part of the same ecosystem, constrained by the same environmental factors. They all suffer from information asymmetries. The whole point is the need to adapt to the environment. Money and human resources have not saved the world's intelligence superpowers from dramatic failures. Those who introduce change in their working methods will be able to exploit the energy available in the ecosystem to their advantage. Who will adapt first?

The Information Society – where it exists – provides the *opportunity* to acquire more information faster, often overcoming constraints of time and space. Today, across the world, the Internet generates an estimated 61 billion queries a month[21]. But will those analysts, diplomats, relief workers, and intelligence officers that only read through the *first* search results page have any form of *information superiority*? More than 4000 TV channels are available through satellite in most parts of Europe. What happens to the organisation that structures its work under the tacit knowledge that television programmes *are* not sources of professional, qualified warnings? What happens to the analytical group that refuses to treat the content of 70 million blogs[22] in order to protect themselves from disinformation? What happens to the diplomat that cannot or does not want to have meetings with all the representatives of a given country's political class? What happens to the relief team that considers as a "negative priority" the costs of online pay-per-view databases for its field operations? What happens to the policy-maker who is unaware of the difference between the BBC World Service and the BBC Monitoring? We have the opportunity to live in and take advantage of the information society, only the opportunity.

One of the tangible consequences of the growth of electronic media is the evolution of the notion of secrecy. While more and more sensitive information is leaked to the press, or through opposition newsgroups and blogs, the number of *functional secrets* is growing geometrically. Countless relevant entities, facts, events, details that nobody wants to conceal *de jure*, are becoming invisible *de facto*. Nobody was hiding the "weak signals" which progressively led Côte d'Ivoire to the 2004 crisis: everyone could have noted the semantic changes in the fabric of public debate on Abidjan.net, one of the most (if not *the* most) relevant discussion forum on the African continent. There was a visible, tangible change of tone: a rupture in the discourse tonality which ended up being matched by violent action. That content was, and still is for many who need to know, a functional secret: something that works like a secret but it is not one.

The phenomenal amount of information available (just think of the number of individual databases available through Factiva or Lexis Nexis) is theoretically within reach for every one of us, but access cost and sophisticated query syntaxes continue to be the main barriers separating decision-makers from mission-critical information. A new form of illiteracy has emerged: we all have Google but none of us knows how to make it work to its full potential. Not to mention Lexis Nexis with its Boolean operators, smart indexing etc. In 2008, it would be hard for any practitioner of CFSP in Brussels to quote an existing educational programme for ministries or security agencies dealing with the issues of sourcing and their relevance for early warning. Far too many continue to consider alternative sources of security-related information as dangerous or simply extracurricular.

The Information Society – we should probably call it the *oblivion society*[23] - is drastically widening the gap between the information we can get hold of and the information we understand. Again, this phenomenon is not new: in the 50s Harold Innis, a disciple of the Canadian Professor McLuhan, wrote "Improvements in communication [...] make for increased difficulties of understanding"[24]. The consequences today are tangible: the intelligence interception capacity (or simply the amount of information projected through various channels to the existing practitioner community) generates volumes of content; so much that the human resources available are unable to group, filter, digest and transform it into action. Those who try to adapt to the new environment without guidance are often discouraged by the fact that these new rules and tools impose a complete redefinition of the workflow and of the tacit assumptions that often hold sway in many professional environments.

With Open Source Intelligence we measure the *relative value* of an organisation's body of knowledge: what we thought was classified turns out to be in the public domain, what we discarded as being an "untrusted source" becomes (sadly, after the event) the clearest form of early warning. When we thought the field operatives had the best information pictures, we realize that the databases we could consult from our offices had more.

If, on the one hand, abundant empirical evidence seems to prove the importance of open sources in terms of early warning, on the other hand practitioners have rapidly understood that turning open source *information* into open source *intelligence* (and warnings) takes time, money and a lot of systematic work. Without sufficient financial support, it is impossible to exploit high volumes of information from multiple types of sources. Without the systematic exploitation of multiple sources (a truly trans-media exploitation) it is almost impossible to overcome the bias of media and the effect of propaganda[25]. Finally, without a multidisciplinary background it is hard to cope with the diversity of open content. Methodology is what makes the difference between watching TV, surfing the web and carrying out OSINT (Open Source Intelligence).

The alignment factor brings an additional explanatory dimension to the issue of failed early warnings. The transition from warning to action is achieved though a form of *centrifugal communication*. It is actually the repetition in eccentric circles of a basic sequence: an important detail is isolated from the stream of information; the detail is amplified and interpreted. Then the interpretation is first shared then agreed by a larger community. Every time the sequence is repeated successfully, energy and speed are added to the process. Without a communication process this energy does not succeed in crossing the borders that separate analytical units, competing risk assessment entities in a single country, and policy units across EU Member States and EU institutions. The opportunities for all these gears to misalign, to interrupt the consensus dynamics are so numerous, and the combination of co-factors generating disagreement is so large[26] that it should not surprise anyone if the system produces sub-optimal results.

When early warning fails it is often because the alignment process has been stopped in one or more locations. When warnings lead to action is because the consensus has been reached in time, or because a given political elite has chosen to act *before* the full consensus has been reached. The greater the decision-making system, the more difficult is to act before a full consensus is achieved. Therefore for most European practitioners of early warning the point is not only being capable of detecting a weak signal, but also sharing the findings with others and developing an *opinion movement* in favour of a given type of action. Advocacy groups such as International Crisis Group, the Crisis Management Initiative, and Human Rights Watch are precisely in that business. They have a chance to shape Europe's political agenda by launching warnings under their own initiative.

There is no shortage of external advocacy. To cope with the new information environment, the EU should act on the motivation dynamics of its crisis responders workforce and should encourage bottom-up initiatives. This would result in novel forms of advocacy, coming from *within* institutions and administrations. Other schools of thought, less optimistic about the chances of an endogenous organisational change of EU's early warning machinery, see in the Lisbon Treaty and in the future External Service an opportunity to *merge* in a single structure all the early warning centres established in the course of the past ten years in Brussels. This could be an effective move. The creation of a central investigative "pool" has been a key factor in the fight against Cosa Nostra. There are however other, equally necessary, moves to be made if the future EU early-warning system is to succeed. First it is necessary to understand that early warning will remain *poly-centric* in Europe. So once the several hundred officials in Brussels are under a single authority, the real challenge will be to encourage sharing, or force sharing (politically) among all the existing early warning centres across the continent. It's the challenge of the *communitarisation* of intelligence and early warning, a debate launched in 2004 by political leaders from Belgium and Austria after the terrorist bombings in Madrid. An investigative pool in Brussels will not alone boost political will. Sharing human resources and competences in Brussels will not be enough without funds and tools, both in Brussels and elsewhere. The EU also needs a "tool-pool initiative", aiming at sharing all the OSINT technology available both in Member States and in Brussels. In this respect the recent creation of both the EUROSINT Forum and of the "Club of Budapest" under the initiative of the Hungarian Minister of Foreign Affairs are encouraging signs of change.

If politics is about selective attention and subjective (if not partisan) decisions, it is unrealistic to assume that priority setting in the field of external relations will in the near future become easy to achieve at national, and a fortiori at European level. It would be equally unrealistic to pretend that *political judgment* – which is above all a matter of responsible choice – will disappear from all the European fora for CFSP, together with the notion of opportunity, prudence, public sensitivity and sovereignty.

The point is having the possibility to choose the best course of action. More intelligence and more warnings will help identify alternatives. Before we can benefit from more shared intelligence, we have to avoid reducing (or attempting to control) complexity arbitrarily. If policymakers do not possess a reference, short-termism becomes the structuring element of political judgement and the political / theoretical discourse is forced (ex post) to adapt to practice. This is another environmental challenge. To adapt to the constraints of 2008, we have to modernize diplomacy, relief work and intelligence.

Cluster analysis is a statistical exploratory tool designed to reveal natural groupings (or clusters) within a data set that would otherwise not be apparent. Cluster analysis is constantly used in electoral studies, political and mass marketing. The External Relations Directorate-General has been using it in the past few years to provide to the inter-institutional early warning community an alternative method to assess monitoring priorities worldwide. This is a method which is both objective and scientifically-based[27] since it uses a wide range of quantitative and qualitative references to assess "families" of countries sharing the same commonalities of risk. The method, as almost everything in nature, is not perfect, since it depends on a subjective selection of criteria (or indicators) of risk. These criteria however are not chosen arbitrarily as they reflect the doctrine of the Community, and data comes from some of the most prominent risk assessment think tanks worldwide. The results of the cluster analysts are very interesting: instead of having a world ranking, the analysis delivers an accurate portrait of the complexity of the world's insecurity. There are groups of countries sharing almost identical patterns of risk although they are located in very different continents. This method has great early warning potential for the entire community of crisis responders, as it overcomes the natural geographic compartmentalisation of both monitoring and project response.

Two years after the first large-scale event dedicated to the enhancement of EU's crisis response capacity, Commissioner Ferrero-Waldner addressed a new consensus conference "From Early Warning to Early action" in November 2007 in Brussels. The conference involved more than 900 diplomats, officers, practitioners, scholars and advocates, representing the complex social network of European crisis responders. This book, builds on the previous publication (Faster and More United?), and aims at extending and consolidating the debate on early warning with a wide range of relevant contributions from all the actors of crisis management, governmental and non-governmental.

The **first part** of the book serves as introduction to the key concepts and the most important changes at EU level, in particular the launch of the Instrument for Stability. It also provides key figures: according to the HIIK Conflict Barometer the overall number of political conflicts has raised slightly since the last measurement. The **second part** provides witness accounts of crisis response projects and initiatives in the Middle East, Africa, Asia and the Balkans. The **third part** is devoted to the issue of resource competition and resource wars, but also to the debate on the impact of climate change on the frequency of hazardous events. The **fourth part** focuses on the practice and organization of warning systems with a focus on conflict prevention, the fight against terrorism and weapons of mass destruction.

This book has been conceived as a manual allowing several reading paths. One, photographic, which reminds the reader of the human tragedies behind political initiatives and projects. Another is more descriptive, aiming at facilitating the learning process of the new generation of practitioners. A third is more technical, aiming at sharing new practices among the existing professionals. This volume benefits from the remarkable quality of seminal papers such as those of Johan Galtung on peacebuilding, Albrecht Schnabel on early warning methodology, and of Cedric de Coning on the unintended consequences of peacebuilding. The book is enhanced by the outspoken tone of all the interviews, particularly those featuring Maggy Barankitse - who has alone saved thousands of children victims of the Rwandan conflict - and Ambrose James on the importance of media as instrument for peace and stability in Africa.

For a more expert audience it is important to point readers with little time at their disposal to the technical quality of the contributions coming from European practitioners (for example Alain Gachet's methodology for uncovering buried aquifers in Sudan and Chad, and Helène Lavoix who delivers one of the first comparative analyses of the existing systems for early warning) and from UN experts working in the most qualified UN agencies. Finally, this book offers EU policy and decision-makers the opportunity to reflect on the growing importance of Track II diplomacy as one of the most interesting tools at the disposal of EU policymakers in the field of peacebuilding.

Official documents on the new Instrument for Stability and practical information on the Peacebuilding Partnership are also annexed to this work to foster the involvement of European non-state actors in peacebuilding and crisis response.

1  'Dealing with natural hazards in Mozambique: the case of the 2000 floods' http://www.fao.org/docrep/007/ae079e/ae079e05.htm
2  "Déjà vu: Early Warning and Late Response—General Reasons for a Recurrent Problem' http://www.fews.net/centers/files/East_200105en.pdf
3  'See http://www.fao.org/wairdocs/ad695e/ad695e04.htm#TopOfPage
4  "Programme performance of the United Nations for the biennium 2004-2005' www.un.org/depts/oios/mecd/a_61_64e.doc
5  "Philippines was aware of risks of landslides ; Manila knew of danger as early as May' - 22 February 2006, *The International Herald Tribune*; by Carlos H. Conde. Also but also 'Danger of Philippine Landslides Often Ignored, Critics Say', 21 February 2006, The New York Times By Carlos H. Conde.
6  "False hopes and real disasters' 27 December 2006, *The International Herald Tribune*
7  "Sumatra jolted by 2 more quakes, but spared a tsunami', 14 September 2007, *The International Herald Tribune*. A radio and Internet early warning system installed in Padang in response to the 2004 tsunami failed to work.
8  'Critics have said the government failed to give people early warnings when the disease first broke out in the country last January. The government finally managed to control the disease in May.
9  "HOW WEST BENGAL ALLOWED BIRD FLU TO FLY' 23 January 2008, *Indian Express*.
10 "'Both early and late warnings of the Rwandan genocide were ignored by policy-makers who denied the facts, resisted calling the genocide by its proper name, refused to consider options for intervention, and finally refused to risk any lives of their citizens. Instead they withdrew 2000 UNAMIR troops and sacrificed the lives of over 500,000 defenseless Rwandans" from http://www.genocidewatch.org/EarlyWarningbyGregoryStanton.htm
11 '31 July 31, 2007 Tuesday 8:45 PM GMT, *Associated Press Worldstream* 'British PM says UK will meet its obligations in Iraq, acknowledges British intelligence failures' Paul Burkhardt, Associated Press Writer
   'White House Missing CIA, Iraq E-Mails', 19 January, 2008 11:55 AM GMT, Associated Press Online
   'Dropping a bomb on Israel', 7 December 2007, *The Jerusalem Post*
   In 2004, a Knesset committee established to investigate intelligence assessments in the run up to the Iraq War found that Military Intelligence and the Mossad had failed to assess the true dangers posed by Saddam Hussein. The probe, headed by Likud MK Yuval Steinitz, then head of the Knesset's Foreign Affairs and Defense Committee, ruled that there had been a serious intelligence failure" regarding the assessments of Iraq's weapons of mass destruction capabilities and that there was a need for a reorganization within the intelligence agencies.
12 'Intelligence failure cited in Korean crisis - Officials say uncertainty hindered diplomacy' 12 October  2006, *The Washington Times* By Bill Gertz
13 27 May 2006, *The Jakarta Post* 'THE HAMAS DEBACLE AND THE THREAT OF CIVIL WAR IN PALESTINE'
14 13 May 2006, *The Guardian* (London) - 'July 7 reports: Intelligence bungles in build-up to 7/7 attacks' 'July 7 reports: Tensions between MI5 and police revealed: Security Service knew of ringleader's violent intent': Ian Cobain, Richard Norton-Taylor and Will Woodward.

15 12 December 2007, UPI. 'Energy Analysis: India intel fails to halt terror. "India says its state intelligence departments are not equipped to take on terrorism following failures that have put their efficiency in doubt".

16 3 October 2007, *The Miami Herald* 'Mexican bombings recall 'dirty war' of decades ago';

17 'ARMS RECOVERY FROM RED MOSQUE REFLECTS PAKISTAN INTELLIGENCE FAILURE – PAPER'. Text of report by Ansar Abbasi headlined "Lal Masjid weapons cast doubts on role of agencies" published by Pakistani newspaper The News website on 13 July (14 July 2007 Saturday ,BBC Monitoring International Reports)

18 'Chronology of a Failure to Stop Genocide: Bush Administration Policy on Darfur since September 9, 2004': http://www.africaaction.org/newsroom/index.php?op=read&documentid=1359&type=15&issues=1024

19 'Why Uganda ignored reports on Kenya's post polls violence', By Grace Matsiko, Nation (Kampala), 19 January 2008. 'Quel mécanisme d'alerte précoce pour l'Afrique?' by Komi Tsakadi in http://www.agoravox.fr/article.php3?id_article=35341

20 French English Spanish Italian German versions of google coupled – observations between 01/06/2007 and 25/06/2007

21 comScore's qSearch 2.0 results in 'Worldwide Internet: Now Serving 61 Billion Searches per Month' http://searchenginewatch.com/showPage.html?page=3627304

22 The State of the Live Web, April 2007 - http://www.sifry.com/alerts/archives/000493.html

23 How many decision makers read in October 2001 the Russian military assessment of the Afghan war which was freely available online ?

24 Innis, Harold. (1951) 'The Bias of Communication'. Toronto: University of Toronto Press, p. 28.

25 Every medium of the Information society has its structural weaknesses: television and monthly press depend, for example, on the availability of images. When images, or recorded witness accounts are lacking, the information shrinks, explaining most of failures occurring in the African context or in several crisis prone rural areas. The diversification of sources, the lowering of the access costs to certain types of channels (newsgroups, blogs, mailing lists) has also given a tremendous impulsion to propaganda. Contemporary forms of terrorisms have become, for example, totally internet-centric.

26 Different working agendas, different gathering and interpretation capacity, the number of targets exceeding the resources available, different definition of risk, different administrative cultures, competition between risk assessment entities etc. Historic links, physical proximity, presence of diasporas in the Member States, economic interests and much more are all good reasons to distance the positions of every EU Member State.

27 Cluster analyses can be performed using the TwoStep, Hierarchical, or K-Means Cluster Analysis procedures. Each procedure employs a different algorithm for creating clusters, and each has options not available in the others. For our application we have chosen to use the TwoStep Cluster Analysis procedure. It provides the following unique features: the automatic selection of the best number of clusters, in addition to measures for choosing between cluster models; and the ability to create cluster models simultaneously based on categorical and continuous variables.

# [ Part 1: Creating Partnership in Peacebuilding ]

# THE GLOBAL CONFLICT BAROMETER

## Global Development

In 2007, a total of 328 political conflicts were identified. Among these, 31 conflicts involved a massive amount of violence (six wars and 25 severe crises), and 99 were conducted with only sporadic use of violence and were, therefore, classified as crises. These crises and highly violent conflicts amounted to 130 violent conflicts. In contrast, 198 non-violent conflicts were also counted and can be subdivided into 118 manifest and 80 latent conflicts. Compared with 2006, the number of wars remained the same (six), five of which were already being fought out at this intensity in 2006: Sudan (Darfur), Somalia (UIC), Sri Lanka (LTTE), Afghanistan (Taliban), and Iraq (insurgents). Two of these, Sudan and Iraq, were therefore classified as wars for the fourth year running. Last year's sixth war, Israel (Hezbollah), significantly de-escalated to a non-violent level following the withdrawal of Israeli troops from Lebanon in October 2006. However, the former severe crisis in Waziristan, Pakistan's border region with Afghanistan, escalated to a war in 2007 (Pakistan, North and South Waziristan).

### Chart 1: Global Intensities in 2006-2007

The number of severe crises decreased from 30 to 25, 16 of which had been classified at the same level in 2006. Six escalated from the level of a crisis in 2006 to

Global conflict intensities in 2007 compared to 2006

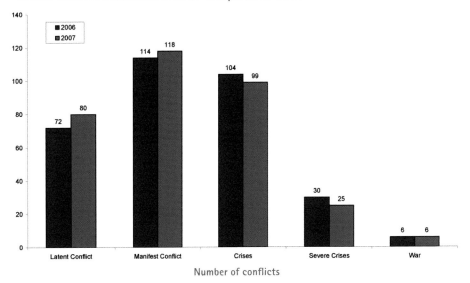

Number of conflicts

a severe crisis in 2007. Two – the conflict between the two main rebel groups in Colombia (FARC - ELN) and the opposition conflict in Burma/Myanmar (opposition) – had been manifest conflicts, i.e. non-violent, in 2006. One severe crisis, Mexico (drug cartels), emerged as a new conflict in 2007. Those of last year's severe crises that were not conducted at this level of intensity in 2007 developed as follows: one, Pakistan (North and South Waziristan) escalated to a war; thirteen de-escalated, ten out of these to the level of a crisis, and three wih the level of a latent conflict.

Overall, 31 highly violent conflicts were

counted in 2007, in comparison with 36 in 2006. This indicates a considerable de-escalation after last year's escalation compared to 2005 during which only 30 highly violent conflicts were recorded, the lowest number since 1984. The number of crises, however, decreased only slightly in relation to their high number: 99 in 2007 compared with 104 in 2006.

### Chart 2: Ongoing global conflicts of low, medium, and high intensity 1945 to 2007

The number of non-violent conflicts grew from 186 to 198, as latent conflicts increased from 72 to 80, and manifest con-

*Nicolas Schwank M.A. is a researcher at the Institute for Political Science at the University of Heidelberg. He is editor of the new conflict database CONIS, which aims on the exposure and analysis of conflict dynamics. His main research interest is in improving methods for the quantitative conflict research.*

*Lotta Mayer has been a member of the board and head of the working group, 'Conflicts in sub-Saharan Africa' since 2005. Mayer has also collaborated with the project 'Humanitarian Impact of Man-made Crises'. Since 2002 she has studied sociology, political science and philosophy at the University of Heidelberg.*

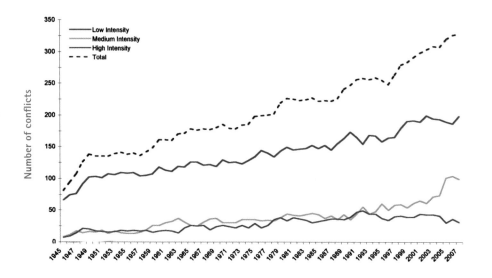

Ongoing global conflicts of low, medium and high intensity 1945 to 2007

flicts increased at almost the same rate with 117 in 2007 compared with 114 in 2006. The total number of conflicts rose slightly from 326 to 328, as eight conflicts had ended in 2006 and ten new ones arose in 2007. One of the terminated conflicts was located in Europe, four in Africa, and three in the Middle East and Maghreb. Of the new conflicts, three emerged in Europe, two in Africa, three in the Americas, and two in Asia and Oceania. While only four of the ten new conflicts were conducted without the use of violence, five were crises and one a severe crisis right from the start. In order to reveal a long-term trend, the five intensity levels are categorized into three groups: the two non-violent levels are summarized as low intensity, crises as medium intensity, and severe crises and wars as conflicts of

high intensity. Chart 2 also displays the total number of conflicts observed. As the graph shows, the number of conflicts observed per year has risen more or less continuously from 81 in 1945 to 328 in 2006, most of which are low-intensity conflicts. When looking at the high-intensity conflicts, a continuous and regular increase is evident, from seven in 1945 to 41 in 2004, interrupted by minor phases of de-escalation. The all-time high was 49 high intensity conflicts in 1992, shortly after the collapse of the Soviet Union. After a spectacular drop to only 30 in 2005, the number of highly violent conflicts rose again to 36 in 2006, but decreased to 31 in 2007. On the other hand, the number of crises soared to previously unknown heights in recent years, indicating a change in conflict conduct. While fewer

conflicts were fought with the systematic use of large-scale violence, more and more disputes were waged with the sporadic use of violence, e.g. ambushes, guerrilla attacks, bombings and the like.

### Analysis intrastate - interstate

The 328 conflicts in 2007 can be categorised as 238 internal and 90 interstate conflicts. The former category comprised four conflicts that can be classified as transnational, since at least one conflict party is a non-state actor. Also, the main base of operations of which is located in a country other than its opponent's, be it a state or another non-state actor. Since the structure of these conflicts (non-state actor vs. state or another non-state actor) resembles the structure of intrastate conflicts, they are subsumed into this category here.

Chart 3: Number of intra- and interstate conflicts in 2007 by intensity level

All six wars in 2007 were internal conflicts, as were all the severe crises, one of which, Chad (ethnic groups), was transnational. Therefore, after last year's severe interstate crisis between Israel and Lebanon [Israel - Lebanon], no conflict between states was fought out at either of the two highest intensity levels. However, six of the 99 crises were interstate [Armenia - Azerbaijan; Chad - Sudan; Uganda - DR Congo (Lake Albert); Colombia - Ecuador; Israel - Lebanon; Syria - Israel], whereas 93 were intrastate (none transnational).

## Number of intra- and interstate conflicts in 2007 by intensity level

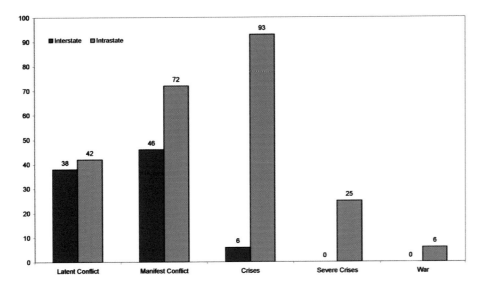

## Ongoing intra- and interstate conflicts of high intensity 1945 to 2007

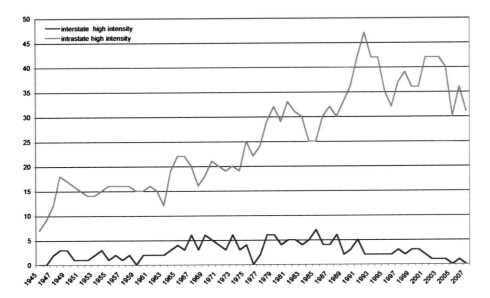

Chart 4: Ongoing intra- and
interstate conflicts of high
intensity 1945 to 2007

Of the six interstate crises, the conflict
between Armenia and Azerbaijan and the
one between Chad and Sudan had already
been conducted at the same intensity level
in 2006, while Israel - Lebanon had been a
severe crisis in 2006. The conflict between
Uganda and DR Congo was new, and the
remaining two disputes had been manifest
conflicts in 2006. Of the non-violent conflicts, 42 latent and 72 manifest conflicts
were intrastate (including one and two transnational conflicts, respectively), and 38
latent as well as 46 manifest conflicts were
interstate. Therefore, intrastate conflicts
outnumbered interstate conflicts not only
in total, but also at every intensity level. The
long-term analysis, for which the two high
intensity levels, severe crisis and war, were
summarized into one group, clearly shows
that the predominance of highly violent
intrastate conflicts can be observed from
the beginning of the period examined. The
current low number of interstate wars and
severe crises, however, was a more recent
development supposedly due to the end of
the Cold War.

### Regional Development

At 109, almost a third of all conflicts
were located in Asia and Oceania. Second
came Africa with 78, third Europe with 55,
then the Middle East and Maghreb and the
Americas with 43 each. Asia and Oceania
also had the largest number of crises with

Ongoing intra- and interstate conflicts of high intensity 1945 to 2007

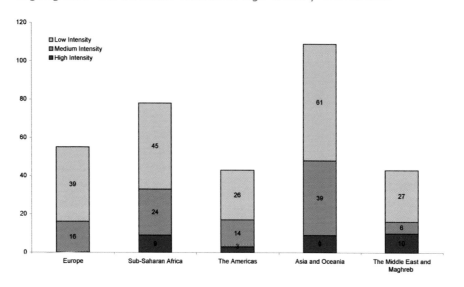

39, as well as the largest number of non-violent conflicts, 61.

Chart 5: Distribution of all conflicts in 2007 by region and intensity type

Concerning highly violent conflicts, the Middle East and Maghreb ranked first with ten, two of them wars and Africa was joint second with Asia, each with nine highly violent conflicts and in each region two of the conflicts were wars. This means that Africa and the Middle East and Maghreb have switched places. This change was the result of a remarkable de-escalation in Africa, with high-intensity conflicts decreasing from 15 in 2006 to only nine in 2007, while their number in the Middle East and Maghreb increased from nine to ten. In the Americas, the number of highly violent conflicts

rose significantly from only one in 2006 to three in 2007. In contrast, no high-intensity conflict was counted in Europe for the first time since 1967, as the previous years' persistent severe crisis in Chechnya [Russia (Chechen rebels/Chechnya)] de-escalated to the level of a crisis and no new highly violent conflict emerged. This is even more remarkable, as Europe had the third largest number of conflicts and with 16 also the third largest number of crises (Asia and Oceania 39, Africa 24). In the Middle East and Maghreb, only six crises were counted, eight fewer than in the America. Therefore, most remarkably, more high-intensity conflicts than crises were fought out in the Middle East and Maghreb, whereas the structure of the distribution of the conflicts between the intensity groups, if summarized

into three groups (low, medium, and high intensity), normally resembles a pyramid, with the high-intensity conflicts on top. If the number of states per region is taken into account and the number of conflicts related to the number of states, the Middle East and Maghreb's pole position becomes even clearer. Not only that, the average number of highly violent conflicts per state was almost 0.5 in this region (the world average being around 0.2), while Africa had 0.2, Asia and Oceania 0.1, the Americas less than 0.1, and Europe zero. Also, the Middle East and Maghreb with 2.1 had the highest overall average number of conflicts per state, thereby replacing Asia and Oceania as the region with most conflicts. The world average was around 1.7. Asia and Oceania as well as Africa displayed values around that mean, while Europe and America had only about one conflict per state on average.

Dynamics within individual conflicts

Approximately two-thirds of all conflicts, some 215 out of 328, remained at the same intensity level from 2006 to 2007. While a total of 36 conflicts escalated – six of these by two levels – 67 conflicts de-escalated. Of the latter, 61 cases de-escalated by one level, two by two levels, and four by three levels. Therefore, the de-escalation from 2006 to 2007 is quite remarkable, with not only the number of high-intensity conflicts decreasing, but also the conflicts de-escalating far outnumbering the conflicts that escalated. In 2006, the overall number of escalating and de-escalating conflicts had been equal, with escalation more often than de-escalation taking place over two intensity levels.

| Change of intensity | Number |
|---|---|
| Escalation by four levels | 0 |
| Escalation by three levels | 0 |
| Escalation by two levels | 6 |
| Escalation by one level | 30 |
| No change | 215 |
| De-escalation by one level | 61 |
| De-escalation by two levels | 2 |
| De-escalation by three levels | 4 |
| De-escalation by four levels | 0 |

Of the six conflicts that escalated by two levels, all went from non-violent to violent. Four escalated from a latent conflict to a crisis [Estonia (Russian-speaking minority); Mexico (EPR/Guerrero); Niger (Tuareg/Aga-dez); Pakistan (opposition)], and two from a manifest conflict to a severe crisis [Colombia (FARC - ELN) and Burma/Myanmar (opposition)]. Therefore, a total of 18 conflicts turned violent in 2007, and in addition, twelve conflicts escalated from the level of a manifest conflict to a crisis. Of the other conflicts escalating by one level, six turned from a crisis into a severe crisis [Ethiopia (ONLF/Ogaden); Kenya (ethnic groups); Pakistan (Islamists); Iraq (al-Zarqawi group); Israel (Fatah - Hamas); Lebanon (Hezbollah, Fatah al-Islam)], and one turned from a severe crisis into a war [Pakistan (North and South Waziristan)]. The remaining eleven remained non-violent, escalating only from a latent to a manifest conflict. One of the four conflicts that de-escalated by three

levels turned from a war to a manifest conflict [Israel (Hezbollah)], as no more violent incidents between the conflict parties were reported after Israel's withdrawal from Lebanon. Three cases went from severe crisis to latent conflict [Ethiopia (Guji - Borena); Guinea-Bissau (MFDC-Sadio); Sudan (Nuer, White Army – SPLM/A)]. In Sudan, this was due to the overwhelming force of the Sudan People's Liberation Movement/Army (SPLM/A), causing the White Army to finally abandon the area in 2006; in Guinea-Bissau, the security forces had succeeded in pushing the rebels over the border to Senegal's Casamance region, where they had originated [Senegal (MFDC-Sadio/Casamance)]. Both conflicts de-escalating by two levels decreased from crisis to latent conflict. Therefore, all six conflicts de-escalating by more than one level turned from violent to non-violent. In addition, 28 crises decreased to manifest conflicts. Therefore, altogether 34 conflicts ceased being violent between 2006 and 2007, underlining the significant de-escalation that took place in 2007.

## Conflict Items

Continuing its position in 2006, the prevalent conflict item in 2007 was system/ideology with 85 cases. This item signifies that the respective disputes were conducted in order to change the political or economic system or concerned ideological differences, e.g. striving for a theocracy as opposed to a secular state; religious differences; seeking democracy in an autocracy; or striving for a different economic order. Resources ranked

second with 67, closely followed by national power with 62. It should be noted that conflicts were often centred on more than one item. Therefore, the same conflict might occur twice or three times in this analysis. Combinations of the three most frequent items were common, as was the combination of territory and resources, regional predominance and resources, or international power and system/ideology.

More than half of the system conflicts as well as the national power conflicts were fought out with the use of violence. Among these, 15 of the system conflicts and eleven of the national power conflicts were even highly violent. Three of each of these were wars. Half of the disputes over regional predominance were violent, including nine highly violent ones. The latter comprised two wars, i.e. Sudan (Darfur) and Pakistan (North and South Waziristan). Disputes concerning autonomy were violent in half of the cases, including two highly violent conflicts. Almost three-quarters of secession conflicts (32 of 45) were fought out violently, featuring six highly violent conflicts, including the war in Sri Lanka [Sri Lanka (LTTE)].

In contrast, conflicts over resources were conducted violently in less than one-third of the cases (however, six of those were highly violent). This might be due to the fact that resources can be shared among the conflict parties, while certain other items, such as ideological questions, power, or self-

**Global frequency of conflict items in 2007 by intensity groups**

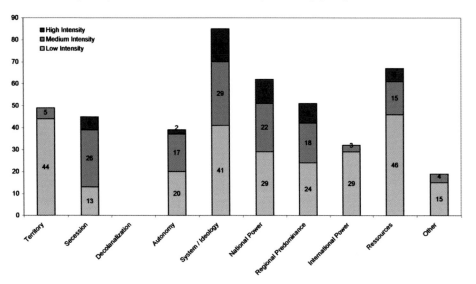

determination can hardly be divided between the conflict parties in a way that satisfies both parties.

Chart 6: Global frequency of conflict items in 2007 by intensity groups

Another factor might be that many conflicts over resources were interstate conflicts, which are far less violence-prone than intrastate conflicts [Panorama: analysis intrastate – interstate]. In fact, violence in disputes over resources occurred only in intrastate cases, with the single exception of the crisis between Uganda and DR Congo [Uganda – DR Congo (Lake Albert)]. The lower susceptibility to violence of interstate conflicts is also illustrated by the fact that only three out of 32 conflicts over international power, an interstate item, were con-

ducted violently in 2007, none of the cases being a high intensity conflict. The same applies to territory, another interstate item, which was pursued violently in only five out of 49 cases. No high-intensity conflicts concerning one or both of these two items were observed in 2007.

Striking differences concerning the frequency of items can be discovered between the regions. In Europe, the prevalent cause for disputes was self-determination; with secession the most frequent item with 16 cases, and autonomy ranking second with 13 cases. In contrast, both internal power conflicts and conflicts over regional predominance were almost unknown (two conflicts over national power, one over regional predominance). This is a quite different

pattern of intrastate conflicts to that which occurs in Africa, where the prevalent conflict item was national power (28), often in combination with the second-most frequent item, resources, and where regional predominance – an item often indicating weakness on the part of the state – came third with 16 cases. Secession or autonomy were, however, sought only occasionally. System/ideology was a rare conflict item in both Europe and Africa (four and six cases, respectively) whereas it was the prevalent item in Asia and Oceania, in the Middle East and Maghreb, and also in America (32, 22, and 21 cases, respectively). Another similarity between Asia and Oceania and the Middle East and Maghreb was the large number of national power conflicts, albeit still considerably less than in Africa. On the other hand, Africa and Asia and Oceania had a very large number of regional predominance conflicts (26) – an item almost unknown in the Middle East and Maghreb (only one case). Asia and Oceania also had a large number of secession or autonomy conflicts (17 and 13 cases, respectively), similar to Europe, but in contrast to Africa, the Americas, and the Middle East and Maghreb. The only analogy between Europe, the Americas, and the Middle East and Maghreb was the relatively large number of interstate conflicts.

### Coups d'état

After 2006's two successful coups d'état in Thailand and Fiji and one attempted coup d'état in the Philippines, only one attempted coup d'état was observed in 2007, again in the Philippines. On 29 November 2007, 50 soldiers mutinied, occupied a luxury hotel in the capital, Manila, and demanded the resignation of President Gloria Macapagal Arroyo. The mutineers were led by Antonio Trillanes, who was due to stand trial that day for another coup attempt in 2003. Trillanes, however, had escaped and, together with the military policemen supposed to guard him, had occupied the hotel. After an ultimatum had passed, Special Forces stormed the hotel. Trillanes surrendered in order to avoid bloodshed.

[    Steeve Iuncker    ]

# Gaza booms – summer rain
Gaza, Palestine

I went to see.
To feel, by myself, something more than what the media shows us every day from one of the most covered regions in the world, from print to TV news, from morning to evening.
Enough of this 'guilty witness' label the press tags on us because we take an interest in the world.
Unable to act and yet entirely responsible.
Am I one of those privileged onlookers who grant themselves the right to express their opinion? Is it legitimate to try and get involved by reporting events that I don't understand myself? For what?
All I can do is take you into what I just saw, into what I just felt.
Otherwise, I remain alone faced with these images.

Steeve Iuncker

*Gaza City.*
© Steeve Iuncker / Agence VU / Palestine, Gaza

*In the city of Gaza, money is missing.*
*rubbish is not being picked up anymore.*
*e is no petrol left for the garbage trucks.*

*At night, at Al Bureij refugee camp -*
*one of the longest resisting camps*
*of the Gaza strip, after a F16 bombing.*
© Steeve Iuncker / Agence VU / Palestine, Gaza

man wearing a Hamas cap during a
monstration at the Jabalya camp in
the Hezbollah firing against Israel.

ve Iuncker / Agence VU / Palestine, Gaza

*Waiting for a cab.*

© Steeve Iuncker / Agence VU / Palestine, Gaza

*Following to the destruction of Nessirat bridge by a F16 bombing, the travellers must walk on both sides of the bridge, until the "traxs" rebuild a road to skirt round the bridge.*

© Steeve Iuncker / Agence VU / Palestine, Gaza

*In Beit-Hanoun refugee camp, Al-Aqsa*
*watch over the main road, which has be*
© Steeve Iuncker / Agence VU / Palestine, Gaza

*Leader of the Al-Aqsa fighters in Al-Bureij camp,*
*just before a F16 bombing of our position.*

*Soldier at the funeral of one*
*of his comrades in arms.*

© Steeve Iuncker / Agence VU / Palestine, Gaza

*A group of men under a tent
in Khan-Ynounes camp.*

© Steeve luncker / Agence VU / Palestine, Gaza

*A soldier at the funeral of one of his comrades in arms.*

© Steeve Iuncker / Agence VU / Palestine, Gaza

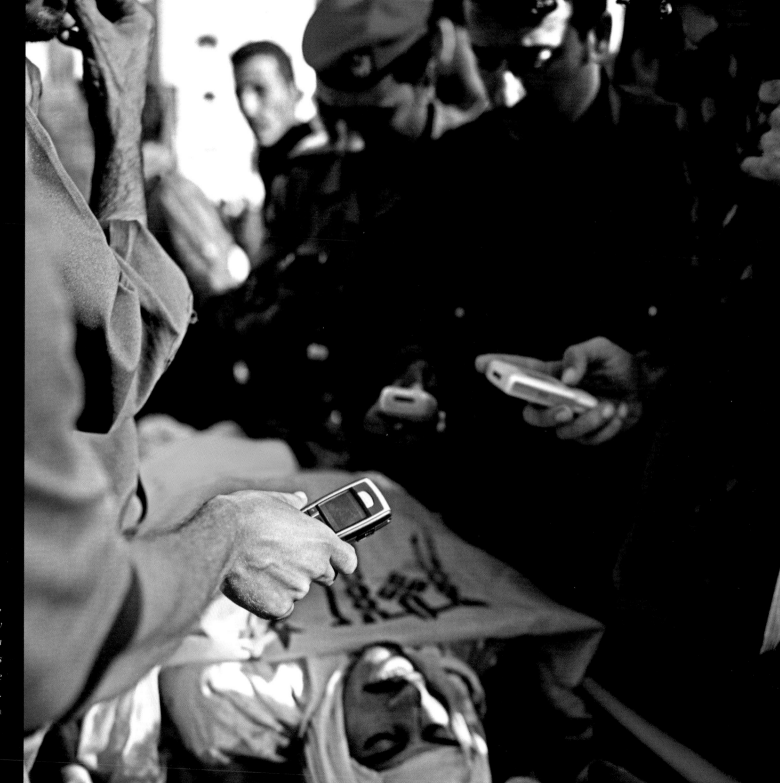

*In Beit-Hanoun camp, funeral of Ahmed Shaheen, 23, shaheed of the Al-Aqsa brigade (Fatah military wing). The body is carried to the cemetery on a military truck. The boy was killed in a minibus after a F16 attack. Soldiers take one last picture of their comrade in arms with their mobile phones.*

© Steeve Iuncker / Agence VU / Palestine, Gaza

*In the camp of Beit-Hanoun, a child mourns
for Ahmed Shaheen, 23, shaheed of the Al Aqusa
brigade (military arm of the Fatah), who died in
a minibus after a F16 rocket attack.*
© Steeve Iuncker / Agence VU / Palestine, Gaza

*In Beït-Hanoun camp, a woman is crying at the*
*funerals of her brother Ahmed Shaheen, 23,*
*a shaheed of the Al-Aqsa brigade (Fatah army*
*wing), killed in a mini bus after a F16 attack.*
© Steeve Iuncker / Agence VU / Palestine, Gaza

# FROM EARLY WARNING TO EARLY ACTION: DEVELOPING THE EU'S RESPONSE TO CRISIS AND LONGER-TERM THREATS[1]

## Introduction

Today's world is characterised by more conflict than ever before; last year 118 violent conflicts wreaked destruction around the globe. Not all raged with the same ferocity; but they were nevertheless united by one fundamental issue: their capacity to destroy human life.

As the Talmud puts it, "Whoever saves one life, saves the world entire".

It is this simple truth which should guide us as we enter these discussions, together with our recognition of the fundamental responsibility we share to protect human life and to promote human security.

Another characteristic of today's world is the vast array of information sources and tools at our disposal. But, does that capacity for early warning translate into early action?

Too often it does not. And that is simply unacceptable in this ever more globalised and sophisticated world.

## EU, early warning and early action

The conference on early warning and early action is part of the European Commission's response. We want to use this occasion to look at how the EU can better react to crises and conflicts. And we want your active guidance as to the future focus of our activities.

The European Union has a comprehensive range of tools at its disposal for crisis management. To maximise their impact we must ensure that at every stage, from planning to the final stages of implementation, Member States, Council Secretariat and Commission work closely together. We have to focus on ensuring all instruments, not only our rapid reaction programmes but also our long term development assistance, humanitarian assistance and ESDP rule of law, police and military missions, are carefully coordinated and complementary.

This conference builds on one held here two years ago, which President Ahtisaari co-hosted with us. Since then we have launched a number of initiatives to further develop our crisis response.

Certainly one of the most innovative developments over the last two years has been our new financing mechanism for crisis management and conflict prevention, the **Instrument for Stability.**

Here I should pay tribute to the European Parliament for its invaluable support in enabling this instrument to see the light of day. It gives the EU's crisis response capacities an important boost. On the financial side it more than quadruples our assistance, from €30 to €140 million this year alone. We have established efficient methods for exchanging information with Member States about our activities via the Council's Political and Security Committee.

The Stability Instrument enables us to fund a wider range of activities than ever before: on the one hand in a range of areas under the broad heading of crisis response and preparedness; and on the other under the heading of long-term trans-regional threats to stability, including non-proliferation, protecting critical infrastructure and tackling major public health threats.

As a result we can now respond more flexibly and rapidly to a major new political crisis or natural disaster; to shore up peace-building processes; and to ensure development needs are addressed from the start by getting children back to school and re-opening health and other local public services.

*Dr. Benita Ferrero-Waldner has been the European Commissioner for External Relations since 2004. She was born in 1948 in Salzburg, Austria. Dr. Ferrero-Waldner received her doctorate in law from the University of Salzburg. She has served as Austria's federal Minister for Foreign Affairs and State Secretary of Foreign Affairs. Between 1993 and 1995, she served as Deputy Chief of Protocol at the Federal Ministry of Foreign Affairs, then Chef of Protocol at the Executive Office of the Secretary General, United Nations Secretariat, New York. Before entering the diplomatic service, Dr. Ferrero-Waldner worked in the private sector and held a number of management positions in Europe and the United States.*

---

1 Introduction speech held by Dr. Ferrero- Waldner at the conference "From early warning to early action: Developing EUs response to crisis and longer-term threats", 12-13 November 2007, European Commission, Brussels, Belgium

### EU's crisis response mechanism

To illustrate the complementarity of the EU's crisis response mechanisms, let me mention the forthcoming (ESDP) mission to Chad. The Commission and Council Secretariat cooperated from the beginning of the planning process, and undertook a joint information gathering mission together with civilian and military staff and the Presidency. The result is a package of EU and EC activities bringing to bear a wide range of EU instruments. The ESDP mission will be complemented by money from the Stability Instrument for training and equipping 850 Chadian Police Officers. They will then be deployed in refugee and IDP camps in Eastern Chad. We hope this will play an important role in securing and stabilising the neighbourhood of Sudan/Darfur. We are also considering additional support, for example funding a population census in Chad to lay the groundwork for future elections.

In Afghanistan the EU is intensifying its efforts to develop a democratic, secure and sustainable Afghan state. Central to that objective is promoting the rule of law, and the Commission has therefore been supporting the payment of police salaries while developing a strategic reform programme for the justice sector and a system of legal aid. All this has been carefully coordinated through joint exploratory missions of the Commission, Council Secretariat and Member States.

We have also been fully involved in the EU's evolving response to the deteriorating security situation in Lebanon. Again, joint planning missions have led to a number of common projects designed to strengthen the country's security sector. We are working closely with the German government on a project for integrated border management, enabling the Lebanese authorities to better control and secure their border with Syria. And we are providing senior police experts to the Lebanese police service, building their capacity for maintaining law and order.

All over the world, from Georgia to Burma/Myanmar, from the DRC to Peru, we are working to tackle ongoing crises and prevent future conflict. An important focus of our work in the coming period will be Kosovo/a. We are engaged in intense planning activities for what we hope will be a smooth transition to its future status.

Another innovative element of the Stability Instrument is the **Peacebuilding Partnership.** We are convinced that the most sustainable approach to resolving conflict is to ensure all partners are involved. We also recognise the deep reserve of technical expertise held by organisations such as those represented here today.

We will set up a broad-based network of specialised European NGOs with expertise in early warning, conflict prevention, peacebuilding, post-conflict and post-disaster recovery. But it also means strengthening our cooperation with Member States' aid agencies, the UN and other relevant organisations. Some financial support will be available for capacity building and the roster of NGOs we establish will give us a readily accessible pool of experts to rapidly mobilise support for any given situation.

We are very excited by the possibility for more collaborative working practises. We hope to build upon the existing capacity amongst our implementing partners, as well as provide innovative mechanisms to deploy these skills in crisis situations.

But the Stability Instrument is not the only way we have been consolidating the EU's crisis response. You may be familiar with the Barnier Report which took a thorough and critical look at the EU's crisis response mechanisms and offered a number of recommendations, several of which we have already begun to implement. Of particular importance to me are consular protection, about which the Commission will publish a Communication later this year, and enhanced coordination of humanitarian aid and civil protection. I want the Commission delegations to play a constructive role in these areas.

In addition, we have released a Communication on the EU's response to situations of fragility, looking at the specific requirements of contexts where institutional capacity is very limited. In such circumstances there is a particular onus on donors to take a whole-of-government approach and ensure development assistance is conflict sensitive. This Communication is complemented by a joint Commission-Council Secretariat paper on security and development to be endorsed by the External Relations Council in November 2007.

I hope in years to come we will no longer speak of forgotten emergencies because they won't exist. And we will play our part in banishing them. We are determined to shoulder our responsibility and ensure that the EU lives up to its ambitious goals for global security.

We have ambitious ideas for the future and I am convinced that the EU will become an ever more powerful force for the good in tackling the world's trouble spots. But we are also conscious that will only be possible through widespread cooperation with others.

# CHALLENGES FOR THE EU IN CONFLICT PREVENTION AND PEACEBUILDING[1]

## Introduction

I want to thank the European Commission for inviting me to speak at this timely conference on developing the European Union's response to crisis and longer-term threats. Finding better and more effective ways to respond to crises rapidly and coherently while maintaining a focus on preventive action is imperative.

This gathering offers a unique opportunity for us Europeans and the many experts from around the world present here to reflect on the priorities the EU should have in conflict prevention and peacebuilding and the best methodologies and tools to support this work.

In the following, I would like to say few words about some particular challenges for the EU in conflict prevention and peacebuilding and to share some of my initial thoughts about the ways and means to move forward in addressing these issues.

A vision of the future nature and context of EU conflict prevention and crisis management activities is essential to inform those near-term decisions that will determine Europe's long-term crisis management capa-

bilities and capacities. Unless globalisation stops or goes in reverse, the world of 2025 is likely to be more diverse, more interdependent and even more unequal. Globalisation will produce winners and losers, as between countries and regions, and within societies, while universal communication will make these disparities evermore apparent. The regions neighbouring Europe will face particular challenges. The prognosis is for tensions and strong migratory pressures in the regions around Europe at a time when it is becoming increasingly dependent on the rest of the world, especially for energy.

## Afghanistan: a key challenge for the European Union

Afghanistan remains a key challenge for the international community. It is a mixed picture, with both progress and setbacks. On the one hand, there has been the tradition of *Loya Jirga*[2], the National Assembly and stronger central government. On the other hand, old warlords remain influential, and political structures at the central and local levels have limited capacity. In addition, corruption permeates much of the government apparatus, and a culture of impunity has continued. The economic situation in Afghanistan is still a major challenge.

Despite increased development efforts, there has been limited real improvements in living conditions.

The country is among the five poorest in the world, the infant mortality rate is the highest in the world and the infrastructure is extremely weak. The drug economy is rapidly growing and has strong political links. This relates not only to the global drug scene, but also to the local political scene. If the Afghan government can not cope with the drug lords it will not be possible to establish good governance, and effective governance is a prerequisite for successful rule by law and reconstruction. In addition, local powerbrokers see reconstruction and development as a threat. Therefore, what we do now will influence people's perceptions of and the level of support for the new political order, thereby determining the chances it has of succeeding. The international community needs to remain committed to Afghanistan and give the country time. Failure to do so would see this native land sliding backwards with disastrous consequences.

Since the Taliban's fall in 2001, the EU has been a major contributor to Afghanistan. A substantial European Commission

*Martti Ahtisaari is a former President of Finland (1994-2000) and a United Nations diplomat and mediator, noted for his international peace work. Currently he is the UN representative and mediator during the Vienna peace talks that will determine the final status of Serbia's southern province, Kosovo/a (which has been under UN administration since 1999). In his proposal to the UN Security Council he has recommended supervised independence for Kosovo/a.*

---

1 Keynote speech held by Martti Ahtisaari at the conference "From early warning to early action: Developing EUs response to crisis and longer-term threats", 12-13 November 2007, European Commission, Brussels, Belgium

2 Loya Jirga is a forum or grand council in Afghanistan, in which, traditionally, tribal elders - Pashtuns, Tajiks, Hazaras and Uzbeks - have come together to settle affairs of the nation or rally behind a cause. Historically it has been used to settle inter-tribal disputes, discuss social reforms and approve a new constitution.

delegation oversees an annual budget of some €200 million in development aid, and a Special Representative is in residence. Furthermore, the EU launched an EU police mission in Afghanistan in mid-June 2007. It is intended that EUPOL Afghanistan will consist of 160 personnel (increasing possibly to 190), with contributions from 17-18 EU Member States and with perhaps additional personnel from third-country states such as Canada, New Zealand and Norway.

However, EU influence is less than it should be. Given its current toolbox of capabilities and institutional strengths, the EU should assume a stronger leadership role in Afghanistan. By assuming a greater coordinating role, the EU could fill one of the biggest gaps in the reconstruction effort. Coordination is a problem on multiple levels – among the hundreds of NGOs, government agencies and international institutions operating on the ground; among EU Member States; and between military and civilian actors. The EU could play a constructive role in all these areas. By establishing a coordination mechanism simply for its own Member States, the EU could significantly reduce the well-documented waste and duplication.

Afghanistan, as a fragile state, has security implications far beyond its immediate neighbourhood. Building viable societies out of failed states and countries that have suf-fered from a long internal conflict is a huge challenge recognised by a growing number of international actors. While there is an increasing demand for state building activities and recognition of their importance for global security, the international community is not united on what the state building agenda should include and what ought to be the means for a successful outcome.

Afghanistan needs time, patience and relentless effort. This is not the time to give up. It is the time to remain fully engaged so that the positive developments can be built upon and produce long-term results.

Even though the EU has, at theoretical and policy levels, adopted a number of important documents on fragile situations, there is still a lack of clarity and coherence on practical state building activities.

Competing and sometimes conflicting agendas are an unfortunate reality and a challenge we face when dealing with fragile states like Afghanistan, which has not had a strong government for a considerable time. Further dialogue on prioritising policies and supporting local capacities in state building activities is needed. The EU could also contribute to the conceptual dialogue process on priorities in state building. It would be important to bring together actors from northern and southern governments, multilateral and regional organisations as well as civil society to discuss policies on state building. This way a more coherent, robust and more rapid approach could be identified regarding what is essential and feasible.

## Tackling changes in Africa

Let me now reflect on some challenges the European Union is currently facing in its relations with Africa.

Africa is changing fast. Growth is historically high, investment from China is sweeping the continent, it has all sorts of environmental assets the rest of the world wants, Africans are more confident, and are more leveraged due to the interests of new investors. But Africa remains fragile. Growth in Africa is not yet being translated into large-scale poverty reduction. The recent 'elections' in Nigeria provide an example of how hard-fought permanent change really is.[3] The EU must deliver aid so that it does not undermine African institutions. We have to review our assumptions about exactly what aid can do given the rapidly changing African landscape – Chinese investment has reminded us about the key role that trade and the private sector must play in Africa's development.

The EU has to insure that its trade policies do not undermine its efforts in the development cooperation field. Europe has repeatedly recognised that global trade is plagued by unfair rules, and that changes could lift

---

3 The last elections were held in April 2007, causing uprisings and killings.

millions out of poverty. However, Europe and the United States still often put their short-term trade interests before development. The principles that should underpin the EU's trading relationship with Africa should be based on a pro-poor development agenda through a mutually beneficial partnership.

We have to treat Africa as part of the global community – not as an item apart. Chinese and Indian engagement with Africa has helped to globalise Africa, both in reality and in perception. If things go wrong in Africa, it spells trouble for the rest of the world. Africa's success affects the chances of success in a wide range of global endeavours – whether economic, political or environmental.

Africa and the African Union are now at the centre of international politics and are emerging as political actors in their own right. It is becoming increasingly clear that Africa matters: as a political voice, as an economic force and as a huge source of human, cultural and natural potential.

In 2005, the EU presented its own Africa Strategy, putting Africa at the heart of its political agenda. However, this strategy has been widely described as unilateral and EU focused. The EU and the African Union are now keen to develop a joint strategy for the future of their partnership. The future partnership has to be based on jointly identified mutual and complementary interests and benefits. Therefore, there has been a public consultation process to develop a Joint EU-Africa Strategy. This new Joint Strategy was adopted by the Africa-EU Summit in Lisbon in December 2007. The main content of the Strategy relates to strategic priorities in the area of peace and security, democratic governance and human rights, trade and regional integration and other key development issues.

The strategy will face serious challenges in translating the ambitions into institutional terms, such as how to treat Africa as one. It is far from being a single entity, comprised of many different actors, each with its own interests and perceptions of security. Another challenge is how to move away from the traditional donor–recipient relationship and how to deal with overlapping initiatives from the EU.

Responsibility is required from both sides, in terms of input and dialogue. In this respect the Joint Strategy should take into account the fact that the partners are equal in terms of rights and responsibilities but not in terms of their level of integration and the availability of their financial and human resources and the strategy must be implemented in a realistic way. 'Partnership' and 'ownership' must be defined in the context of this reality.

## Peacebuilding in Africa

The creation of the African Union in 2002[4] has been an important milestone for Africa. The AU has been instrumental in establishing a security management system that includes the Peace and Security Council. The role of the AU as the central interlocutor on the African side on peace and security issues has to be recognised.

The emphasis in an EU-AU partnership should be on building the civilian capacity for conflict resolution and mediation. The EU should share lessons identified and best practices on conflict prevention and peace mediation efforts with the AU. Creating access for the AU to international networks in the field of conflict prevention and peace mediation would also be an important EU contribution.

Engaging local civil society organisations in formulating and implementing crisis management as well as peacebuilding strategies should also be an important element of the partnership. Local civil society needs to be involved in the monitoring and thus needs to be funded and informed accordingly. The EU should encourage African governments at the highest political levels to create actual political space for civil society. The roles of civil society actors in civilian crisis management cover the broad spectrum of engagement in early warning, prevention, mediation, monitoring, civilian peace-

4 This was the first year of sessions for the assembly.

keeping, and reconciliation. Civil society in new democracies is often unprepared for their roles and EU support will be needed in improving the effectiveness of civil society.

### The crisis in Burma/Myanmar

I would like to look briefly at one of the most acute challenges that the international society is currently facing. I'm sure that the recent developments in Burma/Myanmar, and the savage crackdown of peaceful demonstrations, have touched all of us. Use of extreme violence can never be justified as a means of sustaining order.

While the situation has been an issue of major concern for all of us, it has to be kept in mind that the political stalemate in (and with) Burma/Myanmar is nothing new. The political situation has been deadlocked, military leaders have continued in power and the country has remained in international isolation since the 1988 uprising. Also, the economic situation in Burma/Myanmar continues to be grim. The government is able to generate only a few per cent of its GDP in revenues, the need for civil service and institutional reform is huge and, most importantly, political and democratic empowerment is a necessity for the country's societal development. Authoritarian rule with failed economic policies and human rights violations have created a situation in which simple solutions do not exist.

It is very clear to me that the main re-sponsibility for the welfare of any country's citizens is always with its respective government. That is no less the case with Burma/Myanmar. However, saying this should not prevent us from assessing our own activities critically. To my mind, it is always crucial to look in the mirror and ask oneself, is there something I should do differently? Is there something that we, as representatives of the international community, should do differently? Since the 1988 uprising and 1990 elections Western Burma/Myanmar politics have focused on economic sanctions and consumer boycotts against the junta. This is even more the case now, when we're desperately seeking ways to respond to the current situation in the country. As many of us know, the effectiveness and appropriateness of sanctions has been debated both internationally and also within Burma/Myanmar.

Don't get me wrong, I'm not opposing the use of sanctions. But what I am asking, and asking all of us to seriously consider, is whether sanctions alone are enough to promote democratic changes in the country. Can we find and identify ways and means to complement the policies we're currently taking?

It's obvious that the problems of Burma/Myanmar are located in all the different layers of society. The military leadership has failed to bring about change in the country. The ethno-national realities are complex and diverse. The lack of institutionalised democracy is a risk factor that could lead the country into even more serious turmoil at any point in time; not to mention the alarming economic and humanitarian situation. So how can we support the citizens of Burma/Myanmar in the development of their own home country in a manner that's peaceful and dynamic at the same time?

Ending the turmoil in Burma/Myanmar would seem to require a major dialogue initiative. Promoting initiatives for a dialogue between the government, democratic forces and ethnic groups should be one of the key priorities in European Burma/Myanmar politics, and during recent events we have heard some cautiously promising signals that give us hope that establishing a new dialogue in the country might actually be happening. If this is the case, the international society has to find concrete tools to support this development.

So while we are gathered in this conference, which will critically assess the EU's capacity and readiness to act in the international front, we have to be creative and strategic.

I think that our approach and policies towards Burma/Myanmar can be a valuable entry point to the topic of discussing the EU's crisis response capacity and capability. The questions we are facing now are extremely difficult, but that should not prevent us from discussing and debating the issue.

### The European Union's role

I believe firmly in the potential of the European Union. Eurobarometer opinion polls show the public supports an outward-looking EU – more than two-thirds favour a common European foreign policy. We have the biggest single market in the world, the largest aid budgets, tens of thousands of peacekeepers who are active all over the world and a corps of 50,000 diplomats. We have seen through the process of enlargement that we can make a real difference if we show leadership and abandon our introspection for a serious engagement with the rest of the world. But this takes unity, courage, vision and greater coherence. I think there's a real opportunity for Europe to begin shaping global events. I have convened, together with 50 other Europeans from across the EU, a new organisation that will promote this goal, the European Council on Foreign Relations.

In order to create a vision of the future, global threats have to be understood in a holistic manner otherwise it will be impossible to develop the EU's response to crisis and longer term threats properly address them with targeted policies. One of the most demanding challenges is to understand future threats so that a well-grounded set of responses can be planned.

Foresight should be a continuous process and not an occasional event. The European Security Strategy, adopted in 2003, has often been welcomed as the first important step to build a comprehensive European Security Strategy. However, in the face of the ever-changing security environment there is a need to update the Security Strategy.

The foundation upon which all action for conflict resolution in the EU should be based on is the unity and coherence of the EU's foreign policy action. It is not a new demand but as it still not achieved I will repeat it once again. I anticipate that the new position of High Representative of the Union for Foreign and Security Policy will bring new impetus into the old agenda we all know so well. Establishing an External Action Service and combining the foreign policy spheres of the Commission and the Council, will avoid duplication and make foreign policy more efficient and effective. Only if the EU speaks with one voice can it expect to be listened to and taken seriously.

State building, particularly supporting the rebuilding of civilian administration, should be a key objective in our engagement with fragile states. The EU approach in fragile situations should be embedded in its overall commitment to effective multilateralism. Fragile situations require a greater reliance on multilateral channels and calls for better coordination between the EU and the UN. Both the United Nations, through its Peacebuilding Commission and Peace Support Fund, and the European Union, through its Stability Instrument, are building capacity for sustained engagement in countries emerging from conflict.

It is important that these instruments create synergies and share responsibility without overlapping activities.

We have to be better aware of the impact of our peacebuilding and crisis management activities. Third-party intervention in internal conflicts and crises is increasing and having various short- and long-term effects, at times unintended, on the host's society and economy. In this age of transparency and accountability, evaluation can neither be ignored nor avoided. Understanding the impact dimensions better would help improve the quality of operations through training and planning. The EU has also reached a point in its development where the impact of crisis management and peacebuilding needs to be verifiable and quantifiable.

The European Commission needs to engage in a solid consultation exercise with peacebuilding NGOs to identify needs and areas of cooperation, both at the thematic and geographical level. When it comes to the involvement of civil society organisations in European efforts, the most prominent feature is the Peacebuilding Partnership that was introduced together with the Stability Instrument. It offers an unprecedented opportunity to create genuine partnership. This means that we can start to develop a culture of cooperation between NGOs and the European Commission.

The work of the EU would benefit from the

creation of a mediation support unit, which could assist both European institutions and Special Representatives. Mediation can be an effective instrument in bringing about peace in societies in conflict.

I am quite impressed with the work of the UN Department for Political Affairs in creating a mediation support unit that is developing systematic knowledge about the professional practice of mediation as well as providing support to mediators on specific issues. An EU mediation support unit would help to build a new body of individuals who are capable of engaging in conflict resolution.

The EU also has resources to support the work of non-state actors, creating synergies between the different tracks in mediation. We, the Crisis Management Initiative, have benefited from this. Capacity building by the European Commission and its partners in mediation/Track II diplomacy could be one of the key goals for crisis response in the EU through the use of the Stability Instrument.

The European Union, like all the other actors, is facing challenges in its relations and actions with the changing world. As the challenges are novel and complicated the tools created to respond to these challenges should be accordingly innovative. There are great expectations of the Stability Instrument to deliver. Responding coherently and rapidly to crises while at the same time integrating crisis response into longer-term action will be a challenge. I trust that the new Stability Instrument will contain an innovative dimension and be courageous enough to seek new methods for crisis response and conflict resolution.

# FORESEEING CONFLICT[1]

## Introduction

We live in a context of two major and related processes. First, there is regionalisation based on high-speed transportation and communication. This, however, comes up against cultural borders. In fact, four of these 'borders', or international unions, currently exist: the European Union (EU), the African Union (AU), the South Asian Association for Regional Cooperation (SAARC) and the Association of South East Asian Nations (ASEAN).

As I see it, there are four more to come:

1. United States of Latin America and the Caribbean, ALC (*Estados Unidos de America Latina y el Caribe*);
2. Russian Union, RU, with autonomy for all non-Russians;
3. East Asian community, like the Shanghai Cooperative Organisation, SCO, comprising 50 per cent of humanity;
4. Islamic community similar to the Organisation of the Islamic Conference, OIC, which would be the *Ummah* ('community' or 'nation') from Morocco to Mindanao.

The second process at work is the rapid decline and fall of the US empire, which, if handled well, may be a blessing for the US republic just as it was for the 11 EU Member States formerly colonial powers liberated from their empires.

## Where is the early warning?

Early warning has three components:

1. Direct violence: beyond throwing a first stone. This is the capability and intention proven by a general tendency to participate in wars (which is among other reasons to create hierarchies and hegemonies);
2. Structural violence: a position higher up or lower down in a hierarchy of exploitation–repression–alienation, which can either preserve or destroy the hierarchy;
3. Cultural violence: the cultural justification of direct violence or structural violence.

A 'war participation index', based on the number of wars a state has participated in, divided by the number of years the state has existed, seems to confirm this.

The top four of such an index are:

1. United States of America    0.3040
2. Israel    0.1842
3. Ottoman Empire and Turkey    0.1552
4. England and Great Britain    0.1277

The commonality of the four countries mentioned above is structural violence, both in the sense of settler colonialism within and of regional and world empire-building without. They also share cultural violence based on hard readings of Abrahamic religions – hard-line Protestantism in the USA and the UK, hard-line (not Sufism!) Islam in the Ottoman Empire, and hard-line Zionism (not Martin Buber-esque!) in Israel. In all three cases we find dualism with Manichean overtones: seeing oneself as good, opponents as evil and Armageddon as the final arbiter – the DMA syndrome.[2] Add to this the idea of 'chosen by the eternal', a sense of past and future glory and the significance of past trauma suffered on the road – the CGT syndrome.[3] Both syndromes are important building blocks for deep violence. Of course, dialectically they also inspire the same syndromes in the other side. Today we witness this spiralling cultural escalation.

Two of these empires are now gone, with Turkey as a late bloomer. For the other two, the early warning prediction is obvious: came, went, gone. So what is the early action consequence? Contain the USA and Israel – is this realistic? Some think so, and most of today's violence takes place in these contexts.

*Johan Galtung is a sociologist and principal founder of the peace and conflict studies discipline. He has published several books on peacebuilding and conflict resolution. Professor Galtung is the founder of TRANSCEND – a peace and development network – as well as the International Peace Research Institute and the Journal of Peace Research.*

---

1 Keynote speech held by Johan Galtung at the conference "From early warning to early action: Developing EUs response to crisis and longer-term threats", 12-13 November 2007, European Commission, Brussels, Belgium
2 DMA: Dualism–Manicheism–Armageddon.
3 CGT: Chosenness–Glory–Trauma.

Hierarchies produce intractable conflicts. Peace assumes a high level of equity, or an 'equiarchy'. The road to peace is paved with acceptance of the other(s) as an equal partner in negotiation and dialogue. But if one or more of them is informed by a highly inequitable structure sustained by an entrenched culture, then peace by peaceful means becomes more difficult.

A cornerstone of the EU approach is to promote a culture of human rights and democratic structures. These are excellent – *bene* – per se. But the assumption that peace follows in their wake is based on a logical fallacy with serious consequences.

Violence in general, and war in particular, is a relation between two or more states. So is peace. But democracy and human rights may be properties of none, one or more of them, and may be very good for innerpeace. Make democracy a relation, like in a regional, or even global (the United Nations or national parliaments) relation based on free and fair elections. We are in the interstate, inter-nation peace business. Democracy does not steer major parties to crisis and violence today, but what about the day after tomorrow?

### Where is the early action?
### What is our crisis/threat response?

Another kind of relation worth working on is an unresolved conflict between parties.

This is the fire, and violence is the smoke. Conflict is as human as the body, mind and spirit. 'Conflict prevention' is meaningless, but 'violence prevention' is certainly not. There is no 'post-conflict', but hopefully there is a 'post-violence'. We must get out of the Anglo-American view of conflict as a clash of persons, groups or parties, and see conflict as a clash of goals.

Seeing conflict as a clash of goals makes it a problem to be solved by creating a reality whereby legitimate goals can be accommodated and become compatible. Seeing conflict as a clash of parties usually implies seeing one or more of them as parties to be controlled – often violently. Concepts matter.

TRANSCEND uses one-to-one dialogues with all parties. Mediation means mapping conflicts (parties–goals–clashes), testing goals for legitimacy and bridging legitimate goals. This calls for empathy, nonviolence and creativity. Conciliation means acknowledging past wrongs, elaborating how and why, and then defining a future together. When you enact in the present, you form an image with the parties – a vision of a compelling future – and are sensitive to their traumas and the glories of their past. You are creative.

This is more easily said than done, so let us explore five cases of mediation and five cases of conciliation, based on our own experiences. For more details, see www.transcend-nordic.org and our UN manuals for TRANSCEND and the Sabona approaches.[4]

What would peace in the Middle East, between Israel and its neighbours, look like? It would look much like the European Community imagined by two French statesmen whom we now honour for their creativity. They said, 'Nazi Germany has been so atrocious that it has to be a member of the family'. Few saw it that way at the time; moreover, the European family did not exist then except as a wartime alliance. They painted a compelling future on the wall, a community of six, invoking the future to overcome the past and even the present. In the end it stuck and has been an astounding success, inviting us all here and now to continue the good work.

Peace could look like a Middle East community of six: Lebanon, Syria, Jordan, Palestine (fully recognised), Egypt and an Israel willing to contract to something like its 4 June 1967 borders in exchange for security through peace. The opposite would be a non-starter. Others, like Turkey and Cyprus, might join, maybe in an Eastern Mediterranean community. Israel might develop very tight EU relations and Arab countries could join the Organisation of the Islamic Community. And yet there could be a Middle East community with open borders, rights and obligations.

4 Sabona is a group working on facilitating professor Johan Galtung's conflict concepts.

The six states in the Treaty of Rome could serve as a model, not only as a mediator. Open the archives and invite the countries concerned to share their concerns, while at the same time NGOs continue to stimulate dialogue. This scheme would need work both from the bottom and the top, with open dialogue all around. Western Europe managed to digest Germany. Western Asia and the eastern Mediterranean can manage the same with a more reasonable, more modest Israel.

Right now we are living in the shadow of a major US-Iran nuclear war. How do we solve this problem? This is not a border problem but a conflict rooted in the past. It needs acknowledgment by the United States and the UK of the wrongs committed by the CIA and MI6 in 1953, which deposed a legitimate prime minister and initiated 25 years of dictatorship. This has the possibility of triggering Sura 8:61 in the *Qur'an:* when your enemy inclines toward peace you shall do the same. Iran did so in both 2001 and 2003 but there was no response. Nonetheless, peace is located in this direction, and the nuclear issue would dissolve.

### What is the joint future?

Imagine the world's biggest oil consumer and potentially biggest oil producer join together for large-scale, non-fossil fuel projects! Maybe this could be financed by Norway's big oil fund rather than using a fifth of it to finance the Iraq war? Is this unrealistic? On the contrary: the lack of realism is with the so-called realists. The world would rejoice. But it would take moral courage. And it might take some history and textbook revisionism on both sides, which could build on the work of the masters of this, the Germans, some ten years after conflict resolution was built into the Treaty of Rome.

And what about Iraq? We need to build on past successes. The European Commission, for example, was an internal inter-state success. So was German textbook revision, which created good relations with the 25 invaded countries by today's map and the three peoples exposed to genocide: Jews, Sinta-Roma[5] and Russians. The Helsinki Conference on Security and Cooperation in Europe was also a success. Why not make a Conference for Security and Cooperation in West Asia, financed by the EU? Kurdistan would also have to be on this agenda – how can you have a confederation of four autonomies without drawing new borders?

And what about the artificial birth of Iraq, beginning in 1916? It lingered somewhere between federation and confederation while under the protection of the United Nations Security Council and Organisation of the Islamic Conference.

We have a list of Western aggressions against Muslim countries. We have names, years and particularly traumatic events. There is France attacking Egypt, and England Mysore, in 1798,[6] Italy bombing bases in Libya in 1911,[7] and Spain-Franco-Xauen in 1925.[8] The perpetrator suffers from amnesia, but the victim never forgets.

But what are the motives? Resources no doubt, with well-rewarded autocracies to guarantee delivery. There is also a continuation of the Crusades to subvert and convert Islam. (Italy and Spain, please take note). With luck there may be some serious signs of acknowledgment well before 2011 and 2025 – and not simply to stay out of trouble because it is the right thing to do. True greatness also includes the acknowledgment of one's own smallness.

This leads us to the US/Western world's 'War on Terror', a complex conflict with acts of war like 9/11 in New York and Washington, D.C., 7/7 in London and 11M[arch] in Madrid, and massive killing and torture in Iraq and Afghanistan. Spain, under Prime Minister Zapatero, handled 11M masterfully. Morocco's ambassador was not expelled, nor was Rabat bombed as

---

5 Sinta is a sub-group of the Romany people.
6 The Fourth Anglo-Mysore War (1798-1799) was a war in South India between the Kingdom of Mysore and the British East India Company.
7 During the Libyan war between Italy and the Ottoman Empire.
8 Americans troops under French and Spanish command bombed Xuaen in 1925 causing a large number of causalities.

somebody else might have done. Zapatero travelled to Rabat for top-level dialogue and also no doubt for talks about Ceuta–Melilla[9] (here a 'Hong Kong' solution might have been useful). In October 2005 Zapatero legalised nearly half a million illegal Moroccans in Spain, pulled Spanish troops out of Iraq and launched an 'Alliance of Civilisations'. Brilliant!

Which brings up Sykes and Picot, British and French diplomats respectively, who in 1916 promised the Arabs independence if they fought and helped overthrow the Ottoman Turks. They so did but were colonised: Iraq and Palestine for England and Syria and Lebanon for France. Rulers (leaders) used rulers (straight edges) to define their artificial entities. Maybe an Anglo-French-Arab history book about 1916 is overdue? It is never too late. Arab school children live this trauma even if the English and French do not, and not all wrongs come from Washington.

Let us move from the West-Christian/Arab-Muslim theatre to the Balkans. Here there is the situation in Kosovo/a, where the Serbs have 'clear historical legitimacy' in the territory they call 'Kosovo', while the Albanians have 'clear self-determination, democratic and historical legitimacy' in the same piece of territory they call 'Kosova'. Both status quo as a part of Serbia, and independence as a unitary state, are clearly untenable and will lead to endless violence. Division is untenable for at least two reasons: viability and the right of all to consider Kosovo/a theirs with free travel and interaction. What is the solution? An independent, federal Kosovo/a, with autonomous Serbian cantons, in a confederation with Serbia and Albania. Of course, majority-based self-determination for Kosovo/a sets a precedent for Bosnia-Herzegovina and elsewhere. But then, why not?

There is an Ottoman shadow over the region, which brings us to Turkey–Armenia and the question of conciliation. The conflict seems to have been trilateral with the Kurds being promised freedom if they would do the Turks' dirty work. They did, but got no freedom. The Anglo-French/Sykes–Picot formula, a part of the same zeitgeist, probably passes as an example of the art of statesmanship.[10] But does that exonerate the Turks? No, but it provides a context. Imagine unconditional acknowledgment implies unconditional compensation – could that stand in the way? Of course. How about building the joint future of neighbours around the contested mountain Ararat? How about making Ararat a 'Mountain of World Peace', not only for the three Abrahamic religions, but for humanity? Under joint Turkish–Armenian administration, UN aegis and paid by the EU? Approaching the past via the future – maybe also for Burma/Myanmar?

Why not open the EU for Turkey, Armenia and the Caucasian community? There is conciliation work to be done, as with formerly colonial countries and many EU charter members. But conciliation without conflict solution – à la shake hands, be good friends – is only pacification. This is like a ceasefire or money for development: it may buy time before violence erupts again. All roads to peace pass through deep conflict resolution. And price stabilisation in return for keeping the EU–ACP division of labour is shallow. The East Asian formula was industrialisation with protection and welfare state. Deeper transformation is needed.

The EU-ACP structural conflict has an important dimension: who plans whom? MDCs[11] love to plan LDCs,[12] and the EU the ACP, down to micro-management, as a part of ODA.[13] Imagine the EU inviting the ACP or the whole former Third World (AU + OIC + SAARC + ASEAN + SCO + ALC) to advise the EU and half a billion 'EUians'? Invite experts, host dialogues with their nationals

---

9  Ceuta and Melilla, on North Africa's Mediterranean coast, came under Spanish control around 500 years ago. Spain claims the urban enclaves are integral parts of Spain. They are surrounded by Morocco, which views the Spanish presence as anachronistic and claims sovereignty.

10  The 1916 Sykes-Picot-Sazanov Agreement, between the governments of Britain and France, with the assent of Russia, defined their respective spheres of influence and control in west Asia after the expected downfall of the Ottoman Empire during World War I.

11  MDC: most-developed-countries.

12  LCD: least-developed-countries.

13  Official Development Assistance (ODA) is a category of development aid.

in EU diaspora, elicit good ideas. Symmetry, reciprocity. The EU Commission has little or no hesitation dispensing advice – but is it willing to receive any?

The EU currently faces a very important dilemma: the civilian peacekeeping favoured by the Commission or the military version with rapid deployment favoured by the Council? The latter might like to fill the gap left behind when the USA withdraws troops, like the British did East of Suez in 1965. The Third World, the chosen battlefield like Orwell's Malabar Coast,[14] might have some advice to offer about taming the forces favouring interventions and enhancing those favouring creative solutions.

Maybe the Chinese could offer some advice from among that which they addressed to themselves at the 17th Congress of the Chinese Communist Party? And India might offer some advice about high electoral participation in a country with well above a billion population to one with less than half of that. The world does not need a new empire but rather inter-regional structures for joint planning.

As the South African foreign minister expressed at a conference (with the United States and Israel eloquently absent) on the issue of colonialism, 'this is not about money or compensation but about dignity'. How is dignity promoted? By perpetrators acknowledging, elaborating and designing new ways of entering the future together.

Dignity is a relation with symmetry, reciprocity and equity. One approach, building on the UNESCO German–Polish experience and the German approach in general, would be to invite a major joint history project on colonialism, with slavery included. This would also focus on the Arab–Muslim world and others.

All of these cases illustrate one point: to contribute something to solving big problems you must think big thoughts. Small thoughts will do for small problems, like standardisation of car bumpers. Check your thoughts, and let them grow with the people concerned. This can be done better by NGOs in the field than by diplomats in sterile rooms with linear agendas.

The Track I government vs. Track II civil society with NGOs, local authorities, the young and women, is problematic. Track I often becomes 'Track minus I', hoping that Track II can weigh in at plus I.

The strength of civil society is in direct contact – high on empathy and less inclined to violence. Having no hammer the world looks less like a nail. But creativity remains a crucial commodity. Its scarcity among diplomats geared toward correct process does not guarantee its presence in civil society – except for artists, engineers, architects, etc. Both can be trained in, say, non-Western *ho'o ponopono*[15], *gacaca*[16] and *shir*[17] conciliation approaches and then work hand in hand. There is much to learn.

The civil society can do all three, peacemaking, peacebuilding, peacekeeping. The non-governments can probably do it better than the governments. Thus, civil society can make 10,000 dialogues blossom, within and among conflict parties, find out where the shoes pinch and what future society, region, world they want to live in – like what Middle East, what Kosovo/a. They can let all that information flow together and watch the 'GNIP', the gross national idea product, grow. Something will emerge; peace may be made. Governments may clinch the deal.

But peace also has to be built. Webs of togetherness must be woven; humanising where there has been dehumanisation, and depolarising where there has been polarisation. And peace has to be kept, by non-violent peace forces, which are

---

14  Reference to George Orwell's novel Nineteen Eighty-Four
15  Ho'o ponopono means "to make right" and is a Polynesian ritual for forgiveness and clearing of past hurts.
16  Literally meaning "judgment on the grass" in Kirwanda. Gacaca courts were established after the Rwanda genocides. It is a traditional Rwandan method of resolving disputes by discussing issues with community leaders who were empowered to make a decision.
17  Shir means song in Hebrew and refers to Shir LaShalom - A Song For Peace which has become an anthem for the Israeli peace efforts.

numerous, competent and insert themselves so densely between violent parties that there is not enough space left for battle.

How about gender and generation? This is very important! In general men are more deductive, from grand principles, and women more compassionate – unless they permit PhDs in those grand principles to stand in the way. In general, the older generation has a more closed, and the younger a more open, discourse, and are more sensitive to new aspects and new ideas. Therefore, in a conflict women should meet the women on the other side(s), and the youth meet the youth on the other side(s). And young women should meet. Wherever older men enter a conference room some brigade of young women should get into action. Seduction rather than deduction? Well, those older men happen to run the world. And they often engage in mischief.

To this you may object – watch yourself Professor Galtung – you look like a man who has come of age. Wrong. I am actually a charming young woman, only disguised as an elderly man...

# HUMAN SECURITY IS THE KEY FACTOR

## INTERVIEW WITH ANGELIKA BEER

*What are your expectations concerning the difference that the new Stability Instrument can make in the EU's response to crise worldwide?*

I am fully aware that the new legal provisions still have to be implemented and that there is still much that needs to be done in terms of the EU's capabilities and performance. This is especially the case when it comes to the involvement of civil society organisations in the implementation and in the evaluation of the Stability Instrument.

Together with six other instruments, this initiative represents the legal and financial basis of the EU's common foreign policy activities. With its €2 billion budget for 2007-2013[1], the Stability Instrument significantly strengthens the EU's capacity for civilian intervention. Using a single legal method, the EU will be able to react to crises outside its borders in a rapid, flexible and coherent way potentialy followed by a cooperation based on other EU aid mechanisms.

Concerning both short-term and long-term measures, the Stability Instrument provides for financial and technical support for civilian actions of international and regional organisations, state actors as well as NGOs.

*What are the most important elements of the Stability Instrument in concrete terms?*

Some overdue and promising features in-clude civilian measures against the proliferation of small arms and light weapons, as well as clearance and stockpile destruction of landmines and duds. It also includes programmes to demobilise and reintegrate former combatants and child soldiers. Moreover, the instrument allows for the particular concerns of women in all fields of action. In addition, the instrument features a binding declaration that guarantees the respect for human rights in Europe's fight against terrorism.

The most prominent feature of the Stability Instrument is the Peacebuilding Partnership. This provides for the development of a representative network of NGOs engaged in conflict prevention, early warning, peacebuilding and post-conflict operations. The Peacebuilding Partnership also allows for direct financial support for regional organisations and networks to improve their capabilities. In addition, it envisages European Commission contact and coordination offices, both in Brussels and on the ground that are responsible for providing short-term administrative and logistic assistance. Right now we are revising the Peacebuilding Partnership Action Plan, as more and more NGOs hear about this instrument and could support it.

And there are other areas that need special attention, for instance the situation of weapons in Bosnia-Herzegovina. There are far too many weapons stored in this little country. What is striking is not just how old many of them are, but also the conditions in which they are stored as they flout all safety standards. The Stability Instrument could be used for monitoring and destroying surplus weapons.

*You also mapped out the Greens' new security strategy for Europe. Does the EU need to create a European Army as some politicians are openly calling for?*

In the controversy about 'human security' three things have gone wrong. First, the concept of 'human security' has been stretched so far as to even legitimise, for example, the deployment of armed forces to secure supplies of fossil fuels. Second, as a result of this – justly criticised – militarisation of 'human security', large sections of the peace movement have now rejected their own concept and concern themselves exclusively with civilian instruments. Third, we are being diverted from the need to examine how to obtain more security with less military involvement via the controlled harmonisation of European armed forces.

The Greens are countering the militarisation effort with reinforcement of the civilian instruments of the European Security and Defence Policy, disarmament, and

*Angelika Beer has been a member of the Greens/European Free Alliance group in the European Parliament since 2004. She chairs the EP's delegation for relations with Iran and is a member of the delegation for relations with Afghanistan. She is her party's coordinator in the EP's committee on foreign affairs and in the sub-committee on security and defence. She is a founder member of the German Greens and was their federal chairwoman (2002-2004) and the party's spokesperson on defence policy (1994-2002).*

---

1 Budget refers to the entire Instrument for Stability, not only the crisis response but also more long-term actions.

harmonisation of the armed forces in Europe. We in the Greens are campaigning for a European peace policy that responds to the issues of a fair distribution of resources and fair access on a global scale; pleas for urgent global disarmament efforts, first and foremost with regard to nuclear and other mass destruction arms; and puts the fight against expanding organised crime as one of the EU's top priorities.

*What are the core elements of your security proposal?*

European security policy must always be a human rights policy, too. Human rights are universal. Peacekeeping and peace-enforcement operations, and also the fight against international terrorism, can succeed only if forces deployed under the EU flag respect the European Charter of Fundamental Rights, the European Convention on Human Rights and international humanitarian law absolutely.

With regard to human rights, many problems have root causes in other policy areas as well. Current European foreign trade, agricultural and fisheries policies deprive millions of people in developing countries of their basis of life and drive them to migration. Conflicts over the distribution of water, energy sources and other resources threaten political stability in many regions worldwide. The trade and agricultural policy of the EU should be reformed to ensure fair market conditions for producers and farmers from developing countries and increased standards of living to remove causes for conflict.

It is not acceptable that there exist different standards of human rights within the EU. We cannot explain to other countries worldwide why the Charter of Fundamental Rights does not apply to all European citizens.

*The EU is very much concerned about a sustainable supply of energy and a diversification of its energy sources. When it comes to nuclear energy, do you see the nuclear issue as a threat to Europe's security?*

Energy policy must be a policy for peace. As well as responding to concerns about the security of energy supply, our strategy of moving away from oil and gas removes the cause of many conflicts. Our understanding of 'human security' firmly rejects the deployment of armed forces to safeguard raw materials. We Greens reject the revival of nuclear power as a replacement for oil and gas – one of the reasons being the lessons learnt from the nuclear catastrophe in Chernobyl.

Nuclear power always has a dual purpose. After all, civilian and military use are inseparable. The fight against proliferation cannot succeed while nuclear power is being used – a fact illustrated by the nuclear dispute with Iran. This means that renewable energy sources are not only necessary for the environment, they also increase security, as they tackle the causes of conflicts over fossil resources. Because of their decentralised networks renewables also present less potential for attacks, for example by terrorists. Investment in renewable energy sources is investment in more security and stability, and thus investment in peace. We would like to see

the EU promoting and providing renewable technologies in developing countries at low cost or for free.

*EU accession and the process towards membership is considered to be an extremely effective peace tool for the EU. What will Europe's current enlargement fatigue mean for its security?*

The accession perspective, currently benefiting the Western Balkan countries and Turkey is one of the most powerful security policy instruments at Europe's disposal. The prospect of joining the EU gives our neighbours a unique boost for democratisation and modernisation. However, this will materialise only if the EU advocates its founding values self-confidently and if it acts credibly in its negotiation strategy.

The situation in the Balkans, ravaged by civil war and political instability, is a particularly vivid illustration of the extent to which the prospect of EU accession has given these countries the courage to carry out reforms and the vision of a common European future. By continuing to hold out this prospect of accession on the one hand, and strengthening its neighbourhood policy on the other while recognising cultural differences as an asset, the EU can provide a decisive boost for democracy and human rights in Eastern Europe and Central Asia, in particular.

We do not support the doubts that are being cast on promises of future EU membership that have already been made. Questioning accession pledges would mean relinquishing without good cause one of

Europe's most important instruments for the peace project. The Greens support the EU's promises and firmly oppose a 'third way' between neighbourhood policy and membership that would call these promises into question.

*Will the Lisbon Treaty change the role of the European Parliament in security issues?*

We Greens are campaigning resolutely for effective parliamentary control of all EU military operations. For as long as this is not guaranteed at European level, the rights of national parliaments must be ensured and strengthened. The co-decision procedure, which we managed to secure for the first time with the Stability Instrument, is even more important in the case of Euratom and the military.

We support the new 'double-hatted' High Representative for Foreign Policy, as well as his/her assisting the European External Action Service. We hope that this new construction will strengthen the parliamentary control of EU foreign policy.

# A EUROPEAN PERSPECTIVE ON CRISIS RESPONSE
## INTERVIEW WITH ENEKO LANDABURU

*From an historical perspective what has the Commission learnt in the past 7 years in the field of Crisis Response?*

When we watch on the media the dramatic images of the crises in China, Pakistan, Congo, Burma, Sri Lanka, Somalia, Afghanistan, and when we think that so many other countries are going through a crisis without similar levels of attention from the public opinion, one could really wonder if the construction of peace, or "freedom from fear" are not forms of wishful thinking.

However, we are fully aware that we also have a political and moral duty to try everything to save lives, to transform conflicts that everyone considers as insoluble, intractable. The challenge we face is exceptional, but so are the resources available in Europe.

Our recent history shows that we have tried to use these resources intelligently. In 2001, the Rapid Reaction Mechanism (RRM), the precursor of the Instrument for Stability, provided an initial contribution to the process of conflict prevention and crisis response at European level: there were at that time (and there still are unfortunately) more than 100 political conflicts around the world.

The real change did not occur until the 2004 tsunami. This disaster triggered an overwhelming response worldwide, but this response was uncoordinated, often chaotic and ended up being criticized in an important ICRC (International Red Cross) report.

In Europe we felt we were obliged to lead the resulting debate. For this reason, together with President Ahtisaari we launched in 2005 a first major conference on the enhancement of European Crisis Response. Europe had to respond to these challenges in new ways. One of the most important things we had understood between 2001 and 2005 was that we had to integrate the full range of instruments as well as all available financial, human and technical resources. Coherence in the implementation of our resources became of paramount importance. Since then, we have made significant efforts to enhance the cooperation between the various institutions in Brussels dealing with crisis response, notably the Commission, the Parliament, the EU Military Staff, the Joint Situation Centre and Council Policy Unit. Most of these links are now operational and we have a new and dynamic tool: the Instrument for Stability.

The Instrument for Stability is a financing mechanism which – because of its structure and size – can provide flexibility, width and coherence to our action. We can implement a wider gamut of types of interventions and we can connect our short-term action with long-term cooperation aid, or with EU-led civil military operations.

*Can you give some examples of projects carried out with the Instrument for Stability?*

For example, in Guinea-Bissau we are implementing a Security Sector Reform project which aims at achieving a reform of the security sector, preparing the ground for major EDF activities, and possible activities by other donors in the near future. The project assists the government in the short term in the demobilisation and reintegration of former war combatants. This specific IfS project prepares the ground and facilitates the success for a long-term strategy to stabilize the political and economic situation and to fight the traffic of cocaine towards Europe. In Afghanistan we are enhancing the work carried out by EUPOL, which supports the Afghan police, by reforming the judicial sector through the IfS. In Lebanon, after the clashes between the Lebanese army and the jihadist militants of Fatah al-Islam in 2007, we are working to form a planning committee for the reconstruction of the Nahr el Bared refugee camp and at the same time we are removing 500 000 m³ of rubble; all this in order to prepare the long-term rehabilita-

*Eneko Landaburu* **has been Director General of External Relations at the European Commission DG RELEX since 2003. Prior to this he was Director General for Regional Policy and Cohesion and Director General for Enlargement. He has also served as Director of the Institute of Research on Multinationals and as an alternate Member of the Board of Directors of the European Investment Bank. Since 1996, he has also been a member of the scientific board of the Institute of European Studies, and a member of the administration board of Notre Europe.**

tion of the area and the stabilization of the province of Lebanon that our longer-term reconstruction programme will assist.

*How can the EU better coordinate its efforts in the context of continuously changing conflicts?*

We need to make use of networks of community actors to match the specific context and needs. This means honing in-country capacities. We are also increasingly responding to crises with new approaches; for example, better cooperation and coordination between civilian and military tools. This approach has become unavoidable.

*Can you explain how the civilian and military component integrate in a crisis situation?*

When there is a crisis requiring a form of military presence, the Member States have been able to agree unanimously to lend some of their national military units for joint EU military operations. This has happened on a few occasions, but in peacekeeping functions rather than combat functions.

What the Commission can rapidly offer in this context are the implementation models and the funds for activities that complement what is being carried out by the military component.

For example in Chad the Commission is supporting through the IfS civilian activities (e.g. training of the police, humanitarian aid, development of the local economy), alongside EUFOR CHAD, a military mission launched by the EU. The military and the civilian activities are taking place in the same geographical area and complement each other, but follow different chains of command.

*How would you explain the concept of 'early warning to early action'?*

Moving from early warning to early action is modern crisis response. Conflicts ignite quickly and responses need to be comprehensive and united in order to address them. Recently there has been an evolving public discourse concerning crisis response. Often the international community is taken aback by sudden outbreaks of violent events, particularly in Africa. The term 'forgotten wars' has become commonplace.

Thanks to the abundance of information that we can obtain from open sources, we have today the possibility of taking decisions with a much better situation awareness. The European Commission contributes to this information-gathering through its Crisis Platform Directorate. This directorate hosts one of the "nodes" of the "COREU Network" (CORrespondance EUropéenne), which is the EU communication infrastructure linking the Member States and the Commission for cooperation in the fields of foreign policy. Also operating within the Crisis Platform Directorate is our Crisis Room, which maintains for a user community of more than 1000 officials the Tarîqa open source intelligence system for early warning and risk assessment.

Finally, I should mention our operational links with 135 EC Delegations on the ground, with almost 5000 officials and a continuous stream of political reports on the situations unfolding on the ground. The challenge today for every diplomatic community is to modernize, and to have access to better, more qualified open source intelligence in support to bilateral or multilateral diplomatic activities.

*Is information, then, the key factor to develop a more reliable network of early warning resources?*

Yes, but it is not as simple as it might seem. There are a large number of people who witness conflict in the making, and we need to learn how to connect these people better, and draw on their knowledge and insights. Even with an abundance of information, there is often a gap between what we know and what we digest and put into action. Doing something at European level to address these "missing links" is crucial.

After all, nearly every crisis has relevance for Europe. Just look at the growing international communities living in all major European cities: instability in the Middle East, or in Africa or in South Asia, influences – sometimes directly – the evolution and the stability of these diaspora communities living in our cities.

*On a broader level, the EU has a number of tools available to stabilise potentially complicated global situations. Trade sanctions, for example.*

Yes, there is an array of tools available: joint statements, common positions of Member States, protocols, partnerships and agreements. Trade sanctions by the EU are often the last resort. It is important that all these tools play together. Specifically, our crisis platform has the ambition of bringing together a variety of crisis response tools.

In Aceh[1], for example, there was a rare combination of factors which fell into place in the right moment. After the tsunami the situation ripened locally for peace talks but external facilitation was needed. We were able to fulfil this role. At the same time, in order to underpin the Aceh peace agreement, there was the need for a neutral monitoring role. So there was a window of opportunity which opened the way for the EU's monitoring of the ceasefire and the EU Peace Dividend programme. Aceh illustrates well how the EU can add value and combine different kinds of actors and instruments coherently. Even though our tools remain subject to administrative procedures, we have the flexibility to do things faster now than in previous years.

*Looking to the future, what are the key challenges?*

Concerning the challenges, I think it is important to mention the issue of energy security. Energy today is increasingly being used as a political weapon. There is a resurgence of energy nationalism and re-nationalisation programmes among a number of producer countries, a deterioration of governance principles in the management of those resources, aggressive and non-transparent energy policies from certain important consuming countries and – last, but not least – an absolute need to fight climate change.

It is clear to everyone how these factors are already affecting the security situation of many countries around the world.

---

1 After the 2004 tsunami which hit the coastline of Aceh particularly hard, the rebels and the government agreed to peace talks. It resulted in a peace agreement, ending more than 30 years of conflict.

# ASSISTANCE IN CONFLICT MUST PROMOTE RESOLUTION
## INTERVIEW WITH MARC OTTE

*What is the role of the European Union in trying to make progress for peace in the Middle East? Is it a player or mainly a payer, especially in comparison to US engagement?*

The Europeans are the first to be responsible for giving such a wrong impression. If they have been payers then it is only because they have not always shown the same coherence and unity in pursuing the political goals or the political role they want to play. Europeans have de facto always been political players: it is only that the nature of European external action is different from the foreign policy of a national government.

Without the United States nothing can happen, but it is not only the USA who can move things forward. The Europeans tend to understate their involvement, and the EU is an abstraction: it is a collection of governments who can express a strong political will to act together or express a weak political will to do so. Some European countries are extremely focused and interested in the problems of the Middle East, some are less. But generally speaking, the stronger the EU's common interest in this conflict, the more effective the EU can act in its external policies.

*Has external assistance helped to move the Middle East peace process forward?*

Not really, no. That's not only the case with EU engagement. What we Europeans have been doing in the last few years when the conflict has been escalating, has been to compensate for the humanitarian consequences in the Palestinian population. So, to a large extent, it has been at work on the symptoms, not on the causes. After the Oslo Agreement, and being in the wake of a process, our assistance was successful because the Europeans in general were responsible for a part of the institution building and for a part of the development of economic structures.

But once the parties decide to fight there is little one can do. You cannot replace the parties to the conflict or try to come up with any substitutes for their action. I am not against humanitarian assistance at all. It has always been part of the EU's values – be it the case of Palestinian refugees or in many other areas of the world – to be among the most generous and among the first to respond. However, I always had misgivings about it because its value is to respond to immediate humanitarian need and it does not help to resolve a conflict. It is clearly a moral dilemma, but at the same time morality is only one dimension of foreign policy.

We should have a better system for assessing the impact of what we do in terms of assistance. Here I come back to the idea of being a political player: you use your tools towards a political end, otherwise the tool becomes the policy. If the important criterion is to say that you are the biggest donor, then that is a policy and no longer a tool. Your assistance in a conflict needs to promote the resolution of the conflict. Once external support stops doing that one should review the tools, and not question the policy.

*What is needed to make real progress in the Middle East?*

For a conflict to be resolved the first condition is that the parties want to resolve it. If people want to fight there is very little third parties can do. It is only when they signal a desire to get out of their conflict and they ask for a mediator, a third party or for any other kind of external assistance, that external mediation can start doing something. Numerous studies have shown that in the absence of a real process towards the resolution of a conflict, external assistance tends to prolong the conflict or at least tends not to give the parties involved any reason to end the conflict. That is true in the case of the Israeli–Palestinian conflict as well as in any other conflict in the world.

*How do you assess the results of the Annapolis Conference?[1]*

The main goal of the Annapolis Conference was to launch real negotiations to end

*Marc Otte is the European Union's Special Representative for the Middle East peace process. Since July 2003 he has represented the EU's efforts to help find a final settlement of the Israeli–Palestinian conflict. He worked as adviser on defence and security policy to the EU's High Representative for Common Foreign and Security Policy (1999-2003) and was Head of the European Security and Defence Policy task force in the EU Council. He has also held various positions in the Belgian Foreign Service, including Ambassador to Israel (1992-1996).*

---

1 The Annapolis Conference was a Middle East peace conference held on 27 November 2007 at the US Naval Academy in Annapolis, Maryland, USA. The conference marked the first time a two-state solution was articulated as the mutually agreed-upon outline for addressing the Israeli–Palestinian conflict. The conference ended with the issuing of a joint statement from all parties.

the conflict. This has been achieved. Both parties agreed, in a joint declaration, on the framework of these negotiations. Now we have a table of content, a timeline, a methodology and a monitor. This is already a very good outcome.

Annapolis was not about ending the conflict, but about starting something. Contrary to the last peace talks in Camp David in 2001, which were supposed to be the end of a process, this is the beginning of a process where people will start to solve the conflict. First it will involve the Israelis and the Palestinians, and maybe at a second, later stage the Arabs in general. The conference was a success because everybody has accepted that it was held and more than 40 countries endorsed the joint declaration. Among those were many Arab states that do not yet have diplomatic ties with Israel.

The outcome of Annapolis must now be translated into an efficient follow-up. This has to include productive negotiations and real international support to establish a two-state-solution, which means creating a Palestinian state that has the capacity to run itself. For these reasons and because there is already a lot of pledging for that kind of support, Annapolis is a success because it has given that kind of momentum.

*How do you see the current political weakness of the leaders on both sides?*

Apparently when they are too strong they are too strong to negotiate; when they are weak they are too weak to negotiate. The fact that people are coming to Annapolis shows that they have a reason to do it. I can give a very long list of reasons why it is not a good time to start a negotiating process and why it will not work. It is not the perfect time. But the real question is what would be the cost of failure? What is the cost of doing nothing in the present situation? In this conflict, but also in the region, maybe that is one of the reasons why people start to reflect these days. There is a convergence of interests to start working in a more positive way towards something that is more tangible instead of continuing with some sort of crisis management that has been going on for several years. So, a weakness of leadership is only a relative notion. The cost of failure is the much more important consideration.

*How can Hamas and Fatah move closer together?*

It is the same thing as with the Israelis and the Palestinians: they have to want to come together. What can outsiders do? It is a matter for the Arabs. To the extent that Syria is sponsoring the terrorist activities of Hamas, or at least letting them act or hosting their leadership, they could use their authority to stop it. But if Fatah and Hamas have to work together they have to find common ground. It is very difficult because they fight for two different models of society. But national unity is the only way that the Palestinians can achieve their national goals. However, it is not the first time that this has happened in a national liberation movement. I see it as mainly an Arab issue. The Arab League is offering a peace initiative and all Palestin-

ians should agree to it and end violence. But unfortunately Fatah and Hamas have not given up the idea of fighting each other.

We already have a state within a state. In Gaza, Hamas controls everything. They control the territory, they control the life of the people and it is not a law-abiding leadership. Life is not happy for the Palestinians, especially for people in Gaza. Nevertheless, they continue to support the idea of a negotiated solution, and they are sceptical about what could happen after the Annapolis peace conference. It will have to be demonstrated to the Palestinians that the present situation is a more promising one than just getting on with life.

*Is the extremely complex situation in the Middle East an unsolvable conflict?*

It is all relative. As John Maynard Keynes used to say: in the long-term we will all be dead. The conflict has been already lasted 60 years now; peace deals that Israel has concluded with some of their neighbours have not been particularly warm. But one can see similar situations in other parts of the world. It often needs an awful lot of time.

*Will the Lisbon Treaty change anything in the EU's power to influence the Middle East peace process?*

In principle, these new institutional arrangements that are planned will help us improve the EU's external action and make it more efficient. But it is too early to say whether this will help us solve a certain conflict.

*What were your expectations when you started your job, and how would you describe them today? Are you more disillusioned, maybe even frustrated, or have you been a realist from the very first day?*

The core problem remains the same, but the backdrop has changed. It is the same play but against a different background. A number of elements in my perception have been sharpened. It is like in a picture where you change the focus; some elements have come into closer focus. It has become obvious in the last four years that the strategic concerns of the parties are increasingly shifting. The rise of Iran has become the main strategic challenge – which was facilitated by the disappearance of Iraq as an Arab shield vis-à-vis Iran – leading to an ideological confrontation in the region and the rise of non-state actors, which have become strategic threats. More generally speaking, the contrast between the stagnation in this region and the dynamism of other regions in the context of globalisation is very striking – not to mention the dangers of proliferation of weapons of mass destruction.

# CROSSING THE LINES

## Introduction

Women's organisations are playing an increasingly important role in non-violent conflict resolution. They are frequently the first to take the risks necessary to promote dialogue across divided communities and move towards reconciliation. This works ranges from small local initiatives which often involve an income-generating component. One example of this is a café and pastry shop that women have organised in an ethnically divided town in Bosnia-Herzegovina. Situated on the unofficial border that separates the two communities, the café and pastry shop is the only safe place within miles where members from the different communities can meet and talk with each other. It was started by Croat, Serb and Bosnian women together, as a way to both provide employment for women and to help heal ethnic enmity. The women also collect the names and addresses of possible returnees from the 'wrong' ethnic group, and help provide returnees with practical necessities such as tools and milk cows.[1]

Women's work for dialogue also reaches to the highest political levels. The Northern Ireland Women's Coalition (NIWC), after mobilising broad cross-community support, played a key role in the talks leading up to the 1998 Good Friday Agreement, and conducted a successful door-to-door election campaign that sent two members to the Northern Ireland Assembly. In a radical departure from partisan politics, the NIWC has refused to take a stand on issues such as a constitution for Northern Ireland, emphasizing instead the need for inclusive dialogue and decision-making.[2]

The Liberian Women's Initiative (LWI) likewise helped to transform a previously male-dominated political process by demanding a voice at the 1994 Accra Clarifications Conference. By insisting that all parties disarm before the election, by publishing lists of women qualified to take up positions in government ministries if appointed, and by conducting an energetic voter education programme that emphasized the need for women to be actively involved in peacebuilding, the LWI helped build stability and peace in Liberia. LWI's efforts also laid the groundwork for a founding LWI member, Ruth Perry, to be elected as Liberia's head of state.[3]

Several common understandings and paradoxes inform the work of all these groups. The first understanding is the necessity of involving as many ordinary people as possible in building peace. For peace to be sustainable, peace processes and reconstruction must be owned by the communities involved. Women's engagement in such peace processes are especially critical. Women's political marginalisation paradoxically often provides them with a wider space for peacebuilding. Their motivation in becoming involved in peacebuilding often stems from, or is perceived as, the desire or need to provide for their family, especially children. This concern for their family gives many women the permission to enter formerly forbidden male political territory. Because of their previous marginalised position, women may be perceived as outside the influence of a conflict's major stakeholders. This means that women's peacemaking initiatives may be trusted more by a community than those of peacemakers coming from the political elite.

Angela E. V. King, Special Advisor on Gender Issues and Advancement of Women to the United Nations, pointed out some of these perceptions in analysing the role of women in the United Nations Observer Mission in South Africa (UNOMSA), which she served as Chief of Mission. While she writes of foreign women in the role of observers,

*Shelley Anderson founded the Women Peacemakers Program (WPP) in 1997 and is currently a WPP Programme Officer. The WPP works to empower women peace activists and pioneers gender-sensitive non-violence training. The WPP is a programme of the International Fellowship of Reconciliation (IFOR). Anderson is an experienced non-violence trainer and has conducted trainings in gender and peacebuilding throughout the world. Her articles on women's peace activism have been translated into a dozen languages. In 2005 she was collectively nominated for the Nobel Peace Prize as part of the '1000 Women for the Nobel Peace Prize' initiative.*

---

1  C. Cockburn. 'Picking Up the Pieces: Women's organizations in post-war reconstruction in Bosnia-Herzegovina'. Keynote address to the Trinity College Euroconference on 'Women, Violence and Reconciliation', 10–12 March 2000, Dublin, Ireland.
2  K. Fearon (1999). Women's Work: *The Story of the Northern Ireland Women's Coalition*. Belfast: The Blackstaff Press.
3  'The Liberian Women's Initiative'. International Women's Day for Peace and Disarmament, 24 May 2000, pack 9.

women inside a particular community may also be perceived in the same way. 'The presence of women seems to be a potent ingredient in fostering and maintaining confidence and trust among the local population', she writes. 'In performing their tasks with their male colleagues, women were perceived to be more compassionate, less threatening or insistent on status, less willing to opt for force or confrontation over conciliation, even it is said less egocentric, more willing to listen and learn – though not always – and to contribute to an environment of stability that fostered the peace process'.[4]

Conflict can thus lead to social transformation. In some post-conflict situations, such as in Cambodia and Rwanda, male death rates during the armed violence means that the surviving population may be 60 to 70 per cent female. Reconstruction in such societies often demands that women take on new roles. Whether women keep this new ground and/or use it to promote improvements in women's status after the crisis that has made such an opening possible is over, is an unanswered question. In Western history, during the Second World War, women in the UK, Canada and the US were mobilised in unprecedented numbers to work in jobs and decision-making functions formerly restricted to men. After the war, women were immediately sacked and told to return to their kitchens and more traditional gender roles.

In what ways are community-based women's peace groups promoting dialogue and rebuilding societies destroyed by armed conflict? To answer this question we will first look at the work of the International Fellowship of Reconciliation (IFOR) Women's Peacemakers Program (WPP).

### Empowering women peacemakers

The WPP began in 1997, though its roots go back much further. The WPP's operating assumptions include the belief that without peace, development is impossible and that without women, neither peace nor development can take place. Other assumptions include the belief that peacebuilding, especially in a post-conflict situation, is a long term process, and that the principal actors in such reconstruction should be the affected communities themselves.

The WPP's main goal is to support and strengthen women's peacemaking initiatives and capacities. The WPP does this in four ways:

1. By helping women's groups to organise training in active nonviolence and conflict resolution (as has been with tribal women in the Chittagong Hill Tracts, along the Thai–Burma/Myanmar border, in Romania, Azerbaijan, India, Nepal, Nigeria and Zimbabwe);

2. By organising regional consultations where women from different sides of conflicts can safely meet to discuss strategies for de-escalating the violence, and to deepen their understanding of nonviolent conflict resolution (as has been down for the European, Asian and African regions);

3. By publishing materials that document and analyse the successes and failures of women's efforts in reconciliation and peacemaking (such as the annual 24 May International Women's Day for Peace and Disarmament action pack and the WPP newsletter 'Cross the Lines'; and

4. By helping to promote self-sustaining women's organisations (primarily by linking women's groups with resources and organisations that can provide technical and financial support for peace initiatives).

Some practical examples of how the WPP works are given below.

### The Sudanese Women's Voice for Peace

'Peace comes from talking to your enemies', says Teody Lotto of the NGO Sudanese Women's Voice for Peace.[5] The SWVP is a good example of the role community-based

4  A. King, 'Success in South Africa'. *UN Chronicle* 3, 1997.
5  Sudan: As long as you are alive you must have hope'. International Women's Day for Peace and Disarmament, 24 May 2000. IFOR Women's Peacemakers Program, Spoorstraat 38, 1815 BK Alkmaar, Netherlands.

women can play in the peaceful resolution of armed conflicts. It is also exemplifies the role dialogue on all levels – between communities in violent conflict, between different factions inside particular communities, and between conflictants and the international community plays in nonviolent conflict resolution.

Lotto's attitude reflects SWVP's approach to its work in transforming Sudanese society through peacebuilding and human rights advocacy. Such an attitude is a key element towards a dialogue that makes for reconciliation. 'I am not interested in revenge. Will revenge bring back my loved ones? No!' she states. SWVP teaches conflict resolution skills to villagers. 'We have trained 66 women trainers so far', Lotto says. 'When we come to an area we ask the women to select the women with influence in the village. These leaders are trained in non-violence and reconciliation, so they can train others. We teach women to promote traditional peacemaking, to bring different villages to forgive one another'.

Village women have been empowered to begin a dialogue with guerrilla leaders. 'Sometimes the women come together to talk to rebels who have been raping, looting and burning houses. When the women oppose this, they have made some rebel leaders change. The leaders see how some soldiers took advantage to loot, pretending that they are under orders. Some leaders say even the military needs peace train-

ing. They have given us the okay to build peace demonstration centres', Lotto says. In some areas women stopped the recruitment of child soldiers by negotiating agreements from guerilla leaders to stop abducting children from schools.

The Sudanese conflict has provided some women an opportunity to explore public space and power negotiations with men in a way that peace-time society did not. This opening up of possibilities for positive social transformation during a period of conflict resolution is not unique. The Wajir Peace and Development Committee, a community-based group in north-eastern Kenya composed primarily of women, is also creating a public political role and voice for women. The women's on going work to prevent violence between different clans has mobilised both youth, a group not normally listened to, and the traditional decision-makers, older men, to work together to create peace and stability. 'When one elder asked me how I, a woman, dared to speak in public', says one Committee activist, 'I asked him, "If your house was on fire would you wait to put it out until a neighbour came?" My house is on fire and I must put it out'.

The WPP also helped the SWVP make critical international links during its formation in order to secure non-violence training, office support and funding. SWVP members were invited by IFOR to international gatherings, such as the 1994 'Women, Religion and Peace' seminar in Sweden; the 1995 UN

Fourth World Conference on Women in Beijing, China; and the 1999 Hague Appeal for Peace conference in the Netherlands, in order to put Sudan on the international agenda.

Other international peace organisations are also cooperating with the SWVP. In 1997, Pax Christi started a pilot trauma counselling project in Nairobi, for Sudanese refugee women, and inside Sudan, in Mapel. 'In this project we help women to feel free to tell of their suffering', says Lotto. 'We ask women not to hold bitterness in their hearts, but to go to trained women to be healed of trauma and aggression. You cannot amend the past but you can correct the future'.

### Work in the former Yugoslavia and the Caucasus

Women's groups, like the Women in Black in Belgrade and the Anti-War Coalition in Zagreb, were among the first to publicly oppose nationalist and ethnic violence when war first broke out in former Yugoslavia in the early 1990s. IFOR supported these groups in practical ways, by distributing their statements and manifestos; publicising their work with dissidents, military deserters, conscientious objectors and refugees; helping to relay messages between the two groups when telephone and fax communication between Belgrade and Zagreb were cut; providing safe spaces where Serbian, Croatian and Slovenian activists could meet; and eventually helping these and other anti-war groups to secure computer equipment and in getting online.

IFOR was also a founding member of the Balkan Peace Team (BPT, a cooperative project by some 11 peace NGOs, including War Resisters International and Peace Brigades International). BPT has been sending trained volunteers to Bosnia-Herzegovina, Croatia, Kosovo/a and Serbia since 1994, to support local civil society groups and to assist with dialogue and community conflict resolution projects. One example of how BPT works occurred in 1998, when students in southern Serbia wanted to do something about the growing tensions in Kosovo/a. The students approached BPT to help make connections with ethnic Albanians in Kosovo/a. BPT organised a prejudice reduction workshop for the Serbian students, then accompanied the students on a visit to an Albanian youth group inside Kosovo/a. The Serb students attended a nonviolent march in Kosovo/a as observers. They were able to report back to their community on the Serbian police's aggression against the marchers.

After the 1999 NATO bombing campaign the BPT office in Belgrade was shut down. The BPT in Pristina continues to assist local groups in working for a multi-ethnic Kosovo/a. In order to counter the rigid emerging ethnic enemy images that will perpetuate inter-ethnic violence, BPT is now working on a project to collect and publicise stories of how individuals from one community,

whether Serbian, Albanian, Slav or Roma, saved the lives of members from the 'other' community. 'In working on peacebuilding there are several important points that we need to bear in mind. First and foremost, peace (and conflict) is based on the relationship. Therefore, building peace needs to be focused on the relationship', writes BPT volunteer Erik Torch,[6] '[there is] overwhelming pressure within Albanian society to portray all Serbs and Slavs and Roma as inherently evil [...] how does one begin to deconstruct such attitudes in others? It requires a relationship that is strong enough to challenge such attitudes'.

Similar challenges to enemy images have been undertaken by other community-based peace groups. The IDP Women's Association of Georgia specifically focuses on children and youth in this regard, bringing together Georgian, Abkhazian and Ossetian children in peace camps where they will have a chance to build personal relationships with their enemy counterparts and learn peacebuilding skills. The IDP Women's Association has also been involved in documenting stories where people from one community saved individuals from the opposite side.

'Ethnically induced armed confrontation had one more side: a humane one. The facts are [...] people, at the risk of their own lives,

rescued the lives of other people, belonging to the opposite, "hostile" side of the conflict'. This is explained in the introduction to *Restoring The Culture of Peace in the Caucasus: A Human Solidarity Document.*[7] This 86-page book records the testimonies of some 60 women and men during the conflicts in Georgia, Abkhazia, South Ossetia, Armenia and Azerbaijan. The testimonies were collected by the NGO Assist Yourself, an organisation of mostly women internally displaced people from Abkhazia,[8] explicitly because 'there exists a risk that it [the stories] might disappear some time, and information of a different, negative kind, used by the destructive forces, would promote further separation and distrust'.

During the WPP European consultation, Gulnara Shaninian of Armenia emphasized the importance of such attempts. 'My generation had personal relationships with Azeris, lived side by side as neighbours, had friendships. This generation only knows enemy images and war. This will make it harder to build peace for the future'.[9]

IFOR members remain committed to working with community groups throughout the Balkans. The Fellowship of Reconciliation (FOR) in the United States helped several hundred young Bosnians continue their secondary school and university education in

6 E. Torch, 'The Paradoxes I See: A letter from a volunteer'. *Balkan Peace Team Newsletter,* No. 17, autumn 1999.
7 *Restoring the Culture of Peace in the Caucasus: A human solidarity document.* International Centre on Conflict and Negotiation, compiled by Marina Pagava. Georgia (1990).
8 Abkhazia is a region in the Caucasus.
9 S. Anderson, 'Women Peacemakers: Healing and Reconciliation'. *Reconciliation International,* June 1998: p. 22..

the USA during the war, placing the students with American families, securing scholarships, and helping the participants in the FOR's Bosnian Student Project (BSP) return after the war's end. The FOR also organises annual work camps throughout the former Yugoslavia, which focus on practical work such as rebuilding homes, sharing experiences in peace organising and multi-cultural living, and teaching English.

The FOR also supports the work of Bosnian activists such as Emsuda Mujagic, a survivor of the Trnopolje concentration camp. Mujagic is founder of 'From Hearts to Peace', which works for dialogue between Bosnians and Serbs. Among other work, From Hearts to Peace organises an annual dialogue group where Bosnian and Serb educators can meet to discuss reconciliation. Dolores Gunter, an FOR staff member who participates in the BSP, wrote about a party Mujagic organised for a FOR work camp in Bosnia-Herzegovina: 'Emsuda and others prepared a big barbecue of roast lamb, and invited the few Serbs who live in town (their homes were not destroyed) and who will someday be their neighbours again. The Serbs did not come, but some of their children did. Em-

suda packed up meat and sent it home with them to their parents. And so, in the small gestures of women, the work of reconciliation proceeds'.[10]

## Strengths, weaknesses and contradictions

Women are playing a leading role in reconciliation. This fact is being recognised more and more by conflict resolution specialists, government officials and development agencies. Despite this growing awareness, women's peacemaking initiatives remain under-resourced. There is a danger that women's work for reconciliation and reconstruction can be seen as a 'natural' extension of women's role in society. This means that such work goes unrecognised and inadequately resourced. It is stripped of its political meaning and rendered, like much of women's work, invisible. Women remain marginalised, their problems ignored, their experiences unanalysed, and their skills underutilised. When does capitalising on women's strengths in peacemaking, such as good listening and communication skills, flexibility, and a concern for people above abstract principles, become perpetuating traditional sex role stereotypes?

The functions women have in reconciliation processes are complex, reflecting the multiple roles women have in society. Like women's lives, such functions must be viewed holistically. Women are peace educators inside the family, in schools, in women's and mixed organisations and elsewhere. Their networks and knowledge of local affairs make them effective early warning monitors, alert for rumours, increasing tensions, a sudden influx of weapons and others sign of potential conflict. Their sometimes extensive kinship links, social expectations and training can make women highly effective mediators. Their status as outsiders, the perception that they are not primary stakeholders in conflict, also reveal a role as negotiators and originators of new approaches to peace.

The challenge for people interested in reconciliation is to explore this complexity and to develop an integrated gender approach. Such an approach would investigate both the ways in which women contribute to and oppose armed conflict. Most of all such an approach needs to discover concrete ways to support community-based women's work for peace.

10  D. Gunter, 'Women Reconcilers in Bosnia', *Fellowship*, 1998: 64.11–12:28.

# 'LIGHT IN THE DARKNESS'
## INTERVIEW WITH MARGUERITE BARANKITSE

*You are in Brussels to speak at an EU crisis management conference. Is it sometimes difficult to get your message across to decision-makers who might not have the same life experiences as you?*

When I speak at a conference, I speak from the heart. I do not just give a speech. Speaking about your human calling is easier because you do not need to convince people. I taught for a long time so I know how difficult it is to try and "teach a lesson" to people. It is easier for me just to speak about what happened in my life and about the dreams I have for the future.

I talk about living among a people who experienced a 10-year civil war that others did not even talk. People are aware of Rwanda but they do not talk about neighbouring Burundi, which suffered 10 years of atrocities. We sometimes felt abandoned but I have always said to people that I would like to bring some light into this darkness.

I communicate in the same way with everyone, whether it's a homeless person in a train station or a prince in a palace. I know that everyone is created in God's image. Even if I sometimes come across arrogant people who do not want to listen, I do not find it difficult to meet politicians or decision-makers. I see every handshake as a flow of love and friendship and I have no prejudices against people.

I am the ambassador of all the children

and others back in Burundi. I know I am their voice and I have the chance to speak from the heart to people who can make a difference. My hope is that this voice is heard. For me, just to be invited to this conference shows that decision-makers are thinking about people in my country. At the table of big players, it is important that a place is also kept for others.

*What are the difficulties you face when dealing with governments and decision makers?*

Our work is complex. All the big organisations, for example at governmental level, have bureaucratic systems that can be very time-consuming to deal with. We work in the field and often need to react as a matter of urgency. We see the poverty at first hand and we know that two days waiting for a decision can make the difference between life and death.

We call on the people in power to make the processes less bureaucratic. Our government tends to need endless documents and long reports to be able to see what we want to achieve. Our focus is on the result. I don't mean to criticise the work the government does. I am part of the same nation after all. We just need a better synergy. I call on them to trust us more, to give us the means to make our plans possible. They will be happy to see what we can do!

Organisations always want to have big

advertising boards to show what they are doing. If we took all of those, imagine how many houses we could build! So, sometimes I steal them and use them to build kiosks for the children.

In 14 years, we have progressed a lot at Maison Shalom. When we began, we only had computer boxes to use as cradles for babies. We had love though and I think that shows that love is inventive! At the time, we saw all the buildings and seminars that were being funded. Crumbs were all we got! We are tired of getting crumbs; we are all brothers and sisters in this world.

*What does Maison Shalom represent and how does it make a difference?*

Maison Shalom is more than a project; it is a message. It is a message of peace addressed to everyone, not just policy-makers. We believe in living in dignity and in refusing hate and fratricide, despite the atrocities that surrounded us.

It is about being able to go to school, to receive health care and to say that we live in a country free from war. We welcome children from Congo and Rwanda. We also welcome child soldiers and teach them a trade so they can have a fresh start in a new job.

We give work to people in our care. Our initiatives have included everything from hairdressers to cinemas. I have seen orphaned children grow up and work to

*Marguerite "Maggy" Barankitse is a humanitarian from Burundi. On 25 October 1993, during the civil war in her country, she was tied up and forced to witness the massacre of 72 people. She adopted the 25 children who were orphaned on that day. This action led to a movement, 'Maison Shalom', which has since cared for over 10,000 children of both Hutu and Tutsi origin from Burundi and outside its borders. Barankitse's work has been recognised by numerous international awards including the Council of Europe's North-South prize and the United Nations' Nansen Refugee Award.*

earn their livelihood. Among the children who have been in my charge, one went on to become the governor of a province, another to work for UNICEF. It shows there is hope.

We continue our work. Our latest project is to build a hospital. Of course, there are highs and lows. It is fortunate that we all have crises from time to time, because they confront us with reality and remind us of our limits. There will always be despair but we should put the emphasis on what we can do. One child saved is humanity saved.

*Your work is also spreading outside your country's borders?*

I feel I am a citizen of the world. I am attached to my country but I know I have a wider role to play too. We have recently sent people to help in the Democratic Republic of Congo. If we have to go to Iraq, we'll go there too because we are all part of the same human family.

People talk about Africa in terms of stereotypes and caricatures. They paint a dark picture: the AIDS situation in many countries, the genocide in Rwanda, and the terrible misery in Darfur. All that is true and real. I don't say we should close our eyes. But what people often overlook is our *joie de vivre*. Africa can wake up and surprise people! We have a lot of young people and there is real hope for the future.

I look at other countries and see problems there too. I see Belgium and wonder how in this day and age we can still be worrying about who is Walloon, Flemish,

Hutu or Tutsi. I hear about the number of suicides in Europe and it makes me think about opening a Maison Shalom there too! Trust us. I think Africans can show how to fight problems without becoming disheartened. We could have a real partnership.

The world is constantly changing. Not so long ago Europeans were migrating to America because they were in a bad economic situation. Tomorrow Africa could wake up and make use of the richness it possesses in natural resources. Maybe one day we will be helping Europe and the rest of the world!

*Our capacity to help is perhaps limited because many people have little consciousness of the world beyond their borders. Events that may grab their attention at first are often soon forgotten.*

That is human psychology, but fortunately, there are also people in the world who do not forget. There are always prophets among us who awake others.

When the customs officers ask me what I'm going to do in a country, I say I'm here to see my brothers and sisters! There are so many barriers, real and psychological. In times of war, people suspect you are an asylum seeker. The world is afraid of poor people but it should see sharing as a richness. There is no worse enemy to man than fear. It can even drive us to kill each other.

Maybe I am utopian to wish there were no barriers but imagine a world without passports. Life would be much easier and

we could help each other a lot more than we do now!

*What role can expatriate Burundians play?*

There are Burundians who qualified as doctors back home but retrained as nurses abroad to earn more money and be accepted there. Some highly qualified people are even delivering newspapers for a living. I call on them to come back! We have empty universities and hospitals at home.

Many have returned to Burundi but I do recognise that it is difficult. The government must give our intellectuals and qualified nationals the salary and dignity they deserve. If a university professor earns only €80 a month in Burundi, it is understandable that people do not return. Personally, though, I think it is better to fight for your rights in your own country and maintain your identity.

What does it mean to be rich anyway? It isn't about money. People in material poverty can still have a strong identity and fight together for their civil rights. In Africa, we have a debt to our families who paid for our school studies when we were children. We shouldn't be cowards or forget where we came from.

*You have a very positive message. What hopes do you have that others will be able to move on from the past?*

I believe in the triumph of humanity and in extending the hand of friendship. I will not be discouraged by fatalistic speeches or by bitter, desperate people. My duty is not to change the face of Burundi. I must not take myself too seriously or put the whole of Burundi on my shoulders.

I believe that every situation has a solution. I was tied up when I witnessed the murder of 72 people but I was able to do something afterwards. I took care of their children. Every one of those children has been successful at school and some already have gone to university or got married. For those people killed on that day, they saw in my eyes that I supported them and this gave some small sliver of light and hope. So, I was not powerless. Love is inventive.

I continue to look after young people and hope there will be a new generation who will understand and carry on this message on. We need to approach those who are discouraged or vengeful and make them understand that hate kills. I will not fall into either fatalism or utopianism. I am realistic. I am a hands-on person!

The message to the children is to stand upright, to maintain their dignity, and above all not to be disheartened by statistics from the World Bank or the IMF that rank Burundi as last in the world. What does that mean anyway? If I paid too much attention to the statistics, I'd ask for asylum but that's not me. I want to stay among my brothers and sisters in Burundi and I want to be a daughter worthy of my nation, because a country is like a mother.

*Do you feel women have a special role to play? Would it help your country to have more women in positions of power?*

Fortunately, Africa has always had many mothers. A woman gives life. All human beings were once physically connected to their mothers. It is a fabulous thing but life is not possible without the contribution of a man. What I mean to say is that we need both men and women to play a role.

I don't want to shock anyone but I already see women everywhere in power: even the mother or wife of the president for example. We are pillars of this world and I do not feel that I have been denied anything because I am a woman. I have always demanded that my rights be respected.

Today I am a woman, a mother to 10,000 children and doors open everywhere because I opened my heart. It is for no reason more extraordinary than that.

There is a lot more I want to do but I have limits of health and character. I am not a saint! But I find life beautiful. I want to stop people and tell them that. We should not wait for paradise in the afterlife. It is already here in our hearts!

[   Rip Hopkins   ]

# After Paradise (reportage from 1997-1998)

LIBERIA

In a photo reportage from 1997-1998 Rip Hopkins reflected over the devastation of the Liberian civil war: *"Liberia has been totally destroyed by seven years of civil war. The majority of its infrastructures has been reduced to rubble, and health and education services are non-existent. Out of 2.5 million Liberians, an estimated 150,000 to 200,000 people have been killed, 900,000 have been displaced and 600,000 are refugees in neighbouring countries. The fighting has temporarily stopped, Charles Taylor, head of the NPFL (National Patriotic Front of Liberia) faction, is now president but Liberia is still in a state of shock. Of the 60,000 fighters, 10,000 of which were children, the large majority now suffer psychological trauma brought on by the horror of the fighting. Death from malnutrition, cholera, measles and murder is common. The ECOMOG (Economic Community Ceasefire Monitoring Group) soldiers are still present in a country whose seven-year civil war could easily flare up from one day to the next."*

RIP HOPKINS

*Firestone rubber tree plantation. In terms*
*of natural resources, Liberia is one of West Africa's*
*richest countries. Before the war, Firestone,*
*the world's largest rubber plantation, was Liberia's*
*main source of income along with diamonds,*
*copper, iron ore and timber. The various warring*
*factions financed themselves through the sale*
*of these various resources.*
© Rip Hopkins / Agence VU / Liberia

*Save the Children funds a rehabilitation centre for child fighters. Franklin was a member of the NPFL (National Patriotic Front of Liberia)*
*faction controlled by Charles Taylor. Today, aged 7, he suffers from psychological trauma brought on by the horror of the fighting.*

© Rip Hopkins / Agence VU / Gbarnga, Liberia

*One of the 350,000 Liberian refugees*
*living in the Ivory Coast.*

© Rip Hopkins / Agence VU /

Ivory Coast, Crossroads / Liberia

*Ministry of Health.*
*Children play in front of the half-completed*
*"new" Ministry of Health, where 470 displaced*
*families have taken refuge.*
© Rip Hopkins / Agence VU / Monrovia, Liberia

*African Plaza Hotel. Some 320 displaced families live in the shell of what used to be one of the most expensive hotels in Liberia.*

© Rip Hopkins / Agence VU / Monrovia, Liberia

*Palm oil production is one of the main*
*sources of income for the local population.*
© Rip Hopkins / Agence VU / Bong Mines, Liberia

*Mamba Checkpoint in the capital, Saturday
evening. A boy is mistreated by ECOMOG soldiers.*

© Rip Hopkins / Agence VU / Monrovia, Liberia

*A displaced person demonstrates his wish to fly from Liberia.*

© Rip Hopkins / Agence VU / Ministry of Health, Monrovia, Liberia

*Repatriation to the countryside of some of the 700,000 displaced living in Monrovia. Of 2.5 million Liberians, an estimated 150,000-200,000 have been killed and nearly 1.5 million displaced or living as refugees in neighbouring countries.*

© Rip Hopkins / Agence VU / Monrovia, Town Centre, Liberia

*Save the Children funds a rehabilitation centre for child fighters. Franklin was a member of the NPFL (National Patriotic Front of Liberia)*
*faction controlled by Charles Taylor. Today, aged 7, he suffers from psychological trauma brought on by the horror of the fighting.*

*Save the Children funds a rehabilitation centre for child fighters. Boxing practice is intended to help the boys vent their anger and frustration.*

© Rip Hopkins / Agence VU / Gbarnga, Liberia

on any source other than their own. For a start, there is never a shortage of warning about pending disaster in a host of places. Sometimes that warning turns out to be inadequate. And government action is costly, so there needs to be a degree of certainty to generate action. Governments have limited resources and various emergencies competing for attention and funds. Of course in bureaucracies one will often get into more trouble for urging action and being wrong, than for taking no action when action was needed. Too often the incentives are aligned against early action.

The EU has formally recognised the importance of organised civil society. By adopting the EU Programme for the Prevention of violent conflicts in Gothenburg in 2001, the European Council recognised the importance of conflict prevention as a long-term policy commitment and as one of the main objectives of EU external relations. Furthermore, the ESDP procedures for coherent, comprehensive EU crisis management (2003):

http://11127/03 register.consilium.europa.eu/ pdf/en/03/st11/st11127en03.pdf

provide entry points for consultation with civil society organisations regarding early warning mechanisms, strategic and operational planning, and mission implementation. These procedures explicitly note that modalities for coordination in the field between the EU and local authorities and civil society need to be developed. Moreover,

the EU Action Plan for Civilian Aspects of ESDP (2004) welcomes a regular exchange of views with civil society organisations regarding the general orientation of EU civilian crisis management and states that civil society experience and early warning capacity are valued by the EU. The recognition that greater efforts need to be undertaken to address how civil society experience and knowledge can be better drawn upon led the Finnish Presidency to launch the project Role of Civil Society in Crisis Management (or RoCS I) in 2006.

The new Instrument for Stability (IfS), which was created as part of the reform of Community external financing instruments in 2006 (compare Rapid Reaction Mechanism), provides additional means for developing new mechanisms for increased coherence and for cooperation with relevant intergovernmental and non-governmental actors. It provides the European Union with a new strategic tool to ensure an effective, rapid and flexible response to political crises as well as to strengthen the capacity of civil society organisations over the longer term.

The Stability Instrument takes a broadly based approach, founded on development policy principles. Aid under the Stability Instrument must be:

a) coherent with EC country priorities set under the long-term instruments, and
b) consistent with CFSP objectives. Furthermore, should aid under the Stability Instrument be complementary to EC Human-

itarian Aid it cannot be subject to political considerations. In fact, there are two key elements in the IfS:

• first, crisis response and preparedness that allows timely response to political crisis or natural disaster;
• second, long-term, transregional threats to stability (e.g. on non-proliferation, organised crime, protection of critical infrastructure and major public health threats).

Under the new Stability Instrument crisis response measures include, first, conflict prevention and peacebuilding, which is understood as pre-empting violent conflict; supporting peacebuilding and diplomatic initiatives for political stabilisation; providing incentives to the parties; fostering stability during political transition; and safeguarding human rights and democratic processes. Second, addressing the direct consequences of violent conflict, like de-mining/unexploded ordnance; reconstruction of homes and public buildings; demobilisation and reintegration of combatants; and decommissioning of small arms/light weapons. Third, promoting stabilisation through good governance (elections and constitutional processes, local government, security sector reform and civil society development). Fourth, ensuring basic development needs are addressed from the outset (getting public administration working, getting a national budget in place, getting children back to school, reopening health and local public services and generating employment).[10]

Probably the most significant change in the EU policy instruments is the extended timeframe of its programme to respond. The new procedures allow the European Commission to design a response for a period of 18 (+6) months, whereas the old system only enable a programme of 6 months. Another new requirement is close political coordination between the European Commission, the European Parliament and the European Council. More particularly, it is interesting to note that the European Commission undertook to:

- strengthen policy-making capacity in the area of crisis response and peacebuilding;
- establish a 'Peacebuilding Partnership', including possible 'framework partnership' arrangements with NGOs;
- establish a logistical capacity to support the deployment of civilian experts, and
- give specific commitments relating to counter-terrorism measures.

## Conclusion

At a conference in Berlin in June 2007 (under the German EU Presidency) it was argued that to promote such a strategic partnership further investment is needed in developing a culture of cooperation based on dialogue and mutual trust between the EU and its civil society partners. For the EU, such effectiveness requires the active solicitation of input from civil society organisations in order to benefit from their expertise, their understanding of the long-term situations and contexts, and their engagement with local civil society. For civil society organisations, such effectiveness requires proactive engagement with the EU at Member State and field levels. A framework for engagement and collaboration will make such a partnership more effective.

The new Peacebuilding Partnership programme from the European Commission opens a window of opportunity to develop a strategic partnership with civil society organisations.

The aim of the Peacebuilding Partnership is to mobilise and consolidate civilian expertise on peacebuilding. One of the priorities is to strengthen civil society's early warning capacity. In fact, civil society cooperation with governmental institutions should become part of the EU's 'DNA'. Both the EU and civil society organisations must be prepared to listen to each other, and the EU needs to be willing to provide time, space and resources to civil society organisations to enable them to become respected dialogue partners in mutual cooperation.

10 Information based on a presentation of the IfS given at the Pax Christi International offices during a PeaceNet meeting November 2007 by two members of the Crisis Management and Conflict Prevention Unit.

# REPORT ON THE OUTCOME OF THE MULTI-DONOR INITIATIVE 'EVALUATION AND STRENGTHENING OF EARLY WARNING SYSTEMS' IN COUNTRIES AFFECTED BY THE 26 DECEMBER 2004 TSUNAMI

## Introduction

The 26 December 2004 Indian Ocean tsunami disaster resulted in substantial new demands on the secretariat for the International Strategy for Disaster Reduction (UN/ISDR) and its Platform for Promotion of Early Warning (PPEW), located in Bonn, Germany. While the mode of reaction to these demands were not in the original PPEW work programme, they were fully in line with the goals of the early warning platform established in 2004 as a recommendation of the Second International Conference on Early Warning. The most significant factor was the multi-agency, multi-donor Flash Appeal project proposal that had been quickly produced by PPEW to support tsunami early warning systems in the Indian Ocean, and to which donors contributed US $10.5 million.

The PPEW developed and coordinated the implementation of the project in cooperation with UNESCO's Intergovernmental Oceanographic Commission (UNESCO/IOC), which oversees the coordination of the establishment of early warning systems for tsunamis and other ocean-related hazards in the Indian Ocean, North Eastern Atlantic, Mediterranean and Caribbean regions. The project was financed with contributions from seven donors, namely the governments of Finland, Germany, Japan, the Netherlands, Norway and Sweden, and the European Commission Humanitarian Aid Office (ECHO).

The project was coordinated by the UN/ISDR-PPEW, as part of the larger Flash Appeal overseen by the UN Office for Coordination of Humanitarian Affairs (UNOCHA) and was implemented by 16 partners: the United Nations Development Programme (UNDP) India and Sri Lanka offices, the United Nations Environment Program (UNEP), the United Nations Economic and Social Commission for Asia and the Pacific (UNESCAP), the United Nations Educational, Scientific and Cultural Organisation (UNESCO) Jakarta office, UNESCO's Intergovernmental Oceanographic Commission (UNESCO/IOC), the United Nations Office for Project Services (UNOPS), the United Nations University Institute for Environment and Human Security (UNU-EHS), the World Meteorological Organisation (WMO), the All India Disaster Mitigation Institute (AIDMI), the Asia-Pacific Broadcasting Union (ABU), the Asian Disaster Reduction Center (ADRC), the Asian Disaster Preparedness Centre (ADPC), the Centre for Research on the Epidemiology of Disasters (CRED), Sustainable Environment and Ecological Development Society (SEEDS) and the University of Geneva.

## Building partnerships

A major highlight has been the establishment of partnerships and coordination mechanisms across a wide range of partners and donors, which provides an example of an integrated vehicle for supporting the implementation of the 'Hyogo Framework for Action 2005-15: Building the resilience of nations and communities to disasters'. This PPEW partnership approach has brought an added value to the diversity of activities and a more coherent and coordinated approach to the issue of early warning systems, thus extending the reach and effectiveness of inputs and resources. Although the project was developed in the context of the Flash Appeal process, it fits naturally into the framework of the International Early Warning Programme (IEWP) launched in 2005 at the World Conference on Disaster Reduction and the objectives of the PPEW's work programme.

The project contributed to maximising the effectiveness of inputs and resources by providing strategic direction for the implementation and monitoring of the project activities and avoiding overlaps between the implementing agencies. It was the first time that PPEW under the administration of the UN/ISDR secretariat provided overall coordination to a project under the UN Flash Appeal that was not necessarily focusing exclusively on humanitarian assistance. Nevertheless, the integrated approach and

*Stefanie Dannenmann (Germany), PhD joined the United Nations International Strategy for Disaster Reduction (UN/ISDR) Platform for the Promotion of Early Warning (PPEW) in Bonn, Germany, in April 2005. Among other duties, Dr Dannenmann supports the ISDR's system partners in their assistance to Indian Ocean governments to strengthen the regional and national tsunami early warning system. She has worked in the hazards and risk management field for several years.*

*Douglas Pattie (United States), PhD is the coordinator of the Platform for the Promotion of Early Warning (PPEW) at the United Nations International Strategy for Disaster Reduction (UN/ISDR) in Bonn, Germany. Dr Pattie's works on a number of problems confronting methodological and institutional issues surrounding early warning systems; the use of traditional knowledge for disaster reduction, participatory GIS for vulnerability and risk reduction; mapping land-cover dynamics; and community-based fire management. Prior to joining the UN/ISDR he served as an environmental affairs officer with the United Nations Convention to Combat Desertification.*

coordination proved to be effective. Efforts were mainly on (i) establishing the project administration and underpinnings, particularly partner work programmes and memoranda of understanding; (ii) supporting UNESCO/IOC to develop governance mechanisms and technical inputs for a regional tsunami warning system; and (iii) providing project coordination and integration. More than half of the funds received have been streamed to other key agencies. Partnerships and coordination have been strengthened across many UN agencies, regional and national organisations, research institutes, and local communities.

*Figure 1: Countries supported by the project*

### The project

Although the original UN Flash Appeal was confined to a sub-set of affected countries, a series of consultation meetings led to a general agreement by implementing agencies and donors that all countries affected by the 24 December 2004 tsunami and other countries at risk of tsunamis should be involved in this project for the establishment of tsunami early warning system in the Indian Ocean Region. The project supported all countries that are members of the UNESCO/IOC[1] in the Indian Ocean region. At the outset, the number of Indian Ocean member countries was 27. This increased to 28 *(see Figure 1)* when Djibouti formally joined. However, Djibouti, even as an informal IOC member, had participated in various project activities. Some project activities were attended by all 28 countries, but financial support was provided mainly for the participants from developing countries.

At the national level, the project not only benefited national governments, but also their disaster management agencies, local authorities, scientific and technical institutions, the broadcasting sector as well as other practitioners from the civil society and communities at selective locations. Wider participation was sought for all project activities, in particular, at the regional, national and local level. Gender-related project activities were highlighted by such agencies as AIDMI, CRED, UNDP India and UNU-EHS.

The project components were identified broadly in two different areas, namely warning system development and preparedness. As a cross-cutting theme, the project promoted 'people-centred early warning systems' emphasizing (i) risk knowledge, that is, prior knowledge of the risks faced by communities; (ii) monitoring and warning service; (iii) communications and dissemination of understandable warnings to those at risk; and (iv) response capability and preparedness to act by those threatened aspects.

The PPEW established a Project Overview Plan[2] and developed a web-accessible project database and information system (TEWIS)[3]. PPEW delivered substantial inputs to and

1  http://ioc3.unesco.org/indotsunami/interimsystem/focal_points.htm
2  http://www.unisdr.org/ppew/tsunami/pdf/project-overview-plan.pdf
3  http://unisdr.unbonn.org/index.php

participated at the international tsunami co-ordination meeting in Paris, at the regional tsunami coordination meeting in Mauritius, and at several high-level dialogue meetings. Information was supplied on request to the Office of the Special Envoy on the tsunami (former US President Clinton) in collaboration with WMO and UNESCO/IOC.

Some specific project activities and efforts to facilitate multi-partner initiatives and collaboration include:

- the special session on tsunami warning systems in the Indian Ocean organised at the World Conference of Disaster Risk Reduction (WCDR) in Kobe, Hyogo, Japan (18-22 January 2005);
- a high-level dialogue meeting on the development of tsunami early warning systems was held in Kobe on immediately after the WCDR (22 January 2005);
- policy dialogue for high-level administrative policy-makers on establishing a tsunami early warning system in the Indian Ocean was organised by ISDR secretariat and ADRC (22-24 February 2005);
- two regional workshops in Bangkok on 'Emergency Information Flows in Disaster Situations: the Role of Broadcasters' and 'Public Awareness, Preparedness and Response: the Role of Broadcasters' (13-16 June 2005);
- training and familiarisation event in Japan (11-14 July 2005) and Hawaii (26-29 July 2005) for high-level administrators from the Indian Ocean region;

- public awareness and education workshop in Bangkok, Thailand (7-8 September 2005);
- mid-term review process with participation of implementing partners and donors (25 November 2005). A second review meeting took place (7 December 2005) with the ISDR secretariat project team members, including the ISDR-Asia regional team;
- facilitation of the formation of the new working group on disaster mitigation, preparedness and response of the UNESCO/IOC Intergovernmental Coordination Group for the Indian Ocean Tsunami Warning System (ICG-IOTWS). The working group was officially adopted in August 2006 during the ICG-IOTWS III meeting in Bali, Indonesia;
- side-event on tsunami early warning in the Indian Ocean organised during the 3rd International Conference on Early Warning (EWC III), Bonn, Germany (27-29 March 2006);
- the presence at EWC III of former US President Clinton, the UN's Special Envoy for Tsunami Recovery;
- a Roundtable on Indian Ocean Tsunami Warning and Response Systems in the presence of President Clinton during EWC III (27 March 2006);
- translation of the early warning systems checklist 'Developing Early Warning Systems: Checklist' into 19 Indian Ocean languages;
- regional Workshop on Mitigation, Preparedness and Development for Tsunami Early Warning Systems in Bangkok (14-16

June 2006);
- workshop on the Human Impact of Tsunami and Disaster Risk Reduction in Bangkok (16-17 June 2006);
- production of the report Lessons for a Safer Future.

With the project's groundwork in place, there had been accelerated emphasis on the role of UN/ISDR secretariat in setting the directions and fostering implementation and supporting activities in the region, in particular on the components of integrated risk management, public awareness and education and community-based approaches to stimulate the development of effective end-to-end multi-hazard warning capacities and wider public engagement.

## Sustainability of early warning systems

The Early Warning Strengthening Project has created an enabling environment for coordination and partnership-building necessary for the development of 'end-to-end' and 'people-centred' early warning systems in the Indian Ocean region. However, the project activities are only the first step for establishing a fully-fledged TEWS within a multi-hazard framework. Strong political commitment of the Indian Ocean countries as well as substantial financial and technical supports from the international community are crucial in achieving this goal. The Intergovernmental Coordination Group for the Indian Ocean Tsunami Warning and Mitigation System (ICG/IOTWS), coordinated by the

IOC of UNESCO (UNESCO/IOC), is an excellent example of cooperation between Member States, UN Agencies and donors. It has taken the decisions on the underlying technologies to be employed, the mechanisms for regional governance, funding, cooperation and communications. One effect of the 2004 Indian Ocean tsunami on the political landscape was that it drew more attention towards inclusion of disaster risk reduction as an important aspect of preparedness, response and recovery.

The PPEW, UN/ISDR secretariat and the implementing partners will continue to support the Indian Ocean countries through various mechanisms to ensure sustainability of the project. Resource mobilisation for the development of fully-fledged early warning systems as well as national platforms on disaster risk reduction and preparedness will continue through the Indian Ocean Tsunami Consortium, UNESCAP's Multi-donor Voluntary Trust Fund on Tsunami Early Warning Arrangements in the Indian Ocean and South East Asia, and the Global Facility for Disaster Reduction and Recovery of the UN/ISDR and the World Bank and other efforts of the partner agencies and the UN/ISDR secretariat. The UN/ISDR regional offices in Asia and Africa will continue to provide technical support in developing national plans and proposals in this regard. Regional coordination for TEWS will continue mainly through ICG/IOTWS and technical support will continue to be provided through the UNESCO/IOC and WMO. The UN/ISDR-PPEW will also follow-up establishment of TEWS in the Indian Ocean region within its follow-up activities for the International Early Warning Programme and the global multi-hazard early-ly warning system mandated by the United Nations General Assembly in 2007.

## Success stories

Although occurrence of tsunamis and earthquakes was not frequent in 2006-2007, some success stories have already been reported by the partners to UN/ISDR-PPEW. The interim warning system established under the project has proven to be effective not only for tsunamis but also for other hazards. The UNESCO/IOC and WMO reported that the Global Telecommunications System (GTS) demonstrated its effectiveness during the July 2006 tsunami in Java. Interim tsunami advisory information was issued from the Pacific Tsunami Warning Center (PTWC) and the Japan Meteorological Agency (JMA). Several national warning centres in the Indian Ocean region, including the one in Jakarta, Indonesia, received interim tsunami advisory information from PTWC and JMA soon after the earthquake took place. The UNDP Sri Lanka office reported that the enhanced capacity for early warning and dissemination as well as the in-country partnership among relevant institutions saved some vulnerable communities in Sri Lanka during a landslide in January 2007. Finally, the UNESCO Jakarta office reported that the Standard Operational Procedures (SOP) developed under the project in cooperation with a local NGO, were effectively applied by the disaster control authority in Padang, Indonesia, when an earthquake hit West Sumatra in March 2007.

## Conclusion and recommendations

The international, regional and national efforts in response to the 2004 tsunami disaster provided a sound basis for strengthening early warning systems in the Indian Ocean region, including substantial progress toward the development of capacities and intergovernmental processes.

Despite the challenges described above, the Early Warning Strengthening Project succeeded in achieving the original objectives and intended outcomes of defining core technical elements of the TEWS for the Indian Ocean region, quickly setting up an interim warning system, establishing regional coordination mechanisms, starting the process of integrating early warning into national disaster risk reduction and preparedness efforts, raising public awareness, strengthening the role of communities and local authorities, and starting the resource mobilisation necessary for the establishment of fully fledged TEWS within a multi-hazard framework.

Substantial support is still needed to establish the TEWS in the Indian Ocean region with a sound technical base and strengthened community response. In order to realise the TEWS with a close linkage to other ocean-related hazards, the following actions are recommended:

- the UN/ISDR, UNESCO/IOC, WMO as well as other UN, international and regional institutions working on early warning should continue their assistance to the Indian Ocean countries in enhancing capacities and mobilising resources necessary for both the establishment of the TEWS and of national platforms;
- to generate an enabling environment for TEWS in the Indian Ocean region, the UN/ISDR secretariat, its regional offices and other members of the ISDR system should continue to assist the countries in Asia and Africa to establish and/or strengthen national platforms for disaster risk reduction to effectively implement the Hyogo Framework for Action. Low-capacity, high-risk countries require more international support;
- the regional coordination mechanism for the tsunami warning systems through the UNESCO/IOC ICG/IOTWS should be strengthened to ensure integration of tsunami early warning systems into national and regional mitigation, preparedness and response capability building efforts within a multi-hazard framework;
- understanding of vulnerability and risk should be deepened through strengthening the multi-sector approach. The methodologies for multi-sector vulnerability assessment need to be further explored despite its complexity by building on the activities of the UNU-EHS undertaken under the Early Warning Strengthening Project. Methodology and tools for enhancing community preparedness need to be adapted to local-

specific conditions and context as the local capacity and socio-economic conditions differ from community to community;
- before the 26 December 2004 Tsunami, many of the countries in the Indian Ocean region did not have a well-organised disaster management system except some tropical cyclone-prone countries such as India and Bangladesh. Thus, National Disaster Management Offices in most counties were very weak, and there were few established national platforms for disaster risk reduction in the region. The roles of the National Disaster Management Offices should be enhanced for better coordination within a country;
- constructing measures such as sea walls and shelters should be considered to protect lives, properties and significant infrastructures from tsunami. Currently, very few countries have implemented the structural measures mainly due to lack of information on risks. Countries need to have access to such information;
- accurate tsunami risk assessments based on paleo-tsunami research in the Indian Ocean region is needed. Sufficient scientific information is not available on the historical occurrence of natural hazards in the region, except Indonesia for which some records are available for the last few hundred years. Research outcomes would facilitate policy-making process in each country. In addition, historical and geographical research should be promoted to analyse what happened in the region in the past.

**Follow-up activities**

During 2007-2009, as a follow-up to the Tsunami Flash Appeal Project, an ISDR-coordinated initiative on building resilience to tsunamis in the Indian Ocean is being implemented with the support of the European Commission. This multi-partner initiative aims at building the resilience of communities and nations to disasters by strengthening national and local institutions, mechanisms and capacities for disaster risk reduction in India, Indonesia, the Maldives and Sri Lanka.

A roundtable on Indian Ocean Tsunami Warning and Response Systems was convened by UNESCO/IOC and the UN/ISDR secretariat on 27 March 2006 in the margins of EWC III in Bonn and in the presence of President Clinton, the UN's Special Envoy for Tsunami Recovery. On the occasion of the roundtable, ISDR system partners formed a consortium to assist initially up to ten governments with technical assistance to develop plans for an accelerated implementation of a national tsunami early warning system. The consortium partners include UNESCO/IOC, WMO, UNOCHA, IFRC, UNDP, UNEP and the World Bank, and is being coordinated by UN/ISDR-PPEW, ISDR regional offices in Bangkok and Nairobi, and the ISDR secretariat in Geneva.

By August 2006, 11 governments (Comoros, Madagascar, the Maldives, Mauritius, Mozambique, Pakistan, Seychelles, Somalia, Sri Lanka, Tanzania and Thailand) have submitted official requests with detailed budgeted proposals to receive financial and technical assistance from the Indian Ocean Consortium. The Consortium partners have started direct dialogue with their national counterparts with respect to the needs and the resources available. UN/ISDR secretariat supports the mobilisation of resources to address the needs and gaps raised by the 11 national plans submitted to the Consortium for accelerated implementation. It is envisioned the consortium partners will support the implementation of the national plan until 2008-2009.

[    Isabelle Eshraghi    ]

# Post-war trauma and pain in Bosnia-Herzegovina

A massacre by Bosnian Serb forces in July 1995 was one the worst episodes of war in Europe since the Second World War. An estimated 8,000 Muslim men and teenage boys were murdered.

The UN war crimes tribunal in The Hague described the massacre as a genocide (April 2004). Since the end of the war, 18,000 victims (a majority Muslims) were exhumed from 300 mass graves in Bosnia-Herzegovina. About 6,000 bodies were disinterred from mass graves around Srebrenica. New mass graves are still expected to be found. Over 16,000 people are still considered missing according to International Committee of the Red Cross (ICRC).

Nine years after the end of the war (1992-1995) the government of Republika Srpska said for the first time that it 'sympathises with the pain of the relatives of the Srebrenica victims and expresses sincere regrets and apologies' (10 November 2004).

The women of Srebrenica were the witnesses of this tragedy. In Potocari, the Serb forces segregated the civilian population into a group of men and teenage boys and a group of women and children. Some young girls were taken away, and they never returned. After two nights, women and children were forced into trucks. Men were found later with their throats slit.

Thousands of Bosnian women are still searching for their sons, husbands and others relatives, and they are all waiting for the day when the remains of their loved ones will be found. Then finally they will be able to start the process of mourning.

These women were greatly traumatised during the 1992-1995 war by constant exposure to violence. After the war ended their trauma became obvious. The effects of stress began manifesting itself as a loss of self-confidence, poor concentration, disturbed sleep, nightmares and the reliving of the traumatic experiences. Many are suffering from depression, withdrawal and have contemplated suicide.

It was in the suburb of Sarajevo where I met these women from Srebrenica and the Drina Valley. There are 63 families; 221 women and children and only seven men. They live in a collective centre for refugees and are offered tenancy rights for five years. In May 2005, they were faced with the risk of being expelled with force; once more suffering the pain of humiliation.

They spend their time having coffee and cigarettes. In silence, in their minds they return to this terrible month of July 1995. They are still alive, but never will they smile again.

Isabelle Eshraghi

Adela Mujić, 20 years

*'I remember everything, but please don't ask.*
*I don't like to talk about it. I've never cried'.*

Missing persons

| | | |
|---|---|---|
| Mujić Adil | 1938-1995 | her father *(identified)* |
| Mujić Mujo | 1948-1995 | her uncle *(identified)* |
| Mujić Osman | 1935-1995 | her uncle *(identified)* |
| Mujić Nezir | 1932-1995 | her uncle *(identified)* |
| Mujić Edhen | 1925-1995 | her uncle *(identified)* |

And her cousins

Sakib *(identified)*, Fadil, Kiram, Hamdija.

Azemina Ademović, age 41

'In my village there lived 57 men, only 7 survived.
Back in 1993 my husband was hurt by an
exploding shell. Being wounded saved his life,
otherwise... he would not have been among us now'

Missing persons

| Bekrić Meho | 1978-1995 | her brother |
|---|---|---|
| Bekrić Mustafa | 1960-1998 | her brother |
| | | *(killed by a* |
| | | *landmine)* |

Kadira Mešanović, age 42

*'The worst moments, you can never wipe them from your mind. It is always the same memories that haunt you, always the same'.*

Missing persons

| | | |
|---|---|---|
| Mešanović Avdija | 1955-1995 | her husband |
| Mešanović Mirza | 1979-1995 | her son |
| Handžić Nezir | 1952-1995 | her uncle |

And her father-in-law, her brothers-in-law.

Tima Hajdarivić, 43 years

*'I can't get rid of those three months (of rape).
They took me everywhere they went, from the one
house to the other. I had to go to the Kochevo
hospital and had all my sexual organs removed.
My life as a woman is over'.*

Missing persons

| Hajdarivić Salko | 1954-1992 | her husband |
| Hajdarivić Habib | 1923-1992 | her father-in-law |
| Hajdarivić Nefa | 1922-1992 | her mother-in-law |
| Omerović Mehmed | 1925-1992 | her uncle |
| Omerović Meho | 1942-1992 | her uncle |
| | | *(identified)* |
| Audić Fadila | 1958-1992 | her uncle |
| | | Meho's daughter |

Rajiba Beganović, age 44

*'When I entered the house. I recognised my mother
in law because of her dress, her head had been
separated from her body. I fainted'.*

Missing persons

| | | |
|---|---|---|
| Beganović Mula | 1925-1995 | her mother-in-law |
| Beganović Meho | 1949-1995 | her brother-in-law |
| Beganović Mersed | 1976-1995 | her nephew |
| Jusić Husein | 1978-1995 | her nephew |
| Hasanović Hasan | 1935-1995 | her father |
| | | *(identified)* |

Rusmira Beganović, 49 years

*'I went to Tuzla. I recognised the brown shoes of my husband, the ones you would get when you went to war. They were nicknamed "the shoes of death"... When I saw his shoes, I knew he would never come back again'.*

Missing persons

| | | |
|---|---|---|
| Beganović Munib | 1956-1995 | her husband *(identified)* |
| Beganović Ekrem | 1962-1995 | her brother-in-law |
| Beganović Ramo | 1952-1995 | her brother-in-law *(identified)* |
| Beganović Mujo | 1954-1995 | her brother-in-law *(identified)* |
| Memišević Devla | 1932-1992 | her mother |
| Memišević Mina | 1958-1992 | her sister |

Rejha Jusic, age 51

*'Two years ago my son was found in a mass grave near Zvornik. Only I know how to bear this burden'.*

Missing persons

| | | |
|---|---|---|
| Jusić Nusret | 1952-1995 | her husband |
| Jusić Azmir | 1974-1995 | her son *(identified)* |
| Jusić Fadil | 1955-1995 | her brother-in-law |
| Brdarević Alija | 1923-1995 | her father |
| Brdarević Taib | 1927-1995 | her uncle |
| Brdarević Vahid | 1970-1995 | her nephew |
| Brdarević Said | 1968-1995 | her nephew |

Hamida Hukić, age 53

*'I've seen quite some bodies in front of a house,
they had cut-throat the people. They had cut the
head off with an axe. It was at dawn.
I can still see the axes'.*

Missing persons

| | | |
|---|---|---|
| Hukić Tahir | 1953-1995 | her husband |
| Hukić Mujo | 1977-1995 | her son |
| Hukić Rašid | 1958-1995 | her brother-in-law |
| | | *(identified)* |
| Hukić Ibrahim | 1956-1995 | her brother-in-law |
| Hukić Idriz | 1930-1995 | her father-in-law |
| Beganović Sejad | 1966-1995 | her brother |
| | | *(identified)* |
| Beganović Nijažija | 1954-1995 | her brother |

And her cousins

Saban, Reždo.

Hajrija Beganović, age 53

*'I held my son close to me, they took him, they*
*pushed him. They only wanted to ask some*
*questions, they said. Ever since I am mad,*
*I cannot lose this image, I cannot forget it...*
*I do not dare to live one day without medication'.*

Missing persons

| | | |
|---|---|---|
| Beganović Meho | 1949-1995 | her husband |
| Beganović Mersed | 1976-1995 | her son |
| Smadić Sulo | 1935-1995 | her father |
| Smadić Ferid | 1956-1995 | her brother |
| Smadić Rejid | 1957-1995 | her brother |
| Smadić Izo | 1958-1995 | her brother |

And her nephews

Nessim, Mesud, Džedad, Vahid.

© Isabelle Eshraghi / Agence VU / Bosnia

Rujika Aljič, age 67

*'In front of the bus in Potocari, a Tchetnik pointed a gun at my husband and arrested him. In a film made by the Serbs, which was broadcast on TV, I recognised him. I had to cry'.*

Missing persons

| | | |
|---|---|---|
| Aljić Zilđžija | 1936-1995 | her husband |
| Aljić Mevlid | 1957-1995 | her son |
| Aljić Latif | 1959-1995 | her son |

Timka Karišik, age 83

*'They never found one single body.*
*Maybe they've been burnt'.*

Missing persons

| | | |
|---|---|---|
| Omerović Mehmed | 1926-1992 | her brother |
| Omerović Meho | 1945-1992 | her brother |
| Avdić Fadila | 1964-1992 | her niece |
| Hajdarević Salko | 1953-1992 | her son-in-law |

Hadžira Orić, age 28

*'My husband is a survivor, a survivor of the massacre. His life has lost all sense. My husband drinks. I can't stand it any longer'.*

Missing persons

| | | |
|---|---|---|
| Bekrič Selman | 1955-1995 | her father |
| Orić Ćazim | 1935-1995 | her father-in-law |
| Orić Ćazim | 1979-1995 | her nephew |

© Isabelle Eshraghi / Agence VU / Bosnia

# 'EARNING EACH STEP'
## INTERVIEW WITH MIROSLAV LAJCÁK

*What hopes and ambitions did you have when taking on your current position as High Representative and EU Special Representative for Bosnia-Herzegovina (BiH)?*

I took over my duties in July 2007 with the ambition of anchoring a politically and economically stable Bosnia and Herzegovina irrevocably on the path of Euro-Atlantic integration.

*You have previously said that you see diplomacy as a "science". Is there a risk that a rational approach fails to address the war's legacy of human tragedy?*

During my first few months in Bosnia, I had to spend a lot of time dealing with issues from the past. While I do understand the necessity for BiH and its constituent nations to come to terms with the past, I also firmly believe that politicians need to focus on the future and act as real leaders. Crimes cannot be undone, but those who committed them must be brought to justice. Only when victims have a feeling that justice has been served will they be able to come to terms with what has happened to them. So our task is two-fold: we must insist on justice for the victims, but at the same time, work on building a better future for the country.

*Many in BiH feel that the international community failed them during the war. Has this caused some to be sceptical about what it can achieve in their country today? What assurances do people have that there would be immediate intervention if violent conflict was to break out again?*

Today's battles in BiH are fought at the political level, and there is no danger of armed conflict. It is the military's assessment that there has been no deterioration in the security situation. The environment is safe and secure and, as an example, we are seeing the freedom of the population to voice their political views in public, en masse and in safety. There has been peace here since 1995. EUFOR is here to ensure that this peace remains in place, and it has plans for every eventuality. The European Union has deployed all types of Common Foreign and Security Policy (CFSP) instruments at its disposal in BiH: a military mission (EUFOR), a police mission (EUPM), and a civilian mission (EUSR). This is in stark contrast to 1991-1992, when the EU did not have the right instruments to address the unfolding Yugoslav crisis.

*The European Union initiated a Stabilisation and Association Agreement (SAA) with BiH on 4 December 2007. Until recently, politicians in BiH did not seem to be bothered that their country was the last in the Western Balkans without this kind of link with the EU. What has changed and how should the EU respond to the new situation?*

For a long time, we had a paradoxical situation in BiH. It really looked like the international community was pushing the country into the EU integration process, as if Europe itself had a greater interest in the process than BiH. That was a mistake.

Based on the Slovak experience, I warned the country's political leaders that it is them, above all, who must want this process. After the failure to agree on police reform in September 2007, the EU said "enough, we won't force you into anything", which led to the change of heart among politicians. Suddenly, they started coming forward with their own initiatives. At the same time, it was also important to convince them that Europe would not be deaf and blind in the face of their successes.

More generally, I believe that the EU approach to the Western Balkans should be tailored to the specific situation and needs in each country. While progress towards the EU must be earned, we should also be realistic in our demands. The EU must be careful not set unrealistic requirements that countries cannot meet and which will discourage them. The EU must act as a motivating factor, but make clear that each step forward must be earned. The process of EU integration rests on transformation of a society and its approximation to EU values and standards, and not on the formal status of a country's relationship with the EU.

*Ambassador Miroslav Lajcák, a Slovak career diplomat, is the international community's High Representative and EU Special Representative in Bosnia-Herzegovina. He has extensive experience in South-eastern Europe, and served as mediator and personal representative of the EU High Representative for the Common Foreign and Security Policy, Javier Solana, in Montenegro in 2006.*

*Some voices in the EU are calling for trade or partnership agreements as a preferable alternative to enlargement. What guarantees does BiH have that EU membership will become a reality if it achieves the necessary reforms?*

The EU has repeatedly stressed that it sees the future of the Western Balkans in the European Union. Of course, potential candidates must also fulfil the criteria for membership. There is unity among Member States on this issue, and BiH has no reason to doubt the EU's commitment as long as BiH delivers on its own promises. By rewarding each step in the integration process, as it did when initialling the SAA with BiH, the EU can alleviate any concerns and prove that genuine efforts will bring benefits.

*Russia has not hesitated in making clear its opposition to the independence of Kosovo/a. Is the continued lack of a coherent and unified message from the EU a problem in the face of this?*

There is a general consensus among EU members on the way forward in Kosovo/a, so I would not subscribe to the view that our message lacks coherence and unity. As EUSR in Bosnia-Herzegovina, I have also made clear that there is not a single issue where Bosnia-Herzegovina depends on the future of Kosovo/a. BiH is not a hostage of Kosovo/a. The country has its own problems, and the solutions lie in the hands of its leaders.

*You have repeatedly insisted that any future declaration of independence by Kosovo/a*

should not be linked to calls for a referendum on the secession of Republika Srpska. Was it wise for the EU to initial the SAA with Serbia while these calls continue to destabilise BiH?*

When Serbian officials tried to link the fate of Republika Srpska to the future of Kosovo/a, there was a rapid and firm response from the EU and the US. The international community said, in crystal-clear terms, that the future status of Kosovo/a would not have any effect on the constitutional setup of Bosnia-Herzegovina, as defined in Dayton. Serbia has since stopped drawing such parallels and reiterated its commitment to the Dayton Peace Agreement and the territorial integrity of BiH.

*How far are you prepared to go to maintain the territorial integrity of BiH and to improve the functioning of its institutions? Are the Bonn powers sufficient to achieve your aims?*

The Bonn powers are a part of my mandate as High Representative of the international community. I have stressed from the beginning that I understand these powers as the yellow and red cards that a referee holds in his pocket during a football match. The best game is one when nobody notices the referee. That is how I view my role. However, I have also said that I will not refrain from using the powers of my office to counter attempts to divert BiH from the right path. I prefer to support agreement among local politicians, but the international community also has a responsibility for this state. I have

two hats – the High Representative's hat and the EU Special Representative's hat – and I will always have one of them on my head. I will not keep them both under the table and observe the situation with folded arms.

*Is the future of BiH high enough on the EU's political agenda? Why do you think it is almost non-existent in European media?*

The recent media focus on Kosovo/a is understandable in view of the ongoing discussions about its future. Slovenia has indicated that the EU's relations with the Western Balkans will be in the focus of its Presidency. This will also be an opportunity to review our policies and adapt them where necessary. The challenge of creating a viable and stable country is probably much greater in Bosnia-Herzegovina than any other region of the Western Balkans. The Dayton Agreement ended the war in BiH, but it did not provide for the institutions needed to take the country into the European Union. The challenge for the EU is to support and assist Bosnia-Herzegovina in the process of constitutional change, which is an absolute necessity if the country wants to integrate the EU.

# 'Preserving status quo is dangerous'
## Interview with Peter Semneby

*What kind of instruments does the European Union have at its disposal to deal with the conflicts in the South Caucasus?*

First, there is the perspective that the EU itself represents a way of transforming the conflicts. The Georgian government, society and people living in conflict regions are very interested in a close relationship with the EU and in what the EU can offer. They have been living for the better part of the last two decades in a kind of cocoon without clear perspective of their future. Making people in the conflict regions share their visions and adapt them to a European context will eventually bring them closer together.

*How can this kind of common European identity be created?*

The EU can offer a layer of identity in addition to the national identities. It can offer a framework for a more fruitful cooperation between neighbours by putting them into a larger framework. This includes the neighbours in the narrow South Caucasus region but also in the wider region with Russia and Turkey. This will bring both security to the region, which has been notoriously unstable and plagued by conflict, and ultimately also prosperity.

*How can this objective be achieved even though EU accession is not an option at this point in time?*

EU membership is not on the agenda, but on the other hand the EU can offer avenues of integration that fall short of membership but are still interesting and would still be noticeable for people in these countries. This could include visa facilitation, which would be noticeable for any citizen in this area. It could involve free trade, which would be noticeable for businesses in the countries.

*Has the EU enough to offer as long as accession is excluded?*

Of course there are always desires and ambitions that go beyond what is on offer. That is just natural; it is a healthy sign. But the European Neighbourhood Policy (ENP) contains quite a generous offer. It includes possibilities that are far from exhausted in this region. We have just started in Georgia, Armenia and Azerbaijan to implement ambitious five-year action plans that contain a wide-ranging transformation agenda. This is of course where the focus of attention should be in the next few years. If governments and societies in the region work diligently in fulfilling these tasks, it will make these countries much more similar to the EU. This could be a very good and firm basis for the future, whatever it looks like. I cannot say if any kind of additional new institutional framework will be on offer sometime in the future. But if the countries in the South Caucasus become more similar to the EU's Member States then that would be a basis for a much closer and much more fruitful relationship.

*Looking at the frozen conflicts in the South Caucasus one gets the impression that what is supposed to be conflict resolution is actually more a way of conflict management. Do you see any movement at all?*

At this point in time, yes, the focus is on conflict management and on conflict prevention. At least this is the case of Georgia where the situation is rather tense, and in the case of Nagorny Karabagh [Nagorno-Karabakh] where the conflict is as frozen as ever.

However, the focus also is on conflict transformation. Through the instruments that the EU now has at its disposal we can make proposals and offers that could change the outlook of the conflict regions themselves. We have started to do this in Georgia where we have on the table a set of confidence-building measures that have been worked with the different parties in the region.

*What are these measures and what difference can they make for people in the conflict regions?*

They, first of all, involve the opening up some of the programmes under the ENP and in the Action Plan to people living in the conflict regions. This will change their perspectives; it will show them that there is a more complex environment, that there are other alternatives and additional possibilities to the two poles that they have been caught between for so long. It will make the aspira-

*Peter Semneby has been the European Union's Special Representative for the South Caucasus since 2006. He assists Georgia, Armenia and Azerbaijan on their way to moving closer to the EU by helping to carry out reforms in the fields of the rule of law, democratisation, human rights, good governance, development and poverty reduction. His previous posts include the head of the OSCE missions to Croatia, Latvia and Georgia. He was responsible for European Security and Defence Policy in the Swedish Ministry for Foreign Affairs 1997-2000. Before that he served in the Swedish embassies in Germany, Ukraine and the USSR.*

tions of people living in the conflict regions more similar to the aspirations of people living in Georgia proper.[1] And if we manage to make the mindsets and hearts of the political agendas similar in the conflict regions and Georgia proper this will make an important contribution to transforming the conflicts. Measures could include the opening up of education exchange programmes to people in the conflicts regions.

*Which other channels will the EU use to step up its engagement?*

We also want to engage more directly in activities of various kinds that will create incentives for contacts across the confrontation lines. Already a lot has been done in support for civil society and in assistance with infrastructure development. We will continue along these lines as well as try to build joint interests between Georgia proper and the conflict regions. We also envisage a larger EU presence in the conflict regions by setting up information offices and deploying a few police liaison officers on the ground. This will have a reassuring impact and it will strengthen the message that there are new perspectives that people can reflect on. It will also have a deterring impact and will raise the price of irresponsible action on all sides. If we develop our project-related activities then it will mean that there will be EU people on the ground and each such person has an important role.

Finally, we will assist Georgia further in developing its minority policies, minority rights and social integration. Even where the problems may not be acute there is a need for attention to make sure that the development in those regions will be manageable in the future. It will also condition society in Georgia into making compromises and taking the necessary steps to find a solution to the conflicts in Abkhazia and South Ossetia.

*How can the EU manage to establish fruitful cooperation with Russia in this regard?*

We can engage with Russia and try to find common interests in order to influence Moscow. But if there are aspects of Russian foreign policy that we are not comfortable with, we should also be able to make that clear. In order to be heard in such a situation we have to have a broad relationship with Russia and use every opportunity for engagement. Russia will remain a neighbour of the South Caucasus; it will remain a part of the wider Black Sea region. Therefore, it is impossible to envisage any framework for this region without taking Russia into account.

Since 1 January 2007, the EU is a Black Sea power in its own right with Romania and Bulgaria being littoral states of the Black Sea. This could increase our possibilities in linking up with Russia and with Turkey in a regional framework that may eventually stabilise the whole region. In order to address the problems of the South Caucasus – which

is a very small and weak region with enormous differences between the countries – the region needs to be put into a larger context. Many of the problems that the South Caucasus is facing are problems with the larger neighbours – with Russia, in particular for Georgia, and with Turkey, in particular for Armenia. The EU can play an important role in order to be a catalyst for a larger political framework.

*All these measures are essentially soft-power measures. Is that enough for successful conflict resolution?*

In this context this approach has a very important advantage because the EU as a major soft-power actor should not be perceived as a threat by the parties of the conflicts. Soft-power measures can have quite a considerable influence. If the EU is able to build trust through its soft-power approach, it will also be in a better position to address the more traditional security challenges.

As far as conflict resolution is concerned, we have to keep the ultimate objective in mind: moving towards resolution of the conflict and not falling into the trap of using our instruments to preserve a status quo that is dangerous and untenable in the long-run. Here the EU can play the role as a facilitator not least based on the fact that the EU is an authority that, in many ways, embodies the ambitions and aspirations of the parties to the conflicts.

---

1 Georgia's separatist regions of Abkhazia and South Ossetia are not recognised by the international community.

*Looking back at when you started your job in March 2006, would you say that there is a need for a more coherent EU policy for the South Caucasus? What are your ideas and visions?*

The South Caucasus has, for a long time, not figured in people's minds and therefore it has only recently been discovered by people in Europe. That includes decision-makers, EU politicians and administration in Brussels and in the European capitals. So there is a need for a lot of basic knowledge in order to understand the challenges that we are facing in this region.

It is also a region where many other policies and interests of the EU are involved. The relationship with Russia is one of those policies and it very much colours the European vision on the South Caucasus. The need remains to define how the South Caucasus relates to our policies with Russia, how our interests in the South Caucasus can be balanced with our interests in Russia.

The importance of the region and our attention has increased for a number of reasons. First, the need for Europe to diversify energy transportation routes and energy sources has dramatically increased the importance of the South Caucasus. Second, the political transformation that has taken place in Georgia since the Rose Revolution has also enhanced the attention Europe is paying to the region. So it is a matter of realising

the real importance and the potential of the South Caucasus. This will take some time, but is well under way. We are also realising how the South Caucasus region relates to our other EU policies.

*Is the EU neglecting its eastern neighbourhood and focusing too much on its southern neighbours?*

No, that is the wrong impression. There is no competition or contradiction between our engagement in Europe's eastern and southern regions. Both regions are important in their own right. Some challenges are the same, some are completely different. We have to realise that both are important regions, but that we also need to differentiate our policies by taking into account the particular issues that we face in these two regions.

The South Caucasus, Ukraine and Moldova have their own specific character. They all emerged from the old Soviet Union; they have a very particular transformation agenda and a very special geopolitical situation. However, they are neither less nor more important than the Mediterranean. We have to take into account the specific character of each of these two regions and I expect more of this to be done. The European Commission has already presented a paper called 'Black Sea Synergy', which is an attempt to define a policy that specifically addresses the particular challenges in the region.

# Civilian peacekeeping: how civilian international interventions at grassroots level contribute to human security and stability

## Introduction

There is a widely shared consensus today within the European Union and its Member States that the use of civilian specialists is needed in crisis management and human security. Less acceptable, however, may be the thought that direct peacekeeping tasks could be undertaken by civilians rather than by armed forces, and that this may be an option to consider in cases where there is neither the political will nor the capacity or the acceptance by the country in conflict to deploy armed forces or international police.

In addition, even if political and financial constraints do not prevent the sending of a peacekeeping force, does it always have to be a military force? This question may sound a bit provocative in a context where the almost unquestioned paradigm is that military protection is the only way protection can be achieved, but as I would like to show in this contribution there are examples of initiatives moving in this direction and achieving results by it.

The examples that follow are taken from different places of the world where unarmed civilian peacekeeping undertaken by international (and often also local) civilians is making a considerable contribution to achieving human security at widow community level.

## On the concept of peacekeeping and its role in crisis response

Since the Secretary General of the United Nations, Boutros Boutros-Ghali published his *Agenda for Peace* in 1992, the terms peacekeeping, peacemaking and peacebuilding have become well known. But it wasn't Boutros-Ghali who invented these terms but Johan Galtung, who 20 years before him called them 'approaches to peace'.[1] Since then these terms have been refined by other authors. Together, these three approaches formulate a general theory of achieving or maintaining peace: 'With reference to the conflict triangle, it can be suggested that peacemaking aims to change the attitudes of the main protagonists, peacekeeping lowers the level of destructive behaviour, and peacebuilding tries to overcome the contradictions which lie at the root of the conflict'.[2]

Unlike Boutros-Ghali, these peace researchers emphasize that peacekeeping, peacebuilding and peacemaking need to be applied at the same time, not subsequently, as in Boutros-Ghali's model. Peacekeeping without peacemaking and peacebuilding would be very difficult because the violence might overwhelm the process, and any group wishing to sabotage a peace initiative would find it easy to provoke armed clashes. If peacebuilding is ineffective, the decision-makers might lose the support of their communities, and if peacemaking is ineffective, the perceived disagreement that caused the conflict will remain unresolved, and the probability that violence would start (again) soon is high.

In this definition, peacekeeping is defined by its function – the lowering of the level of destructive behaviour, or more simply put, preventing violence. This function can be achieved by military as well as by non-military means.

As the concept of civilian peacekeeping is rather new in the international relations debate, it shall be defined here as peacekeeping by un-armed civilians who take a non-partisan stance to the conflict.

## Some examples for civilian unarmed peacekeeping

### Nonviolent Peaceforce in the Philippines (Mindanao)

Nonviolent Peaceforce (NP) is a young international NGO based in Brussels, founded

*Christine Schweitzer is a trained social anthropologist; she was born in 1959 and lives and works in Hamburg, Germany. She is currently working as Programme Director for the Nonviolent Peaceforce (www.nonviolentpeaceforce.org), an international NGO founded to carry out and promote civilian peacekeeping. Is a member of the German Institute for Peace Work and Non-violent Conflict Transformation (www.ifgk.de). In the 1990s Schweitzer co-founded, and for some time coordinated, the international Balkan Peace Team. She has published work on subjects including civilian-based defence, non-violent conflict intervention and peace work in general.*

---

1 Johan Galtung, Anders verteidigen. Beiträge zur Friedens-und Konfliktforschung 2, Reinbek b. Hamburg: Rowohlt Taschenbuch Verlag, 1982.
2 Hugh Miall, Oliver Ramsbotham and Tom Woodhouse (1999). *Contemporary Conflict Resolution. The prevention, management and transformation of deadly conflicts.* Cambridge: Polity Press, p. 22.

with the goal to develop unarmed peace-keeping, in the sense of having direct impact for the human security of populations caught in an armed conflict through the presence of large numbers of international trained professionals using purely non-violent means.[3]

For over 30 years, more than 120,000 lives have been lost in the struggle for independence waged by Muslim groups against the Christian majority in Mindanao, the second largest island in the Philippines. The main guerrilla group, the Moro National Liberation Front (MNLF), signed a peace treaty with the Philippines Government in 1996.

MNLF leaders joined the government structures in Mindanao, mainly in the then newly created Autonomous Region of Muslim Mindanao (ARMM). But another group that split from MNLF, the Moro Islamic Liberation Front (MILF), continued the fight and it took many years and several ceasefire agreements before fighting more or less stopped, with violent incidents still occurring in central Mindanao. Negotiations for a comprehensive peace agreement are currently being conducted.

The ceasefire is being monitored by an official mechanism that includes both the government and the MILF and has four elements: the Coordinating Committee on the Cessation of Hostilities (CCCH), local monitoring teams, an international monitoring team staffed mostly by Malaysia, and an ad hoc joint action group. The CCCH has set up Monitoring Posts in the conflict areas, which are manned by government and MILF soldiers as well as with representatives of local civil society initiatives. The extraordinary feature of this setup is the close involvement of several hundred local civil society peacekeepers who mostly work in a voluntary capacity.

These local peace groups have invited NP to send an international team to provide support and protective presence to local groups working to enhance civil society initiatives and prevent violence. Beneficiaries of the project are the vulnerable communities, individuals and civil society groups whose lives and work are threatened by the continuing violence or threat of violence, in particular women and children.

Nonviolent Peaceforce sent its first team of six peole to Mindanao in May 2007. In the few months of their work, they have been able together with local groups to work successfully on several smaller and larger incidents in central Mindanao as well as the Sulu archipelago, including Basilan, helping to prevent such incidents leading to full-scale military confrontation. The tasks of NP teams are:

- to enhance the scope and quality of locally based people's organisations and peace/human rights advocates;
- to reduce the incidence of violence in the vicinity of NP field sites through means of unarmed international civilian peacekeeping and thereby aiding in the maintenance of the ceasefire(s);
- to support human rights reporting mechanisms in remote conflict areas and assist/connect local and international advocacy groups that work for peace and justice by responding to people's grievances;
- to localise grassroots conflicts so that they are resolved through dialogue at the lowest level and do not escalate into larger crises.

In our analysis, there is a double mechanism of protection at work here as in regard to the work of international civilian peacekeepers: they are providing the 'eye and ear of the world', and being outsiders, are able to talk to all sides of the conflict without being seen as partisan. Their own security is based on the trust the local communities and the civil society partners of NP give the international peacekeepers. The result is a relationship of mutual support and protection, with its outcome being an increase of the impact the joint peacekeeping efforts have.

## Nonviolent Peaceforce in Sri Lanka

NP launched its first project in Sri Lanka in

---

3  NP is a federation or organisation of about 85 member organisations (mostly groups with an explicit non-violent action or resistance background) from all continents. It has currently field projects in Sri Lanka, the Philippines and Guatemala. For general information and reports of the two projects presented here, see www.non-violentpeaceforce.org

late 2003 at the invitation of and in partnership with local groups. Sri Lanka is of course no longer an example of a country moving from a ceasefire to real peace. The ceasefire agreement from 2002 that was meant to end almost 20 years of war has de facto broken down and the situation is characterised by open warfare between the government and the Tamil Tigers (LTTE) fighting for independence of those parts of Sri Lanka where Tamils are a majority.

NP in Sri Lanka (NPSL) consists of five teams comprising of 25 internationally recruited field team members (the majority from countries from the Global South), applying unarmed peacekeeping methods such as protective accompaniment, mediation, observing and reporting in volatile areas in the north and east of Sri Lanka. Their objectives are to prevent or reduce the level and potential for violence; support and improve the safety, confidence and ability of Sri Lankan peacemakers and other civilians to address conflict in non-violent ways; and work with Sri Lankans to provide human security and deter resumption of violent conflict.

Primary partners and beneficiaries of NPSL's work are community-based organisations working to prevent violence and protect human rights on the ground. NPSL is also partnering and working with international NGOs and UN agencies such as UNICEF and UNHCR. It has played key roles in resolving disputes among ethnic and other groups, securing the release of child soldiers, providing a protective presence in Internally Displaced People (IDP) camps, at temple festivals, and monitoring the delivery of aid to tsunami-affected areas, accompanying local aid workers who are under threat in certain areas.

A major element of the work aside from accompaniment, presence and monitoring is linking people to authorities or agencies, as well as training and dialogue at the community level. Neither of the last three would fall under 'peacekeeping' if that was defined as a purely dissociative approach. But since the goal of most of these activities has been to increase people's well-being by helping them to get access to aid, or solving conflicts that would otherwise likely lead to communal violence and killings, and helping civil society groups to come together to develop their own activities against violence and human rights violations, they are part of a strategy to provide human security.

Also, NP staff security is also based on the acceptance and trust by the local community and also on their international linkages, while the source of its impact is in being non-partisan outsiders with intimate knowledge of the communities in which they work, and thereby being able to offer at a local level what in a diplomatic context would often be called 'good offices': they also make a concrete contribution to the health and security of groups at risk (youth at risk of abduction by armed groups, for example).

### Balkan Peace Team

The Balkan Peace Team (BPT) was an international volunteer project working in Croatia and the Federal Republic of Yugoslavia between 1994 and 2001.[4] Its mandate was broader than that of NP although it shared with the goal of opening space for local actors rather than being one of the countless NGOs in the area following their own agendas and doing their own externally planned projects. Protection and supporting of dialogue were its two focuses, with protection being more important in Croatia, and the support of dialogue at the civil society level among activists from Serbia and Kosovo/a.[5] Many activities of BPT in Croatia had to do with human security (though that term was nearly unknown then). The teams accompanied local human rights activists on many of their missions, be it to prevent the illegal eviction of people of the 'wrong' ethnicity from their flats, or monitoring the situation in newly reintegrated Croatian Krajina after 1995. In the Krajina this international presence was intended to deter harassment and worse (arson, killings) of

4   The Balkan Peace Team was founded and run by a group of mainly European-based peace organisations. Its coordinating office was based in Germany.
5   See Barbara Müller (2006), *The Balkan Peace Team 1994-2001, Non-violent Intervention in Crisis Areas with the Deployment of Volunteer Teams.* Stuttgart: ibidem-Verlag; and Christine Schweitzer and Howard Clark (2002), *Balkan Peace Team – International e.V. A Final Internal Assessment of its Functioning and Activities,* ed. Balkan Peace Team/Bund für Soziale Verteidigung. Minden: Bund für Soziale Verteidigung, Hintergrund-und Diskussionspapier, Nr. 11.

those Serbs who remained behind after the reoccupation. All internal assessments as well as the study by Müller done later on the project confirm that the presence made a difference at those places they regularly went.

BPT was an experiment in combining several roles that other projects tended to keep apart. Unlike many peacebuilding projects, it focused on human security/protection (civil peacekeeping) without rigidly limiting its role to this one aspect. It also allowed itself to get involved in a large variety of peacebuilding activities without feeling that doing so it would lose its character or endanger its non-partisanship.

The ways in which BPT made a difference included:

- serving a *preventive* function in regard to potential human rights violations;
- fulfilling a *mediating* role between local NGOs and international organisations or NGOs. In Croatia, BPT teams were often called upon because, as an international NGO, it had easier access to other 'internationals' than local activists. Unfortunately, this was not only a question of language, but also whether internationals were prepared to take local groups seriously;
- serving as a *bridge* between local NGOs or private citizens and local authorities in the same way as NP does in Sri Lanka;

- facilitating *contact* between NGOs from 'different sides'. As internationals, BPT had more freedom of movement between the conflict areas than local NGOs — between Croatia and Krajina, between Serbia and Kosovo/a, between Croatia and FR Yugoslavia.

This placed the organisation in the position to support dialogue between organisations, and eventually to arrange meetings. The meetings between Serbian and Kosovan students and activists that BPT mediated have had a very different character from other dialogue meetings because they did not happen abroad (as most dialogue projects prefer), but they accompanied people visiting each other in their own towns, which gave the participants a much bigger feeling of ownership over the meeting than any international workshop can do;

- carrying out an *active advocacy* role. BPT alerted other international organisations about, for example, the policy of Croatia regarding refugees from Bosnia-Herzegovina (especially the town of Bihac); the sometimes less-than-helpful role the UN protection forces (UNPROFOR) played in Croatia; the situation in the Krajina and Eastern Slavonia; the situation in Kosovo/a after the war of 1999 when local experts were picked up by international organisations that were able to pay them much better.

These different functions BPT was able to play because it was an international project. And in many instances its efficiency can probably be explained by the deterrence theory. But there is one important modification: The former Yugoslavia was an arena with a multitude of international interveners, many and the most conspicuous of them being backed by military force-though until 1995 of a limited sort and not being entitled to enforce its protective mandate. BPT made a point of distancing itself from the interventions of the international community both on the symbolic level and on the practical by seeking dialogue rather than invoking the threat of international power, and striving to be tolerated in the countries by keeping a low profile. So while it certainly profited from this power, its approach was different from that of the NGO Peace Brigades International, and the sources of its influence were different from the rest of the international community which had a sort of clout.

## Unarmed peacekeeping by governmental missions

There are a large number of other projects, organisations and initiatives by civil society involved in non-violent peacekeeping initiatives.[6] Neither BPT nor NP have been the first, and the reason why they have been singled out as examples lies solely in the author's personal involvement with these three examples.

6  See Christine Schweitzer (ed.), *Nonviolent Peaceforce – Feasibility study*, contributions by Donna Howard, Mareike Junge, Corey Levine, Christine Schweitzer, Carl Stieren and Tim Wallis. Hamburg/St. Paul, September 2001. See http://www.non-violentpeaceforce.org/ en/feasibilitystudy

But there have also been, and still are, civilian missions sent out by governments or international organisations whose mandate does include or is even fully focused on protection, such as UN Monitoring Missions. Many missions by the OSCE can be considered to belong to this category. An interesting example is the Truce/Peace Monitoring Mission that was set up in Bougainville[7], an island that belonged to Papua New Guinea (PNG). Starting in 1988 Bougainville went through a serious civil war between the Bougainville Revolutionary Army, fighting for the independence of the island from PNG and the PNG defence forces supported by Australia. The war was brought to an end by two agreements in 1997 and 1998, and as part of the agreements an unarmed Truce Monitoring Group (TMG) was established. In 1997, under the leadership of the New Zealand military, approximately 370 soldiers and civilians from New Zealand, Australia, Fiji and Vanuatu were sent to Bougainville to monitor the ceasefire and the implementation of the agreement. All members of the TMG had to be unarmed and wear civilian clothes, as an armed peacekeeping force would have been refused by the parties in conflict. The operation was set up according to military standards and rules, using a military infrastructure and approach. Most of the staff today is based in a tent camp in one central location. From there they go out to patrol in the villages to explain the ceasefire agreement and through their presence prevent new violence.

### How does civilian peacekeeping work? The theory of non-violent deterrence

Liam Mahony and Luis Enrique Eguren in 1997 and Liam Mahony in 2004[8] described a theory of deterrence without threat of arms; a deterrence based on the concern a conflict party has for its international image:

*International accompaniment can succeed in deterring attacks because the decision-makers behind these attacks seldom want a bad international image. They don't want the world to know about what they are doing. They don't want diplomats making them uncomfortable mentioning human rights problems in their meetings. They don't want to read in the international press that they are being called monsters or criminals. They will avoid all that if they can.* (Mahony op. cit.: 7)

Mahony and Eguren describe that the protective effect of international presence is one of an indirect threat – the threat with an international reaction in case an attack or human rights violation occurs in the presence of the international monitor/ accompanier, thereby increasing the political cost.

It does not only affect the decision-makers – those at the top of the line of command – but also the individual perpetrator:

*We should not assume that the thugs who pull the trigger are unaffected by international presence. No one wants an unexpected witness around when they are carrying out a crime. The volunteer's presence may have a moral influence on individual perpetrators. It also introduces an uncertainty factor – the attacker does not know what the consequences of this witness will be, so unless he has explicit orders that take the accompaniment into account, he is likely to restrain himself rather than risk getting in trouble with his superior.* (Mahony op. cit.: 8)

According to Mahony (op. cit.:18) a series of conditions must be met in order for this deterrence to 'work':

1. There must be a clear source of the threat.

2. The perpetrator has to be sensitive to international pressure, and the accompaniers have to gauge how much sensitivity there is. The assumption of this theory is that the

7   See Volker Böge (1999), *Friedenskonsolidierung in Nachkriegszeiten. Der Fall Bougainville*, arbeitspapier Nr. 3/1999 der Forschungsstelle Kriege, Rüstung und Entwicklung der Universität Hamburg, Hamburg; and the INP Feasibility Study 2001 a.a.O.
8   Liam Mahony and Luis Enrique Eguren (1997), *Unarmed Bodyguards. International Accompaniment for the Protection of Human Rights*, West Hartford: Kumarian Press; Liam Mahony (2004), *Side by Side. Protecting and encouraging threatened activists with unarmed international accompaniment*, ed. The Centre for Victims of Torture, Minneapolis.

perpetrator makes an assessment of costs and benefits and then decides that the perceived costs are higher than the benefits.

3. The organisation has to have the leverage to exert pressure, which is achieved by making itself known to all levels of the military and civilian authorities, and through a global emergency alert network adding grassroots pressure.

4. The abusing party must know of the presence of the accompaniers and their power.

5. The accompaniment and the activist have to communicate clearly to the aggressor what types of actions are unacceptable.

6. The aggressor must believe that an organisation is capable of carrying out its resolution.

Accompaniment or non-violent peacekeeping alters the political space local activists have. Mahony and Eguren describe in detail the problems that go with widening space because there may be a difference between perceived and real space. So in the worst case scenario the presence of internationals may also cause a false perception of space that is not really there, thereby making people take risks they should not take.

Deterrence fails when the aggressor decides that attack is worth it, because other benefits outweigh the political costs. 'All that is left is to apply the threatened consequences as firmly as possible after the attack, in the hope of changing the calculation next time around' (Mahony and Eguren op. cit.:162).

## Unarmed approaches to human security

Human security refers to freedom for individuals from basic insecurities caused by gross human rights violations, and is distinguished from state security.[9] Human security widens the understanding of security to include other threats than those from an invading army, and includes protection of human rights as well as provision for other basic needs.

Looking at how NGOs provide human security, Hugo Slim and Luis Enrique Eguren[10] distinguish five main modes of action:

1. Denunciation is pressuring authorities through public disclosure into meeting their obligations and protecting individuals or groups exposed to abuse.

2. Persuasion is convincing the authorities through further private dialogue to fulfil their obligations and to protect individuals and groups exposed to violations.

3. Mobilisation is sharing information in a discreet way with selected people, bodies or states that have the capacity to influence the authorities to satisfy their obligations and to protect individuals and groups exposed to violations.

4. Substitution is directly providing services or material assistance to the victims of violations.

5. Support to structures and services is empowering existing national and/or local structures through project-orientated aid to enable them to carry out their functions to protect individuals and groups.

These five, they say, can put a stop to violations, punish the perpetrators, prevent violations or limit their effect. Methods used include humanitarian assistance, presence and accompaniment, monitoring and human rights reporting, and humanitarian advocacy.

At least four of these five 'modes of action' have direct reference to our topic here, namely the goal to open space and give protection to civil society in resistance. Only substitution seems not to fit well. And we find here again the strategy of deterrence when authorities are being pressured to act through denunciation but also two other

9   A Human Security Doctrine for Europe. The Barcelona Report of the Study Group on Europe's Security Capabilities, Barcelona, 2004.
10  Hugo Slim and Luis Enrique Eguren, Humanitarian Protection. A guidance booklet. Pilot Version, ALNAP, February 2004, p. 372. See http://www.alnap.org/alnappubs.html

clearly different mechanisms: persuasion defined as making authorities act at their own accord, and substitution, defined as the NGO acting in place of the authorities.

As described in the three examples above, there is one major factor other than deterrence at play in unarmed civilian peacekeeping: the relationship the non-partisan civilian peacekeepers build with the local community, and the trust resulting from this relationship.

Perhaps the best examples aside from those quoted above are the effective work of local or national initiatives. Probably the best-known examples are the Pakistani and Indian 'peace armies' as developed by Abdul Ghaffar Khan and Gandhi, and a number of local peace teams or peace monitoring missions that can be found in such different countries as Croatia, Indonesia, the Philippines, Sri Lanka and of course India today.[11] Their effectiveness is mainly derived from respect in the community, being centred

inwards - not outwards - to the international world. The focus of the Indian Shanti Sena is and was convincing to those ready to apply violence, and strengthened the communities to resist that violence using methods of dialogue, counteracting rumours, physical inter-positioning and aid and reconstruction.

## Conclusions

This article has tried to argue that civilian peacekeeping is an efficient instrument in dealing with potential violence in the volatile initial time after a ceasefire ends open warfare in a country. Of course, it cannot enforce peace, but then again: how good and convincing is the record of military peacekeeping really in doing so?

Civilian peacekeeping is used in at least two different scenarios: on invitation by civil society groups who use non-violent means of dealing with conflict, or as an outcome of official negotiations when one or both sides reject a military force for whatever reason.

The costs of civilian peacekeeping are probably much lower than that of military peacekeeping because it requires less infrastructure and less hardware. If carried out professionally, it may also have fewer undesired side-effects, such as having a population already traumatised by many years of war and being faced with new heavily armed soldiers.

There is of course still an enormous task ahead. Currently civilian peacekeeping often lacks political support; initiatives involved in it have to struggle for funding (often through budget lines that are not really intended for this purpose); civilian personnel, if sent by civil society, cannot expect the same kind of framework support as soldiers or police can – they most often have to give up their work at home with no right to reclaim the job they left. They also don't enjoy unemployment, pension or other insurance through state schemes, and the recruitment and training of qualified staff is only at its infancy.

11  See NP Feasibility Study 2001 a.a.O., and the literature references given there.

# CREATING COMPREHENSIVE ACTION IN PEACEBUILDING — SHIFT (SHARED INFORMATION FRAMEWORK AND TECHNOLOGY)

## Introduction

After the Cold War, NATO tried to find its new role in the changed world and became more involved in crisis management. Twelve years ago NATO sent its troops to Bosnia-Herzegovina, a mission which UN peacekeepers had failed to complete. NATO's intervention was effective and the situation was brought under control. As a result of its self-evaluation and development work, NATO had created a vision of comprehensive crisis management in which all parties would work towards the same goal. All that was needed was coordination, and that was tested in Sarajevo 1996.

'It was like forcing wild cats into the same cage,' described an officer who was a member of the coordination group. Actors involved in civilian crisis management, let alone different organisations, felt very distressed about all military coordination attempts as they were afraid that soldiers would take control. Some of the organisations even had a legitimate reason to remain completely neutral in their relations to others. In the worst case scenario the results gained for attempting to dictate to crisis management organisations, international organisations and the broad spectrum of NGOs were possibly more chaotic than those gained from random methods. What was left was a tender interface between civilian and military efforts in peacebuilding.

## The problem and its solution

Almost everyone involved has gradually admitted that lack of coordination is one of the key problems in crisis management. Over time the prevalent way of thinking has begun to emphasize a comprehensive approach in all peace efforts: from preventative measures and peacebuilding to hardcore crisis management. Main actors such as the EU encourage creating partnerships that enhance cooperation between organisations — even if that may not necessarily lower the walls between different organisational alliances.

Hundreds of independent organisations may still be working in the same major crisis area without very much knowledge of each other's actions or experiences. Many of them may have pieces of information, seemingly valueless but important to somebody else, but they do not know what they know. More importantly, such small pieces of information when collected and analysed may form an adequate early warning system that triggers successful preventative action in the international community.

The result of this analysis is not new, as many great organisations already work as forewarners and coordinators. Several organisations have been established to coordinate relief work or development aid but none of them covers the whole scope of action. Furthermore, coordination is not understood in the same way by everyone, because many actors have well-founded reasons to act separately from each other. Organisations may also see each other as competitors, for example, because they have the same funding sources or a different ideological or religious approach.

The common denominator accepted by all actors is open and voluntary sharing of information between organisations. It is considered to be beneficial to all parties. However, so far there has been no generally accepted concept and no user-friendly collaboration tool. Even in crisis areas the Information Communication Technology (ICT) possibilities used in information sharing have been limited. The problem is triple- headed: potential users feel uncomfortable with systems owned by somebody else, all organisations want to preserve their freedom of action and the existing collaboration tools are limited in one way or another.

Finland has in turn taken a leading role in financing and developing a user friendly ICT tool suitable for information sharing in

*Kalle Liesinen is the Executive Director of the Crisis Management Initiative (CMI). Before joining CMI, in October 2007, he worked in the Finnish Ministry of the Interior as national coordinator for civilian crisis management training, evaluation and research. His previous engagements include serving as Deputy Head of Mission and previously Chief of Decommissioning in the Aceh Monitoring Mission, Chief of Operations in the Sri Lanka Monitoring Mission, Commanding Officer of the Nordic Battalion I in UNPROFOR and UNPREDEP in Macedonia, and Deputy Chief of Operations in UNIIMOG in Iran.*

any crisis area. The Finnish Government's aim is to provide its solution to the international community as a free, open framework and tested technology. The project is called Shared Information Framework and Technology; SHIFT. It is both an operating model and an internet service together with programmes.

The project aims to create an environment that is not owned by any of the organisations involved but which serves them all. The SHIFT organisation has no other interest than to create a collaboration platform. Only against this background can we try to achieve new unbiased and diverse synergy.

### Credible enough to be used

Developers financing the project are the Finnish Ministry of Foreign Affairs, Ministry of Defence and Ministry of the Interior. In Finland these actors cover both civilian and military crisis management, development cooperation, security matters and rescue services. The Finnish Defence Force is responsible for the practical implementation of the SHIFT vision. Civilian partners include Crisis Management Initiative (CMI), Helsinki University of Technology and the Futures Research Centre in the Turku School of Economics. Commercial partners include several established enterprises that accept the idea of an open and scalable environment.

The Multinational Experiment 5 (MNE5) process has been used as one of the test beds in developing the SHIFT concept. MNE5 is a programme focusing on multinational development and experiments. It pays special attention to the civil–military interface – a well-needed learning process interlinking the US military with European thinking.

When enhancing the SHIFT concept, it is important to establish what the role of the security authorities is as well as what the need is for information sharing between public authorities who carry out the immediate reconstruction work and those who develop democracy on a long-term basis. Furthermore, the solution is not credible unless, in addition to public authorities, non-governmental actors involved in crisis management make a considerable input to its development. Only an open approach can create the critical mass of users needed to gain maximum synergy benefits.

SHIFT focuses first on designing an operating model and developing a technology that supports the concept of open information sharing. At the same time it encourages participants to transfer to a new kind of information management environment where open information sharing adds value to all participants.

As a technology, SHIFT examines information flows between different actors and the use of new internet services in crisis management, such as network meetings and user-created wiki pages. In addition, common graphics and a data model for visualising and sharing situation pictures of crisis areas at international level have been developed.

As an operating model, SHIFT focuses on the fact that actors in crisis management inform each other of their objectives and actions. The solution based on well-developed information sharing can also be applied at strategic-political level as an early warning tool, whereas present research and modelling focus on field-level work. It is believed that common situational awareness helps to minimise overlapping functions, to identify common objectives or operational needs, to locate any gaps in action and to increase security.

### SHIFT in short

The SHIFT environment promotes the situational awareness of all the actors in crisis management, namely, military and civil authorities, international organisations, NGOs and local actors. SHIFT is not owned by any of the authorities or the interested actors. A SHIFT organisation, for example, a particular association dedicated to providing SHIFT services, does not have any operational ambitions; instead, it provides different actors with a forum for open information sharing.

SHIFT is accessible via the internet and provides authorised users with a wide range of ITC services, such as a portal, virtual meetings and the 'Shiftpedia' where up-to-date and user-relevant information is gathered, just as in the Wikipedia. SHIFT technology includes a situation picture that all actors implement. For the situation picture, a culture independent — or as universal as possible — set of symbols has been developed. The situation picture is considered to be self-sustainable because it is, as a rule, in the interests of all actors that the picture is accurate. However, the open system may also leave the way open to misuse. This is why the developers have carefully examined how to prepare for misuse in the right way.

At national level, the SHIFT principle and technology have been used in preparedness exercises like the Barents Rescue 07 exercise in the wilderness of Lapland. The purpose has been to explore ways of using this technology when public authorities, Finnish actors in crisis areas and NGOs cooperate with each other. International testing will be linked to MNE5 events in 2008 and 2009 and the Viking 08 exercise in Sweden.

The objective is to make an international breakthrough utilising current technology and translating it into practical action. The reality is that field-level crisis management and peacebuilding does not clearly make full use of the possibilities available today. Potential development steps are huge, which is in fact the biggest obstacle to any advance on the present situation. People's working methods and ways of thinking have to change to improve the outcome. When the needed steps are finally taken, crisis management organisations will wonder about the odd old times without adequate information exchange in crisis areas.

# UNINTENDED CONSEQUENCES OF PEACEKEEPING

## Introduction

This article deals with the poorly understood and as yet inadequately conceptualised phenomenon of the unintended consequences of peace operations. We now know from recent literature, public criticism and international debate that some unintended consequences, for instance sexual abuse and exploitation, can be extremely damaging to individuals and communities where peacekeepers are deployed. These unintended consequences and others, such as the impact of a rapid and large external intervention on a fragile host society and economy, can weaken the ability of a peace operation to achieve its intended objectives. In fact, some unintended consequences can harm the very concept of peace operations and undermine the legitimacy of the organisations that are responsible for their deployment.

Our aim is to improve our understanding of how unintended consequences come about, and to explore ways in which those planning and managing peace operations can improve their ability to anticipate, mitigate and manage potential unintended consequences. The overall purpose of this article is to contribute to the improvement of peace operations. Traditional peacekeeping was intended to have a neutral impact on the ceasefires or peace agreements they were mandated to observe. They were not meant to have any impact on the future direction of the peace process other than to bolster the fragile peace that existed by monitoring the status quo.[1] In the post-Cold War era, however, the focus of peace operations has gradually shifted from peacekeeping to peacebuilding, in that they have become complex, integrated, whole-of-government, multifaceted operations aimed at supporting and facilitating the implementation of comprehensive peace agreements.[2] This modification in the role and scope of, especially United Nations (UN), peace operations has taken place over the last decade and a half and has exposed peace operations to a new range of potential unintended consequences it has not had to manage before. We consider peace operations to be an indispensable instrument in the international conflict management toolbox. It is therefore in our collective interest to learn lessons from both our successes and failures.

The authors of this article co-edited a volume under the same title and this article is meant to share the insights gained from that study with the broader peacekeeping community.[3]

## What do we mean by 'unintended consequences'?

No intervention in a complex system like a human society can have only one effect. Complex systems are dynamic and respond to interventions in a non-linear fashion.[4] We may be able to anticipate some of the ways in which a complex system will respond to an intervention, including the responses we intended to stimulate through our intervention. However, the system will also respond in ways that we could not anticipate.[5] Those reactions that fall outside the scope of the response we intended to elicit are the unintended consequences of our intervention.

If we accept that unintended consequences are a natural outcome of the dynamic nature of complex systems, then we also have to recognise that they cannot be avoided altogether. This implies that we should anticipate that despite our best efforts to limit

*Cedric De Coning is a Research Fellow at the Norwegian Institute of International Affairs (NUPI) and the African Centre for the Constructive Resolution of Disputes (ACCORD). He served as a diplomat for South Africa in Washington, D.C. and Addis Ababa (1995-1997) and has monitored elections in Ethiopia, Sudan and Algeria for the Organisation of African Unity (1995-1997). He was a civil affairs, and later political affairs, officer for the UN Transitional Administration in East Timor (1999 and 2001), and a training officer in the UN Department of Peacekeeping Operations (2002). De Coning holds a MA from the University of KwaZulu-Natal and is a DPhil candidate at the University of Stellenbosch.*

*Chiyuki Aoi is an Associate Professor of International Politics at Aoyama Gakuin University in Tokyo, Japan.*

*Ramesh Thakur is a Distinguished Fellow at the Centre for International Governance Innovation and Professor of Political Science at the University of Waterloo, Canada.*

---

1  Lester B. Pearson, quoted in Brian Urquhart, *Hammarskjold*. Norton: New York, 1994, p. 176.
2  On the transformation of peacekeeping there is an abundance of literature. See, for instance, Ramesh Thakur and Albrecht Schnabel (eds) (2002). *United Nations Peacekeeping Operations*: Ad hoc missions, permanent engagement. Tokyo: United Nations University Press.
3  C. Aoi, C.H. de Coning and R. Thakur (eds) (2007). Unintended Consequences of Peacekeeping. Tokyo: United Nations University Press.
4  For more information on the dynamics of complex systems, see Anatol Rapoport, 'Systems analysis: general systems theory', *International Encyclopaedia of the Social Sciences*, vol. 15 (1968). New York: Free Press, p. 453; and Ludwig von Bertalanffy, *General Systems Theory: Foundations, development, applications*. Braziller: New York, 1986: 55.
5  Paul Cilliers (1998). *Complexity and Postmodernism: Understanding complex systems*, London: Routledge, p.3.

our actions to those necessary to achieve a desired outcome, unintended consequences are likely to occur.

The unintended consequences of a peace operation are those effects, outcomes and impacts that have come about as a result of the operation but that were not intended in the mandate of the operation, nor in its implementation. UN – authorised peace operations have mandates that are formulated in the form of a UN Security Council resolution. The intended consequences of these operations can be determined by analysing these resolutions.

Some unintended consequences should have been foreseen or anticipated, especially if they have occurred under similar circumstances in the past, while others may be totally unexpected. These nuances may have important implications and will be discussed in more detail. It is also important to note that not all unintended consequences are necessarily negative; some may be neutral and others may actually be positive. Our focus will, however, be on the negative unintended consequences, because they are the harmful to the local communities that peace operations are intended to serve, harmful to the very notion of international peace interventions aimed at supporting and facilitating local peace processes, and harmful to the organisations that mandate and deploy such operations.

A few qualifications need to be made. First, unintended consequences need to be distinguished from failure to achieve intended consequences.[6] Second, unintended consequences need to be distinguished from the 'mixed motive' phenomenon in intervention decisions. We accept states participating in peace operations may have motives for supporting such operations other than those stated in the formal mandate of the operation. We do not consider such mixed motives to be unintended consequences of peace operations. We do recognise, however, that they may cause or aggravate unintended consequences and will then be addressed in that context.

## The scope of 'unintended consequences'

It is also important to note at the outset that the fact that this article is devoted to unintended consequences is not meant to suggest that this phenomenon occurs at a scale that implies that peace operations are doomed to failure. We argue that peace operations will always generate some consequences that will be unintended, but we do not address the frequency or scope of such unintended consequences in this article.

We were unable to make a meaningful assessment of the overall scale and impact of unintended consequences in peace operations, and further research will be needed before any definitive findings can be made in this regard. If we use the cases covered in our study[7] as a sample, there are no missions that have failed as a direct result of the unintended consequences they have generated. There are many, however, whose effectiveness has been negatively affected by some of the unintended consequences they have generated. And there are some that have generated consequences far beyond specific peace operations. The sexual exploitation and abuse by UN peacekeepers of those that they have been mandated to protect, has undermined the credibility of the UN, its Secretary General and of peace operations as an international conflict management instrument.

Albert Hirschman points out that straightforward effects, i.e. intended consequences, are common and often dominate perverse ones.[8] Jervis argues that if this were not the case, it would be hard to see how societies can make progress or how any stable human interaction could develop.[9] In other words, the fact that unintended consequences will occur does not render futile the whole enterprise of mandating, planning and

---

6  For a critical view of strategic effectiveness of peacekeeping deployments see Richard Betts, 'Delusion of Impartial Intervention', *Foreign Affairs*, November/December 1994. Fortna also tests realist as well as institutionalist propositions about the impact of peace processes accompanied by peacekeeping deployments. See Page Fortna, Peace Time: *Cease-fire agreement and the durability of peace*, Princeton University Press, 2004.
7  Aoi, de Coning and Thakur, op. cit., footnote 2.
8  Albert Hirschman, *Rhetoric of Reaction*, quoted in R. Jervis, *System Effects: Complexity in political and social life.* Princeton: Princeton University Press, 1997, p. 68.
9  Jervis, op. cit., footnote 8, p. 68.

managing peace operations. The central message of this article is that we have to recognise that unintended consequences are a predictable side-effect of peace operations. They should therefore be factored into the mandating, planning and managing of peace operations so that their potential effects can be anticipated and managed.

## Why is the focus of unintended consequences new?

We were struck by the absence of literature on, or even remotely related to, the phenomenon of unintended consequences of peace operations. Most of the references that were available are anecdotal. The failure to take unintended consequences into account probably stems from the fact that researchers and practitioners have been preoccupied with the intended consequences of peace operations.

We have been concerned with improving the ability of peace operations to achieve their intended objectives. We have studied peace operations to find out whether they have been successful, and in measuring their success our focus has usually been on whether they have achieved the mandates with which they were tasked. Where they were not, we focused on what could have been done differently to make them

successful. However, a number of incidents have come to our collective attention over the last decade and a half that made us realise that peace operations can also generate unintended consequences.

## Liberal assumptions about peace operations

This lack of attention to and awareness of the unintended consequences of peace operations is also due to deeply embedded and uncritical liberal assumptions about peace operations.[10] Not only are peace operations expected to serve largely liberal-internationalist purposes of creating stable, market-oriented, democratic polities,[11] which are regarded as inherently 'good', but they are at the same time expected to be successful. Decision-makers, practitioners in the field and analysts operate according to the belief that peace operations authorised by the Security Council reflect the will of the international community and therefore are inherently 'good'. Peace operations are therefore expected to produce positive outcomes such as promoting stability and durable peace; they are expected to rebuild and develop and they are expected to generate respect for the rule of law, human rights and democracy. Participation in peace operations by troop-contributing countries is thus a contribution to the global good and the risks involved,

including casualties, is regarded as a noble sacrifice for the greater good.[12]

After the failures of the missions in the early 1990s in Somalia, the Balkans and Rwanda, the liberal assumption has been tempered to accept that peace operations may, for a variety of reasons, fail to produce these intended results. Some may even concede, after the highly publicised sexual abuse scandals, that peace operations may, under exceptional circumstances, have unintended consequences. But such incidents have been viewed as exceptional, once off, phenomena, caused by a handful of 'bad apples' acting outside the norm. The liberal assumption has not yet matured to the extent where it is recognised that peace operations, as a matter of course, generate unintended consequences, including negative economic, social and political side-effects that are contrary to the liberal intent. It has not yet absorbed that unintended consequences come about as part of the non-linear and dynamic behaviour of complex systems, and are thus a systemic consequence of peace interventions.

The fact that peace operations will generate a variety of unintended consequences, some of which may be negative and even pathological to the mandate or intended consequences of the mission, is thus counter-

10 For the classic critique of the liberal agenda of modernisation, see Samuel Huntington, *Political Order in Changing Societies*. Yale University Press, 1968.
11 On the liberal-internationalist agenda of peacebuilding missions, see Roland Paris, 'Peacebuilding and the Limits of Liberal Internationalism'. *International Security* 22(2), fall 1997, pp. 54-89; and from the same author (2004) *At War's End: Building Peace After Civil Conflict*, Cambridge, UK: Cambridge University Press.
12 A. Sotomayor, 'Unintended consequences of peace operations for troop-contributing countries in South America: The cases of Argentina and Uruguay', pp. 171-92 in Aoi, de Coning and Thakur, op. cit., footnote 2. See also, Charles Moskos (1976). *Peace Soldiers: The Sociology of a United Nations Military Force*. Chicago and London: University of Chicago Press.

intuitive to many observers under the influence of the liberal assumption.

This article aims to stimulate awareness that all peace operations generate 'unintended consequences', so that it becomes common practise for decision-makers, practitioners and researchers to anticipate, mitigate, manage and respond to potential unintended consequences in the planning, execution and evaluation of peace operations.

### Examples of unintended consequences

If we accept that unintended consequences are likely to occur, and that they can have a significant impact on the outcome and impact of a peace operation, then we have to improve our ability to anticipate and take steps to try to prevent some of the negative unintended consequences. In others we may have to be satisfied with merely containing and managing the potential negative effects of these unintended consequences. And if we manage to do so with some success, the result should be an improvement in the overall effectiveness of peace operations.

In this context it may be useful to discuss a few examples of unintended consequences. Our study covered a number of other topics related to the unintended consequences of peace operations, such as: sexual and gender-based violence and abuse, distortions of the local economy, impact on host systems, impact on humanitarian action, civil—military coordination, impact on troop contributing countries, the legal position of the United Nations and institutional responses to unintended consequences by the UN and others. For the purposes of this article we have grouped some of the major findings generated by the study under the following topics: permissive environment, impact on local economy, impact on local civil service, and impact on troop contributing countries.

### Permissive environment

The breakdown of law and order, socio-economic infrastructure and social-cultural norms, the prevailing post-conflict condition in which most peace operations operate, create a fertile ground for unintended consequences to occur. A breakdown of this nature implies that the natural checks and balances that would otherwise identify, contain and manage potential negative effects are absent. For instance, it is now recognised that sexual and gender-based violence is often part of a conscious strategy to demoralise the opposing side in a conflict. Kent argues that such violence can become institutionalised in post-conflict societies when the conditions that created the violence remain in place.[13] She points out that extreme poverty, lack of economic opportunity, lack of employment and the loss of family and community support networks, all account for the vulnerability of women and girls to sexual violence, exploitation and abuse in post-conflict societies, not only by local predators but also by international peacekeepers. This would explain, for instance, why human trafficking seems to thrive in post-conflict societies.[14]

### Impact on local economy

The deployment of a peace operation, involving tens of thousands of international civilian, police and military peacekeepers over a relatively short period of time, have various positive and negative effects on the host system. It most cases considered in our study, the presence of the peace operation, humanitarian community and other external actors making up the expatriate community distorted the local economy and stimulated the development of a dual economy, one which served the needs of the expatriate community and another that served the local population. In general, the impact the expatriate community is likely to have on the host system is related to the degree of poverty that existed in that society at the time of the intervention, and the extent of the devastation caused by the conflict. In most cases the budget of the peace operation alone is several times that of the GDP of the host system. The direct effect on the host system, financially speaking, is limited to the funds injected by the peace operation, and the peacekeepers individually, into the host system.

13 V. Kent, 'Protecting civilians from UN peacekeepers and humanitarian workers: sexual exploitation and abuse', pp. 44-66, in Aoi, de Coning and Thakur, op. cit., footnote 2.
14 S. Koyama and H. Myrttinen, 'Unintended consequences of peace operations on Timor Leste from a gender perspective', p. 41, in Aoi, de Coning and Thakur, op. cit., footnote 2.

Ammitzboell's research in Afghanistan and Kosovo/a found positive evidence that large expatriate communities have a range of unintended economic consequences on their host systems, most of which have a negative effect on the host economy.[15] These effects may range from, but are not limited to, a rise in basic commodity prices, an increase in salary disparities and higher rates of unequal standards of living. Ammitzboell points out that peace operations may have a positive impact on the local economy by creating job opportunities and by increasing or creating a demand for certain services and goods, but cautions that this impact will not necessarily result in the enhancement of local infrastructures or capacities, as much of this additional demand is taken up by the international private sector. A large portion of this economic stimulation is linked to the temporary deployment of the peace operation and an influx of international assistance, and the positive economic impact that it has in the short-term can thus not be sustained.

Shin-wha Lee makes the point that humanitarian assistance in these contexts may also give a false sense of relief and distort the local economy, with possible negative unintended consequences.[16] Ammitzboell notes, for instance, how the provision of food assistance allow farmers the opportunity to turn to cash crops, some of which may be undesirable not only from a food-security perspective, such as with poppy-growing in the Afghanistan context.

### Impact on local civil service

Ammitzboell recorded the effects of the 'brain-drain' phenomenon and the 'dual public sector syndrome' on the host public sector, both of which contribute to a dysfunctional and unreliable public sector. The perversity of this effect becomes even clearer when we take into consideration that it not only has a negative effect on the local economy, but it is in fact directly opposite to the effect the peace operation intends to have on the local public sector, which in most mandates are to build the capacity of the public sector and to support the extension of state control throughout the territory of the host state. Another example would be, as noted by Ammitzboell, the combination of weak local administrative capacity and the inflow of considerable amounts of aid and/or direct budgetary assistance, resulting in an increase in corruption by state officials.

### Change in gender roles

Another aspect of the impact that the international community tends to have on a host society is the way in which international assistance programmes empowers certain types of individuals, for instance, those with Western language and cultural skills.

Another category that has become popular over the last decade is women who tend to be the focus of various types of 'empowerment' programmes by international aid organisations, and whom are often given preferential access to jobs, training and other economic and career opportunities. The intended consequences of these programmes are to have a positive impact on development and stability by empowering women to play a more assertive role in their society. The medium- to long-term effects of these initiatives are the subject of various studies, but Koyama and Myrttinen have identified some negative short-term consequences on women, for example, by inviting resentment against them within families and society in general for their newly gained economic independence and power, which in some cases may result in an increase in domestic violence.[17] They also point out that while such programmes may have a short-term and direct impact on the women involved, it takes longer for society to adapt and this may have further unintended consequences. If there is a sudden increase in the employment of women it may impact on their traditional roles at home, where women bear the disproportionate share of child-rearing and household work. It may, for instance, result in burden-shifting to younger children and the elderly.

15 K. Ammitzboell, 'Unintended consequences of peace operations on the host economy from a people's perspective', pp. 69-89, in Aoi, de Coning and Thakur, op. cit., footnote 2.
16 Shin-wha Lee, 'Unintended consequences of peace operations on humanitarian action', pp. 90-108, in Aoi, de Coning and Thakur, op. cit., footnote 2.
17 S. Koyama & H. Myrttinen, 'The unintended consequences of peace operations on Timor Leste from a gender perspective', in Aoi, de Coning and Thakur, op. cit., footnote 2.

Koyama and Myrttinen's research into the Cambodian and Timorese cases touch on the direct link between the deployment of peacekeepers and the influx of aid workers, the growth of the local sex industry, and an increase in the number of cases of sexual exploitation and abuse. They also note the link between a declining sex industry and the departure, or significant withdrawal, of a peace operation and the humanitarian aid community.

### The impact on troop contributing countries

Peace operations give rise to a range of opportunities and costs for troop contributing countries (TCCs), be they financial, social or political, to which TCCs have responded in varying manners. Some of these opportunities and costs gave rise to unintended effects, some significant, some not as significant as is generally believed. For instance, there is a widely held perception that some developing countries contribute troops to UN peace operations because it is considered a 'financial opportunity' by both military institutions and individual troops. In Aning's study of Ghana,[18] financial gains from participation in peace operations for both individuals and the state seem substantial, while Sotomayor points to similar perceptions in Argentina and Uruguay. Murthy's chapter on India and Pakistan finds, however, that such gains did not constitute a significant

effect given the proportionally small number of units participating in peace operations in relation to the overall size of these armies.[19] In more than a few countries examined, participation in peace operations offered some opportunities for corruption to occur. Aning and Sotomayor discuss cases of corruption such as the manipulation of appointments to peace operations (where selection implies significant financial gain for individual soldiers and officers), and the misappropriation of funds received from the UN to reimburse countries for some of the costs of their participation in peace operations.

### Integrating unintended consequences into the planning and managing of peace operations

Most of the research cited noted the importance of institutionalising accountability in peace operations. In the past, the weakness or lack of clarity in accountability mechanisms in itself created a 'permissive' environment within which unintended negative side-effects went unreported and therefore fell outside the realm of that which should be managed. When they did occur at such a scale that they could not be ignored they were usually managed as exceptional phenomena that require a temporary, once-off, response.

For example, Kent, Koyama and Myrttinen's findings indicate that peace operations

have not meaningfully anticipated the reality of sexual exploitation and abuse before the late 1990s, and that it is only half-way through the first decade of the 21st century that various steps to anticipate, prevent and manage sexual violence and abuse in UN peace operations have become institutionalised. Before these latest developments, peace operations rarely addressed enduring violence on women and girls, due to a lack of consciousness of the problem, the severity of the implications of the problem for all concerned, and most importantly a lack of institutional preparedness to identify, contain and manage the problem. There are very few examples of UN peace operations identifying, containing and managing unintended consequences outside of the sexual exploitation and abuse realm. It is thus not yet a widely understood, discounted and institutionalised phenomenon.

### Planning

In order to improve our ability to manage complex peace operations, we need to improve our understanding of the dynamics of complex systems, including complex social systems. This article makes the point that unintended consequences are part of the natural feedback cycle of complex systems and cannot be avoided. However, we can improve our ability to anticipate, mitigate and discount specific potential negative unintended consequences, and in so doing,

---

18 K. Anning, 'Unintended consequences of peace operations for troop-contributing countries from West Africa: The case of Ghana', pp. 133-155, in Aoi, de Coning and Thakur, op. cit., footnote 2.
19 C.S.R. Murthy, 'Unintended consequences of peace operations for troop-contributing countries from South Asia', pp. 156-70, in Aoi, de Coning and Thakur, op. cit., footnote 2.

improve the overall effectiveness of peace operations.

This knowledge leads us to the understanding that in a complex system unintended consequences should not come as a surprise. Once we realise and accept this fact, it follows that whenever we plan or undertake action in the complex peace operations context, we have to discount the potential unintended consequences of our actions.

As the system is dynamic and we can therefore not predict all the ways in which it may respond to our actions, it means that we have to anticipate that despite our best planning efforts, we will still not be able to foresee all the potential unintended consequences our actions can have. However, through research of past actions and by systematically thinking through the consequences our actions are likely to evoke, we should be able to significantly reduce some of the obvious negative consequences of the past. Anticipating the potential unintended consequences of our actions should thus become a standard aspect of our planning procedures and processes.

### Real-time monitoring and evaluation

If we accept that despite our planning efforts some unintended consequences will still occur, then we should introduce, as standard practice, monitoring systems that can identify emerging unintended consequences, so

that we can try to contain or counter their potential negative effects. In fact, peace operations should have monitoring systems in place to study whether the missions are having their desired effect on the system. If such systems are in place, an important sub-set of such systems should be the identification of any unintended consequences, especially negatives ones that may be emerging in response to our actions. The alertness to potential negative unintended consequences should thus be integrated into an overall awareness of the dynamic nature of the complex systems that peace operations are trying to influence. Such awareness should inform a willingness to continuously adapt the planning and management of peace operations, and its various aspects, to the way the system is responding to the peace intervention. Real-time monitoring and longer-term evaluation are tools that will assist those responsible for managing peace operations to detect, at the earliest opportunity, when unintended consequences occur.

### The 'do no harm' approach

One methodology for anticipating unintended consequences that has been developed in the context of humanitarian assistance is the *Do No Harm*[20] approach. In short, this approach is built on the realisation that aid cannot be provided without becoming part of the wider conflict, and provides a model for planning, continuously monitoring and adjusting the effects of any assist-

ance programme by identifying and downplaying the negative influences while at the same time identifying and encouraging the positive influences of the programme. It thus implies (a) recognising that unintended consequences will occur, (b) putting systems in place that will identify the effect one's action is having (both positive and negative), and (c) steering and refining that effect by countering potential negative effects and encouraging and modulating the positive unintended consequences towards the intended impact. It implies that one needs to understand that intervening in a complex system requires a continuous process of adjustment.

### Unintended consequences that cannot be avoided

Through planning and monitoring efforts, like the *Do No Harm* approach or others, we are likely to identify unintended consequences that cannot be avoided if we want to continue to pursue a specific course of action. This implies that we may be faced with situations where we have to discount the potential negative consequences of our actions with the potential good that those same actions are intended to generate. This predicament is not unknown, and has been addressed before in the context of the *Double Effect* and *Just War* theories.

We do not intend repeating these theories here in detail, but the principle of dou-

---

20 M. B. Anderson (1999). *Do no Harm: How aid can support peace or war.* London: Lynne Rienner.

ble effect is a moral principle for assessing actions that produce side-effect harm that has wide-ranging utility. In short, it states that, although actors are responsible for the harmful side-effects that ensue from their actions, actions that produce harmful side-effects are nevertheless permissible provided that: (1) the primary goal of the action is legitimate; (2) the side-effects are not part of the actor's intended goal; (3) the side-effects are not a means to this goal; (4) the side-effects are permissible only if the actor aims to prevent or minimise them; and (5) no alternative courses of action could have been taken that would have led to fewer or no side-effects.[21]

There are thus existing theories and approaches that can assist us in developing practical means of containing and managing unintended consequences when they cannot be avoided altogether. However, we should always be cautious of overestimating our ability to 'manage' outcomes when dealing with complex systems. A further insight we need to gain from our study of complex systems is that managing the host system, in the sense of controlling it, is impossibly complex. Our definition of managing unintended consequences in the peace operations context is purposefully interacting with the system with the aim of continuously adjusting our actions to the feedback generated by

the system with a view to minimising any negative unintended consequences our interventions may have caused. When we talk of containing and managing unintended consequences the emphasis is thus on being alert to system feedback through institutionalised monitoring and evaluating mechanisms, and constantly adjusting our planning and operations accordingly.

Planning for peace operations can thus not rely on a 'fire-and-forget' planning model where a peace operation is planned prior to deployment, and then perhaps annually reviewed against the original plan, or in some cases only after the situation has fundamentally changed to the extent that significantly more troops are required. In the complex peace operations context each action result in the system responding in various ways that will require a range of further actions. The analogy most apt is that of steering a ship. Although the destination is known at the outset, and although it is possible to plan the journey in great detail, the actual voyage requires thousands of route adjustments, some minor some more significant, to reach the destination. The reality of peace operations is, however, even more complex in that the destination is a very broadly defined desired end state and the exact journey is unclear beyond the milestones contained in peace agreements, and these are typically unrealistic

political ideals formed by the need for compromise and mutual assurance, rather than realistically achievable timeframes. Managing complex peace operations thus necessitates an ongoing planning process that constantly monitors and evaluates the feedback generated by the system so that peace operation can continuously adjust its programmes or initiate new actions accordingly.

### The accountability debate

The attempt to establish clear accountability in peace operations is hampered by two factors. One of them concerns *authority*, the issue of *to whom* a peace operation is accountable. The second issue concerns the *control* of the mission.

Hampson and Kihara-Hunt address accountability in the context of the responsibility to address criminal conduct or breaches of applicable disciplinary codes.[22] This relates to the 'control' of the mission issue through the management of the behaviour of individuals and it covers unintended consequences such as sexual exploitation and abuse, corruption, theft, etc. Mégret, on the other hand, addresses authority in the broader sense of unintended consequences caused by the actions or omissions of the mission itself,[23] and it covers the kind of unintended consequences addressed by Ammitzboell (economic consequences),

---

21 G. J. Rossouw, 'Business is not just war: implications for applying the principle of double effect to business', in L. Bomann-Larsen and O. Wiggen (eds), *Responsibility in World Business: Managing harmful side-effects of corporate activity*, Tokyo: United Nations University Press, 2004, p.39.

22 F.J. Hampson and A. Kihara-Hunt, 'The accountability of personnel associated with peacekeeping operations', pp. 195-220, in Aoi, de Coning and Thakur, op. cit., footnote 2.

23 F. Mégret, 'The vicarious responsibility of the United Nations', pp. 250-67, in Aoi, de Coning and Thakur, op. cit., footnote 2.

Shin-wa Lee (humanitarian consequences) and Gordon[24] (civil–military coordination consequences).

## Who has authority over the mission?

For this latter category, the question of authority, or to whom a peace operation reports to, two models may be relevant, namely the delegation and participation models.[25] These models capture two separate potential accountability mechanisms. In the delegation model, power is exercised by those who are delegated with the authority to do so, making them accountable to those who delegate the power to them. In the participatory model, those in power are accountable to individuals in the polity. In the international sphere, different perceptions about accountability create tensions and conflicts. Whereas some perceive international organisations – such as the UN, World Bank, etc. – as reporting to their member governments (delegation model), others hold that these organisations' actions should be made accountable directly to the people who are affected by these organisations' actions (participation model).

Thus in the UN peace operation context,

some would argue that a peace operation is accountable to the UN Security Council, the body responsible for establishing and supervising the mission, while others would argue that a peace operations should be accountable to its host community, i.e. the people whom the peace operation are meant to assist. Mégret notes that there is a shift observable in various areas of governance from a 'shareholder' view of accountability to one emphasizing the importance of 'stakeholders'. Ideally, a peace operation should establish a balance between these two models, for neither seems sufficient ground for accountability by itself. Whereas the accountability of the peace operation to the UN Security Council, and indeed the UN General Assembly for budgetary matters, are established practice, mechanisms still need to be developed for meaningful host community participatory accountability.[26]

One such mechanism was addressed by Hoffman, in the form of the ombudsperson model, which provides us with one example of a mechanisms that may empower the local population to submit claims against the peace operation.[27] However, much more can and should be done to develop meaningful

accountability towards and by the host community, not just in the context of legal accountability related to some form of wrong doing – for which a range of practical recommendations has been made in the studies by Kent, Koyama and Myrttinen, Hampson and Kihara-Hunt, and Mégret – but also through ongoing and proactive political accountability. This can come about through a process of consultation and participation in order to, among others, seek advice and input from the host community on future plans and to receive and monitor feedback from the community on programmes being undertaken.[28]

One obvious question is who constitutes the host community? And one can respond that the host community should be represented through a range of institutions and mechanisms at all levels of society, and should include civil society. In a post-conflict context, which is the condition in which most peace missions operate, most of the official institutional positions and mechanisms will undergo considerable change under contested circumstances, and the peace operation would thus have to be resourceful in ensuring that the mechanisms it is

24 S. Gordon, 'Unintended Consequences of civil-military cooperation in peace operations', pp. 109-30, in Aoi, de Coning and Thakur, op. cit., footnote 2.

25 For a theorisation of these models in the context of international relations, see Ruth W. Grant and Robert O. Keohane, 'Accountability and abuses of power in world politics' in *American Political Science Review*, vol. 99, no. 1, February 2005, pp. 29-44.

26 For one such attempt, see for instance the 'Principles and Good Practice of Humanitarian Donorship', *Humanitarian Exchange*, No. 29, March 2005, p. 7.

27 F.F. Hoffman, 'A beacon of light in the dark? The United Nations' experience with peace operations ombudspersons as illustrated by the Ombudsperson Institution in Kosovo/a', pp. 221-49, in Aoi, de Coning and Thakur, op. cit., footnote 2.

28 Note the February 2003 Rome Declaration on Harmonisation signed by 28 developing countries and 49 donor organisations. The four main principles highlighted in the Declaration are: recipient countries coordinate development assistance, donors align their aid with recipient countries' priorities and systems, donors streamline aid delivery and donors adopts policies, procedures and incentives that foster harmonisation. See www.aidharmonization.org

interacts with, or facilitates, reflect the broadest possible representation of popular will and opinion.[29] As Mégret points out, the challenge is no longer to determine whether the UN should be accountable, the challenge is now to determine what accountability means by examining the various options for accountability.

### Who has control over the mission?

The other issue that hampers the establishment of clear accountability in international peace operations concerns the *control* of the mission, i.e. those who are responsible for the peace operation do not necessarily have effective control over the responsibility to address criminal conduct or breaches of applicable disciplinary codes of all the individuals that are perceived to be its employees.[30] The most obvious case in this context is the fact that personnel that are deployed as part of a military contingent to UN peace operations remain under the legal authority of the sending state when it comes to criminal and disciplinary issues. Although the conduct of these personnel are also governed by international humanitarian law, international human rights and other bodies of international law, these instruments need to be applied through the national legal systems of the troop contributing country. Hampson and Kihara-Hunt also discuss the full spectrum of other categories of UN peace operations personnel, including military observers, UN police, international civil servants, international and local UN staff, etc. and the various challenges related to the ensuring criminal and disciplinary accountability for these categories of personnel in the peace operations context.

### Conclusion

We were struck by the absence of literature on, or even remotely related to, the phenomenon of unintended consequences. Most of the references that were available are anecdotal. Our recommendation is thus to encourage further research into the unintended consequences of peacekeeping.

However, even within the scope of the limited research undertaken into this topic, and to which our study is a modest contribution, it has become clear that unintended consequences is an important, yet neglected subject. It is an important subject because some of the unintended consequences that come about in the context of peace operations are morally and ethically unacceptable, while others can seriously hamper a mission's capacity to achieve its mandate. In fact, we have seen that some unintended consequences can question the value of peace operations itself, while others have brought sending institutions, like the United Nations, into disrepute and have been ma-

jor drivers for reform and calls for greater accountability within these international organisations.

Those responsible for the planning, managing and supervision of peace operations need to recognise that unintended consequences are a natural consequence of the complex dynamic nature of complex systems. As such, all peace operations should develop the capacity to identify, contain and manage unintended consequences. This implies that the United Nations and other institutions that undertake peace operations need to develop institutional mechanisms for addressing unintended consequences, and should institutionalise planning, real-time monitoring and evaluation mechanisms that will enable it to anticipate and respond to emerging unintended consequences.

The overriding message of this article is that we can no longer pretend that these side effects do not occur, or that when they do, that they are exceptional phenomena. An awareness of and sensitivity to unintended consequences should be integrated into the routine management processes of UN and other peace operations, so that they can be proactively prevented, contained or managed as part of the normal day-to-day reality of complex peace operations.

---

29 See the report of the 'Building Effective Partnerships Conference: Improving the Relationship between Internal and External Actors in Post-Conflict Countries', 7 October 2004 available at www.ipa.org
30 Issues concerning the control of power in international relations are discussed in Grant and Keohane, op. cit., footnote 24, pp. 37-8.

[    Philip Blenkinsop    ]

# Women at war

As photographers we are witnesses and messengers. I endeavour to preserve moments which faithfully portray the people and the situation in which they find themselves in as accurately and compellingly as possible. My photographs say, unambiguously: 'this is the situation'. This is what these people face each and every day of their lives.

The underlying question is always the same: what are you going to do about it? The closer you can come to feeling a place and immersing yourself in a situation, the more revealing your images. It is very rare that I do not feel moved by the people I spend time with. Moved to the point of tears and anger, and so many times left in awe of their spirit and selflessness.

If my photographs, taken in these pathetic theatres, fail to disturb and anger viewers where I myself have been so disturbed and angered, the work is of no merit. My search for the image is always free of thematic or storyline constraints. Arriving in a place with a fixed idea of what you expect to see and photograph is a recipe for disaster.

What do you do when, no matter what you try to isolate within your viewfinder, the reality outside is ten times more shocking and threatens to swallow you up as you pick your way through it.

Philip Blenkinsop

*I returned to the hospital after a week in the Delta area and entered an empty hospital room. Sunita had died that morning. In her village, by the side of the road that would eventually lead her to her final resting place, relatives grieve by her corpse.*

© Philip Blenkinsop / Agence VU / Nepal

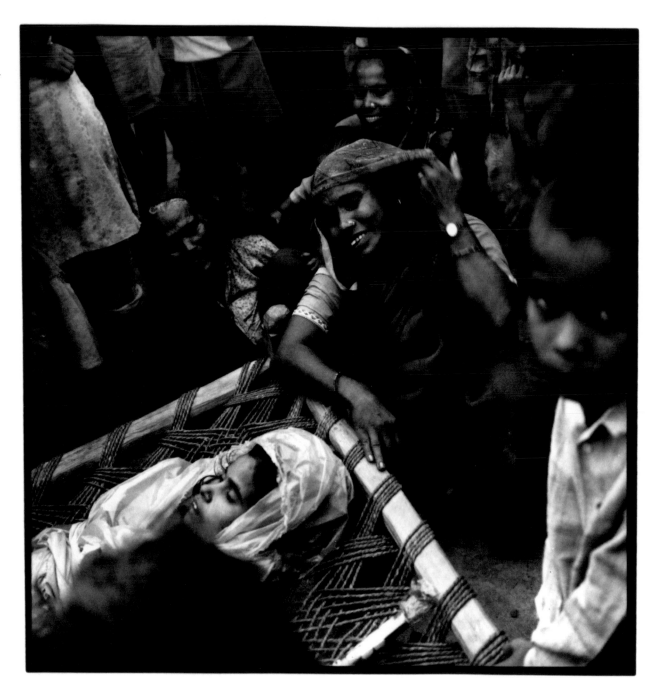

*The road out of Nepalgunj to Bardiya is scarred by Maoist ambush sites. This particular blast claimed the lives of two women.*

© Philip Blenkinsop / Agence VU / Nepal

*Policewomen stand with batons ready, during anti-monarchy demonstrations.*
© Philip Blenkinsop / Agence VU / Nepal

*Royal Nepalese Army (RNA) women recruits outside of their Kathmandu barracks. This represents the second batch of female recruits into the RNA.*

© Philip Blenkinsop / Agence VU / Nepal

RNA recruit, Karki Puspa, age 20

*"My husband, Karki Jeevan (age 20), was killed
in an ambush by Maoists at the birthplace of Lord
Buddha, Kopil Bustu in southern Nepal, ten months
after we were married. I joined the army to fulfil
my husband's dream of saving the nation.
We are not scared to be ambushed. We will fight."*

© Philip Blenkinsop / Agence VU / Nepal

RNA recruit, Shrestha Ram Kumari, age 20

*"My husband, Shresthaa Rambahadur (age 26), was ambushed by Maoists while on patrol in Shinduli Bhadrakali 15 months ago."*

© Philip Blenkinsop / Agence VU / Nepal

Comrade Rojana, age 19

*"I have seen women being beaten by security forces*
*at a religious fair in Malakot, Kalikot District*
*two years ago. Nirmala (another female Maoist*
*combatant) and I were in the cultural team and*
*decided to join the armed movement together."*

© Philip Blenkinsop / Agence VU / Nepal

Comrade Nirmala, age 19,
Chetri from the Mid-west hills

*"I joined the cultural wing of the movement when
I was 16 years old. It was Rama Roshan people's
cultural group. I joined because I was aware of
western cultures supporting the old government.
My uncle was killed by RNA troops two years ago.
He was in a cultural team and was sheltering in
a village in the Kailaali district. He was 26 years
old. He was captured at 07h00 by RNA and taken
away with two others and tortured. They had nails
pushed under their fingernails. Their hands and
feet were tied and they were shot. I heard that my
uncle's body was found in the forest. That is what
my friends informed me of. I joined the military
wing about six months ago, but I took part in an
attack on Atcham HQ Mangalesen in the North-
western hills in 2002 while I was still part of the
cultural team. I was slightly back from the front
wave, playing my madel (drum). I felt no fear...
I received encouragement from the leaders and
brothers who were becoming martyrs. The blood
of the people made me more angry. Where I was I
saw 26 people killed. We celebrated by telling the
villagers we had won the battle and showed them
the sophisticated weapons. The villagers welcomed
us, giving us garlands and playing musical
instruments for us. That day there were 175 dead
military and police. After the war I would like
to liberate all the women of Nepal. They have no
income or status."*

© Philip Blenkinsop / Agence VU / Nepal

Comrade Bargiya, age 20, of Taru ethnicity

*"The security forces knew I was a Maoist activist with the women's organisation. Two years ago, at 09h00, 150 RNA arrived in my village in Rajapur. They beat 20 to 22 villagers and encircled our house to ask my mother where I was. She told them she didn't know where I was. They beat my mother and my brother's wife with guns and kicked them. This was in November 2002, and in January I joined the military wing. I have participated in one raid, numerous encounters and five ambushes. I am not sure how many people were killed by my bullets but I am sure they died. In an ambush in Ghariha with another group, they blew up a vehicle and I have seen seven dead bodies. Those I have killed deserved to be killed. I was excited to see their dead bodies and encouraged to kill others because they [security forces] are the enemy of the proletariat. I'm married. My husband is also in the military in the hills. It was less than a year ago that we got married. The last time I have seen him was a month ago. We have no plans for children at the moment. I haven't even thought of it. If I am pregnant, the Party would assign me to a different position in the political wing. It would make no difference to me."*

© Philip Blenkinsop / Agence VU / Nepal

RNA recruit, Tharu Mina Kumari, age 20

*"My husband, Tharu Patiram (age 23) was killed in an ambush while patrolling in the Chitwan area. I will marry again after the war if I can find a good man."*

© Philip Blenkinsop / Agence VU / Nepal

Comrade Rekha, age 19, Kamaiya
(members of the system of bonded labour
in Nepal go under this name)

*"I joined the women's wing of the Communist Party of Nepal (Maoist) three years ago. One year later I joined the armed wing of the Maoists. The senior comrade visited our village and convinced us of the persecution and suffering of the poor. I saw the chance to join the party and achieve things from within the party. I have taken place in two raids, in Lamki and in Beni. In Lamki it was my duty to care for the wounded and oversee the disposal of the dead bodies. In the Beni attack I was part of the defence group, supporting the main assault group. I saw the lights in their bunkers. The RNA knew we were coming and ambushed the main assault group but they managed to overrun them and we attacked from all sides. My brother (age 25) has been with the RNA for the last six years. He used to be in Kailali barracks but not any more. We used to write to each other but not anymore... he stopped a year ago. My parents asked me in the beginning: "why did you join the Maoists if your brother, Rambahadur Choudhari, is with the RNA?" They do not ask me anymore. I don't want to meet him again because he is our enemy. If I meet him on the battlefield I am in a position to kill him, I will kill him."*

# Arms and the Girl

## Women in conflict situations

Women and girls perform many roles in conflict, such as hostages, spies, porters, cooks, nurses and propaganda symbols. They secure food and firewood and provide sexual services. One role has remained largely invisible – that of combatant. Women form over 10 per cent of regular armed forces in Australia, Canada, Israel, New Zealand and the United States.

The number of women and girls in irregular, or guerrilla, armed forces is even higher. One-quarter of El Salvador's Farabundo Martí National Liberation Front (FMLN) and 30 per cent of Nicaragua's Sandinista National Liberation Front were women and girls. Today, women and girls comprise one-third of Sri Lanka's Liberation Tigers of Tamil Eelam (LTTE) and the same percentage in several of Colombia's armed opposition groups.

Girl combatants have been particularly ignored. Girls, defined by international conventions as females under 18 years of age, are approximately 40 per cent of today's 300,000 child soldiers. The groundbreaking study *Where are the Girls? Girls in Fighting Forces in Northern Uganda, Sierra Leone and Mozambique: Their Lives During and After War* by researchers Susan McKay and Dyan Mazurana, discovered that between 1990 to 2003, girls were part of fighting forces in 55 countries and took part in armed conflicts in 38 of these countries.

Girls become combatants for different reasons. Some are abducted or kidnapped. Others join voluntarily in order to confront social injustice or to achieve national goals. Some armed groups, such as the New Peoples Army (the Philippines), LTTE (Sri Lanka) and former Maoist guerrillas in Nepal, specifically emphasize gender equality in their recruiting efforts.

Researcher Yvonne E. Keairns identified poverty as a key factor in girls joining, or being abducted by, armed movements. Her research is based on interviews with girl soldiers from Angola, Colombia, the Philippines and Sri Lanka. With little or no food at home, girls joined armed movements in order to empower themselves and their communities, or because they did not want to accept an arranged marriage or be hired out as a domestic servant. Many girls interviewed were escaping sexual abuse or other violence at home.

Disarmament, demobilisation and reintegration (DDR) programs fail girl soldiers. The Save the Children report *Forgotten Casualties of Wars* revealed that in the Democratic Republic of Congo, only 2 percent of those going through Save the Children's demobilisation programs were girls, despite the estimated 12,500 girl soldiers there. In Sierra Leone, the percentage of girls in such programs is 4.2 per cent. The only option for many girl ex-combatants is prostitution.

Women and girls who challenge traditional gender roles by becoming combatants face stigmatisation upon their return home. Female ex-combatants are seen as violent, disobedient and promiscuous. This is especially true for girl ex-soldiers who return home pregnant or with children. Stigmatisation means many girls are reluctant to identify themselves as former combatants.

In Sierra Leone children who could prove they knew how to dismantle and fire a gun were eligible for a DDR package, i.e., a school uniform and payment of school fees for three years, or a vocational training course. Girls were put off by this military orientation, which also excluded girls who worked as cooks or porters. In other DDR programmes, where money or food was given to soldiers in return for weapons, male soldiers stole guns from girls, or commanders confiscated the money girls received for their weapons. The lack of gender awareness in planning demobilisation camps also led to an increase in sexual violence: in some camps girls were raped when they were housed next to men from enemy units.

It is essential for gender assumptions to be re-examined if the needs of girl ex-combatants are to meet. The invisibility of women and girls in conflict must be broken. The voices of women and girl combatants must be heard. Only then will sustainable peace be possible.

*Shelley Anderson founded the Women Peacemakers Programme (WPP) in 1997 and is currently WPP Programme Officer. The WPP works to empower women peace activists and pioneers gender-sensitive non-violence training. The WPP is a programme of the International Fellowship of Reconciliation. Anderson is an experienced non-violence trainer and has conducted trainings in gender and peacebuilding throughout the world. Her articles on women's peace activism have been translated into a dozen languages. In 2005 she was collectively nominated for the Nobel Peace Prize as part of the '1000 Women for the Nobel Peace Prize' initiative.*

# STREAMLINING OF MEDIA AS A CFSP INSTRUMENT

## Introduction

It is evident that media has played a significant role in escalating conflicts. This is true for almost all violent conflicts — Yugoslavia, Rwanda, Gujarat, Iraq, Kosovo/a and many more. Media is also employed to radicalise young people into terrorists.

Nevertheless, media may also be used to contribute to the prevention of conflicts and the building of peace. Even in conflict management during a crisis, media and communication strategies are essential. To be successful in its civilian response to conflicts, in its ambitions to spread democracy and fundamental rights and in its ambitions to support social development and regional cooperation in third countries, the European Union has to make use of media as a catalyst for change.

The EU's Common Foreign and Security Policy provides the European Commission with all necessary instruments to deal with civilian prevention of conflicts and to support peacebuilding, including working with the media. Humanitarian Aid (ECHO) along with programmes for human rights and democracy (EIDHR), development cooperation (DCI), neighbouring countries (ENPI) and the Instrument for Stability (IfS) ensuring rapid response in urgent crises and medium-term support under more stable conditions are among the instruments available to the Eu-

ropean Commission. As is often the case, the challenge is to develop and implement coordinated, comprehensive strategies based on these instruments. This is definitely necessary in the field of media, which constitutes a relevant tool in all phases of a conflict, be the objective democracy, human rights and social development, or be it peacebuilding and prevention of conflicts. Due to the prominent role of the media in achieving these objectives, strategies connecting short-term rapid actions with medium- and long-term measures are essential. This implies tools and mechanisms ensuring the capacity to react rapidly and comprehensively in situations of urgency, crisis or emerging crises.

## Media and structural conflict prevention

When working with local media in conflict areas a delicate balance must be maintained between our immediate goals — conflict prevention, democracy, fundamental freedoms and peacebuilding. Most conflicts are rooted in structural inadequacies, but triggered by dynamic causes often featuring the political leadership of the conflicting parties as participants. The distinction between structural and dynamic factors is very useful when looking at the scope and goals for media assistance.

The prevention of conflicts — recurring or not — requires a public sphere with open discussion of social inadequacies where po-

litical leaders are held accountable. Critical and constructive debates on adjustments to prevent problems from escalating into a violent conflict require independent, professional media as well as a well-functioning civil society.

In the former Yugoslavia it was possible to discuss almost everything in the media, but impossible until the immediate pre-conflict phase to criticise and debate the ruling Communist Party or the fundamental construction of the Yugoslav federal state, characterised by a multitude of national groups. In other conflict countries it has been very difficult to question unfair ethnic and economic divisions, geographical claims on sovereignty and natural resources, or other issues, which may eventually cause an escalation of the conflict.

Rather than merely serving as the government's mouthpiece, the media must be allowed to discuss any issues of relevance to the local community in an early pre-conflict phase, thus opening a new role for the media as a catalyst of social change. It is also essential to ensure that a common media platform is accessible to all population groups to maintain national identity and coherence. The goals and means used by international actors in the early pre-conflict phase are identical whether the objective is conflict prevention, democracy, fundamental

*Bent Nørby Bonde is a manager, academic and consultant working with the constructive use of media in conflict prevention, peacebuilding and democracy development in the Balkans, Asia, Africa and the Middle East. He was co-founder and executive manager for the Baltic Media Centre Fond, working with a staff of 70 in 23 countries, promoting peace and democracy. He was co-founder and member of the board of the European Coordination of Film Festivals, and the Bonn Network. He has a PhD in Communication and Conflict and is a member of the Danish Foreign Policy Society and of the European Communication Research and Education Association.*

freedoms or sustainable peace and conflict transformation.

### Dilemmas of media in structural conflict prevention

When international actors enter a conflict area during conflict escalation or in the phase immediately before the outbreak of violence, the situation is much more complicated.

One of the dilemmas faced after the conflict has escalated is that the very legitimate foreign policy goals of supporting a transition to democracy and promoting fundamental freedoms may easily threaten the peace. Research demonstrates that totalitarian systems in transition to democracy and fledgling democracies are vulnerable to conflicts. When Yugoslavia introduced multiparty elections at the federal level, nationalists were elected leaders in four of five republics. One year later the country was engaged in several severe wars. Similarly, the genocide in Rwanda took place shortly after the first democratic multiparty elections.

The conflict vulnerability of countries in transition does not make the goal of democracy irrelevant, but it indicates the necessity to time and prioritise realistic goals to prevent a country from the gradual escalation of violent conflicts.

Similarly, a free and diverse media landscape accessible to all groups of the population is usually considered an important step forward in a democratic development. In the phases right before and after a peaking conflict, there is no guarantee that a quick liberalisation of media laws helps prevent the conflict or that a mushrooming of independent media will stabilise peace. Again, the Yugoslav example is illustrative. Less than two years before the internal wars, new media legislation was passed after heavy internal and international pressure. Private, commercial media were allowed and the state media were required to adhere to international public service standards, including independent and impartial reporting. It is common knowledge that the state media in Yugoslavia acted as a mouthpiece for the political leadership in each republic, supporting violent conflicts with each other.

With the political escalation of conflicts the new legislation was never implemented and the state media ended up as useful propaganda tools. Most of the experienced, professional journalists were dismissed, sent on leave or removed from the screens and loudspeakers. Young, inexperienced staff without journalist educations replaced them, and eventually only patriotic or nationalistic journalists and editors were in control. The Yugoslav example is far from alone in demonstrating the importance of international focus in the conflict escalation phase on the practical protection of the safety, rights and independence of journalists and media rather than concentrate on

pushing for new legislative measures. Timing and priority is crucial.

After the ending of a war where the media has been a means in the escalation of conflict, many international donors have often assumed a need to liberalise the media sector as much as possible, particularly the mechanisms for issuing licenses to new broadcasters. What seems a logical reaction to biased media escalating a conflict may involuntarily sow the seeds for the next conflict as in the former Yugoslav republic, Bosnia-Herzegovina, where 400 broadcasters started up in a war-torn country with a non-existing market. Media without financial resources, almost no professional journalists and hardly any ethical standards tend to associate with political factions which may harm rather than facilitate peacebuilding. An international focus on freedom of speech standards is seldom enough to establish peace in an immediate post-conflict situation or prevent an outbreak of violence in a pre-conflict context, while in a stable democracy it might be one of the most important prerequisites for sustainable peace. Again timing, priorities and a balanced approach are necessary.

Thus, strategies to promote democracy and human rights must necessarily be coordinated with strategies to prevent conflicts or build peace. Consequently, the EU must consider these strategies as interdependent and integrated elements in other development activities.

## Working with media to change conflict dynamics

Timing and approach is even more critical when it comes to actions playing directly into the dynamics of a conflict dealing with content, advocacy and policy.

Numerous violent conflicts demonstrate that most media become biased in their reporting and fuel prejudice against their adversaries once the conflict begins to escalate. In this phase the top leadership of governments, opposition parties, independence movements or threatened minorities attempts to control the media. The media institutions become the scene for internal fights between professional management and journalism on one side and staff submitting to political pressure on the other. In this phase the goal for international media interventions must be to support genuine media ideals like impartiality, diversity and objectivity. Often this can be achieved by combining capacity building, advocacy and increased involvement of local media representatives in international cooperation.

In the immediate pre-conflict phase all significant media are under control or have been harassed and closed down. The space for questioning the top leadership in its fuelling of the conflict is minimal or non-existent. Media contributes to moral panic by propagating prejudice, stereotypes and even hatred against the 'others'. Some media even actively encourage popular participation in killings and fights, making it virtually impossible for the population to rely on any media as neutral. In this phase international media interventions should support cross-conflict, self-regulatory means to prevent media from broadcasting and distributing conflict-escalating journalism. This phase also calls on international actors to make conflict-escalating media aware of the risk of being held accountable to the International Criminal Court. Alternatively, the interventions must be in the form of reliable, trustworthy sources beyond the control of the top leaders.

In this case international organisations, donors and implementers need to consider their media policy carefully. If international donors in crisis situations produce content with unsupported messages or convey particular policies they will fail. This is partly because communication research today shows that the recipients do not uncritically accept and appropriate such messages, and particularly not if their own reality is different from the conveyed messages. And it is partly because constructed messages or positive 'propaganda' for peace hampers the credibility of the local media and makes it difficult for the local population to believe that the content in media is independent and free. If a journalist in one situation pursues one goal as peace, however important it is, she might be seen to pursue other interests in the political life of a democracy. At its best, media content may help set the agenda for discussions among the recipients. In a short-term perspective international actors must respect that editorial freedom and autonomous control over editorial content remains with publishers, broadcasters, editors and journalists of the local media we support, while increasing their capacity to make professional, impartial and responsible editorial judgements.

Particularly in news and fact-based journalism, international actors must maintain a careful balance, respecting the integrity of the local journalists, while helping to develop their professionalism. Less controversial than news programmes are fiction series, sports and entertainment, which may be highly efficient to set the agenda for popular discussions and contribute to re-establishing relations, re-conciliating populations or increasing awareness about the causes of conflict.

In the charts next page different genres and content are related to the phases of conflict mentioned above and the aims of international conflict prevention or peacebuilding.

| Possible interventions/period | Distant pre-conflict | Pre-conflict | Immediate pre-conflict | During conflict |
|---|---|---|---|---|
| Aim | Removal of root causes of the conflict | Mediation between adversaries and solution of conflict issues | High-level negotiations, monitoring, protection of diverse identity groups | High-level negotiations, humanitarian assistance |
| Focus of content | Debating existing systemic weaknesses and visions for the future | Debating conflicting issues of concern to the adversaries and allowing access for all identity groups | Strengthening relationship between identity groups, discuss solutions to issues of conflict, and reduce stereotyping in media | Providing neutral humanitarian information and news about political and international development |
| Genres | News, Documentaries, Debates, Investigative journalism | News, Current Affairs, Debates with phone-ins, Documentaries | News, Current affairs | News, Public service announcements |
| Media | Existing mainstream, New local, Net media | Existing mainstream, Community, Net media | Existing mainstream, Community media | Existing niche, Main stream, UN, International media |

| Possible interventions/period | Immediate post-conflict | Post-conflict peacebuilding | Transformation of conflict society |
|---|---|---|---|
| Aim | Humanitarian assistance, re-establishment of relationship and state structures | Reconciliation, social change, civil networking between adversaries | Involve society in the development of joint values, visions and systems |
| Focus of content | Providing neutral humanitarian information and news about post-conflict and discuss solutions to the triggers of conflict | Re-establishing relationship through dealing with human life of enemies, providing common platforms for interaction, communication and cultures | Analysing and debating economic, social, structural and political inadequacies, search for solutions and common visions for future society |
| Genres | News, Current affairs, Public service announcements | News, Current affairs, Documentaries, Public debates, Fiction, Sports | News, Current affairs, Documentaries, Public and political debates |
| Media | Existing mainstream, UN, New local media | Existing mainstream, Niche, Net, Local, Community media | Existing mainstream, Niche, Net, Local and community media |

A coherent EU-strategy employing all instruments in coordinated efforts to prevent conflicts, build peace and secure fundamental rights across the world is in high demand. But media also plays an important role in preventing long-term threats by helping to avoid radicalisation and the recruitment of youngsters to Islamist-based terrorism.

In the Federally Administered Tribal Area (FATA) in Pakistan the sense of isolation and negligence from the national authorities combined with very active religious leaders in the villages of the FATA, bordering Afghanistan, has fuelled increased radicalisation of the local population, and particularly youth. The strong basis for bitterness and hostility towards the national authorities and rest of the world can only be removed if the isolation is breached and the empowerment of the local population is increased. The only broadcaster transmitting in the area is Pakistan radio, which has very little credibility with the local population. A neutral network of community radios providing independent public service programming including important news and social reporting could help in creating a common public sphere within the FATA, give the local population a voice in the Pakistani community and strengthen their sense of inclusion in the national and international communities. It would be very important to include also neutral reports about events in rest of Pakistan and the region.

Another example where EU intervention could be useful is in dealing with the Bolivian media to prevent violent conflicts, as land reforms, nationalisation of the hydrocarbon sector, and the election of a constituent Assembly to agree on a new constitution has drawn protests from the dominant city-based broadcasters, representing primarily the middle and upper classes. As a contrast to the very critical private media a new public radio network covering also the rural part of the country may ultimately prove to develop into a mouthpiece for the government defending the government's reforms rather than becoming the balanced and much needed public service broadcaster providing access for the marginalised, poor parts of the population. The division between the government and opposition is now reproduced in the media structure, which makes it urgent to encourage private and public media to act professionally, to be balanced and impartial, reflecting all parts of the population. The EU could prevent an escalation of conflict by facilitating an interim Forum for Dialogue involving private and public media, journalists, politicians and regulatory bodies to agree on guidelines such as:

- codes of ethics and systems for media self-regulation;
- public service broadcasting – programme standards and goals;
- private media – roles, programme standards and markets;
- community media – social role, programme standards and funding;
- license allocation procedures, including programme standards;
- principles for capacity building of journalists and editors.

This step is supported from the Bolivian government and willing partners from the European public service broadcasters and the NGO community.

Lebanon is another example, where media could help prevent internal violent conflicts and conflicts between Israel and Hezbollah. The stakes are high for the involved politicians and the media is an important tool. Inter-cultural dialogue is virtually non-existent so it is crucial and urgent to establish a mutual, neutral, diverse and moderate platform for dialogue and debate to keep peace and promote unity in the country. The political leaders from all factions seem most focused on their own private media, which has made it difficult for the public broadcaster, Télé Liban, to reflect the diversity of all the popular groups and strengthen national coherence. Nevertheless, the public broadcaster would be an obvious platform for running a project focusing on programmes with dialogue and debates among the population groups, and independent and diverse news programmes. To succeed, such a project should be managed by all conflicting parties in the country and probably be facilitated through ASBU, EBU and relevant representatives from the NGO community working with media in conflict.

Together with other measures such as diplomacy, mediation, civil society collaboration, travel, trade, disarmament and non-proliferation, media can make an important difference to peacebuilding and conflict prevention.

### Steps to be taken

For EU there are plenty of challenges in making media an integrated and efficient tool in its efforts to prevent conflicts, build peace, democracy and development. The Common Foreign and Security Policy still needs to streamline the use of media.

It is crucial to ensure coherence within short-, mid- and long-term strategies. The impact from rapid short-term measures must not be counterproductive, but rather support long-term goals of conflict transformation, democracy and development. Therefore, it is important that the thematic media strategies are coordinated. It is also essential that the coordination between the EC delegations, the geographical units and the important instruments such as IfS and EIDHR is proactive and action-oriented.

Finally, it is important to build the strategic, human and technical capacity for the EU to act rapidly and comprehensively with media in conflicts and crises. With a capacity to react rapidly the media can act as a lifeline by contributing accurate and life-saving information about humanitarian assistance as it does in Darfur and did in Afghanistan. The media can through rapid actions take the first steps to re-build relationships and confidence across conflicting communities, or the right and timely steps to prevent escalation of a conflict.

It would be logical for the EU to make a dedicated media taskforce ensuring internal coordination at all levels including the capacity to react rapidly. It would however be more efficient to enter a genuine partnership with the Bonn Network and make use of the strategic, technical and human capacity of the member organisations, which are all actively working with media in conflicts.

The Bonn Network has more than 25 member organisations worldwide – among them the Council of the European Union, OSCE, UNDP-BCPR, EBU, numerous media development organisations, researchers and the international media. By partnering with the Bonn Network, the EU would take an important step towards a global collaboration and coordination of media strategies with governmental, non-governmental and intergovernmental actors working actively with media in peacebuilding and conflict prevention.

# TUNED INTO SIERRA LEONE: A SEARCH FOR COMMON GROUND APPROACH TO CONFLICT TRANSFORMATION

## INTERVIEW WITH AMBROSE JAMES

*What is the mission of Search for Common Ground (SFCG), both generally and in Sierra Leone particularly? How is the organisation's programme shaped?*

Search for Common Ground is an international NGO with an ambitious mission: to change the way the world deals with conflict. This is what most of the organisation's 16 field offices around the world contribute towards. Each country programme is based on its own context, and when the country context changes so does the programme. There are a lot of tools we use in SFCG, and in Sierra Leone specifically we are using media as well as outreach work.

SFCG approaches conflict transformation through the media, and in Sierra Leone radio is the best way to reach people. More than 80 per cent of people there tune into the radio. SFCG established the Talking Drum Studios, which are multi-media studios producing issue-based programming. This is in partnership with 24 radio stations across Sierra Leone. We aim not only to add value to programming, we also try to impact the editorial and media landscapes in the country. Several other radio stations are copying our model, which is a good thing. This is what the whole mission is about: to change the way the world deals with conflict!

*What are SFCG Sierra Leone current priorities?*

We are coming to the end of a two-year strategy in which current areas of focus are corruption, governance, education and youth/women. We have field officers working around these thematic areas; they let us know what people are thinking about these issues.

Our field officers know what issues are on people's minds because they are based there. And wherever you are, the issues are mostly the same throughout the country. Field officers bring in information from all directions, examine what people are saying, produce a programme about it and send it back to radio stations for airing. You end up hearing voices from all parts of the country from the person who is really a stakeholder.

We're trying to build a sense of nationhood! Through the radio we are learning and sharing. We want people to know and to feel that their issues are being taken on board and that people are responding to them. It's not about radio news; it's about a sustained campaign around specific issues. As an organisation, we move with the context and the context determines how the programming goes.

*Through Talking Drum Studios' programming do you bring people from the conflict together?*

Yes, by bringing together people from opposing sides we're trying to deepen the analysis. We need more voices – diverse voices! And the more people you talk to, the deeper the analysis. More people are able to decide, for example, about politicians and see if they are really serious or jokers.

Our national programmes encapsulate the nation and its issues in general. We have mini-studios based in the south and the north. These studios respond to needs on the local front and feature stories about local councils, mining or culture. The bigger studio in Freetown responds to the international aspect.

In addition to the radio front, at Search for Common Ground we're also doing video. Video is not as big as radio, but it supports and complements the radio aspect. In our context it is targeted at policy-makers, who are mostly based in Freetown. We know that a lot of policy-makers listen to the radio, but when you really want them to act they have to see something visual. This is what we have learned.

Politicians and even the Ministry of Education will get behind a policy statement

*Ambrose James is country director of Search for Common Ground (SFCG) Sierra Leone. He liaises with stakeholders in Sierra Leone and throughout its vast network, including media and civil society organisations working on conflict transformation. SFCG Sierra Leone uses media and outreach as tools to help find solutions to ongoing and new conflicts, in part by promoting local, national and sub-regional dialogue. The SFCG programme in Sierra Leone works in conjunction with partner organisations in Liberia and Guinea for greater peace and stability in West Africa.*

such as 'free basic education for all by 2015'. Then you get out a video camera and go to rural schools where children are sitting on rocks and have no benches, no chalkboards and no books. We capture this and then go into a city where the children are dressed up nicely and have current textbooks. We show the contrast.

We reproduce our videos and give them to institutions like OXFAM, CARE International and others working on governance issues. They use these videos to generate discussions about what is happening, particularly on the political scene.

*Are politicians receptive to this kind of medium and willing to be held accountable?*

Sometimes. We are not just generating accountability and pressure from our side; we are allowing people on all sides to have a say. For example, councils in Sierra Leone run in four-year terms. After two years we check on them and what they have done. People talk! They talk about what they know and what they have seen. We want to generate discussions about accountability, and we need to be because of widespread corruption.

For example, there is a local programme we do called 'Accountability Now', which is mostly about the local councils. These councils are supposed to post their income expenditure statements every month. A lot of people are not used to reading, and literacy rates are not so high in rural communities. So we take microphones to the notice board and read what is there – the income and expenditure – just so people know. After a period of

5 months or so, people start comparing and saying, 'last week you were talking about 1 million spent on communications and now you're talking about 10 million. Why?'

People begin to question things, and this is very good. The citizens need to know how their money is being used. In one of the videos shot for the local councils, a local market woman sat down and said, 'I heard yesterday that they spent 2 million on entertainment for the month. What is this? What does entertainment money mean?' The working woman wants to know more! She wants to know where her money is going. If people know how their money is being used they feel OK to pay their taxes.

*Following up on issues of transparency, the Sierra Leonean media was heavily affected during the war. What's the state of media now? How free is it?*

Search for Common Ground started operations in Freetown in 2000, and at that time there were just four or five radio stations. Now we have about 40. The landscape has expanded, and it's continuing to expand. There are community radio stations all over the country. Every district except one has a community radio. There is religious, private and government radio, too. All of those voices are out there, and it's quite developed right now.

Radio is far better than print, which is very much Freetown-centred. The media landscape has grown so much in the last six years that even the government cannot understand how to respond because they are still in the

old mode. The old mode focused on public relations, not real issues. Now the bigger media groups are starting to catch on, which is great.

*In your presentation at the conference you spoke about the priority areas for SFCG, one of which is gender equality. Could you talk more about the situation of women in Sierra Leone and if gender equality is difficult to implement as a priority?*

The gender issue is a cultural and societal issue. Gender equality is something that we really struggle with. We have a specific programme for women focusing on the post-conflict challenges women face; for example, inheritance property rights, abuse and a variety of discriminatory practices. We want women to be at the forefront and raise their voices. Community radio is a strong tool for women to be part and parcel to do just this: the more women's voices you have the better to be able to get women's issues on board.

One of the challenges we're taking on is to see how we can get more women into the radio so they can start mobilising other women. If we can do this, it's a first step to getting women to speak out. Women often do not think it's safe to be on the radio — many times they are called names or perceived to be prostitutes. They think that they make mistakes or that they're not articulate enough. It's a struggle, but it's also an investment. We won't see the results in two or three years, but in ten years you'll really see a change. These are the seeds we're trying to sow now.

This is already going on in the bigger towns because there you have a lot more women who can challenge issues. It will take some time for us to get the momentum going in the rural areas. Gender discrimination is really rife. Even when the president was making a big fuss about bringing in more women he was just talking about three or four women ministers. Come on – in a 40-member cabinet! They talk about 'not enough qualified women', but it's obviously not about this.

There is another problem as well: a lot of 'elite' women do not like to go into politics, they prefer the advocacy side of things. So instead they are engaged in civil society.

*Regarding the political front, Sierra Leone had successful presidential elections earlier this year. How was Search for Common Ground engaged?*

We contributed significantly and were commended for our role. SFCG worked on a few major fronts, one of which was the National Elections Watch, a coalition of civil society groups monitoring the democratic process.

Search for Common Ground is the chair of the National Elections Watch and we house the secretariat in our office. We organised more than 6,000 electoral observers; there was at least one observer at each polling station. This was the first time in history of mobilising civil society in such a way. It wasn't just about monitoring; it was about the entire process such as voter registration and voter education. This was a huge effort by civil society, which complemented international bodies like the EU and the AU.

Another contribution we made was through the Independent Radio Network (IRN), which has been an investment for SFCG over the past four years. The Independent Radio Network is a coalition of about 20 radio stations. The network brings in what we call a 'Common Ground approach' to the media landscape. During elections the Network broadcasted simultaneously across the country. We worked with the national electoral commission, for example, giving them free airtime on a weekly basis. We also gave politicians equal space, which really supported the electoral process.

During the election we had some 400 reporters covering the country who called in and explained the situation on the ground. We put them on the air from the most remote places in the country. This was also a problem-solving mechanism for the police – they could know where to react, and fast.

When the election results came in – which took quite a while because we don't yet have computerised mechanisms to tally votes and roads are bad – our reporters were calling to tell us what that polling station got. This really decreased the tension, and by the time the official results came in it was no longer a huge issue. People knew what was happening and felt it to be transparent.

*What's the climate like post-elections? Are people more inclined to trust their leaders?*

You can't really say the climate is optimistic yet, but there is a new wave of politicians in sight. Let us see what happens. A lot of people are looking at what the politicians are actually trying to do. For me personally, it's not too impressive as of yet. We need to do a lot of social accountability programming right now, to hold them responsible for what they said. For example, during the election period SFCG organised in local communities debates between different parliamentary candidates. There was a big forum outside the town hall, which was hooked up to the radio and people could ask [the candidates] questions. This was the first time this happened, and we did it in nearly all constituencies. There was a huge demand on us to do more and more so that people could hear what the candidates had to say!

We recorded all of these events, and we're going to go back and check after a year and ask, 'this is what you said; now, what have you done?' We want to push them to deliver on what they said before.

We also did a 'situation committee' video about women and youth and their participation in elections. It was very powerful. This was also the first time for us to do video around this. For example, we would go to a women's hairdressing salon and hosted a debate there. The discussion that takes place is incredible! They talked about the real issues that people face.

All of the different fronts we worked on about elections focused on stabilisation. After all, if you are not able to stabilise the situation you will definitely slide back into conflict. Search for Common Ground provides information that helps people to make informed decisions and informed choices.

*You mention 'sliding back into conflict'. In your opinion, what are the chances of that? How dangerous is a short institutional memory?*

It's dangerous; you can't just leave. During my presentation at this conference I mentioned a couple things I think that post-conflict you have to pay attention to in the Sierra Leonean case – like the Truth and Reconciliation (TRC) report, for example. Its recommendations have been on the table for a few years and yet no one has made any profound movement around them. The TRC report is the history of the war and its recommendations are on the table so we don't slip back into conflict. Equally important is the Human Rights Commission.

The independent media also needs attention because the landscape is expanding. People's independent voices need to be heard and Sierra Leoneans need to feel that it is truly independent! During the elections a few people questioned if we were doing propaganda. But at the same time, the level of trust is generally very high. When the Independent Radio Network was broadcasting, everybody was tuned in. We need to hold on to that space because if we don't bad things can happen. The political parties had their own radio stations, and you can imagine the propaganda and terrible things they were doing.

I've been speaking about the media a lot, but Search for Common Ground is also working on the outreach side of things. The media complements our outreach work – alliance building, coalition building and networking. Some issues throughout the country are very sensitive and if as an organisation or an individual you try to take these on, you are simply not going to be able.

Society is closely knit. Since groups everywhere basically have the same issues, we bring them together to discuss. SFCG provides a space for alliances on all kinds of issues, and we hook them up to the radio, too. Search for Common Ground has several kinds of alliances and coalitions, like for example motorcycle taxi drivers. These are mostly ex-combatants who were part of the war, and now the police chase them because they have no licence, no helmets or don't follow traffic laws. There were violent clashes between them and the police all the time. We organised a coalition called the 'Transport Stakeholder Taskforce'. We invited everyone to come around the table and talk about the issues. When we dug a little deeper we discovered that even the government officials were not talking to one another, and the taxi drivers were just stuck in the middle. We started having regular forums, and the situation started to calm down. This is a very practical thing we provide as an outreach arm of our work.

SFCG also does trainings for local drama groups, most of which are based in Freetown. We are trying to develop community resources so we train a small drama group around message design, and it's a ready resource. Any time we have a message to pass on we can use these drama groups. They have become increasingly successful because they know how to tailor messages. People are seeing more and more how effective this is.

*Like you said, the TRC report came out nearly two years ago and its recommendations are still not being implemented. Do you think it's because they are not realistic? Or is it a general lack of support?*

It is a general lack of support and will of the government. This was really where the government lost its credibility, and so they were voted out. These recommendations need to be carried out because they lead to the war. The recommendations say 'if we do this we won't go back to conflict'. If the government isn't willing to move forward then it is a problem and people get frustrated. You have all of these amputees and reparation issues – people are frustrated and they showed in their voting! They vented their views about it.

*During your presentation at the conference you spoke about a possible regional Disarmament, Demobilisation and Reintegration (DDR) strategy. Can you speak more about what such a scheme might look like?*

When war breaks out in a particular region or country, remember that a lot of people are criss-crossing as refugees and displaced people. Idle youth are often targeted by those on the other side saying 'hey, come over here and help us fight'. And they give them money to do so. Even when a war is finishing a lot of these people return home and they go back with their two or three guns. They will bury one and wait for the next good deal because they know there will be a violent uprising in future.

Thus far the implementation of the DDR has been really country specific. It basically just looks at a single country and how to take away the guns. You do this in one country, but the implementation strategy is different in the next country. In West Africa people are just hanging around with their guns waiting to go to, for example, to Guinea. Why don't we have a well thought out regional strategy that encompasses all of these young people? Let's have a strategy that accommodates a large number of people and not just moves guns from one place to another. This is what is happening.

*After such a brutal civil war do you think Sierra Leoneans are really ready for peace? Is there still a sense of retribution?*

People are ready for peace; they don't want to go into war again. Nobody wants to hear about guns, about coups or anything con-nected to war. The war in Sierra Leone was around resources and the centralisation of resources. You had one group who for 24 years marginalised an entire other group of people and centralised everything in the capital city. People in the border areas of the country turned to their neighbouring border for help.

When the uprising started people said 'we are tired of being ignored and we need to be part of our society'. It was nothing religious, tribal or ethnic – it was about resources and the class system. A lot of young people felt marginalised and the few people who were benefiting from the system were targeted: rich people, chiefs and government officials, even if they weren't corrupt. This is why the war was so hard to deal with because there was no ethnic or tribal element to it.

When the war was finally over, a pro-gramme of decentralisation was put in place whereby people have more real power. It aimed to bring development to the doorstep of the people. The next elections are in 2008, and it's only after four years that people re-ally realise what this is about. The upcoming elections will be pretty tense.

*What are your thoughts about the recent Hollywood film 'Blood Diamond' and about all of the international media attention about Sierra Leone?*

I saw the film, but I didn't pay much at-tention to it. I think we've passed that stage. People say, 'Aw, I saw Blood Diamond and I know Sierra Leone'. But the country is at a different level now. The movie was really old stuff, and this should not be the perception. It's exactly what we are trying to get away from. We should be talking about what's go-ing on in the country now. There are huge issues about decentralisation and disarma-ment. The government is moving forward and there has been security sector reform. Also, the media landscape is open and we had successful elections. These are the is-sues going on, and this is what we need to be talking about. The international media jumped on *Blood Diamond*, but it's just not the right picture now.

# MEDIA COVERAGE ON THE TSUNAMI IN ASIA VS. THE EARTHQUAKE IN PAKISTAN: INTERNATIONAL ANALYSIS OF GERMAN, UK AND US MEDIA COVERAGE[1]

## Discrepancy in coverage between the tsunami (December 2004) and the earthquake (October 2005)

There was a perceptible difference between the coverage on the tsunami that hit South-East Asia in December 2004 and the earthquake that hit Pakistan in October 2005. The tsunami received far more extensive coverage in all countries analyzed in both television and print media.

The earthquake in Pakistan, India and Afghanistan did not cause as high a death toll as the tsunami, but left more than 3 million people homeless in freezing weather in comparison with 1.5 million displaced people in tsunami-affected areas of moderate temperature. Low media presence contributed to the fact that timely help did not reach the thousands of people living in rugged, mountainous areas which could be accessed only by 70 available helicopters. By contrast 4000 helicopters were available to the areas affected by the tsunami.

Both disasters resulted in an out-pouring of global donations and fund drives. The magnitude of both disasters was different in terms of the death toll and economic devastation, and this could be a factor as to why the tsunami received far more coverage which in turn affected private donations. The tsunami affected tourist areas which could also explain why there was more reporting and global solidarity. In either case, the volume of coverage was very low given the fact that hundreds of thousands of lives were lost. If this reporting trend continues, it will lead to lower international awareness and consequently an avoidably high death toll from lack of aid and relief efforts.

It is evident from the analysis that coverage differs a lot in all the analyzed countries. For example, in Germany, the tsunami received 666 reports in the three TV channels in comparison to 66 on the earthquake. Those 666 reports resulted in private donations amounting to US $178 million while for the earthquake only US $8 million have been collected so far.

The US' contribution to tsunami relief work was US $350 million and this wasn't even the largest contribution which came from Australia and amounted to US $819.9 million. In the TV and print media monitored in the US there were 804 reports on the tsunami and 210 on the earthquake. Humanitarian organisations received US $13.2 million from the private sector. Governmental support did not vary as much as public support, as governmental offices have more direct information and connection to reality than the audience and public at large whose perceptions and issue stances are shaped by media coverage. Media Tenor has been researching these connections for the past several years and this study supports the 'Theory of Agenda Setting and Cutting'.

*Media Tenor was founded in 1993 and is based in New York but has offices in Germany, South Africa, Namibia and UK. It has established itself as a media research institute focusing on continuous media analysis serving partners in the corporate, government and scientific world with strategic media intelligence. In addition to this it helps organisations make better and more efficient use of media.*

---

1 Edited version of full study covering German, UK, US, Czech and South African media coverage.

## Tsunami vs. earthquake in Pakistan[2]

| Possible interventions/period | Tsunami | Earthquake in Pakistan |
|---|---|---|
| Total death | 289,273 | 79,000 - Unofficial: 100,000 |
| Homeless/ displaced | 1,500,000 | 3,000,000 – 4,000,000 |
| Area | Flat, easy to approach | Rugged, mountainous terrain |
| Helicopters provided | 4,000 | 70 |
| Weather conditions | Moderate | Temperatures below zero centigrades and snow |
| Speed of aid | 80 per cent in two weeks | Up until now 12 per cent of promised aid |
| Tourism in the country | High | Low |
| Media reporting vs. private aid | High/high | Low/low |

2 Media used: US media (Wall Street Journal, Time, Newsweek, CBS, NBC, ABC and Fox), German TV media (ARD, Tagesschau und Tagesthemen, ZDF heute und heute journal, RTL Aktuell, SAT1, NEWSPro 7, Newstime) British media: BBC one News at 6, BBC One News at 10, BBC Two Newsnight), Czech media (Czech TV – Udalosti, TV NOVA – Televizni noviny, TV Prima – Zpravodajsky denik), South African media: SABC Afrikaans, SABC English, SABC Zulu/Xhosa, SABC Sotho, e-news), Other sources used: Red Cross (SA, DE, CZ), United Nation, BBC, www.nationmaster.com, www.saquake.org, Embassy of USA, Wall Street Journal.

# MEDIATION AS AN INSTRUMENT FOR CONFLICT PREVENTION AND CRISIS RESPONSE: AN OPPORTUNITY TO MAXIMISE THE IMPACT OF THE EU'S SOFT POWER

There are dozens of cases where Track II diplomacy has worked successfully – from the Middle East to Mozambique. And there are many more opportunities that could help solve conflicts, from the South Caucasus to Burma/Myanmar.

Why is it that one private person – Martti Ahtisaari – is asked to mediate a seemingly intractable conflict (Aceh, Indonesia), negotiates a peace agreement (Memorandum of Understanding) and then enjoys the support of EU Member States to monitor the peace process (the Aceh Monitoring Mission)? At least part of the answer is that the former Finnish President is trusted, is seen as impartial and has excellent negotiation skills. While the practice of private diplomacy (or Track II diplomacy) is not new, it seems to be blossoming with the EU appointing a growing number of envoys and representatives. A reason could be the resurfacing of conflicts that are often intra- rather than inter-state, whose victims are mainly civilians and which are waged with unconventional weapons and methods, including terrorism.

One argument for private diplomacy is that independent, non-partisan actors can successfully complement or replace governments and international organisations when these (because of restrictive mandates, bureaucracy or shrinking budgets) are prevented from taking part actively in crisis management and conflict resolution. A second argument is that traditional diplomatic instruments of negotiation and conflict management have proved to be ineffective, calling for new approaches. Post-modern diplomacy is a profession that includes other agents than states or state-like structures. Some actors in need of mediation would be more inclined to trust a private diplomat (a small 'entity') rather than a state actor, especially when needing a rapid intervention. A third argument, which is gradually surfacing, is that the practice of mediation has not had the opportunity to professionalise itself. Mediation, in fact, is a rubber concept that is being stretched for the political purpose at hand. Conflict mediation is a voluntary and confidential method through a structured process where one or more impartial third parties assist warring factions to reach a mutually satisfactory solution. The mediator provides a framework and conducts and facilitates mediation, but makes no substantial suggestion or decisions in this case. The use of this 'soft' instrument in an adequate and systematic fashion could indeed add weight to the 'soft' power of the EU on the world stage.

## NGOs as natural partners for bolstering the EU's ability to act and react in crises

The complex institutional set-up of the EU could benefit from the use of parallel diplomatic efforts. The current approach of European diplomacy is multi-dimensional, involving the Council of Ministers, the European Commission, the European Parliament and the EU presidency. If decisions are taken through this complicated diplomatic machinery, they could actually have a strong impact on third countries. But more often than not, such a heavy decision-making structure hampers rather than facilitates crisis management and too often it does not produce quick results.

More than 60 wars are waged around the world with many more tense situations that might evolve into conflicts. The Council has nine special representatives at its disposal. These special representatives are often given a negotiating brief based on the lowest common denominator between EU Member States, which limits their ability to broker deals and solve crises.

Many actors in private diplomacy in non-state groups, such as think-tanks, non-governmental organisations (NGOs), the private sector or religious organisations carry years of experience on the ground and as facilitators of dialogue, and have the advantage to having gained trust – a rare commodity in conflict ridden areas – with parties. The case of a successful trust-building exercise for

*Antje Herrberg is a Senior Adviser for Mediation for the Crisis Management Initiative, the Director of Europe for Interpeace and the President of the European Peacebuilding Liaison Office. A political scientist, economist and mediator by training, Dr Herrberg has worked for 15 years in the public and private sector on issues relating to EU external relations and conflict resolution. She is currently working on various initiatives that aim to professionalise mediation for it to be considered as a foreign policy instrument of the EU and beyond.*

conflict resolution in Mozambique through the Community of St Egidio is just one case example.

At the same time, NGOs provide early warnings of impending conflicts and often act as information brokers and mediators or facilitators of official or unofficial negotiations. Some are deeply immersed in conflict prevention, crisis management and conflict resolution at the grassroots level, working for and with local populations, bringing relevant information to civil servants who spend most of their time analysing information in Brussels. And it is NGOs that are the organisations that stay after the conclusion of a peace agreement, oftentimes continuing the mediation processes with deeply divided societies to prevent further outbreaks and to allow for reconciliation.

The EU, in particular the Commission, has now, through the Stability Instrument, an important potential to unleash the partnership that can help to build professional practice. This requires shifting the relationship with NGOs from one where they are executors of projects to a situation where they provide a service to the EU foreign policy. At the same time, for that to happen the NGO community needs to show increased professionalism and to demonstrate that its interests are not always driven by the need to secure funding. The EU can help build these capacities through provision of core support.

The European Commission's Conflict Prevention Network, a cooperative effort by NGOs active in the field of peacebuilding, is one step to bring in some lessons learned from Track II initiatives. It will assess what Track II diplomacy has done so far to help solve conflicts, why it is needed and how it can best be used. This initiative realises that mediation is just one element in peacebuilding, which needs to be embedded and accompanied with dialogue processes for civil society to allow for political participation of societies in post-conflict environments.

## Realising the potential of mediation

More can be done, especially on the EU institutional front. As the impressive work done by the UN Mediation Support Unit has shown, there is a need to and use for, on the one hand to professionalise and systematise know how, but on the other, showing an ability to implement lessons learned in a coherent way. In many ways this requires a paradigm shift in how (European) foreign policy will be implemented in this century and beyond. This would include the creation of a culture of foreign policy that looks beyond zero sum (win-lose) terms or power-based mediation and which will shift to supporting conditions that create mutually acceptable and locally owned agreements. Some governments in Europe which are not members of the EU, such as Switzerland and Norway, have managed to nurture such a culture and are supporting the practice of mediation in many regions of the world, ranging from the Middle East, Nepal, Sudan and Sri Lanka. And these countries are rec-

ognised for their contribution, professional work and impartiality, as the driving interest is to assist countries to transform conflicts to sustainable peace rather than historically driven or economically driven interests.

While the core principles of mediation are well known — impartiality, confidentiality and party driven — the professional practice of facilitation and mediation are less known in the EU peacebuilding policy community. For example, mediators need to be able to see through positions the underlying interests of parties, which requires specific skills to do so. There are no specific and systematic set of instruments in the EU to date that can support the mediation of a peace agreement while a number of elements that could be drawn into this already exist.

Drawn from the enormous experience at hand in the field of security sector reform, disarmament demobilisation and reintegration (DDR), transitional justice, constitution building and gender mainstreaming, could be synthesized and developed to fit the needs of a mediation process. The translation of knowledge and experience into operational tools, would need to go hand in hand with training and sensibilisation on mediation practice. A team or the access to staff that can support mediation processes with expert knowledge will increase the chance of translating interests of the parties into peace agreements that have a chance to be sustainable. As any new policy venture, it requires devoting financial and human resources to develop this blossoming but somewhat yet unstructured field of peace mediation. The investment will be well worth it, as it will bring back a peace dividend.

The Stability Instrument could and should support the development of capacity that can be utilised by state and non-state actors alike, in the name of an effective European foreign policy. A stand-by team of Track II organisations could well assist in this process.

# MEDIATION BASED ON CONFIDENCE AND FRIENDSHIP
INTERVIEW WITH MARIO GIRO

*What is Sant'Egidio's membership base and scope of work?*

Sant'Egidio has a membership of around 55,000 and across 70 countries. It works on combating poverty and undertaking social actions. In the last 20 years, it has also invested a lot of effort in the field of conflict resolution, but of course it continues the social work that it has always been involved in.

Regarding conflict resolution, our first involvement was in 1982 in Lebanon. Since then, we have mediated in Mozambique, Guatemala, Burundi, Algeria, Kosovo/a, Liberia, Togo, Rwanda, the Democratic Republic of Congo, Ivory Coast, Colombia, Sri Lanka, Nepal and most recently Darfur.

*How does Sant'Egidio decide to become involved in a mediation process?*

It is a question asked today that we did not ask in the past because nobody was working on "conflict resolution". In the case of Mozambique, we simply went because nobody else did. There was no civil society organisation at that time that was tackling crisis management or conflict resolution at all levels. How we make such a decision today depends on the requests we receive. We can receive an invitation to become involved from a wide variety of different actors. It can come from groups, states, civil society, or churches.

*No doubt, partnership is essential when you are engaged in a mediation process. What is the so-called 'Sant'Egidio Formula'?*

At Sant'Egidio, we talk in terms of synergies. A peace process is invariably a long one. When it tries to move too fast it never works. Every situation is unique and that requires a certain expertise. You have to harmonise yourself with the reality of a conflict, so of course we need a lot of partnerships. We need local partners in particular, because they have direct experience of the conflict.

You also need institutional partners. We don't believe in parallel or privatised diplomacy. The term 'track II diplomacy' is often used but I prefer the term 'track I and a half' because you need a synergy between institutional and non-institutional.

A non-institutional civil society organisation such as Sant'Egidio is able to intervene in a conflict with much greater ease than an institutional actor because we are able to wait. We can keep time management open, have patience, and keep faith in a situation until the time and situation is ripe.

Many representatives from NGOs ask me how Sant'Egidio can act in competition with states. My answer to them is that we have the opposite problem: getting state actors involved. You also have to consider that states are always needed to guarantee and arbitrate, in signing or implementing a peace agreement for example.

So, a mix is essential. The 'Sant'Egidio Formula' was a term coined by Boutros Boutros-Ghalli when he was UN Secretary-General and it refers to exactly that blend of the institutional and non-institutional.

*What are the other challenges that you face?*

Involving governments is one issue, but it is not the only problem or the largest one. When we began, there was a transitional phase between the Second World War and the Cold War. Many powerful states did not want to get involved in conflict resolution in Africa because they considered that war and conflict were inevitable and nothing could be done about it.

This pessimistic mentality has spread. Now, many people have a tendency to think that all conflicts are inevitable. Some even talk about something on a far bigger scale: there is the rhetoric of a "clash of civilisations". At Sant'Egidio, we believe in the opposite of that. We believe that you can always count on humanity and that it is possible to turn a fighter into a politician.

This is not to say we delude ourselves and deny that there will always be conflict. What I mean to say is that we can move conflict from the battlefield to the political arena. We can progress from an atmosphere of hate and exclusion to one of dialogue and negotiation.

*Mario Giro is a member of Sant'Egidio, an international, ecclesiastical community that was founded in Rome in 1968. His role has a particular focus on West Africa and he is responsible for Sant'Egidio's international relations as a whole. With an involvement in the Sant'Egidio that stretches back over two decades, Giro has personally mediated in many conflicts worldwide.*

*What is the first step to take in mediation talks if you are confronted by the kind of pessimistic attitudes you describe?*

The first step is to build confidence between the actors. It is always possible to convince the actors that there is another way to achieve their objectives. Most civil wars – remembering that 80 per cent of conflicts are internal ones – are a question of exclusion and recognition. We can show a path to guarantee recognition of rights without the use of arms.

You need patience for that. Consider Uganda where we negotiated with the Lord's Resistance Army from 1996 to 2006. After the first contact in 1996, there were 10 years of intermittent contact, silence, and re-establishing contact. That is the nature of the work that needs to be done, so you must have political conviction from the start. Only then can the peace process also take hold among the population.

Peace requires a long process of reconciliation that must be taken on by the parties concerned. You cannot impose peace on people. It is that attitude that leads to frozen conflicts. The major example of that is Bosnia-Herzegovina. We can deploy thousands of troops but if you want to get to the root of a conflict and resolve it, you have to take the necessary time to convince the people involved to move towards peace.

A mediation based on threats does not work either. As we saw in Darfur, a peace agreement can be signed but immediately renounced afterwards. These situations call for long-term work and that requires confidence and friendship. You could say it's a pedagogical process too.

You have to harmonise yourself with the root causes of the conflict, which are almost never economic. Economic factors are there but they come in at a second level to perpetuate or give sense to a conflict. Other reasons are usually at the root. You have to listen and be patient enough to let others have their say. This can be done more easily by a non-institutional organisation, ideally working in partnership with institutions, of course.

*Apart from patience and willingness to listen, what does it take to be a good mediator in your experience?*

The best mediator is one who also has other work to do. Allow me to clarify that. Mediators from civil society, outside an institutional context, can only count on their personal credibility or that of their organisation. A mediator who is too professionalized runs the risk of being personally dependent on the success of the mediation. That is a potential weakness. The advantage of the non-institutional mediator is the right to failure and that is a luxury that states cannot afford.

There must always be a synergy. When states are able to do something, it's better that they are the ones to do it. What they can't do can sometimes be done by the non-institutional sector.

I have another job to get on with. I am a trade unionist, and I am responsible for the international matters for Sant'Egidio. When there is mediation to do, I dedicate myself entirely to it. It's good to have other things to do and then focus all efforts on mediating talks when the time comes. In between, it is about maintaining links and contacts. It requires a long-term engagement.

*What are your hopes for the future?*

It seems to me that conflict resolution has become fashionable. A lot of people are studying or discussing it. But what I also see is that very few people are actually taking action on the ground. You could say there are fewer than 10 organisations, not counting the institutions, which are engaging hands-on in that way.

We do far too little mediation and facilitation. We talk a lot: maybe too much if you consider just how many conflicts are ongoing in the world. Personally, I think there is a lot of scope to do more than what is happening at the moment. What we need is fewer words and more action!

[   Philip Blenkinsop   ]

# Hmong secret war continues, Laos

In January 2003, photographer Philip Blenkinsop and the reporter Andrew Perrin travelled to the remote jungles in the Pha Sie Region of northern Laos. They were the first journalists to cross the Laotian communist boarders since 1975.

Together with the Hmong fighters they travelled on foot to the secret camp, which is one of the last pockets of the Hmong resistance in Laos.

Threatened by Laotian communist troops and regular Vietnamese troops, these men, women and children are not only living with munitions and food shortage but are also living in fear of a relentless of helicopter, artillery or chemical weapons attacks.

The 'secret war' in Laos, as its name suggests, was a total secret.

PHILIP BLENKINSOP

*Hidden among the trees,*
*Hmong huts in the morning mist.*
© Philip Blenkinsop / Agence VU / Laos

*Hong Pao Yang, age 71. Fought with the CIA during the secret war from 1967-1975.*

© Philip Blenkinsop / Agence VU / Laos

*We continue to approach... and this sea of humanity crumbles like a wave, crying, wailing and wailing at us (hands clasped together). We are the first white faces any of them have seen since they were abandoned by the Americans 27 years ago.*

© Philip Blenkinsop / Agence VU / Laos

*The sea of faces that greets us is void of any expression of hope. In the centre of the image, Bang Yang, age 14, cries, like she did almost each and every time we saw her over the next three days. Her story is tragic; she is an orphan. Her husband, age 15, Koua Pao Lee, was recently shot and killed a few days before their child was born. Yet she holds no monopoly on grief.*

© Philip Blenkinsop / Agence VU / Laos

*Malnutrition*
© Philip Blenkinsop / Agence VU / Laos

*Tdu Bi Xion, age 18, received shrapnel wounds in the chest from a B-41 rocket attack in December 2000 and had his left hand crippled by an AK-47 round in a separate incident.*

© Philip Blenkinsop / Agence VU / Laos

*Sai Tong Wang, age 30, with his son, Tdu Tong, age 6. Tdu Tong was wounded in the face by a shot fired from an AK-47 on 1 November 1999.*

© Philip Blenkinsop / Agence VU / Laos

*Yaeng Hua is 9 years old and severely traumatized.*
*His parents were both killed during a mortar attack*
*and as well as the shrapnel injuries he sustained,*
*his jaw was broken by an AK-47 round.*
© Philip Blenkinsop / Agence VU / Laos

*Pbai Lo, age 28, shot in the neck by an AK-47 round on 19 November 2001. Only four days earlier her husband, Teng Kong Wa, lost his leg to a landmine.*

© Philip Blenkinsop / Agence VU / Laos

*Father and son.*

© Philip Blenkinsop / Agence VU / Laos

*Teng Kong Wha, age 40, with his son,*
*Wha Hua, age 7. Lost his right leg to*
*a landmine on 23 November 2001,*
*four days after his wife, Pbai Lo, was*
*shot in the neck and leg by AK-47 rounds.*
© Philip Blenkinsop / Agence VU / Laos

*Three generations of resistance, left to right: Song Der, age 80 (fought with the French), his son, Sai Tua, age 40, who fought with the CIA, and two of his sons, Shua Yung, age 26, and Sai, age 10, who, with their father now face the Laos Communist troops.*

© Philip Blenkinsop / Agence VU / Laos

*On the afternoon prior to our departure,*
*Commander Moua Toua Ther with assembled*
*villagers delivers a message and pleas to*
*the USA and the international community.*

© Philip Blenkinsop / Agence VU / Laos

*A Hmong woman with her children.*
© Philip Blenkinsop / Agence VU / Laos

On the afternoon prior to our departure, the whole village gathers to send their collective voice to the governments of the world for their prayers to be heard and for salvation. They know that we are their only chance for survival. Sai Tua, age 40, breaks down, holds himself and weeps during the proceedings.

# KEY ISSUES CONCERNING THE HMONG PEOPLE IN LAOS/THAILAND

## Historical background

The secret wars of Laos date back to the Laotian Civil War (1962-1975) where the Communist Pathet Lao and the Royal Laotian Government fought for control over the Laotian panhandle, which the North Vietnamese had occupied to use as a supply corridor. The war was supported by North Vietnamese, American and South Vietnamese military forces. The Pathet Lao emerged victorious in 1975, along with the general communist victory in Indochina that year. An estimated 80 per cent of men from the Laos Hmong people were recruited to fight the Communist Pathet Lao. After the communist victory the Hmong people were targeted for retaliation and persecution. Many fled the country but of those who were left in Laos, 2000-3000 were sent to re-education camps. Many Hmongs died in these camps. Thousands more fled to the remote mountainous areas of the jungle from which they staged rebel attacks on the ruling government. An estimated 2,000-12,000 Hmongs are still displaced in these remote areas from fear of government retaliation.

## Lao Hmong in the Huai Nam Khao camp

There are currently approximately 7,500 Lao Hmong living in confinement in a camp in Huai Nam Khao while awaiting their repatriation to Laos following a bilateral agreement between the Thai and Laotian governments.

While UNHCR has never officially been allowed to carry out a status determination in the camp it is estimated that the majority of the Hmong population consists of economic migrants. However, the group also comprises a few hundred cases of Lao Hmong who credibly assert to have fled persecution in their country of origin and who hence have legitimate protection claims.

The Thai government refuses to recognize the Hmong people in Huai Nam Khao camp as refugees or people of concern, and considers them as illegal immigrants. In this regard the Thai government has argued that sending illegal immigrants back to their country of origin is not a violation of international law.

While the Lao authorities depict the living conditions of the Hmong returnees as bright, the experience of other Lao Hmong refugees who have been forcibly returned to Laos presents quite a different picture (e.g. the group of 27 children that went missing in late 2005 - the girls among the group claim to have endured repeated beatings, rapes, and other abuses during their detention in Laos following their deportation, the five boys are still missing). On the other hand, there have not been any reports of ill-treatment of more recent returnees (270 in the first half of 2008).

The Thai authorities have announced that they intend to screen all the inhabitants of the camp before sending them back to Laos in order to determine whether some of them qualify for protective status. Resettlement to third countries is being refused by the Thais in fear of the often-cited 'pull-factor' that such an operation might exert. In spite of several demands, UNHCR has not been allowed to participate substantially in the screening process on the Thai side. They have merely been asked to provide minimum input in form of a briefing on UNHCR's standard Refugee Status Determination criteria and procedures to Thai MFA staff who would supposedly be involved in the screening process. The 37th Sub-General Border Committe of Laos and Thailand approved the return of all these Lao Hmong by the end of 2008. Some 270 have already returned this year, seemingly voluntarily, but at the end of May the expectation that the rate of return would be accelerated incited the refugees to burn some 850 houses in the camp (over two thirds of the total), and many are now living under tents.

## The Lao Hmong caseload in Nong Khai detention centre

Since early December 2006, a group of 153 Lao Hmong have been jailed in a detention centre in Thailand under inhumane conditions. Among the 153 refugees - that are recognised to be in need of protection by UNHCR - are 90 children. Several coun-

*Carl Bjorkman is a Swedish national who has lived in Europe, Africa, Southeast Asia and the Middle East. He studied at the University of St. Andrews in Scotland where he was awarded an MA in International Relations and Geography and then a post-graduate MLitt in Economics, Management and Politics.*
*Carl has previously worked as a journalist for Bloomberg, as a terrorism analyst with the United Nations and is now employed by the European Commission in E.C. Delegation in Vientiane where he focuses on aid effectiveness, governance and human rights issues.*

tries had offered to accept this caseload for resettlement but the Thai authorities refused by again citing the pull-factor as well as their bilateral commitment to Lao PDR to return the group to Laos. Two deportation attempts of the Thai authorities have failed due to strong protests of the international community as well as fierce resistance by the refugees themselves leading the Thai government to agree to halt deportation (while at the same time refusing to release them). Tensions have risen in this camp recently as a result of the placement of three Lao Loum who are perceived as spies by the Hmong.

## What is the European Commission's position?

The European Commission is following the issue of the Lao Hmong very closely both from Headquarters and from its Delegations in Laos and Thailand. The EC position is shaped by protection and human rights concerns for the Hmong refugees. As regards the Huai Nam Khao caseload, the EC will insist vis-à-vis the Thai authorities that a proper screening mechanism should be put in place in order to determine their protection needs and effectively identify people of concern. The EC insist on the importance of engaging an independent third party, such as IOM, to be associated to the repatriation process to ensure that it is voluntary and have conditioned support to the resettlement of Hmong on these principles being followed. The Lao Government also needs to ensure a satisfactory level of access to the resettled population groups after their voluntary repatriation

to Laos as an essential pre-condition for EC support to be forthcoming. In addition, the EC advocates for an exploratory mission of Hmong refugees' representatives to be organised in order to allow them to visit the foreseen resettlement site on the Lao side as a confidence-building measure. To end the stalemate surrounding the Nong Khai caseload consisting of recognised refugees, the EC will continue to push the Lao authorities to agree to a "face-saving" solution for the detained Hmong in form of resettlement to third countries as migrants.

## The Lao position

The Lao Government had made the firm demand that no third party should be included in the repatriation process as a precondition for any negotiation with Thailand on the Hmong issue. However, during discussions with the EC, various high-level interlocutors on the Lao side have signaled some degree of openness to associating IOM to the repatriation process of the Huai Nam Khao caseload as well as to ensuring a certain 'traceability' of the returnees by the diplomatic community and to allowing NGOs access to the resettlement sites. However, no concrete steps have followed.

The situation of the Nong Khai caseload is in a stalemate as the Lao government refuses to authorise the Royal Thai Government to resettle the group in third countries.

The Lao Government has recently stated that they might be agreeable to allowing re-

settlement in third countries provided that the Lao Hmong group return first to Laos and leave Thailand with a migrant rather than a refugee status. First contacts with the US Embassy in Vientiane suggest that this may be an option. This solution would provide a face-saving approach to ending the deadlock that these 153 refugees have been caught in since almost one year now.

## Progress to date and activities in 2008

Over the last year the Delegation in Laos has sought to improve the policy dialogue with government interlocutors on the issue of the Hmong through bilateral meetings and through the framework of the Informal Group of Likeminded Donors. European Commission employees have also participated in several missions organized by the Government to visit resettled emigrants, amongst which are frequently groups of ethnic Lao Hmong. In a very encouraging step, the French Human Rights ambassador was also given access to visit the new Hmong villages in Taklak.

In 2008, the EC Delegation in Vientiane plans to pursue the policy dialogue on these issues through the joint Lao-EC working Group on Governance and Human Rights. High profile visits, such as that of the Commissioner for External Relations, Ferrero-Waldner (expected at some point in 2008/9), will also be used to put the spotlight on the Lao Hmong issue and emphasize the importance that the European Union has bestowed on it. More specifically, the European Commission will:

- Request that the 153 Lao Hmong that are currently in detention in Nong Khai (on the Thai-Lao Border) be allowed to leave Thailand (several countries have offered) in a low-profile manner (resettlement to third countries is being refused by the Thais in fear of the often-cited 'pull-factor' that such an operation might exert).

- Monitor the situation of the 7,500 Lao Hmong living in confinement in a camp in Huai Nam Khao (Thailand) while awaiting their repatriation to Laos following a bilateral agreement between the Thai and Laotian governments. While UNHCR has never officially been allowed to carry out a status determination in the camp we estimate that the majority of the Hmong population consists of economic migrants. However, the group also comprises a few hundred cases of Lao Hmong who credibly assert to have fled persecution in their country of origin and who hence have legitimate protection claims. The Thai government refuses to recognize the Hmong people in Huai Nam Khao camp as refugees or people of concern, and considers them as illegal immigrants. In this regard the Thai government has argued that sending illegal immigrants back to their country of origin is not a violation of international law. One option to facilitate the voluntary repatriation of the Lao Hmong in Huai Nam Khao camp would be an exploratory mission of Hmong refugees' representatives and Hmong elders to visit the foreseen resettlement sites in Lao PDR and see for themselves what the condition of the returnees is like. In 2008, the EC will ask the Lao Government to look into the possibility of taking this initiative forward.

- Seek information related to the 5 Hmong boys who were part of the group of 27 children who crossed the border from Thailand in December 2005. While the girls have been reunited with their families in the camp in Petchabun (Huai Nam Khao) there is concern as to the whereabouts and the condition of the five boys.

# FROM MANAGING THE EMERGENCY TO CONSOLIDATING THE STABILITY — LEBANON AND ITS BORDERS AFTER THE 33-DAY WAR IN 2006

## Introduction

In crisis management and post-conflict situations we often realise that the formal crisis state was triggered too late and the end of the crisis was announced too early. The question of when exactly a crisis comes to an end is a theoretical one, and an exact time cannot usually be determined. However, the important lesson is that the phase of consolidation should be initiated as soon as possible. This is clearly apparent from the 33-Day War between Israel and Lebanon in 2006. In this case the crisis itself was already obvious long before the Israeli bombardments began. The crisis status was triggered too late, so that crisis indicators according to the key words 'Early warning- Early action' had to be detected earlier and led to earlier consultation and conflict reduction.

Under international law the crisis in Lebanon still exists, as at the time of writing no ceasefire agreement or peace contract was in place. The suspension of hostilities has been declared between the two countries but no further resolution has occurred. UN Resolution 1701 calls for the prevention of weapons smuggling with a view to the arming of Hezbollah. The discussion about contributions to the UN resolution 1701 by enforcing the United Nations Interim Force in Lebanon (UNIFIL) mandate or executing

an international police or military mission turned out to hamper rather than help stabilisation. To give an example of action in the stabilisation phase after the 33-Day War in Lebanon, Germany provided federal police officers and customs officers who were intended to be the focus of an adviser operation to support the Lebanese security agencies, with the aim of enhancing their capability to execute their duties. In the political arena, this presence was a precondition for lifting the air embargo and opening the airport to permit the import of goods urgently needed to meet the inhabitants' daily living requirements. The suspension of hostilities and the lifting of the air embargo, and one day later the sea embargo, which was lifted due to the presence of the German Maritime Task Force close to Lebanese territorial waters, helped the population to step back into a regular pattern of life.

## Transition phase and multi-level approach

In the transition phase it is important to work with a multi-level approach. Essentially the stabilisation of the socio-economic situation and public security need to be pursued as priorities. This seems to be very important in conflict areas where the population have suffered a lot from violent actions. This is more difficult if, in addition to governmental organisations (GOs),

donor states and opposition organisations are trying to influence the population and use the reconstruction phase to enhance their reputation. In Lebanon, for example, Hezbollah supported the Shiite population in South Beirut's *Dachieh*, the Shiite district, which was heavily damaged by Israeli bombardments in the war. The financial emergency support ranged from cash to goods to meet people's daily needs. People's misery was mitigated as a result. The same support went to the south of Lebanon, where villages were badly damaged. The government of Lebanon appeared to be somewhat paralysed, and was not able to provide sustainable aid for this part of the population. In the security sector, we faced the same needs.

An analysis of the state of the German Adviser Team exposed an imbalance between the equipment of the different security agencies. While in the socio-economic sector, a huge number of support offers were coming in and NGOs provided the basic work required for stabilisation, the security sector encountered problems because of the different preferences of the participating countries. Especially in security sector reform, the individual interests of donor states play a role that should not be underestimated. These encompass economic as well as political interests, and can pro-

*Detlef W. Karioth was a law professor at the Federal University for Applied Sciences and Public Administration in Lübeck, Germany, before heading to Lebanon in September 2006 as Brigadier General and Head of the German Adviser Team Federal Police/Customs. He is responsible for the first project in Integrated Border Management on Lebanon's border with Syria. He has held various management positions in the Federal Police and also has legal affairs experience at the German Embassy in Bangkok. He works as a national expert for the EU Commission and Council in border management and organised border crossing crime. He also has five years' experience as a project leader and expert in EU projects in Romania. He is a national expert for Schengen Evaluations of the EU Council.*

vide the impression that aim of the exercise is less efficient aid and the improvement of physical security than the achievement of the donor's own objectives. In effect, the project is used as a basis for donors to achieve their own selfish aims.

In Lebanon at the start of the transition phase, the different security agencies worked totally separately and there was no exchange of information or cooperation. They were self-sufficient. The equipment and training of each participating agency were extremely different. While some of the donor countries provided equipment and training that seemed to be based exclusively on their own interests, the German Adviser Team chose a comprehensive multi-agency approach. In a pilot project all security agencies were encouraged to develop common responsibility for Integrated Border Management. Donor states were motivated to contribute according to their capacities and budgets.

## Donor coordination and local ownership

The coordination of the activities of donor states is an important role, which should usually be handed over to the conflict countries themselves. They should be obliged to fulfil this task. However, long-term experience has shown that conflict countries often do not have the capability to manage the task. The huge number of donor states, GOs and NGOs acting in a very enthusiastic and engaged way during the stabilisation phase

does not make the task easier. There is a dual risk in the performance of aid and provision of contributions to consumers. One the one hand, there is sometimes too much equipment that is not appropriate and not utilised as forseen. On the other side demands are not met because needs were not detected in time, or the available finance had already been used for other purposes. Nevertheless the recommendation remains that conflict states should be required to take responsibility for the coordination of donors and aid for reconstruction and development. This behaviour would facilitate the idea of local ownership and overall responsibility for the whole reconstruction process. Although the crisis in Lebanon still exists at least in a formal sense, the German Advisor Team strictly maintains a role as merely an adviser in the Border Management. The Lebanese authorities have the responsibility for the elaboration and implementation of the Integrated Border Management.

There are also security reasons for donor agencies to play no more than an advisory role. For political reasons a considerable number of conflict countries refuse to accept the presence of international uniformed police forces. Lebanon is one of them. One reason is that the presence of uniformed international forces would be seen as a hostile act by Lebanon's neighbour Syria. From this perspective it is important to focus on the right approach and the use of the right formulas and tools. It is always important to be aware of the impact of the aid activity.

## International formulas and methods

Choosing the right method is the key. International organisations often tend to use standard methods, systems and intervention mechanisms without adapting them sufficiently to the political, cultural and religious specifics of the situation. If these specifics are taken into consideration a clear road map should materialise. The lessons learned in Lebanon in 2006-2007 support this thesis. There must be an in-depth analysis of the current situation – based on all open sources and intelligence work – in every conflict area before any decision is made on the kind of international intervention mechanism that should be implemented. So, in September 2006 the indications were clear that no uniformed military or police mission would be welcome in Lebanon in addition to the long-term United Nations Interim Force in Lebanon (UNIFIL) contingent based in the south of the country. These facts played an important role for the Syrian border. According to this philosophy, the toolbox contained only a limited range of mechanisms. There was no room either to extend the UN mandate to cover an executive police mission or to establish a uniformed EU police mission (e.g. European Union Border Assistance Mission [EUBAM] or European Security and Defence Policy [ESDP]). The government of Lebanon clearly pointed out that the bilateral engagement of adviser missions or EU project management (in twinning projects) could be successful and would be welcomed. This led to the quick elaboration of a pilot project in

North Lebanon, and also to a feasible perspective from which to initiate a bilateral or EU project on the eastern border.

We should be careful not to copy experience from Afghanistan or the Balkan states in the field of border management and the public security sector without careful reflection. It is rather difficult for police and military practitioners to avoid taking an executive role and adhere to an advisory mandate. But this seems to be important, to ensure there is e.g. Lebanese 'ownership' of the project management in Lebanon. The acceptance of an intelligent and independent partner, and the right alongside to decide how far the country wants to go is a key factor for success. Specific note should be made of unarmed international missions, which could be seen as a bridge or compromise between an advisory role and a uniformed armed mission. International missions usually have high prestige, but it is questionable how successful an unarmed international mission can be. The limitation of its capabilities immediately reduces the intervention capacities.

Further mention should also be made of the importance of neutrality in the field of crisis stabilisation. Although countries and regional unions may take clear political positions in political, military or policing matters, these should be translated into action in the 'transition zone', which should maintain a strictly neutral stance. Neutrality is often important in countries with multi-religious population. In Lebanon, there are 18 different major religious groups. All security agencies will be perceived as favouring one or more religions, due to the known faith of the director-general of the organisation. Strict neutrality and a united front in executing the road map ease up the procedures in the stabilisation work. However, experience has shown that although this common front is desirable, it is often missing in reality. It is more common for the specific interests of donor countries to be apparent than for a common approach to be followed. To establish a united front, strong leadership is necessary.

## Project management and road map

The form of project management applied depends mainly on the political situation and the goal it is hoped to achieve. It is necessary to have project management with a firm theoretical and scientific foundation in order to develop effective approaches and achieve the project goal within the timeframe. However, the intensity of the project management should be related to the conditions on the ground. Each project should have an individual road map which takes into account the specific local conditions. A paste and copy system takes this into account only in a limited way. The German Adviser Team evolved a pilot project for Integrated Border Management for North Lebanon based on a European philosophy: to test the capacities and the willingness of the Lebanese authorities in surveying their border with Syria. There was heavy pressure to execute UN Resolution 1701. This meant that the project had to be implemented in a short period of time and the impact on the project management structure and timeframe was obvious. Some 750 members of the different security agencies had to be educated in border management, a training centre and a common operation centre had to be set up, and it was also necessary to procure the equipment needed. In a short timeline, experts had to elaborate a training concept to prepare the officers on the ground. Beside these measures, there was a need for careful public relations, to explain to the population in the border region that Integrated Border Management would not interfere with their daily livelihood and that they would still be able to cross the border.

The international pressure on the Lebanese government to execute resolution 1701 was very intense, and remains so at the time of writing. A deliberate decision was made to carry out the pilot project in a area with a low profile in the region. This was done with the aim of minimising the risks for financial investment and security. The pilot project was intended to show the international donor community whether the Lebanese security agencies and the government were capable of securing their borders. This should give a clear perspective for further investment and engagement in the future. The donor community saw the project as an optimal test run, to discover how far equipment and capacity building is sustainable, before the much farther-reaching strategic planning process and investment planning started to survey the eastern border.

## The pilot project 'integrated border management' North Lebanon
### Area of responsibility

The pilot project is to be confined geographically to the area of competence of the 5th Brigade of the Lebanese Armed Forces (LAF) along the northern border between Lebanon and Syria, taking in the crossing points El Aarida and Aboudiyeh.

The operational area will begin in the west at the Gulf of Sidra at El Aarrida and will end to the east of Hmairé.

### Project objectives

The project is intended to be both the nucleus and actual test phase for future integrated border management of Lebanon. The Lebanese security authorities involved are to be acquainted with the benefits of integrated border management.

Specified indicators are to highlight whether or not the project has been a success and following subsequent evaluation they will provide the basis and set the trend for the development of a state-of-the-art national border strategy for Lebanon. When evaluating the success of the project, the findings of monitoring and the experience gained by the Lebanese side will need to be taken into account in order to finally be able to develop a viable system of integrated border management for the whole of Lebanon that will take the conditions in Lebanon adequately into account.

The specific definition of project objectives will be based strictly on the evaluation report drawn up by the German Project Bureau and on the common defined need for action. The project specifications stipulate that efficient use will be made of personnel, that optimised equipment and facilities will enhance cooperation and hence communication between the security authorities involved, and that tactical changes will be made. Furthermore, interfaces are to be reduced and optimised cooperation between the individual authorities is to open up the possibility of using synergy effects.

At present, there are no plans to modify the statutory task and competency allocations of the security authorities involved. This would contravene the current political conditions and pose certain risks. It is not the objective of the pilot project either to demilitarise control of the green border or to set up a higher-ranking border control authority. However, this does not rule out the possibility of structural and organisational changes being made by the security authorities in due course.

### Project implementation in phases

The pilot project is to be implemented in three phases: a preparatory phase followed by an implementation phase, with the pilot project being concluded by a follow-up phase.

The preparatory phase is marked by working through the specified work packages; the specifications of these work packages will follow separately containing details and timeframes. In principle, it will not be possible to enter the implementation phase until all phase-specific work packages have been successfully completed.

### Project duration

The time required for the preparatory phase depends on the level of cooperation shown by the Lebanese side, the delivery times of the required equipment and facilities and on the length of the necessary advanced training measures. It is therefore not possible to say yet how long it will take. However, the estimation that this phase could take five months seems to be realistic.

The implementation phase of the pilot project is to be limited to three months maximum.

The follow-up phase is to last one month. During this phase, the tasks are to be performed within the meaning of the project in order to ensure it can begin immediately in the north-eastern and eastern section of the border once it has been completed successfully.

### Opportunities offered by the pilot project

During talks with other donor countries, it became evident that apart from the pilot project proposed here, there is also a lack of reliable concepts worthwhile investing in. By and large, individual measures are implemented on the basis of bilateral agreements or at the request of the Lebanese security authorities. However, the endeavours of the international donor countries are focusing specifically on structured concepts, which is precisely why this particular pilot project has met with such widespread international acceptance. The pilot project has already prompted several donor countries to offer the prospect of funding.

The pilot project offers huge opportunities. In view of the explosiveness of the situation within Lebanon, which calls for incisive optimisation measures along the Lebanese borders, the project happens to be the right step at the right time, without demanding too much in an initial approach. The carefully selected operational section for the project will help matters as no special interests dominate. This will make it easy to implement any such undertaking in terms of interior policy. The pilot project will make it possible to glean valuable organisational findings that may well apply to the whole of Lebanon. The establishment of a joint operations centre can also be seen in this light as it will bring the individual players together and will have a confidence-building effect. The Lebanese authorities reserve the right to take organisational decisions themselves. It is noted irrespective of how the project develops that the current situation can only

be optimised in the near future if equipment aid is provided.

The simplicity and clarity of the pilot project is also expressed in the targeted application of the principles governing project management and quality management, and is hence likely to be a success without necessitating any far-reaching organisational changes or even modifications to the statutory job descriptions of the security authorities at this early stage.

It also needs to be mentioned that with this type of pilot project the German orientation of integrated border management in Lebanon will be maintained if the German project work is transferred to the project framework of the European Union. Once the structures of a successful pilot project have been established, it would no longer be that easy to deviate from them.

### Risks involved in the pilot project

The positive international response can be attributed not least to the fact that the investment tied up in the pilot project did not involve any risks. If the project were to fail, against all expectations, this would not necessarily mean the investment would have been wasted because, for instance, any equipment and facilities procured could certainly be distributed expediently according to other criteria and any accompanying advanced training measures could be appropriately diverted.

### Outlook

The pilot project for implementing integrated border management will lead to the development of a national security network between the various security authorities involved with border control and customs duties in terms of its overall configuration.

If the project objectives are achieved, it is planned to expand the pilot project to other border regions within the framework of a national border strategy for Lebanon. As such, it is up to the Lebanese decision-makers to perhaps consider setting up a national border control authority. This should go hand in hand with considerations to enhance the infrastructure at crossing points and the green border. Furthermore, the location of some border crossing points should be reconsidered given their distance from the actual borderline itself. In addition, the need for clear demarcation of the land border with Syria should be taken into account.

In particular, any social and financial changes resulting from the follow-up project would need to be taken into account in future. They would have to be made up for by social projects concomitantly.

The final objective is to continue with the project management under a European umbrella in future.

# 'PEOPLE ARE TIRED OF WAR!': SUPPORTING THE PEACE PROCESS IN NORTHERN UGANDA
## INTERVIEW WITH OLOO OTIENO

The rise of Ugandan President Yoweri Museveni and his National Resistance Movement in 1986 coincided with the escalation of a notorious rebel movement, the Lord's Resistance Army (LRA). The group, led by Joseph Kony, has been engaged in an armed rebellion against the Ugandan government in what has been one of Africa's longest-running conflicts. Based in northern Uganda and southern Sudan, the LRA is accused of widespread human rights violations, including mutilation, torture, rape, the use of child soldiers and a number of massacres. The scope of the violence is almost unbelievable: nearly two million northern Ugandans have been forced to flee their homes, most living in over-crowded, unsanitary and dangerous camps. The LRA has abducted an estimated 20,000 children in northern Uganda to serve as soldiers or sex slaves. In 2006, peace talks began in Juba, Sudan, and later that year the government and the LRA and the government signed a truce, which both sides have violated. Arrest warrants of Kony and his top commanders by the International Criminal Court (ICC) remains a political stumbling block for genuine peace in northern Uganda.

*How did Nonviolent Peaceforce evolve, and what is the organisation's mission?*

The idea for Nonviolent Peaceforce started at the 1999 Hague Appeal for Peace. A group of American individuals with similar ideas bumped into each other after one of them had shouted about the need for civilian peacekeeping. After the meeting they went back home and started organising and devising their approach. They managed to organise support from different civil society groups working in peacekeeping, peacebuilding and non-violence. When the group secured support from a number of organisations all over the world a conference was organised in India in 2002. There they founded the Nonviolent Peaceforce.

A number of countries were proposed to begin with: Burma/Myanmar, Sri Lanka, Colombia, Guatemala, Palestine—Israel. After doing a thorough assessment of each country they settled on Sri Lanka. A feasibility study was quickly initiated. A group of three people went to Sri Lanka to meet with civil society groups and government officials to assess if there was a need for an international civilian peacekeeping organisation. This need was established, fundraising started and the first team was sent in September 2003.

I was a member of the first field team that was recruited, interviewed and sent for specialised training. We had 18 days of rigorous training in teambuilding, theories of third-party, non-violent intervention, communication, as well as skills that would be needed with the police and public administration. Also during the training there were psychological and stress tests. Our team of 11 internationals from nine countries was deployed in Sri Lanka to work alongside Sri Lankan civil society and peace activists.

*The NP programme in Uganda is in its preparatory phase. Can you describe the background of the conflict and what NP aims to do?*

The conflict in Uganda has been ongoing for 25 years. It mostly centres around issues of alienation and marginalisation of certain communities in terms of distribution of natural resources, employment, education, etc. This is the basis on which the rebels started this war. When the top rebel commanders were indicted by the International Criminal Court (ICC) [in 2005], this was a tremendous attempt to pressure the rebels to start thinking of alternatives to violence. The government had also intensified the military operation against the rebels. This meant the rebels started to withdraw and think twice about their next step. I think this prompted them to take seriously the issue of negotiation and the peace process. The government of southern Sudan also started putting pressure on the rebels because they were operating from Sudanese bases. Southern Sudan was just signing the Comprehensive Peace Agreement and things were moving along. They did not want any negative groups operating from

*Oloo Otieno is project director of the Nonviolent Peaceforce (NP) project in northern Uganda, where the project is currently in its planning phase. Otieno, who is based in the northern Ugandan city of Gulu, is experienced in protective accompaniment and as a trainer in non-violent conflict resolution. One of the goals of NP in Uganda is to have a civilian-based grassroots foundation for sustainable peace. Prior to his post in Uganda, Otieno was a member of the NP pilot project in Sri Lanka.*

within their territory that could jeopardise the peace agreement.

This process of peace negotiations in the southern capital city of Juba had really brought some hope among internally displaced persons (IDPs) to start returning home. There was good political will from both opposition parties in Uganda as well as the ruling party. The government asked people to go back home and gave assurance that the ground situation had improved and they were safe. So, people started moving back home. Some started going through transit sites because they had suspicions that things might turn worse. Also, they wanted time to visit their ancestral home, to have that psychological connection before they made the final return. For us in Nonviolent Peaceforce this process presented an opportunity to help support the efforts and initiatives of local peace activists, civil society and human rights groups working there.

Two of our partner groups in Uganda had asked NP to consider setting up a programme to help support them in their work. They wanted us to share experiences about what we had achieved in Sri Lanka and to also have international community support behind them. This is how we decided to move into Uganda. In June 2007 we really started to concretise the expectations from our local partners and what they could expect from us. It is important that we all move forward with a common understanding, or else there will be big problems. We will be pursuing several approaches in terms of strengthening community dialogue, rec-

onciliation, the overall peacekeeping and protection of vulnerable community members. Also, we are working alongside the framework of the Ugandan government. The government created an elaborate document this year called the recovery and reconstruction strategy for northern Uganda. This is a document on which the government insists all humanitarian and peace organisations base their interventions.

We are currently liaising with local government representatives at district level as well as the police. This is particularly centred on community policing and trying to strengthen the relationship and confidence between the community and the police. In the past people shied away from reporting criminal cases, so they established a 'community police' that addresses this relationship.

Meanwhile local governments are involved in settling land wrangles between communities and individuals. After 25 years of war and people staying in refugee camps, a lot of boundaries and landmarks have been removed. For example, land demarcations had been trees, rocks or anthills. Now people are coming back and trying to figure out where their land was. In northern Uganda there are no permanent structures or buildings. There are just temporary shelters such as huts, so it is almost impossible to find out where your house was. These are some of the things the communities are facing.

Also, there are issues of identity and reintegration. During the conflict in northern Uganda young ladies have been forcibly

abducted into the rebel ranks. Some were raped and they came back with two or three children. Now the community is questioning the 'moral identity' of these children, claiming they are bad blood coming back into society to wreak havoc. The young mothers are also facing stigma, and they need our support, protection and someone to speak on their behalf.

*NP is a non-violence-based organisation. How does this figure into a context in which violence is so present? Do people think non-violence is relevant?*

Yes, they do. People are tired are war! They want to go back to their homes; they're tired of camp life. Everyone wants to start a meaningful life and find a role to play in rebuilding community and society. Anything that promotes non-violence, promotes peace or promotes coexistence is welcome in Northern Uganda. Particularly ex-combatants returning to their communities are struggling to find a safe place to discuss what happened during the period of violent conflict. They need a forum to express the aspirations they have and the roles they want to play in society. For us, this is what Nonviolent Peaceforce is looking into doing: creating a safe place for these people to share their stories, to come to terms with reality and how to overcome the stigma and psychological trauma they went through. Some of these young people were forced to kill their family, forced to kill small children and forced to kill pregnant mothers. It's just awful.

Also, there is a problem of people being harmed by 'evil spirits'. In Africa we believe in these spirits – in this case the spirits of people that were killed. I was talking to a woman recently who cannot conceive a child; every time she tries to conceive she miscarries. She visited a diviner who said, 'you shot a pregnant woman, and this woman is having an effect in your life'. The diviner told her she needed to have a cleansing ceremony before she could appease the spirit and have a child.

There are some within international humanitarian organisations who are trying to raise funds to help with this kind of thing. A cleansing ceremony to become whole again is very expensive. You have to buy certain number of animals for slaughtering and cleansing. The total cost is about €120 per individual. Most of these people are poor and cannot afford a full cleansing process.

Many young men and women who have come back from the bush are recruited by vocational training centres. Once they graduate and start a trade in carpentry, metal working or dressmaking they are really eager to start working. But you often find they get customers who say, 'I don't want this person who has killed somebody, who has spilled blood, to do something for me! I don't want these people to construct my house or make me a chair to sit on'.

This is an attitude which frustrates the efforts of ex-combatants who then say, 'Ok, I will go grab a gun, go back to the bush and exercise my power'. At NP we really want

to engage the community in dialogue and look for solutions to re-integrate and coexist with ex-combatants. They, too, have a role to play in society. Most of them were abducted against their will and the community must come to terms with this. They have lost a lot of energetic young people who want and need to be instrumental in rebuilding the society. This is an area we want to continue to engage both communities and also the government.

*You've spoken a bit about the indictments made by the ICC. There had been some organisations subtly working with the Lord's Resistance Army (LRA) to broker a peace agreement before the ICC came out with its indictments. Were the ICC indictments a setback?*

There are a few reactions to this. First, the indictments made by the ICC at The Hague were a major push for the rebels to sober up and start thinking about a more positive, constructive way to end the conflict. Generally, it was agreed that the indictments were a wake-up call that the international community will not let the rebels go without punishment. It really made them stick to the peace process. On the contrary, local communities, both religious leaders in northern Uganda and the Acholi diaspora, are advocating for the ICC to slowly withdraw the arrest warrants issued for the LRA's leadership. The argument is that withdrawing the indictments would let the peace process proceed.

Second, people throughout Uganda have

an entrenched traditional justice and reconciliation mechanism regarding how to deal with crime. I think they are the only community in East Africa that has strong traditional leadership for settling disputes and offering judgment against community members. Recently the Acholi Paramount Chief was involved in negotiating between a politician and a military general over a land dispute. He summoned both parties to sit down, discuss and look for a solution. Within one month it was solved, and it couldn't, or hadn't, been solved by the national court system. Ugandans have a very strong sense for this traditional way of dealing with conflict. It is what they want to see in the case of the LRA, too.

During a series of consultations about the accountability and reconciliation protocol that was signed between the government and the LRA, many people said they didn't want The Hague process. There was a feeling that if they simply arrested [LRA rebel leader] Joseph Kony and his commanders, they would be hanged in The Hague. No one would see the bodies or have a chance to talk to Kony to hear him apologise.

This is obviously a huge lack of information; people do not know that in The Hague they do not have the death penalty. People did not understand what happened to Milošević – they thought he was murdered. They want Kony to come out of the bush, whereby there would be an elaborate cleansing ceremony and a process of justice and reconciliation. They want Kony and his top commanders to meet the victims and have them apologise publicly. This should be done by the traditional leadership, and they would determine the punishment.

This kind of traditional justice system is not like the typical Western system where a convicted criminal is locked away forever. People want to see you back in society. In Africa, people want criminals to admit publicly what they did and what their motivations were. They want to hear you say sorry. The community gives criminals their punishment; for example, one can be banished for a certain number of years. Alternatively a criminal might have a cleansing ceremony and he or she is responsible for providing all that is needed. People want to see your contribution to the community, and they want to engage and use your expertise and experience – no matter what you have done. They do not want to see you locked away where you are not seen or heard from again. In Africa, our justice system is restorative. Despite the fact that someone has committed atrocities, at some point in our coexistence we need each other.

*With the looming ICC indictments, does Kony have a reason to leave the bush?*

Kony cannot leave and instead he is saying, 'come and get me'. Recently one of the other LRA commanders whose name is not on the ICC indictment list, Opiyo Makasi, surrendered after Kony arrested his deputy commander. Makasi surrendered to UN peacekeepers, who in turn handed him over to the government of the Democratic Republic of Congo and was put under ar-

rest. The government of Uganda, through their embassy in Kinshasa, tried to intervene. They tried to access Makasi; after all, he is a Ugandan national, and they wanted to talk to him and bring him back to Uganda. Up to now the government of Congo has not allowed Uganda to access him. This is just a political game. The president of Congo, Joseph Kabila, is not comfortable with the Ugandan government because of a potential threat that Uganda may invade Congo.

Of course, having Congolese police go into the bush to arrest Kony and the LRA leadership cannot work. This is the on-the-ground situation that the ICC faces. They don't have practical way of arresting Kony and his commanders. The government of Uganda supports the traditional justice system, and this is why they are also consulting their citizens to find out their views about the procedure and whether they favour it or not. The community and the victims have not been heard properly. LRA negotiations have started very recently, and it has been very emotional. The rebels conveyed an apology from Kony and his commanders. Now people are expecting to hear from Kony himself when he comes out of the bush.

*Especially in lieu of these recent LRA negotiations the conflict seems to be at a tipping point. At such an important juncture, what does the international community need to know?*

It's not really about what the international community should know, but rather what they should do to support this process. The

European Union has never made a strong political statement in support of the peace process in Juba. One of the active players has been the United States. But when the US Assistant Secretary of State for African Affairs came to Kampala recently, she made an inflammatory statement that the United States will wipe out the LRA if they don't behave. The LRA spokesperson basically said in response, 'we are waiting in the bush for you; come anytime you like. It seems you did not learn to listen in Somalia, and you cannot solve problems in Iraq and Afghanistan – we are ready to receive you'.

The statement by the US Assistant Secretary of State for African Affairs angered northern Ugandan leadership. One Anglican bishop, Rt. Revd Ochola, who is very instrumental in the peace process, wrote a protest letter to George W. Bush. He said, 'we want you to support the peace process but we don't want you to jeopardise it'.

This RELEX-sponsored conference has made it even clearer to me that the EU is applying a 'soft power' strategy in dealing with violent conflicts. This is what we're calling for, and we want the EU to play a major role in sustaining the peace process in northern Uganda.

During his presentation at the conference, Johan Galtung posed a powerful challenge that the EU will have to fill a vacuum, as the United States is beginning to become rather infamous. We hope its role will be to fill this vacuum non-militarily and support civilian peacekeeping. The EU has the potential to support organisations that are already engaged in civilian peacekeeping and learn from their experiences. In civilian peacekeeping the strategy should preferably be about regional intervention. You would ideally not want someone from Mexico, Canada or Europe to intervene in Asia, for example. My suggestion is for the EU to train civilian peacekeepers throughout the world and have a pool that could be sent if there was an issue in a certain region. These would be people from that area, backed up an EU mandate and EU training. This would really go a long way in shaping the image of the EU around the world as a unique entity that is pursuing a different kind of approach to solving conflict.

# No development without security: Nonviolent Peaceforce in Mindanao
## Interview with Atif Hameed

Mindanao, home to a majority of the country's Muslims, is a region suffering from poor infrastructure, high poverty, and violence that has claimed the lives of more than 120,000 in the last three decades. Conflict in Mindinao, the easternmost island in the Philippines, has been largely concentrated in the Muslim-majority areas of central and south-western parts of the island. Clashes have been partly characterised by resistance to central government control and resentment of an increasing number of Christian settlers. Several armed rebel factions are operational, including the Moro National Liberation Front (MNLF), the Moro Islamic Liberation Front (MILF), Abu Sayyaf and the New People's Army. Although religious differences have partly shaped the conflict, the roots of the conflict have been clashes of interest in land and other natural resources, and the identity issues emerging from the secondclass status of much of the Moro, or Muslim, population.

*Can you tell me about how Nonviolent Peaceforce (NP) established a programme in the Philippines and what steps were involved to deploy a team on the ground?*

Local civil society in Mindanao felt it needed a non-violent intervention to strengthen its efforts and the overall peace process, especially on the ground level. On that basis they extended an invitation to Nonviolent Peaceforce. As always, we work in areas only where we have an invitation.

We then sent an exploration team to the Philippines in 2005 and conducted focus groups especially in the field locations. The NP mandate is specifically in peace-keeping; we don't do any development or other kind of work. In the first assessment we didn't get the right kind of 'results' and thought perhaps we were not very much needed. At the same time the local civil society were persistent in asking us to set up a programme.

The next step was to send two NP people for three months in Mindanao. Before, this kind of work was done by local people on behalf of NP. In this case we decided to do our own assessments on the ground as to whether we were really needed or not. We checked whether other organisations were doing a similar kind of thing and if it was working or not.

Two people were sent; one was myself and the other someone else who had also worked with NP in Sri Lanka. We already had some kind of understanding about the NP mandate; the way we make interventions and how we assess the project realities. First, we identified the key civil society actors who were playing a proactive role in terms of contributing toward sustainable peace. They helped us to identify six or seven different platforms where the conflict started – the real hotbeds.

A colleague and I spent time in different communities and met with local leaders and commanders from the Moro Islamic Liberation Front (MILF) paramilitary. We also met the leadership of the Moro National Liberation Front (MNLF) and had a series of consultations with them. Equally important was meeting with the Department of Foreign Affairs in Mindanao and finding out how would they see a group of internationals coming in and making an intervention. At the same time we continually consulted with other leading activists in that area.

We soon realised that no internationals stay and work at the grassroots level doing the kind of work NP does. First of all because of security reasons and second because it's not easy to maintain a relationship with the local civil society. Civil society is very demanding; they're very experienced. They wanted expertise from NP and they wanted us to bring an international team of well-trained civilian peacekeepers who could work hand in hand with local peacekeepers.

Civil society wanted us as international actors, who are the eyes and ears of the international community, to be there. They also wanted NP to help build the capacities of local peacekeepers. Finally, they wanted us to link local civil society with the key organisations at the national and international levels working for peace. These are also three key areas where NP thought we could play a pivotal role.

*Atif Hameed is the project director of the Nonviolent Peaceforce (NP) project in the Philippines, which is based in the heart of the conflict in Mindanao. He also served on the team of civilian peacekeepers in the NP pilot project in Sri Lanka. In both cases he and his field team members carry out the mission of accompanying civil society activists, provide protective presence to vulnerable groups and communities and monitor ceasefire agreements.*

On this basis we formulated a proposal and submitted it to the Nonviolent Peaceforce international programme committee. They gave us the green light to go ahead with the Philippines project. But of course you cannot go ahead with a project without financial support, and it took a lot of effort to secure funds. We contacted all donors who were funding some kind of work in Mindanao. When about 65 per cent of the total funds needed had been gathered we decided to go ahead with the project. Our partners wanted us there immediately.

*Concretely, what kinds of activities do you engage in the field?*

Often we are involved in what is called 'protective accompaniment' when, for example, families are threatened. We come and we bring a presence. Occasionally we engage in something called 'inter-positioning': if the chances for conflict look high, we put ourselves there in the middle. We would only engage in this in areas where NP is recognised by all sides – namely, where we have field sites.

We engage in early warning and early response so local people can come to really believe in peace and dialogue. They are more likely to do so when they have a support structure and they do not feel alone. As far as early warning, we do a daily assessment where we analyse different indicators. Ideally, I would like the team be between 25 and 29 people. Then I think we could really be a *'third force'* in the peace process.

*How is the conflict in Mindanao characterised and what can a team of international civilian peacekeepers bring?*

In Mindanao there are so many cycles of war. It's not like there is violent conflict all over the place all the time. Conflict will happen all of a sudden in this or that location. Last year there were two 'mini-wars'. Institutional donors were interested in NP because no one else was doing this kind of work, and it was helpful to have people who could effectively ensure safety and security at the flash points.

Initially our team was to be made up of six or seven international civilian peacekeepers deployed in two areas around Mindanao. We decided not to have our head office in the capital, Manila. Most internationals operating in the Philippines are based in the capital. We decided to put up our head office in the heart of the conflict, which is the city of Cotabato. Then we set up two field sites around central Mindanao.

The situation on the ground is troubling. In one year people are sometimes displaced 12 to 14 times. There are many factional fights, sometimes involving rebel groups and sometimes paramilitaries. People are really on the move.

The other location we identified is in Sulu Province. This is in an area famous for Abu Sayyaf, which is associated with Al Qaeda. There are a lot of Philippine Army soldiers and US Marines in that area, and it is also the base of the MNLF. We decided to put up an office there because it is so

isolated – it's like an island – very disconnected, and like another world. We work in such locations to directly contribute toward the maintenance of peace and to link these isolated areas to the rest of 'mainstream Mindanao'. If the links are there – and if there is peace – then more internationals will go and there will be development income generated. NP doesn't do anything in development directly, but we want to link these isolated areas up.

From there we contacted the Department of National Defence and the Department of National Security, and we met all the army generals and chief commanders of all the rebel groups. You need to get permission from everybody to ensure your own safety and security and to be more effective. It's also a way to ensure our own non-partisanship.

NP was in Mindanao for those initial three months working with the community, which was a way of securing our legitimacy. It was important for the communities to know why we were there and that we really wanted to be there. During the assessment period there were conflicts in the area and because of the presence of our team the level of the conflict was minimal.

*How do conflicts typically start?*

Sometimes conflict starts because of rumours. For example, there was a case where one of the rebel groups was getting very close to the buffer zone. The rebels were actually going there to have an internal meeting. However, the Armed Forces of the

Philippines (AFP) thought maybe they were planning to attack the checkpoint near the buffer zone, so the AFP also moved their troops close to that location. Normally both parties are supposed to maintain a distance around the zone of about 2-3 km, but at that point it was reduced to 300 m.

Meanwhile the communities thought there would be an attack, so hundreds of families started evacuating. We got the news quickly. Immediately we got in touch with the commanders at the ground level and told them that the rebels said they didn't have any plans to attack but were having an internal meeting. And on the other side we told the rebels we had had contact with the AFP and that they were thinking there was going to be an attack. This goes to show that passing information at the right moment really helps a lot. It also reinforces that as an organisation you cannot go to a place for a short time. Stay there. If you move out it makes the people feel more vulnerable.

In such situations only one gunshot is needed. After that first gunshot you then see rockets and shells everywhere. Our presence has avoided many conflicts, and this is a great example of early response. There is often a lot of talk about Track I and Track II mediation, but you hear very little about Track III – the grassroots. This is really key.

The NP operational structure is simply 'do no harm'. All NP interventions at all levels have regular checks at each field site. We want to hear directly from the lo-cal people and have them comment on our goals. This helps to share each others' work, as what we're really doing is creating a network of networks.

*Not just in your work, but also living in a conflict zone, how difficult is it to stay non-partisan?*

It's extremely difficult. There are so many groups and stakeholders. You have the MILF, the MNLF, Abu Sayyaf, the AFP, the US Marines and civil society. We have regular communication with each in some way. If you have one intervention with an affected group of Christians, for example, you also have to have one in a Muslim community. Otherwise you can be accused of favouritism or taking sides. It really helps to have a multi-religious team as well. On our team currently we are two Buddhists, two Christians and two Muslims. We also aim for a gender balance.

Since 1917, more than 165,000 people have been killed in this conflict and millions have been displaced. About 60 per cent of the population of Mindanao are IDPs (internally displaced persons). But according to national law, if you leave an area and are present somewhere else for six months, you lose IDP status. But of course you can't go back to where you came from because someone else is living where you were.

Mindanao is sometimes called 'the land of promise' because it is so rich in everything in terms of natural resources. The people there say you don't even have to throw a seed and you'll get fruit. But people cannot use all of these resources. After 80 years, Mindanao is 18 per cent Muslim. Many were killed, and the government resettled many from the north of the country in the region. Local people can only have 14 hectares of land while outsiders [settlers] can have 24 hectares.

Peace talks are continually held up because of issues related to territory, governance and natural resources. The MNLF signed a peace agreement in 1996 that created the Autonomous Region in Muslim Mindanao. Since then billions of dollars have been spent, but the conflict continues. Bridges are being built, but communities have no food to eat.

In 1996 they achieved autonomy, but the reality of the agreement has had no impact. There are more paramilitaries in the equation. Back then there were two; now there are six.

I can't emphasize this enough: we cannot talk about development; we need to talk about security. I hear people say, 'We don't want noodles, we don't want sardines – we want security'. Actually, the cycle of violence revolves around the growing season. When the crops are ready, that's when the AFP attacks. The people say the armed forces cultivate the fruits and send them off to the capital city, Manila.

If you ignore the people, new actors enter in and play a part in violence. When people feel involved in the process, though, they are more likely to stick to peace agreements. People are often involved in so-called development. For example, they can get funds from the World Bank to carry out projects in which you can see the results: roads, houses and other tangible things. This is done in the name of measurable progress and development. After all, development workers need to show results: 'we built 500 houses', and it is much easier in a way.

But I know someone who has had his house burned down six times. Each time it was built with development funds and personal money. But even concrete things do not last forever. Meanwhile there are brutal things going on that people just don't know about. Have you ever seen a baby with its head cut off? This is the kind of thing that happens – targeted killings. Cutting off heads and genitals are marks of honour.

Donors need to think about the real impact of their funds. You can build a road, but only the rich people live by the roadside. The poor people live far away from the road, and that's where the conflict is. Donors, including the EU, need to generate funds for civilian peacekeeping. It is so much more effective than military peacekeeping, which revolves around monitoring because this it can do. Military peacekeepers have no interaction with the community or with civil society and therefore have no way to establish trust. This is our advantage.

# Swords into ploughshares — Disarmament, Demobilisation and Reintegration in Zimbabwe, Namibia and South Africa[1]

## Introduction

In the past three decades Zimbabwe, Namibia and South Africa implemented the disarmament, demobilisation and reintegration (DDR) of redundant combatants as part of war to peace transitions. Successful DDR is seen as a *sine qua non* for long-term peace and stability. The immediate goal of the process is to restore security and stability through the responsible management of weapons of combatants. The gradual goal is to enable former combatants to become productive members of their local communities. DDR thus has the potential to facilitate security and development by ensuring the human security of ex-combatants through their long-term sustainable reintegration in secure post-conflict frameworks.

The United Nations was deliberately excluded from playing a pivotal role in Zimbabwe's independence process. Britain, the former colonial power, desired to exclusively control and influence a short transitional period that would not include a burdensome post-conflict peacebuilding role.[2] Following the Lancaster House Agreement on Rhodesia of 21 December 1979, a small British-led Commonwealth team supervised Zimbabwe's ceasefire monitoring and transitional elections leading to genuine majority rule and legal independence. The post-independence regime tackled the integration of a new army amidst DDR. Namibia experienced UN-managed disarmament and demobilisation. In 1989–90, Namibia was host to the multidimensional UN Transitional Assistance Group (UNTAG), which successfully supervised the country's transition to independence. UNTAG's mandate was specifically on the disarmament and demobilisation of all armed groups. Following UNTAG's exit, the independence government established a new and professional military while having to formulate a reintegration policy. In South Africa DDR was internally activated, locally owned and state managed. It was closely linked to the high priority establishment of the new South African National Defence Force (SANDF).

This paper reviews the country-specific DDR processes and the outcomes in Zimbabwe, Namibia and South Africa. It does so in four sections. The first three deal with the three countries on an individual case basis. The concluding section then draws some practical policy recommendations and food for thought for enhancing future DDR efforts.

## Zimbabwean case study

### Background

Zimbabwe's DDR was formulated and implemented after the end of a protracted, widespread and bitter liberation war, or Second Chimurenga. The 1960s and 1970s liberation war pitted the military wings of the Zimbabwe African National Union (ZANU) and the Zimbabwe African Peoples Union (ZAPU),[3] ZANLA and ZIPRA, respectively, against the Rhodesian Security Forces (RSF). In October 1976, ZANU and ZAPU merged into the short-lived loose Patriotic Front (PF) tactical alliance in a bid to wage a unified military strategy against the RSF via the Zimbabwe Peoples Army (ZIPA). However, just as a mutual inter-force hostility existed between the PF and RSF, intra-force hostility existed within the liberation armies' alliance.[4] Zimbabwe's experience of a

*Gwinyayi Albert Dzinesa is a doctoral fellow at the Centre for Africa's International Relations, University of the Witwatersrand. This article draws from his doctoral research: 'Disarmament, demobilisation, reintegration, repatriation and resettlement (DDRRR) in Zimbabwe, Namibia and South Africa', conducted under the supervision of Professor John Stremlau.*

---

1 This article has prior been published by ISS, Pretoria

2 See S. E. Rice, 'The Commonwealth Initiative in Zimbabwe, 1979-1980: implications for international peacekeeping', (D.Phil thesis, New College, Oxford University, 1990), pp 67-8. J. Ginifer (1995). Managing Arms in Peace Processes: Rhodesia/Zimbabwe. New York: United Nations: p. 2.

3 ZAPU, led by Joshua Nkomo, was established in 1961 as successor to the banned National Democratic Party. ZANU was formed as a splinter group from ZAPU in 1963 under the leadership of the Reverend Ndabaningi Sithole. ZANU established ZANLA in 1964 and ZAPU established ZIPRA in 1965 as their military wings to wage a liberation war against the Rhodesian Government.

4 Zimbabwe's liberation war movement had competing ethnic, ideological and strategic components. ZANLA was mainly Shona while ZIPRA was mainly Ndebele in composition. ZANLA's liberation war strategy was Chinese-influenced and relied on mass mobilisation to sustain a protracted liberation struggle. ZIPRA's strategy was Soviet-oriented and placed emphasis on conventional warfare strategy.

long and brutal armed liberation struggle, in which two fully-fledged guerrilla armies (ZANLA and ZIPRA) actively engaged the RSF against a background of mutual hostility and suspicion, called for a complex post-liberation war DDR process.

## Lancaster House Agreement and DDR: Ending the war at the cost of long-term stability?

The Lancaster House Agreement – a 'largely pre-conceived British settlement plan'[5] – that was not specific on integration and DDR, ended the war. Integration and DDR were neither sticks nor carrots in the peace negotiations and agreement, despite attempts to have these issues discussed.[6] The British/Commonwealth mediators, preoccupied with expediently ending the war, conveniently sidestepped these issues, arguing that this would be the responsibility of the elected government. This played into the hands of the RSF commanders who had predicated their participation in the Lancaster talks on the maintenance of the military status quo prior to elections.

While envisaging their military victory, albeit at an enormous human and material cost, the PF were pressured into signing the Lancaster House Agreement.[7] Mozambique and Zambia had issued ultimatums threatening to withdraw bases for the PF, given savage punitive RSF raids on guerrilla sanctuaries and general infrastructure in these neighbouring countries. The possibility of Britain legitimising the incumbent Muzorewa-led Rhodesian coalition government, the 'second-class solution' in the event of a PF pull-out from the negotiations, also permanently hung over the peace conference. In addition, the PF predicted electoral victory that would enable them to preside over the post-independence integration and DDR processes. The elite's concurrence to the Lancaster House Agreement, that skirted DDR and the post-independence status and recompense of PF forces, did not find favour among the common combatants.

The Lancaster House Agreement, effected through a ceasefire agreement between the RSF and PF forces, and enforced from midnight on 21 December 1979, provided for a demilitarisation process by means of the separation and containment of the liberation combatants in designated Assembly Points (APs), and of the RSF in their established bases. The Ceasefire Commission (CFC) and a modest Commonwealth Monitoring Force (CMF) provided the institutional framework for the implementation of the Agreement. Operational deficiencies and organisational flaws did not impede Zimbabwe's successful transition. Since the Lancaster House Agreement did not provide the legal framework for the process, Zimbabwe's post-independence government implemented practical DDR alongside the military integration of the three former warring parties, namely the RSF, ZANLA (Zimbabwe African National Liberation Army) and ZIPRA (Zimbabwe Peoples Revolutionary Army), into a national army.

## Pre-integration disarmament and demobilisation

Prior to the integration of the three forces, some units of the RSF, including the Selous Scouts, Guard Force, and Muzorewa's Auxiliary Forces, were disbanded. These units were not eligible for wholesale integration, as they had been established for specific counter-liberation purposes and were not intended to be permanent forces.[8] Moreover, these units were associated with atrocities during the war and had become wholly political during the negotiations; reminiscent of the Koevoet in Namibia. Many RSF members also withdrew from the forces prior to the integration process. RSF conscripts simply opted out and returned to their pre-enlisting employment. Regular RSF members also took advantage of the Inducement Scheme that provided for the upgrading of officers by one rank on retirement for

5  NAN A.636/2, E. S. Landis Accession S. Graves, Rhodesian Lessons for Namibia.
6  See PF's opening address at the Constitutional Conference Held at Lancaster House, London, September to December 1979. While ZANU and ZAPU negotiated as a unitary PF at Lancaster the two split afterwards and contested the independence elections separately.
7  N. Krieger (2003). Guerilla Veterans in Post-War Zimbabwe: Symbolic and violent politics, 1980-1987. Cambridge, Cambridge University Press: p. 37.
8  Zimbabwe Parliamentary Debates, House of Assembly, vol. 1, 14 May 1980 to 26 June 1980 and 23 July to 15 August 1980.

pension purposes. The war-disabled ex-RSF could also claim compensation in terms of a Rhodesian Act of Parliament.

In addition to the disbandment process, PF combatants who were in the Assembly Points, and were unfit or unwilling to enlist in the military forces, were demobilised. While these combatants were given questionnaires in the APs to compile their profiles and preferred post-war occupations, no elaborate reintegration policy was designed, besides the provision of a demobilisation grant of Z $400. The opportunity to plan a comprehensive DDR strategy at the earliest possible stage was lost. The limited monetary reintegration strategy resulted in the ineffective reintegration of these demobilised combatants, the majority of whom re-registered under the Demobilisation Programme of 1981.

As the Lancaster House Agreement had failed to provide for practical disarmament, Robert Mugabe, then Prime Minister and Minister of Defence, outlined the government's policy of disarming combatants as they demobilised, while those awaiting integration would retain their weapons.[9] The retention of weapons by ex-combatants during the long idle months spent in APs awaiting integration and demobilisation proved

catastrophic, as ZANU–ZAPU ethnic-based tensions spilled over from the liberation war. The passage of time did not heal the wounds, distrust and tension between ZANU and ZAPU; this played out against a backdrop of incomprehensive Ndebele–Shona reconciliation. Apartheid South Africa, the major economic, political and military force in the region exploited these mutual hostilities to further entrench the wedge between the two parties.

The insecurity threats posed by the retention of weapons materialised in the eventual clashes in the APs between the ZANLA and ZIPRA combatants. Following the prominent Entumbane clash of 9-11 November 1980, the government disarmed the guerrillas. Perceiving disarmament as disparate, and designed to buttress the political and military power of the Shona, 'many ZIPRA guerrillas left the armed forces and the camps, joining the ranks of those armed members of the lumpen elements who could be a reservoir of future destabilisation'.[10] These mutinies were spontaneous and were not part of ZAPU policy.[11] However, Zimbabwe experienced armed dissident activity in Matabeleland and parts of the Midlands 1981-1987, during which some former ZIPRA combatants took up arms against the government.

The government responded to this internal security problem by deploying integrated army units[12] and the specially created, North Korean-trained 5th Brigade, also known as Gukurahundi (Shona for 'the rain that washes away the chaff from the last harvest, before the spring rains')[13] to counter the 'dissident' menace. An estimated 10,000 civilians lost their lives and thousands more were harmed during the 5th Brigade's campaign, as violence and insecurity rocked Matabeleland and parts of the Midlands until the signing of the historic Unity Accord of 1987 by ZANU and ZAPU. This dealt a major blow to post-independence peace, and to nation building and reconstruction.

Zimbabwe's security policy framework shifted, as it also had to strengthen its defences against apartheid South Africa's 'Total National Strategy' against those southern African states that were inclined to Marxism and supportive of African liberation and ANC operatives. The total strategy was in part prescribed the military equipping of the RENAMO surrogate forces, as well as some dissident elements that launched incursions into Zimbabwe. Information that came to light during the South African Truth and Reconciliation Commission revealed the South African Defence Force's involvement

9  Ibid.

10  H. Campbell (2003). Reclaiming Zimbabwe: The Exhaustion of the Patriarchal Model of Liberation. South Africa: New Africa Books: p. 51.

11  Interview with Minister of Home Affairs, Dumiso Dabengwa (retd.), head of ZIPRA in the cease-fire arrangement, 2 April 2004, Harare. Interview with Col. Tshinga J. Dube (retd.), Zimbabwe Defence Industries managing director, 1 April 2004, Harare.

12  These included the ZNA's four brigades, Police Support Unit, Central Intelligence Organisation and Paratroopers.

13  R. Werbner (1992). Tears of the Dead: The social biography of an African family. Harare: Baobab: p. 159.

in Zimbabwe.[14] Force expansion and official procurement of arms gained momentum in order to safeguard newly won independence by ensuring an efficient, well-equipped defence force. This was an enforced antithesis to demilitarisation.[15] The resultant increase of the army by 10,000 to 51,519[16] was accompanied by constant and substantial defence expenditure.[17] The relegation of DDR meant that the envisaged peace dividend, which should have been characterised by the release of resources for social and economically productive projects, remained elusive.

### Demobilisation policy of 1981-1983: demobilise and scatter?

The integration process resulted in a new army of about 70,000 members, against an initial projected target of 30,000. Fiscal and security objectives underpinned the government's policy decision to plan and implement demobilisation of the over-manned army. The government set up the Demobilisation Directorate in July 1981, appropriately under the Ministry of Labour and Social Welfare, to implement demobilisation and reintegration with relevant sister ministries.

The demobilisation policy did not make specific provisions for the rehabilitation and reintegration of special categories such as the physically disabled and psychologically disturbed ex-fighter, and female ex-combatants, all with specific needs.[18] The demobilisation programme, outlined in a policy document titled Demobilisation within the Zimbabwe National Army revolved on the provision of:

- further education for those demobilised combatants who had not finished their primary or secondary education and wished to continue;
- technical training in motor mechanics, welding, agricultural courses, medical courses, local governance, customs and immigration;
- expert guidance to ex-combatants interested in seeking employment, self-employment, or forming co-operatives; and
- a demobilisation allowance comprising a monthly stipend of Z $185 spread over a two-year period, or a lump sum of Z $4,440.

Employed former combatants were not eligible for the demobilisation allowance.[19] Demobilised combatants were provided with Post Office Savings Bank account books, and

### Table 1: Post-demobilisation combatant status

| Status | Number of demobilised combatants |
|---|---|
| Completion of interrupted education | 5,700 |
| Training programmes | 2,900 |
| Formal employment | 5,041 |
| Self-employed | 2,179 |
| Cooperatives | 6,383 |
| Unemployed | 13,500 |
| Total | 35,763 |

Source: Zimbabwe, Zimbabwe Parliamentary Debates, vol. 18, no. 68, March 1992

14  For more, see D. Dabengwa (1995), 'ZIPRA in the Zimbabwe War of National Liberation' in N. Bhebe and T. Ranger (eds), Soldiers in Zimbabwe's Liberation War, vol. 1. Harare: University of Zimbabwe Publications: p. 28; and. D. Martin and P. Johnson (1989). Apartheid Terrorism: The Destabilisation Report. London: James Currey: pp. 51-76.
15  G. Mazarire and M. R. Rupiya, 'Two Wrongs Do Not Make a Right: A Critical Assessment of Zimbabwe's Demobilisation and Reintegration Programmes, 1980-2000', Journal of Peace, Conflict and Military Studies, vol. 1, no. 1, March 2000, p. 72.
16  Sunday Mail, 11 August 1996, 'Why ZNA being downsized'.
17  Zimbabwe, Parliamentary Debates, House of Assembly, vol. 7, no. 4, Wednesday 29 June 1983.
18  A National Rehabilitation Centre was later established to offer disabled ex-combatants a six-month rehabilitation program. However, the absence of a coherent plan meant the centre was yet to realise its full potential when it was abruptly closed to former combatants in 1985.
19  The Herald, 5 January 1982, 'Ex-guerrillas on parade for demobilisation'.

identification documents authorising them to withdraw the demobilisation allowance from bank outlets countrywide.

At the end of the physical demobilisation exercise in June 1983, 35,763 combatants had been demobilised. *(See Table 1.)*

Notwithstanding the existence of a dedicated Demobilisation Directorate, there were programmatic and institutional gaps. These included the lack of a broad and consistent socio-economic profiling of combatants, the failure to implement financial management skills training for the many ex-combatants inexperienced in handling (demobilisation) money, incompetent and corrupt directorate staff, an absence of elaborate and workable business or cooperatives support mechanisms, and the lack of a proactive monitoring mechanism. The majority of the ex-combatant enterprises collapsed due to these factors, while agro-based enterprises were also hard-hit by drought. The ex-combatants had been 'thrown into a sophisticated world without adequate preparation'.[20] Compounded by unfavourable post-independence economic, social, and politico-military frameworks, the DDR process disintegrated. This translated to the absence of a dedicated reintegration policy by government, impacting profoundly on the independent state's economic, social and political configuration.[21]

Despite these obvious programmatic limitations the Zimbabwean Government stressed that 'those (ex-combatants) who had not furthered their education or gained some skills or training, or were unemployed, would be on their own after the (demobilisation) payments expired'.[22] By 1990 up to 25,000 ex-combatants were unemployed, as indicators of human insecurity dominated their livelihoods. Since the government did not initiate further reintegration assistance beyond the ill-fated 1981 program, ex-combatants perceived this as official indifference to their plight. Instead of turning ex-combatants into productive civilians, (ineffective) DDR transformed them into war veterans, an identity they would later violently mobilise to achieve varied aims. The Zimbabwe National Liberation War Veterans Association (ZNLWVA), established after the Unity Accord of 1987 between ZANU and ZAPU, offered the ex-combatants the platform to launch their demands.

The groundswell of discontent, and the threat to national stability posed by ineffectively reintegrated and disgruntled ex-combatants, exploded in 1997. This followed the Zimbabwean government's suspension of the War Victims Compensation Fund (es-

tablished by government in 1980 to cater for all war-injured persons) in March 1997, and the appointment by President Mugabe of a judicial commission to inquire and report on the administration of the Fund. The suspension was intended to stop further abuse of the Fund, but nonetheless, and understandably so, infuriated many war veterans, given that the Fund had become their most important escape route from destitution, following problematic reintegration. This created an explosive situation, and the government soon found itself at loggerheads with disgruntled ex-combatants who held rolling protests against perceived bureaucratic bungling and mistreatment.[23]

In response to the demonstrations, the government implemented the 'second policy on demobilisation and reintegration'. Coincidentally, the President is also the patron of the ZNLWVA. The relationship between the ruling ZANU PF and the war veterans has consistently been characterised by 'power-seeking agendas, their appeals to the revolutionary liberation, their use of violence and intimidation,' and their 'simultaneous conflict and collaboration as party and veterans manipulate one another'.[24] The costs of this programme including an initial outlay of more than Z $4.5 billion on gratuities and lifetime pensions for over 52,000

20 PARADE, April 1990.
21 G. Mazarire and M. R. Rupiya, op. cit., p. 1.
22 The Herald, 30 June 1983, 'No extended demob pay'.
23 R. Werbner (1998), 'Smoke from the barrel of a gun: post-wars of the dead, memory and reinscription in Zimbabwe', in R. Werbner (ed.), Memory and the Post-Colony. London: Zed Books: p. 81.
24 N. Krieger (2003). Guerilla Veterans in Post-War Zimbabwe: Symbolic and violent politics, 1980-1987. Cambridge: Cambridge University Press: p. 208.

war veterans and the negative impact on the country's broader economy meant that Zimbabwe did not experience the financial dividend of DDR. To date the government is burdened with war veterans' pensions, which constantly have to be adjusted to keep pace with rampant hyper-inflation.

## Namibian case study
### Background

Namibia's liberation war mainly pitted SWAPO's military wing; the People's Liberation Army of Namibia (PLAN) against the SADF from August 1966-1989. This meant that Namibia's DDR would involve one liberation army. The SADF, whose presence in Namibia was declared illegal by the UN, was an external army that could be easily withdrawn from Namibia in the post-war era. South Africa established indigenous forces to fight against PLAN alongside the SADF, such as the South West Africa Territorial Force (SWATF), and citizen and commando forces. The San, also disparagingly known as the Bushmen, whose tracking and hunting skills were considered invaluable in the bush war against SWAPO, were recruited as SWATF soldiers. South Africa also trained the counter-insurgency unit Koevoet ('crowbar'), which terrorised Namibians. These forces had to be included alongside PLAN combatants in the process to establish Namibia's national armed forces and DDR programmes.

### UNTAG and DDR

The New York Accords of 28 December 1988 (signed by Angola, Cuba and South Africa) facilitated the implementation of Namibia's independence plan as outlined in UN Security Council Resolution 435 (1978). Disarmament and demobilisation were part of the Settlement Plan and were concretely enshrined in the mandate of the United Nations Transition Assistance Group (UNTAG). UNTAG's tasks included:

• monitoring the ceasefire;
• ensuring that troops (both SADF and SWAPO) were confined to bases; and
• supervising the rapid reduction and eventual removal of South African military forces from Namibia.[25]

Resolution 435 also provided for the disbandment of all 'ethnic and paramilitary' units that had been established by colonial South Africa. Disarmament and demobilisation were thus incorporated into the overall strategy to create secure conditions for Namibia's transition to independence. As UNTAG did not have a post-conflict mandate to assist with the reintegration of the demobilised combatants, this was left to the devices of the independence government.

UNTAG's implementation of disarmament and demobilisation was marked by an inauspicious start. The delay in the full emplacement of UNTAG in Namibia had serious consequences for the maintenance of the ceasefire. On the day on which the ceasefire was to come into effect, 1 April 1989, South African forces clashed with PLAN combatants who had crossed the border from Angola into northern Namibia. UNTAG has since confirmed PLAN's explanation that it had been engaged in establishing military bases inside Namibia that would be monitored by UNTAG, only to be ambushed by South African forces. However, at the time, South African forces, authorised by the UN to deploy and enforce the ceasefire, engaged in a major onslaught against the outnumbered and less well-equipped PLAN combatants, in which more than 375 PLAN combatants were killed.[26] UNTAG's operational and logistic capacity was expeditiously boosted to enable it to credibly carry out its mandate. The parties' ultimate commitment to the independence process and amenability to UNTAG pressure facilitated significant disarmament and demobilisation.

UNTAG subsequently demobilised the SWATF and the citizen commando forces. The arms, military equipment and ammunition collected from these units were deposited in 'double-locked' drill halls guarded by UNTAG infantry.[27] However, South Africa's attempt to maintain its tactical presence in Namibia's security sector, and SWAPO's alleged retention of a strategic reserve force threatened to blot disarmament and demo-

25 United Nations (1996). The Blue Helmets: A review of United Nations peacekeeping. New York: UN Department of Information: pp. 209-10.
26 As we write, reports on the mass grave expose of PLAN fighters reportedly killed by South African forces during the ensuing confrontations abound in South African media.
27 United Nations, The Blue Helmets: A review of United Nations peacekeeping, op. cit., p 221.

bilisation. For instance, the majority of the SWATF retained their camouflage, maintained contact with their 'former' commanders, and remained on the payroll. In addition, instead of disbanding the paramilitary Koevoet unit in line with UN recommendations, South Africa 'infiltrated' about 2,000 of its original 3,000 members into SWAPOL, thereby bypassing the demobilisation provisions. These 'demobilised' personnel were responsible for widespread intimidation and destabilisation activity, including hunting down and eliminating PLAN combatants and threatening the masses, particularly in the sensitive and populous northern areas. Under pressure from UNTAG, South African administrators eventually agreed to the demobilisation of 1,600 ex-Koevoet members of SWAPOL under UNTAG supervision by 30 October 1989. The remaining 1,500-strong 'Merlyn Force' was withdrawn after the certification of the elections on 21 November 1989, completing the withdrawal of the SADF and its concomitant military equipment.

Disarmament of PLAN was carried out in Angola. PLAN troops who had been in Namibia on 1 April 1989 were assembled at designated camps before being escorted under UNTAG supervision to assembly points north of the 16th parallel in Angola. In spite of a slow start, more than 5,000 were ultimately confined to bases in Angola.[28] The initial difficulties can probably be attributed to the dispersal of PLAN fighters, following the clashes of April 1989,[29] and the intimidating visible presence of South African forces outside their bases. UNTAG's small team of 31 military monitors, based in Lubango, Angola, and known as UNTAG A (Angola), supervised the disarmament of PLAN by the Angolan military and their confinement to Angolan camps. Angolan General Ndalu later asserted that all SWAPO personnel retreated north of the 16th parallel.[30]

## Creating a time bomb?
### Post-independence reintegration

The success of the two 'Ds' in DDR was undermined by the independence government's failure to plan and implement comprehensive reintegration programmes. Namibia had no constitutionally established defence force at independence. One of the priorities of the new government was the formation of an integrated Namibian Defence Force (NDF) against a backdrop of mistrust and suspicion. The successfully established NDF and the transformed Namibian Police combined absorbed between 8,000 and 10,000 combatants, offering them and their dependants some stability. However, this accounted for but a fraction of the over 50,000 total demobilised. Prioritising the powerful political imperatives of national reconciliation and nation building, the Namibian government embarked on stopgap reintegration measures for the superfluous ex-fighters.

Ex-SWATF members were better placed than their ex-PLAN counterparts. For instance, SWATF ex-fighters continued to receive salaries from South Africa after discharge, until Namibia's independence. This was meant to facilitate their reintegration into civilian life, and to retain their loyalty to the SADF in case Namibia's transition to independence collapsed.[31] In 1991-1992 South Africa implemented a compensation scheme comprising 'a once-off payment of 12,000 Namibian dollars (US $2,600) to former Koevoet and SWATF forces as a gratuity to tide them over until they found employment'.[32] In any event, their possession of the standard 8 level of education entry requirement stood them in good stead for civilian employment and reintegration.

The same cannot be said of the ex-PLAN fighters, whose employment prospects were restricted by their lack of formal qualifications. The majority, unable to be absorbed into limied public sector employment, remained a part of the mainstream unem-

28 L. S. Howard, 'UN peace implementation in Namibia: the causes of success', International Peacekeeping, vol. 9, no. 1, Spring 2002, p. 109.
29 Interview with Peter Shivute, Permanent Secretary Ministry of Defence, Windhoek, 12 November 2004.
30 C. Thornberry (2004). A Nation is Born: The onside story of Namibia's Independence. Windhoek: Gamsberg Macmillan Publishers: p. 125.
31 N. J. Colleta, Beyond Repatriation: The demobilisation and reintegration of ex-combatants in Namibia, p. 21.
32 The Financial Gazette, 10 July 1997, 'Namibian war veterans protest for jobs'.

ployed population years into independence. This was at a time when the transition to independence was accompanied by a neo-colonial economic structure and a small private sector that was not immediately restructured to facilitate economic growth and job creation. The government also did not develop the potential of the informal sector to meet the reintegration goals of creating jobs and alleviating poverty among unattached ex-fighters.

Former PLAN combatants were each paid a nominal once-off gratuity of 1,400 rand in 1991.[33] The intention was that this gratuity would be complemented by the succeeding two-year (1991 and 1992) Development Brigade (later Development Brigade Corporation) training programme, designed to impart practical agricultural and construction skills sufficient for sustainable post-graduation income generation to the unemployed ex-combatants, but which did not quite work out as planned. The Development Brigade was strategically placed under the Ministry of Lands, Resettlement and Rehabilitation (MLLR), as land reform was to be central to its success. However, Namibia's slow and cumbersome land resettlement programme has resulted in the perpetuation of skewed land ownership patterns. Access to land has been problematic, in particular for

ex-combatants who are not treated as a specific preferential target group under the national land reform programme. About 3,800 mainly white farmers continued to own 44 per cent of arable land.[34]

Other institutional and operational problems, including a lack of funding, a lack of technical expertise and qualified personnel, as well as inappropriate training, resulted in the Development Brigade programme failing to acquire self-sufficiency status and wean the trainees into productive employment or viable projects. Bilateral donors such as the Swedish International Development Cooperation Agency (SIDA) and later the European Community withdrew sponsorship on the basis of negative evaluation reports on the performance and viability of the Development Brigade.

Namibia's initiatives broadly failed to facilitate ex-fighter reintegration. This presented a potential threat to national stability and security. The public disruption and rioting by ineffectively reintegrated and disenchanted former fighters in the mid-1990s demonstrated this.[35] In a gratifying response to avert full-scale instability, the government decided to implement the aptly named Peace Project, aimed at affirmative job placements, mainly in the public service,

for around 11,950 unemployed and registered ex-fighters. A larger civil service was the price that the Namibian government had to pay for earlier botched reintegration. Instead of mollifying the disgruntled and riotous former combatants in the short term with monetary pay-offs, the Peace Project enhanced prospects of the long-term reintegration of its beneficiaries. Instructively, the Peace Project has for seven years managed to prevent new security threats posed by the ex-fighters.

### South African case study
#### Background
South Africa's violent anti-apartheid conflict involved seven major armed antagonists. The apartheid security forces were the SADF and the armed forces of the Transkei, Bophuthatswana, Venda and Ciskei (TBVC) homelands. The liberation movements, the African National Congress (ANC) and Pan African Congress (PAC), established their respective military wings; Umkhonto weSizwe (MK) and the Azanian Peoples Liberation Army (APLA). The involvement of varied armed formations in South Africa's anti-apartheid struggle meant that the country had a heterogeneous, ex-fighter population to deal with under its DDR process. However, a major feature of the anti-apartheid conflict was that there were limited military

---

33 This followed demonstrations by ex-fighters in Windhoek, who demanded recompense for their liberation war efforts. The funds derived from R36 million offered to the Namibian Government by the South African Government. Initially meant to cater for ex-South Africa forces, the amount was split to cater for the ex-PLAN fighters as well after protestations by the Namibia Government and eventual negotiation with South Africa.
34 'Namibia's second president since independence is sworn in' (accessed on 12 April 2005).
35 The protests were extensively covered by *The Namibian* at the time.

engagements between the larger and so-phisticated SADF and the liberation armies inside South Africa. Jacklyn Cock described South Africa's conflict as a 'low-level civil war'.[36] The fact that armed conflict was low-key may inadvertently have resulted in the low emphasis on the planning and execution of DDR.

The settlement of South Africa's violent conflict was concluded in a series of minutes and accords. These included the Groote Schuur Minute, Pretoria Minute, National Peace Accord and CODESA Declaration. The Multi-Party Negotiating Forum with the National Party Government and ANC elite as major players recommended the creation of an internal Transitional Executive Council (TEC) to supervise South Africa's transition to democracy. A Sub-Council on Defence (SCD) was established as part of the TEC to implement the military aspects of the transition. The multi-party negotiations emphasized the establishment of a new, unitary SANDF. While this was important as part of a broader strategy to ensure control of the levers of the new state in an uncertain political environment, the plan of an essential and comprehensive DDR gave way. For instance, the SCD's major tasks included ensuring compliance by all armed forces with the objectives of the TEC, and research and planning for the new

defence forces. Whereas the formation of the SANDF was structured and well thought out, 'the demobilisation of former APLA and MK soldiers was an afterthought'.[37]

Disarmament, demobilisation and reintegration: the process and the impacts

Against a backdrop of significant meetings between the apartheid government and the un-banned ANC, the ANC suspended its armed struggle in August 1990. This was under the framework of the Pretoria Minute of 6 August 1990, which reaffirmed both parties' commitment to 'moving as speedily as possible towards a negotiated peaceful political settlement' By agreeing that 'no further armed actions and related activities by the ANC and its military wing Umkhonto we Sizwe [MK] will take place', the nationalist movement ostensibly opened the opportunity for self-managed disarmament. The Pretoria Minute, however, did not end mistrust, competition and military machinations. The ensuing volatile political and security framework constrained disarmament efforts.

Against this unstable backdrop the South African Government and the ANC signed the D.F. Malan Accord of February 1991. The Accord reiterated the parties' commitment to the upholding of the most pertinent

points of the Pretoria Minute that touched on weapons control. The provisions of the Malan Accord included the control over the cadres and arms of MK, which had been increasingly infiltrated into the country. One of the results of the Accord was the registration and legalisation of specific MK firearms after the ANC 'raised concerns about the need to protect our leadership', and 'this was one of the processes that helped in the disarmament process'.[38] In addition, a facilitative Government Gazette of March 1991 authorised automatic indemnity for MK members who received military training and engaged in armed military activities up to 8 October 1990.[39]

A result of the above initiatives was the disarmament of some 4,000 MK fighters, and their return to South Africa from camps in Uganda and Tanzania as 'unarmed civilians' during the UNHCR voluntary repatriation operation.[40] Interviews with MK ex-fighters confirmed this. Disarmament and repatriation under the UNCHR was not elaborately linked to ex-fighter reintegration. The repatriated fighters received limited rehabilitation assistance, provided for under the repatriation process.

The weapons collected 'went back to the headquarters of the liberation move-

36 J. Cock, 'The role of violence in State Security Strategies: 1984-1988', CSVR Seminar No. 1, 1989 (accessed on 17 August 2004).
37 L. Mashike, '"You are a time bomb ...": Ex-combatants in post-conflict South Africa', Society in Transition, 2004, 35(1): 87.
38 Interview with SAPS Deputy Provincial Commissioner Africa Khumalo, Ex-MK Commander, 25 April 2005, Johannesburg.
39 Business Day, 8 March 1991, 'MK commanders arrive in South Africa', Sunday Star, 10 March 1991, 'Stunned return to the new South Africa'.
40 L. Mashike, op. cit., p. 88.

ments because there were some form of records on the movements' weapons and which units were given what. They may not have returned all but people returned their weapons'.[41] The liberation movements then handed over these weapons to the Transitional Executive Council, established by the multiparty negotiations to deal with military aspects of the transition, and they were supposed to be destroyed.[42]

Further attempts at disarmament included a July 1993 month-long amnesty period, during which people could hand over weapons and be immune from prosecution. However, in a statement that could be strongly construed to imply the retention of weapons by ANC cadres, ANC spokesman Ronnie Mamoepa said, 'The ANC will never hand over weapons to this illegal government'.[43] Notably, only three days before the amnesty ended, only 18 weapons had been handed in.[44] However, South African police spokesman Captain Louis le Roux attributed the poor response to the possession of arms by criminals who feared to be linked with other arms.

Disarmament was not in any way complete. This may have contributed to South Africa's multi-causal and destructive small arms scourge. For example, firearms are said to 'feature prominently in violent crime and contribute directly to the distinctively high murder rate in SA'.[45] South African Police Services (SAPS) Deputy Provincial Commissioner Africa Khumalo, a former MK commander in charge of disarmament, noted: 'Finally, not all firearms were collected. Some of them we have found in the cash-in transit robberies. Thus (until) today, the government is still giving amnesties with regards to handing in of illegal firearms'.[46]

Demobilisation was secondary to the establishment of the SANDF. It was implemented on the basis of a cabinet decision of 16 August 1995, as an exit strategy for personnel listed on the liberation armies' Certified Personnel Registers (CPR) but ineligible or disinclined to join the SANDF. In 1995 the then Minister of Defence, now late, Joe Modise, announced the demobilisation process as involving the voluntary release of members of the former liberation armies (referred to as Non-Statutory Forces), who, despite being constitutionally part of the SANDF, did not wish to serve in the full-time force or who could not do so due to age, ill health or did not meet the minimum requirements for service in the SANDF.[47] Lephophotho Mashike argues that the result of the expedient nature of the demobilisation process was that 'there was no proper planning for the reintegration of former soldiers into civilian life'.[48]

The legislative framework for demobilisation and reintegration was only put in place in 1996 with the institution of the policy White Paper on the Defence and Demobilisation Act. As demobilisation had started in 1995 after the democratic elections, this had to work retrospectively. The demobilised were supposed to be catered for by a three-legged demobilisation and reintegration strategy:

- a gratuity payment, calculated according to length of service in the liberation armies, and at scales approved by Cabinet, with sums in excess of 30,000 rand; subject to normal taxation;
- counselling and advisory services to guide the ex-fighters on how to manage their gratuities, as well as to advise on the options available to support their reintegration;
- a skills upgrade via the Service Corps training scheme.

41 Interview with Tsepe Motumi, Chief of Policy and Planning, Department of Defence, 5 April 2005, Pretoria.
42 Interview with SAPS Deputy Provincial Commissioner Africa Khumalo, Ex-MK Commander, 25 April 2005, Johannesburg.
43 The Star, 29 July 1993, 'Amnesty for arms gets poor response'.
44 Ibid.
45 R Chetty (ed.), 'Firearm use and distribution in South Africa', National Crime Prevention Centre Firearm Program, 2000, p. 10.
46 Interview with SAPS' Deputy Provincial Commissioner, Africa Khumalo, Ex-MK Commander, 25 April 2005, Johannesburg.
47 'Voluntary release from service', SALUT October 1995, vol. 12, no.10, p. 10.
48 L Mashike, op. cit., p. 88.

The once-off gratuity for the common ex-fighter without financial management skills did not effect the up-liftment and sustainable reintegration of most ex-fighters. While a noble gesture, the flash-funding gratuity would have needed to be relatively substantial and partnered by a solid skills development and entrepreneur-friendly scheme in order to sustainably reintegrate the ex-fighters.

The good intentions of the Service Corps were unhinged by the absence of an enabling and appropriate institutional framework. The location of the Service Corps in the Department of Defence, and its management by military officers was problematic. The military can quite easily train civilians to become military personnel, but is least fitted to reverse the process. In any event, the military was averse to sponsoring a perceived 'non-core' project at a time when international and non-government funding for the resource-intensive venture was limited (except for an initial 141 million rand grant by the Taiwanese government to set up the first vocational training centre). Further technical and financial assistance promised by Taiwan was precluded by the government's political decision to break diplomatic ties with Taiwan in favour of mainland China.[49]

The absence of a timely and comprehensive DDR strategy was aggravated by the post-apartheid economic context, characterised by 'jobless growth', making the large-scale and sustainable reintegration of ex-combatants impossible. Several scholarly studies have confirmed the ineffective reintegration of ex-fighters. For instance, Ian Liebenberg and Marlene Roefs[50] state that 37 per cent of their sample was unemployed. The Centre for Conflict Resolution's study[51] on the livelihood of ex-combatants found that 66 per cent of ex-fighters interviewed were unemployed, with a third suffering psychological problems. The situation was particularly depressing for ex-fighters who had hoped that independence would translate into guaranteed human security.

The fact that the demobilisation and reintegration process lacked clear monitoring and follow-up mechanisms meant that no corrective measures were designed to assist ex-fighters who had failed to reintegrate. This created a potentially disruptive sense of neglect, betrayal and marginalisation among the ex-combatants. The threats to security and stability posed by ineffectively reintegrated ex-fighters became a reality in the form of armed criminal activities, mainly cash-in-transit heists.[52] Small-scale protests by ex fighters[53] were held, largely 'motivated by the needs of the individuals concerned to highlight their grievances'.[54]

The government has since enacted the Military Veterans Affairs Act of 1999 as part

## Table 2: Demobilisation payments

| Category | Years of Service | Amount paid | Numbers |
|---|---|---|---|
| A | 22-23 | 42,058 rand | 172 |
| B | 18-21 | 34,313 rand | 144 |
| C | 12-17 | 28,721 rand | 534 |
| D | 5-11 | 20,201 rand | 1,049 |
| E | 0-4 | 12,734 rand | 2,003 |
| Z | Unspecified | | 242 |

Source: James Higgs (1998). The Critical Component: Personnel Strategies for the SANDF to 2000 and Beyond. Johannesburg: SAIIA: p. 15

49 P. Frankel (2000). Soldiers in a Storm: The armed forces in South Africa's democratic transition. Boulder, Co: Westview Press.
50 I. Liebenberg and M. Roefs (2001). Demobilisation and its Aftermath II: Economic reinsertion of South Africa's demobilised military personnel. Pretoria: ISS.
51 L. Mashike and M. Mokalobe, 'Reintegration into civilian life: the case of former MK and APLA combatants', TRACK TWO, vol. 12, no. 1.
52 Opening Address of the Deputy Minister of Defence, Mr Mluleki George MP, at the occasion of A Symposium On Military Veterans, University of South Africa (Florida Campus), 25 August 2004.
53 See, e.g. Natal Mercury, 20 August 1993, 'Ten-day sit by ANC exiles ends'; Sunday Times, 22 August 1993, 'Defiant MK Cadres end siege after meeting with Mandela'; City Press, 22 August 1993, 'Sit-in at ANC offices'; L. Mashike, '"You are a time bomb ...": Ex-combatants in post-conflict South Africa', Society in Transition, 2004, 35(1), pp. 101 and 102.
54 L. Mashike, op. cit., p. 101.

of the new initiatives to correct the deficiencies of past reintegration strategies. Slow steps are being made towards the establishment of a representative national war veterans association that would facilitate implementation of the support provided under the Military Veterans Act. The full implementation of the Act would mean public expenditure on war veterans translating to an elusive peace dividend, more than a decade into democracy. At the time of writing, the Department of Defence is also working on the reorganisation of the Service Corps, mainly on matters relating to its appropriate location and partnerships.

## Conclusion

This paper has outlined Zimbabwe, Namibia and South Africa's experience of DDR. DDR featured strongly in the three countries' transition to independence and democracy, following negotiated settlements to lengthy armed anti-colonial struggles. The transitional environment, in all three cases, was characterised by historical mutual mistrust and animosity, as preceding conflict dynamics influenced the establishment of post-conflict unitary armed forces and DDR. The resultant insecurity and uncertainty posed challenges to integration and DDR. DDR was the flipside of the logically strategic establishment of unitary and legitimate national defence forces that were crucial for post-conflict peace and nation building.

Notwithstanding the strategic imperatives of the swift establishment of integrated national defence forces, and the demobilisation of superfluous fighters, the equally important reintegration component of DDR was inadequately addressed in all three countries. The government-led reintegration strategies were poorly implemented where policy statements were in place, but worse when they were an afterthought. This effectively created a gap between the two Ds of DDR (disarmament and demobilisation) and the R (reintegration). Despite the fact that some former fighters managed to secure cabinet, government, parastatal and diplomatic postings, the sustainable reintegration of most former liberation fighters remained a problem. The governments that had failed to properly reintegrate ex-combatants later found themselves with a price to pay, as restive ex-fighters threatened national stability. This was a red flag that national authorities could hardly ignore, resulting in the implementation of various new reintegration initiatives.

While DDR occurs in unique settings, the following broad recommendations can be taken from the three case studies, and should be considered when undertaking future processes:

- crafters and implementers of DDR should understand the dynamics of the preceding conflict of which the process is a product;
- DDR should be an integral part of the peace negotiations, agreement and succeeding peace process;

- there is a strong need to conceive DDR as an interconnected and integrated process with no gap between the two Ds and the R;
- the various stakeholders should follow a comprehensive, coordinated and sustainable approach with regard to DDR;
- The reformulation of the wider economic framework is critical, since DDR is unlikely to succeed in a stagnant or imbalanced economy;
- genuine national reconciliation should be nurtured, as DDR symbiotically relates to post-conflict accommodation between former antagonists;
- remedial measures that do not disrupt the national economic fabric should be devised;
- ensuring the human security of ex-fighters through effective DDR facilitates regime and national security, allowing DDR to achieve its promise of supporting peacebuilding.

While UN peacekeeping operations may have exact mandates to implement under specified timeframes, there is a need to ensure continuity through post-withdrawal synergy with relevant local bodies.

### About this article

This paper explores the processes in the peace agreement and transitional arrangements from 2003 and 2005. It seeks to put into perspective the challenges faced thus far and argues in favour of a long term approach to defence transformation as opposed to short-term political considerations. It also laments the slow progress and urges stakeholders involved to move as quickly as possible and without delay in order to reap the benefits of peace before the winds of change die out.

Funder

This article and the research upon which it is based was made possible through the generous funding of the government of the United Kingdom, Department for International Development (DFID).

[    Alvaro Ybarra Zavala    ]

# Ramadi, Iraq

Since the beginning of the war Iraq has caught itself in a hornet's nest with a very difficult exit. As a photographer I have tried to show a realistic view of real daily life, far away from politics, away from what is associated with the conflict and everything that comes with it.

In general every war is analyzed from a political angle forgetting that, in most cases, the supporters are human beings.

Human beings form in one way or another part of the drama called Iraq. This is a drama that not only affects the Iraqis who have to say goodbye to their family before leaving their homes; it has also influenced the firmest beliefs of people who have voluntarily embarked in a conflict defending their values and who have with time seen themselves become relegated to a simple and primitive political weapon.

Iraq is the birthplace of broken ideals – a place without future – which for those who survive marks them for life, regardless if they are Iraqi or part of the international forces. It is a scenario which every day suffers from increasing dehumanization and with every passing day becomes an even sadder and more forgotten armed conflict.

Iraq is a conflict forgotten by the media, as the coverage of the war diminishes day by day. Statistics and numbers are the only reality shown to the rest of the world to describe this tragedy. Since when can you summarise a human life into a figure? A conflict forgotten by the large non-governmental organisations who barely approach or speak about the situation in Iraq. Why are they actually there? A conflict forgotten by the large powerful nations, who no longer see solutions to introduce order in a country which bleeds to death.

As photographer I have committed myself to showing Iraq from the inside, from the daily life, from the familiar side. I wanted to show that daily life in Ramadi, Faluja, Baghdad... isn't very different to ours in the tranquillity of our own homes. The only – and biggest – difference is that our days aren't marked by death, while in Iraq they are.

ALVARO YBARRA ZAVALA

*Ahmet, a former Suni militia man,
now works for the special unit
of the Iraqi police in the Karrada
neighbourhood in Baghdad.*
© Alvaro Ybarra Zavala / Agence VU

*Iraqi police recruits line up to be screened
at Camp Defender, an Iraqi Army base linked to
the Americans' Camp Ramadi. These recruits will
become part of a new quick reaction police team
called the Emergency Response Unit.*
© Alvaro Ybarra Zavala / Agence VU /

Iraq, Ramadi, November 2006

> Iraqi police recruits wait to be screened at Camp Defender, an Iraqi Army base linked to the Americans' Camp Ramadi. These recruits will become part of a new quick reaction police team called the Emergency Response Unit.
© Alvaro Ybarra Zavala / Agence VU /
Iraq, Ramadi, November 2006

< Policemen from the special unit of the Karrada neighbourhood inside their base before going out on patrol.
© Alvaro Ybarra Zavala / Agence VU /
Iraq, Baghdad, November 2006

*Lieutenant Larson and Iraqi chief of the Iraqi*
*special police of Karranda neighbourhood*
*preparing a mission.*
© Alvaro Ybarra Zavala / Agence VU /
Iraq, Baghdad, November 2006

*Checkpoint on the road*
*to Ramadi from Baghadad.*
*(Iraqi policemen are ex-members*
*of a local Suni militia in Ramadi).*
© Alvaro Ybarra Zavala / Agence VU /
Iraq, Ramadi, November 2006

<
*Police unit searching a house in their
own Karrada neighbourhood in Baghdad
with Bravo Company, second platoon of
the first cavalry division, from Fort Hood,
Texas, USA*
© Alvaro Ybarra Zavala / Agence VU /
Iraq, Baghdad, November 2006

>
*During a house search by Iraqi police
and American forces in the Karrada
neighbourhood of Baghdad, a policeman grabs a
little girl while her father is searched.*
© Alvaro Ybarra Zavala / Agence VU /
Iraq, Baghdad, November 2006

*Checkpoint on the road into Ramadi from Baghadad. (Iraqi policemen are ex-members of a local Suni militia in Ramadi).*
© Alvaro Ybarra Zavala / Agence VU /
Iraq, Ramadi, November 2006

*Iraqi police and US army working together in a police station in Ramadi*
© Alvaro Ybarra Zavala / Agence VU /
Iraq, Ramadi, November 2006

Major Megan Mc Lung, 43, from
Coupeville, is taking a picture of the
son of one of the most important tribal
families in Ramadi, the new ally of the
US army in Ramadi. The new strategy
of the US troops is to create an alliance
with the local Suni tribal groups to fight
against Al Qaeda.
One hour after this picture was taken,
Major Megan Mc Lung died in an ambush
set up with an IED (improvised explosive
device), in the territory of this tribal ally,
in Ramadi.

© Alvaro Ybarra Zavala / Agence VU /
Iraq, Ramadi, November 2006

[ Part 3: National Disasters and Resource Wars ]

# RESOURCE COMPETITION IN THE 21ST CENTURY

## Introduction

As in previous epochs, the world of the 21st century faces a variety of political, economic, social and ecological pressures that threaten stability in many areas of the globe and embody a potential for violent conflict. Many of these pressures are akin to those that have imperilled regional and international stability in the past: ethnic and religious antagonisms, the struggle for dominance between aspiring and established powers, territorial disputes, economic competition, and so on. It is likely, however, that additional sources of friction and instability will arise in this century, emerging from the distinctive features of the current era. Of these, one of the most significant will be global competition for access to scarce or vital supplies of critical resources: water, oil, natural gas, arable land and key industrial minerals.[1]

## Facing resource competition

The significant role played by resource competition in sparking conflict is evident in many of the recent outbreaks of armed violence, such as those in Aceh, Angola, Chad, Chechnya, Chiapas, Colombia, Congo, Congo-Brazzaville, Iraq, Liberia, Sierra Leone, Somalia and Sudan. Like all human conflicts, these upheavals have more than one cause; all, however, are driven to a con-siderable extent by competition over vital or valuable resources: diamonds in the case of Angola, Liberia, and Sierra Leone; oil in the case of Aceh, Chechnya, Colombia, Congo-Brazzaville, Iraq and Sudan; timber and minerals in the Congo; arable land in Chiapas and Zimbabwe; and so on.

It is true, of course, that competition over scarce and vital materials has long been a source of conflict. Indeed, many of the earliest recorded wars – notably those occurring in ancient Mesopotamia, Egypt and the Jordan River valley – were driven by struggles over the control of critical water sources and arable land. Similarly, many of the wars of the 16th through to the early 20th century were sparked by competition between the major European powers for control over resource-rich colonies in Africa, Asia, the East Indies and the New World – struggles that culminated in the First World War. The rise of Nazism and the US-Soviet rivalry of the Cold War era tended to overshadow (but not eliminate) the importance of resource competition in the mid-20th century, but the end of the Cold War brought this factor once again to the fore, as evinced by the conflicts identified above.

One can argue, then, that the re-emergence of resource conflict in the current pe-riod is nothing more than a return to the *status quo ante*: to the long stretch of time in which resource competition was a domi-nant force in world affairs. But it is the con-tention of this chapter that the situation we face today is not just more of the same: it is, instead, a qualitatively different situation, in which resource competition has assumed a more decisive and central role in armed conflict than has been the case in the past. To appreciate this, it is necessary to con-sider both the importance of key resources to contemporary human endeavours and the unique pressures on the world's resource base at the onset of the 21st century.

Some resources are, of course, essential for human survival. All humans need a cer-tain amount of food and water, plus access to shelter, clothes and, in northern climates, heat. At a very primitive level of existence, human societies can function on relatively modest quantities of these materials, so long as their numbers remain few. As societies grow more complex, they require more re-sources for their own use and to produce trade goods to exchange for the things they lack, including luxury items sought by their elites. Modern means of warfare also con-sumes vast quantities of resources, especially petroleum to fuel the tanks, planes, helicop-ters and ships that have come to dominate

*Michael T. Klare is the Five College Professor of Peace and World Security Studies (a joint appointment at Amherst College, Hampshire College, Mount Holyoke College, and Smith College and the University of Massachusetts at Amherst), a position he has held since 1985. Professor Klare has written widely on US defence policy, global resource politics and world security affairs.*

1 The author first articulated this argument in Michael T. Klare (2001). *Resource Wars: The new landscape of global conflict*. New York: Metropolitan Books.

the contemporary battlefield. The more developed, urbanised, and prosperous a society, the greater its requirement for all resources of all types.

The dilemma that confronts us at the dawn of the 21st century is the fact that human consumption of almost all types of materials is growing at an ever-increasing rate, imposing growing and possibly intolerable pressures on the world's existing stockpile of natural resources. Until now, humans have been able to mitigate these pressures by developing new sources of supply – for example, by digging deeper into the earth for metals and oil – and by inventing alternative materials. No doubt human ingenuity and the power of the market will continue to generate solutions of this sort. At some point, however, the demand for certain vital resources will simply overwhelm the available supply, producing widespread shortages and driving up the price of what remains; in some cases, moreover, it may prove impossible to develop viable substitutes. (There is no known substitute, for example, for fresh water). As resource stocks dwindle and prices rise, the divide between those with access to adequate supplies and those without will widen, straining the social fabric and in some cases leading to violent conflict.[2]

Even if disputes over the distribution of resources do not result in violence, the stresses engendered by resource pressures will affect human society in several ways. For many countries, the tempo of economic growth will decline as domestic supplies of vital materials contract and the price of imports rises. For those states still in possession of valuable resources, the impulse to extract and sell as much as possible while prices are high could lead to severe and costly environmental damage. And the entire planet will suffer from the by-products of unrestrained resource consumption – among them, increased greenhouse-gas emissions, the build-up of toxic wastes, fisheries collapse, biodiversity loss and severe soil degradation.

It is apparent, then, that resource competition will play an increasingly significant role in world affairs as time proceeds. Just how substantial its impact will be will depend, to a considerable extent, on the evolution of human consumption patterns. The greater the pressure we bring to bear on the world's existing resource base, the higher the risk of major social and environmental trauma. It is essential, then, to consider the implication of five key trends in contemporary human behaviour: globalisation, population growth, urbanisation and resource depletion.

## Globalisation

The growing internationalisation of finance, manufacturing and trade is having a powerful effect on many aspects of human life, including the demand for and consumption of basic resources. Globalisation increases the demand for resources in several ways. Most significant is the spread of industrialisation to more and more areas of the world, producing a dramatic increase in the demand for energy, minerals and other basic commodities.

The spurt in demand for energy is especially evident in the newly industrialised countries of Asia, which are expected to continue growing at a rapid pace in the coming decades. According to the US Department of Energy (DoE), energy consumption in developing Asia (including China, India, South Korea and Taiwan) will grow by an estimated 3.2 per cent per year during the first three decades of the 21st century, producing a net increase in demand of more than 215 per cent over this period. The growth in demand for petroleum will be particular pronounced, with total consumption in developing Asia jumping from 14 million barrels per day in 2001 to 30 million barrels in 2030.[3] A similar pattern is evident with respect to consumption of natural gas and coal – both of which are projected to experience a substantial increase in demand in this region in the coming decades. The rising consumption energy, along with other materials needed to sustain economic growth in the newly industrialised countries, will

---

2 For discussion, see Thomas Homer-Dixon, 'Environmental scarcities and violent conflict', *International Security*, vol. 19, no. 1 (summer 1994), p. 5-40.
3 US Department of Energy, Energy Information Administration (DoE/EIA), *International Energy Outlook 2007* (Washington, D.C.: DoE/EIA, 2007), tables A1 and A5, p. 83, 88.

significantly increase the pressures already being placed on the global resource base.

Globalisation is further adding to the pressure on resources by contributing to the emergence of a new middle class in many parts of the world. As families acquire additional income, they tend to acquire more goods and appliances, eat higher-end foods (such as beef, pork and chicken), and to move into larger living quarters – all of which generates a steep increase in the consumption of basic materials. Most significant in this regard is the growing international demand for private vehicles, a process known as the 'motorisation' of society. The motorisation rate (usually measured in number of vehicles per thousand population) is skyrocketing in many developing countries as economic growth accelerates and personal income rises. 'In many urban centres, such as Bangkok, Manila, Jakarta, Shanghai, and Mumbai, car ownership is among the first symbols of emerging prosperity'.[4] By 2020, the global population of motor vehicles will grow to an estimated 1.1 billion units – 425 million above the level for 1996.[5] Just to produce all of these vehicles will entail the consumption of vast amounts of iron, aluminium and other minerals; once in operation, they will consume millions of gallons of oil per day, year after year.

Finally, globalisation affects the global resource equation by extending the worldwide reach of multinational companies (MNCs), generating significant economic benefits for many poor and isolated countries but also providing incentives for cash-starved governments to permit the extraction of raw materials beyond sustainable levels or the destruction of forests to make way for export-oriented ranching and agriculture. The ever-expanding reach of MNCs also facilitates the entry of warlords, insurgent groups and corrupt military factions into resource-related enterprises. In many cases, these actors have used their ties to such firms to finance the illicit acquisition of arms and other military items. In Liberia, for example, the rebel force once led by Charles Taylor traded timber and mineral rights for the cash needed to purchase arms and ammunition; in Sierra Leone and Angola, the rebels traded diamonds for guns.[6] These transactions have increased the duration and severity of a number of internal conflicts, producing vast human suffering and placing a mammoth burden on the world's humanitarian aid organisations.

### Population growth

Rising population is further adding to the pressures on the world's resource base. According to the World Resources Institute (WRI), total world population will reach approximately 8 billion people in 2025, or two billion more than the number in 2000. These two billion additional people will need to be fed, housed, clothed and otherwise provided with basic necessities – producing a corresponding requirement for food, water, wood, metals, fibres and other materials. Although the earth can supply these materials, at least in the amounts needed for a relatively modest standard of living, it cannot continue to sustain an ever-growing human population and satisfy the rising expectations of the world's middle and upper classes. At some point, significant shortages will occur, intensifying the competition for access to remaining supplies and producing severe hardship for those without the means to pay the higher prices thereby incurred.

Of all basic necessities, the one that is most likely to be affected by population growth is fresh water. Humans must have access to a certain amount of water every day, for drinking, personal hygiene and food production. Fortunately, the world possesses sufficient renewable supplies of fresh water to satisfy current requirements and to sustain some increase in the human population. But the pressure on many key sources of supply is growing, suggesting that severe shortages will develop in some water-scarce areas over

---

4  Doe/EIA, *International Energy Outlook* 1999, p. 133.

5  Ibid., p. 117.

6  On Liberia, see William Reno, 'Reinvention of an African patrimonial state: Charles Taylor's Liberia', *Third World Quarterly*, vol. 16, no. 1 (1995), pp. 109-20.
   On Sierra Leone, see Douglas Farah, 'Diamonds are a rebel's best friend', *Washington Post*, 17 April 2000.

the next few decades. This is especially true in the Middle East and North Africa, where fresh water is already in short supply and population growth rates are among the highest in the world. For example, the number of people who will be relying on the Nile River, the Jordan River and the Tigris–Euphrates system for all or most of their water supply will grow from approximately 325 million in 2000 to 740 million in 2050 – without any appreciable increase in the net supply of water in the region. Unless the existing sources of supply are used more efficiently, or the desalination of seawater proves more affordable, competition over access to water will become more intense in these areas and could lead to war.[7]

Population growth is also likely to place growing pressure on the world's supply of arable land. This is especially true in the developing areas, where many people still rely on agriculture for their basic survival or for family income. As population expands, farmers tend to crop their existing plots more intensively or to bring marginal lands into cultivation, thereby depleting the soil of essential nutrients and risking the onset of erosion. The ever-growing demand for cropland also leads to the accelerated clearing of virgin forests, eradicating the habitats of many unique plant and animal species.

## Urbanisation

Closely related to population growth but adding distinctive pressures of its own is the growing concentration of humans in large towns and cities. Throughout the world – but especially in the developing world – people are moving from rural to urban areas, and from small to large cities. According to WRI, the world's urban population surged from 1.5 billion people in 1975 to 2.6 billion in 1995, and is expected to jump again to 5.1 billion by the year 2025.[8] In many cases, moreover, people are moving to very large cities: by 2015, an estimated 1.7 billion people (nearly one-fourth of the world's total population) will be living in cities of over 1 million people.[9] This has enormous implications for global resource stocks, as urban communities tend to consume more energy, water and building materials, and to generate far more waste products than rural areas. The outward expansion of cities and suburbs is also usurping areas previously used for agriculture, thereby adding to the pressure on the world's remaining supply of arable land.[10]

From a resource perspective, the impact of urbanisation cannot always be distinguished from that of globalisation and population growth. All of these phenomena are adding to the worldwide demand for water, energy and other basic commodities. But the concentration of more and more people in large cities does have a particularly pronounced impact on global water supplies, as urban areas require vast quantities of water for sanitation and personal use, and also because cities produce copious waste products that are often poured into rivers and lakes – thereby diminishing the amount of clean water available to other users. Providing adequate supplies of water to large urban centres and neighbouring areas, therefore, prove to be one of the most demanding tasks facing local and national leaders in the 21st century.

## Resource depletion

The three factors described above – globalisation, population growth and urbanisation – are combining to create a fourth: the irreversible depletion of some nonrenewable resources. While the earth contains large amounts of many of the most vital materials, these supplies are not unlimited and can be exhausted through excessive extraction or utilisation. And, in the case of some vital resources, humans have reached this point or are likely to do so in the early decades of the 21st century. For example, humans have harvested some species of fish (such as the once-prolific cod) so intensively that they have virtually disappeared from

7 For background and data, see Peter H. Gleick (ed.), Water in Crisis: *A guide to the world's fresh water resources* (New York and Oxford: Oxford University Press, 1993); Sandra Postel, *Last Oasis: Facing water scarcity* (New York: W.W. Norton, 1997).
8 World Resources Institute (WRI) (1996). *World Resources 1996-1997.* New York and Oxford: Oxford University Press, p. 150.
9 See World Resources Institute (1996), op. cit., p. 9.
10 For discussion, see World Resources Institute (1996) op. cit., pp. 57-80.

the world's oceans and are not expected to recover. Similarly, some valuable types of hardwood have largely disappeared from the world's forests.

Of the resources that are facing depletion in the decades ahead, none is more important to human life and society than natural petroleum. Oil supplies about two-fifth's of the world's basic energy supply – more than any other source – and provides about 97 per cent of the energy used for transportation. It is an essential feedstock for many valuable products, including plastics, fertilisers, pesticides, asphalt and certain pharmaceuticals. Petroleum is also a non-renewable resource: once we consume the existing world supply (produced by geological processes many eons ago), there will be none left for future generations. So far, humans have consumed nearly one-half of the earth's original petroleum inheritance (1.0 trillion barrels out of the 2.2 trillion barrels that are thought to have existed in 1860, when commercial extraction began), but we are extracting oil at such an intensive rate that much of the remaining supply could disappear in the next 30-40 years. The introduction of new technologies and fuel sources – such as ethanol, coal-to-liquids and hydrogen-powered fuel cells – could slow the rate of oil depletion in the years ahead, but at present we are continuing to increase our total consumption year after year.

Fresh water is a renewable resource and so will never disappear, but it can be viewed as a non-renewable substance because the earth's habitable areas only receive a certain amount of it each year in the form of precipitation. Of this amount – approximately 110,000 $km^3$ – a large share is lost to evaporation, discharge into the oceans and absorption by plants and the soil, leaving only 12,500 $km^3$ for use by humans. At present, we are using approximately half of this supply, and are increasing our utilisation at such a high rate (because of population growth, urbanisation, industrialisation and irrigated agriculture) that we will begin to approach full utilisation by the middle of the century – at which point billions of people can be expected to suffer from severe water shortages.

## Global climate change

All of these problems are bound to be exacerbated by the effects of global climate change. Although climate scientists cannot be certain about the future effects of climate change on any particular locale, they are increasingly convinced that large parts of the plant will suffer from persistent droughts, diminished rainfall, and the invasion of coastal areas by a rise in the sea level. This will, in turn, jeopardise water supplies and food production in many tropical and temperate areas of the world, forcing millions of people – perhaps tens or even hundreds of millions – to abandon their ancestral lands and migrate to other, less-severely affected areas. The result could well be an increase in conflict over access to fresh water and arable land.[11]

Climate change will also effect the planet's energy equation in various ways. An increase in severe storm activity, for example, will endanger oil and natural gas production in such key producing areas as the Gulf of Mexico, the Persian Gulf and the North Sea. Because so much of America's oil production, distribution and refining is concentrated in the Gulf of Mexico area, future storms like 2005's Hurricane Katrina will have a devastating effect on the nation's oil output. The reduced levels of rainfall expected from global warming in many parts of the world will also reduce the flow of water into many rivers that have been dammed for the purpose of generating electricity; with less rainfall, these hydro-electricity plants could sit idle for long stretches of time.

## The potential for conflict

Together, these factors are producing increasing pressure on the world's resource base – pressure that can only increase as we proceed deeper into the 21$^{st}$ century. The resulting shortages are likely to produce or magnify antagonisms between and within societies as governments and factions compete for access to or control over major

11  See the 2007 report of Working Group II of the Intergovernmental Panel on Climate Change (IPCC), *Climate Change 2007: Impacts, adaptation, and vulnerability*, available on-line at www.ipcc.ch.
     See also Michael T. Klare, 'Global warming battlefields: how climate change threatens security', *Current History*, November 2007, pp. 355-61.

sources of vital materials. In the extreme case, such antagonisms can lead to the outbreak of armed violence.

In general, violent struggle over resources can take one of four forms: first, territorial disputes between competing states over the ownership of contested border zones or offshore areas harbouring valuable supplies of critical materials; access conflicts arising from efforts by an outside power to gain or preserve access to a foreign source of critical materials; allocation disputes arising from disagreements over the distribution of supplies from a shared resource source (such as a multinational river system); and revenue disputes arising from struggles between contending factions for monopolisation of the rents or profits generated by control over a valuable resource source, such as an oil field or copper mine, or the illicit traffic in 'lootable' goods, like diamonds or old-growth timber. Most of the conflicts of the post-Cold War era embody aspects of one or another of these conflict types.

### Territorial disputes

Territorial disputes, arising from disputed claims to contested lands have been a source of friction and conflict throughout human history and still occasionally provoke armed violence – the 1998-2000 war between Eri-

trea and Ethiopia being a conspicuous example – but have become less frequent in recent years as states have slowly but surely resolved outstanding boundary disputes.

Conflicts over offshore territories, however, appear to be becoming more frequent as governments fight over contested maritime EEZs (exclusive economic zones) with valuable fisheries and undersea resources, such as oil and natural gas. For example, China has fought with Vietnam and the Philippines over ownership of the Spratly Islands in the South China Sea, a potential source of energy; likewise, Iran and Azerbaijan have clashed over disputed offshore territories in the Caspian Sea.[12] So long as states see a vital national interest in controlling such areas, disputes over contested EEZs will be a recurring factor in international affairs.

### Access conflicts

Access conflicts arise from efforts by a resource-importing nation to ensure its ability to procure needed resources from a distant source and to transport them safely to its own territory. Many of the colonial wars of past centuries were sparked by such efforts, as was Germany's 1941 invasion of the Soviet Union (intended in part to seize control of the oil fields of the Caucasus region) and Japan's subsequent invasion of the Dutch East

Indies (also sparked by the pursuit of oil). Great Britain's determined efforts to retain a presence in Iraq after the Second World War and to retain control of its refinery at Abadan in Iran after its nationalisation by Prime Minister Mohammed Mossadegh in 1951 also fit this pattern.

For the United States, ensuring access to the oil supplies of the Persian Gulf has long been a major military objective. This was made an explicit strategic objective in the so-called 'Carter Doctrine' of 23 January 1980. Asserting that '[a]n attempt by any outside force to gain control of the Persian Gulf region' – and impede the flow of oil – 'will be regarded as an assault on the vital interests of the United States of America', Carter warned that his country would repel such an assault 'by any means necessary, including military force'.[13] This basic principle was then cited by President George H. W. Bush as the justification for going to war against Iraq when it invaded Kuwait in 1990 (and, it was said, posed a threat to Saudi Arabia) as well as for the subsequent quarantine of Iraq by Presidents Bush senior and Clinton.[14] From a strategic perspective, it can also be viewed as the impetus for the 2003 US-led invasion of Iraq.[15]

---

12 For background on the disputes in the South China Sea and the Caspian, see Klare (2001), op. cit., pp. 81-137.
13 From the transcript of Carter's address in the *New York Times*, 24 January 1980. For background on this policy, see Michael A. Palmer (1992). *Guardians of the Gulf*. New York: Free Press, pp. 101-11.
14 For background on these developments, see Michael T. Klare (2004). *Blood and Oil: The dangers and consequences of America's growing dependence on imported petroleum.* New York: Metropolitan Books, pp. 49-53.
15 For background and discussion, see Klare (2004), op. cit., pp.94-105.

## Allocation disputes

Allocation disputes arise when neighbouring states jointly occupy or rely on a shared resource source – a river system, underground aquifer or oil field. In such cases, conflict can erupt from disagreements over the distribution of materials taken from the shared resource. For example, Iraq, Syria and Turkey have been fighting over the allocation of water from the Tigris–Euphrates river system, which originates in Turkey but travels for much of its length through Iraq and Syria. The Jordan and Nile Rivers have also provoked allocation disputes of this sort, both in ancient times and in the present. The extraction of petroleum from a shared underground reservoir can also be a source of conflict, as demonstrated by Iraq's dispute with Kuwait over the prolific Rumaila field.

## Revenue disputes

Revenue disputes usually occur in deeply divided or failing states where the national government has lost control of much or part of its territory and competing factions – warlords, ethnic or tribal militias, separatist groups and the like – are fighting for control over an oilfield, mine, diamond field or some other resource that represents a significant source of revenue. Such struggles can prove particularly intense, as the outcome will often determine which faction will secure the revenues they need to procure arms and ammunition, pay its soldiers and otherwise ensure its survival; these revenues can also become a major source of personal wealth for the key figures involved. Hence the tenacity with which groups like UNITA (National Union for the Total Independence of Angola) and the RUF (Revolutionary United Front) of Sierra Leone fought for control over their nation's diamond fields and resisted all attempts at a negotiated settlement.

Conflicts over the possession of valuable resources sites can also figure in efforts by ethnic groups living in areas adjacent to such assets to establish a separate enclave and the corresponding efforts by the dominant state to retain possession of the region – a pattern seen in Indonesia's struggle to retain control of oil-rich Aceh and copper-rich Irian Jaya (West Papua). This pattern is also a key factor in the sectarian fighting in Iraq, with the Kurds in the north and Shiites in the south seeking exclusive control over the abundant oil reserves in their respective regions and the Sunnis in the middle (which mostly lacks oil) struggling to prevent this from occurring.

Violence is not, of course, the only possible response to resource competition: as will be argued below, there are many other plausible responses to scarcity. But the risk of violence is always latent when states perceive the possession of certain materials as national security matter – that is, as something so vital to the survival and a well-being of a nation that it is prepared to employ military force when deemed necessary to ensure access to that resource, even if this means that other countries will be forced to make do with less. Indeed, the exigencies of national security have been cited by government officials to justify the onset or continuation of combat in many of the conflicts mentioned above.

For some countries, notably those with very limited supplies, water has been portrayed as a national security matter. For example, Israel has declared that access to the waters of the Jordan River is vital to its survival, just as Egypt as long viewed the Nile River in this fashion. For other nations, especially the United States and China, it is oil that has been viewed as a matter of national security – as exemplified, for example, in the 'Carter Doctrine' of 1980. So long as vital resources are viewed through the lens of national security, governments will often respond with military force when possession of or access to critical sources of supply is deemed to be at risk. Violence is also likely when internal factions in divided states believe that control over a valuable resource site is essential to their survival. Only by posing an alternative perspective – one that posits the advantages of cooperative, non-violent outcomes to such disputes – will it be possible to avert recurring conflict over scarce and valuable resources. Devising such outcomes and promoting their benefits is, therefore, an essential precondition for lasting peace and stability in the 21st century.

## Averting conflict over scarce resources

Assuming that the necessary political will can be generated, friction arising from resource scarcity can be channelled into constructive, non-violent outcomes through three types of initiatives: technological innovation; adjudication, mediation and cooperation; and conservation.

### Technological innovation

Technology can go a long way to reducing the threat of conflict over scarce resources by providing alternative materials and less resource-depleting processes. For example, improvements in desalination technology would make it possible to convert sea water into fresh water at an affordable cost (existing methods consume large amounts of energy and are very costly). Similarly, the consumption of petroleum in transportation could be substantially reduced through the widespread use of hybrid (gas/electric) vehicles and fuel efficient diesel engines. Eventually, the use of petroleum products for ground transportation could be eliminated altogether through the introduction of alternative fuels derived from biomass or the widespread utilisation of hydrogen-powered fuel cells. Improved methods of harnessing solar and wind energy would also reduce the need for petroleum. Technological innovation can help eliminate or minimise a wide variety of other resource constraints, greatly reducing the risk of conflict.

### Adjudication, mediation and cooperation

Given the risky and costly nature of war, states and other parties often conclude that it is preferable to resolve resource disputes through mediation and adjudication, or through schemes for the joint exploitation of a shared or contested resource site. Boundary disputes are particularly well suited to international mediation and adjudication: a number of such disagreements have been resolved in recent years when the parties involved agreed to seek a determination from the International Court of Justice (ICJ) in the Hague. For example, the ICJ has taken up the disputes between Bahrain and Qatar over Hawar Island, and between Cameroon and Nigeria over the Bakassi Peninsula. (Both areas are thought to sit above significant reserves of oil or natural gas). Mediation by the World Bank also led to the adoption of the Indus Waters Treaty in 1960, thus averting war between India and Pakistan over the distribution of water from the shared Indus River system. Joint development of contested resources is another approach that is gaining favour in some areas: China and the ASEAN countries have discussed the joint development of oil and gas in the South China Sea area, and Egypt and its upstream neighbours have met to consider plans for the joint development of the Nile River system.

### Conservation

Technology and adjudication can help address some resource problems, but ultimately the best way to avert significant shortages of scarce or limited supplies is to consume less of what we do possess of these materials. Indeed, conservation is often the least costly and most practical method of expanding the long-term supply of a resource. For example, the imposition of tougher fuel efficiency standards on American automobiles and trucks would reduce America's petroleum consumption by millions of barrels per day. Likewise, the widespread use of drip irrigation would greatly reduce the wastage of water through existing irrigation techniques. The systemic recycling of materials also helps to reduce the depletion of scarce resources.

These and other such techniques can be employed to slow the consumption of vital resources and to channel conflict into productive, non-violent outcomes. Many scientists, economists, environmentalists and government leaders perceive the urgent need for such efforts, and have advocated them in every available setting. As a result, progress is being made in many critical areas. But strong resistance to such efforts has been mounted by some companies that benefit from existing modes of consumption and from politicians who view vital resources from a traditional national security perspective, with its zero-sum, all-for-us-and-nothing-for-them outlook. For example, the major US auto companies have fought against any increase in minimum fuel efficiency standards, and some conservatives in the United States have advocated efforts to constrain China's access to the petroleum supplies of the Persian Gulf. Many consumers, especially in the wealthier countries, are also reluctant to reduce their consumption of water, petroleum, rare timber (like teak and mahogany) and other scarce or limited materials.

It is evident, therefore, that efforts to reduce the depletion of vital resources and to avert conflict over critical sources of supply will require a substantial change in attitude toward the utilisation of these precious materials. Only by recognising a shared human obligation to serve as stewards of the earth's precious bounty and to work in concert to preserve vital materials for future generations will we be able to take the necessary steps to avert severe shortages and the very real risk of rising bloodshed over diminishing resources.

# Illegal logging and the illegal trade in timber and wood products—Fuelling conflict

## Introduction

The World Bank estimates that up to US $10 billion (€6.8 billion) of the global market in timber is lost through stolen wood. Of the 1.2 billion people living in extreme poverty over 90 per cent depend on the forests for their livelihoods.[1] Within the EU, as a major consuming region of illegally sourced timber and wood products, it is estimated that we are responsible for up to €3 billion of lost revenue.[2] This crime costs developing countries €10.7 a year through the theft of public assets and non-payment of taxes.[3]

Illegal logging funds armed conflicts and helps to fuel violence against those dependent on the forest. It creates conflict within communities and is a tool by which those who seek power obtain great wealth. Undermining the rule of law, corruption and the ruin of any possible sustainable development are also symptoms of illegal logging.

## Indonesia: a case study

Illegal logging in Indonesia has been called the world's largest environmental crime. Ten per cent of the world's tropical forests are found in Indonesia, which are disappearing at an unprecedented rate. Already around 70 per cent of the country's original 'frontier' forest has been lost, leaving around only 100 million hectares of forest cover. The rate of deforestation is accelerating at an alarming pace – in the late 1980s the annual loss was around one million hectares, but by 2002 it had doubled to over two million hectares every year.

In 1999 the Environmental Investigation Agency (EIA) and Telapak went to investigate illegal logging in a national park called Tanjung Putting in Central Kalimantan on the island of Borneo. What we found was shocking. A massive commercially viable illegal trade in timber was happening right under the noses of the Indonesian Government and law enforcement officials. This forest crime was so big that it took 11 separate EIA–Telapak undercover investigations to actually find out what, or rather who, was behind this violent and extremely profitable business.[4]

Under the Suharto dictatorship, the President and his cronies presided over a centralised system of natural resource kleptomania. After Suharto, a new breed of timber bosses started to operate – this time from a regional power base. They tend to dispense with the masquerade of owning legitimate forest concessions, preferring to operate totally outside the law and to enlist the politicians, police and military through pay-offs. In the last seven years these bosses have orchestrated a rapid acceleration in illegal logging, which afflicts virtually every protected forest left in Indonesia.

What we found we made public. Using undercover cameras we showed visual evidence of the major culprits behind this crime. We provided dossiers to the police, the Ministry for Forests and to the Governor of the Province. At the same time the international community was alerted. Through a donor forum called the Consultative Group on Indonesia (CGI) we took the issue of Tanjung Putting to their annual meeting. We talked to the EU, and our own government in the UK. The media showed considerable interest, both national and international. Indonesian journalists were also involved in their own investigations. We made Tanjung Puting a test case for the Indonesian Government, if they couldn't address this then how on earth could they cope with the rest of this enormous archipelago where it was clear that illegal logging was rampant?

*Faith Doherty was born in Malaysia and has worked in the South-East Asian region and Europe on environmental and human rights issues for the past 20 years. Doherty is currently working with the Environmental Investigation Agency (EIA) and is a senior campaigner working for the organisation's Forests For Life Campaign. She has worked to combat illegal logging and the illegal trade in timber with EIA since 2000.*

*The Environmental Investigation Agency (EIA) and Telapak have been at the forefront of the fight against illegal logging and the subsequent illegal trade in timber for over seven years. In that time they have conducted numerous undercover investigations that have resulted in the exposure of organised criminal syndicates. From the illegal logging gangs usually run by wealthy 'untouchables' from producer countries, to the middle men that supply the trade of timber, the crisis that faces the forests and the people who are dependent upon them from these actors still exists.*

*www.eia-international.org*

1 www.worldbank.org: Forests and Forestry.
2 *Failing the Forests, Europe's illegal timber trade.* Report. 102 pp. 6 bis 7 bis 8 WWF
3 The World Bank, 'Strengthening forest law enforcement and governance: addressing a systematic constraint to sustainable development', August 2006.
4 See *The Final Cut.* EIA/Telapak. www.eia-international.org

Since that time seven years ago Indonesia has come a long way. We have witnessed a flowering of civil society groups campaigning on a host of issues such as corruption, labour rights, press freedom, land rights and the environment. The strengthening of civil society has been the key in advancing the fight against corruption, exposure of abuse and violence in the forest and part of the solution to conflict within this environment. Such was the pressure and public exposure of the role Indonesia was playing in the global trade of illegally sourced timber and wood products that in 2001 it hosted a ministerial conference in Bali that resulted in a declaration to combat this crime. In essence what we had was an acknowledgement from some of the biggest producer countries that illegal logging existed and at the core of this was corruption.

Following the Bali conference the EU responded. What is now known as the Forest Law Enforcement Governance and Trade (FLEGT), an action plan has been agreed to by Member States.[5] The FLEGT Action Plan focuses on improving governance in timber-producing countries, and establishing systems to exclude illegally sourced timber into the European market. Further it allows for timber producing countries to enter into a bilateral agreement with the EU called a Voluntary Partnership Agreement (VPA). Within the VPAs will be commitments followed by actions to halt the trade in illegal timber.

Over the past three years Indonesian civil society has taken the lead on this issue. They have led a process within Indonesia in obtaining common positions with regard to the many issues from independent monitoring, money laundering, indigenous rights and access to land. They have together with the government and industry worked toward a definition of legality. This definition was concluded this year and is now in process through the Ministry of Forestry. Indonesia is the first country to look at the myriad of laws and recognise that reform was needed in this sector and has gone ahead together with stakeholders to set the standard for other countries negotiating VPAs. Civil society has been so much in the forefront that they are part of the negotiating team for Indonesia with the EU.

## Legislation

But it's not enough. For years the international trade in timber has literally been able to get away with profiting from crimes committed in producer countries. The responsibility from consuming nations had to be addressed. But how?

We believe that the EU must bring into effect laws that prohibit the sale of illegally sourced timber and wood products from entering our markets. Much of the wood products and sawn timber has been laundered through a third country. Some of that timber has come from conflict areas and traded il-

legally through the same routes that is used by non-conflict timber. For example, logs illegally sourced in Indonesia and then smuggled out of the country to another country are then manufactured into sawn timber or furniture, which can be sent to a third country, which then ends up in our markets in Europe as origin the third country not Indonesia. Circumvention is not being addressed through the FLEGT Action Plan.

For three years ICS travelled to various Member States and the European Commission to lobby for new laws. They wanted additional measures that would tackle the consumption, the demand, and drive for timber and wood products. With pressure from other civil society and the international NGO community a process is now in place to look at what laws could be brought to bear that would stop illegally sourced timber and wood products from entering the European markets.

There are currently four options on the table to be considered as new laws:

- expanded coverage of the bilateral approach through VPAs;
- private sector measures like codes of conduct, certification schemes, etc;
- an import ban on illegally harvested timber;
- legislation prohibiting the placing on the EU market illegally harvested timber or

5 Council Regulation (EC), No. 2173/2005, December 2005

products derived from such timber. These included two variants: one making it an offence to trade or process timber and timber products harvested in breach of the laws of the country of origin, and one that would require that only legally harvested timber and timber products be placed on the market: proof of legality.

To our surprise one of the most active leaders on legislation is the United States, which is the largest consumer of wood products. Recently The House Committee on Natural Resources unanimously passed the bipartisan Legal Timber Protection Act.[6] This act will allow for enforcement from the United States against illegally sourced timber and wood products within its own borders, something the EU has yet to agree to. Given the EU has led on this issue for the past five years it is disappointing that following warning after warning it has still to actually put in place laws that will address our role in supporting the trade in stolen goods.

If you look at conflict timber from a country such as Burma/Myanmar the only thing in place to address this is the sanctions imposed against the country from the United States under the Freedom and Democracy Act. Within that, these sanctions only deal with direct trade from Burma/Myanmar to the United States. In the case of the EU, proposed sanctions will only do the same thing, and it won't work. Unless the circumvention of timber and wood products is addressed direct trade sanctions do not do anything other than encourage timber traders to continue with business as usual. With a world shortage of raw materials countries that are vulnerable where the barrel of a gun decides who gets what, logs, sawn timber and wood products will continue to be a highly valued commodity as long as its consumed by markets such as the EU and United States without any penalty.

6 (LTPA), H.R. 1497.

# FIGHTING EXPLOITATION OF NATURAL RESOURCES AND INTERNATIONAL TRADE SYSTEMS
## INTERVIEW WITH PATRICK ALLEY

*Why did you create Global Witness?*

Global Witness is a British-based NGO, which I founded in 1992 together with two colleagues, Simon Taylor and Charmian Gooch. At the time, we were working for an environmental agency that looked at issues such as the ivory trade. We created Global Witness because we realised there was a whole area not being addressed: the crossover between the exploitation of natural resources and conflict and corruption.

This became clear in 1992 when the UN was brokering elections in Cambodia. At the time, it was the most expensive intervention in the UN's history. According to news reports, the Khmer Rouge rebels had boycotted the elections and were trading timber with the Thais.

The rainforest was being cut down and was obviously providing some kind of revenue to the Khmer Rouge, which they were using to fight the war. We saw that no one was looking at this link. We also thought, with the campaigning knowledge that we had, that if we closed the Thai-Cambodia border to that trade, we would cut funding to the Khmer Rouge and stop the war. Perhaps that sounds simplistic and naïve, but it worked.

*What progress has been made in tackling the illegal timber trade since then? Can you explain your role as an independent monitor?*

One of the problems with industrial logging around the world is that tropical forests are very often regarded by economists as a resource that can kick-start an economy in a post-conflict or economically vulnerable country. We have seen that attitude in many countries from Cambodia to Cameroon. In reality, illegal logging, incredible levels of corruption, and the over-cutting of trees mean the forests do not deliver the durable benefits that the economists expect. On the contrary, poverty is usually exacerbated.

In Cambodia, after our work on the Khmer Rouge issue, we investigated the government's role in the allocation of forests to private logging companies. It was very corrupt and in one particular year, a minimum of US $187 million of timber was smuggled out of the country and only US $12 million made it into the exchequer.

Eventually the international community called on the Cambodian government to introduce independent oversight of the trade and Global Witness was appointed to do that. Our role was not law enforcement but monitoring of law enforcement.

Our work was effective in terms of the reduction in illegal activities but the vested interests went right to the top level. Exposing that kind of information put us in an uncomfortable position and in Cambodia our contract was terminated, while in Cameroon, a similar contract expired and could not be renewed with terms that would have maintained our independence.

*What needs to be done at the 'demand' end of the supply chain?*

Currently, it is not illegal anywhere in the world to import illegally sourced timber. If illegally cut timber from Cameroon is exported, it is effectively laundered as soon as it reaches international waters.

The US is on the verge of passing into law the Legal Timber Protection Act and in the EU, NGOs have lobbied for a law to prohibit importing illegally sourced timber. However, under the FLEGT (Forest Law Enforcement, Government and Trade) process, this has morphed into bilateral licensing agreements between EU states and producing countries. These kinds of voluntary partnership agreements between two countries are much easier to bypass. Smuggled timber could still originate from other countries or be sold to those who have not signed the agreement.

We hope that there will eventually be an EU regulation on this. It is crazy to allow a trade in stolen goods. It is not allowed for cars so why should it be allowed for timber?

*How did Global Witness pick up the issue of conflict diamonds? Why did the campaign gain such a high profile and how did it lead to the Kimberley Process?*

The civil war in Angola, which took place throughout the 1990s, was killing hundreds of thousands of people. On the UNITA rebel side, the conflict was funded primarily by

*Patrick Alley is a co-founder and director of Global Witness, an NGO that tackles the links between natural resources, conflict, and corruption. The first major campaign by Patrick and his colleagues brought an end to the illegal trade in timber that was generating income for the Khmer Rouge rebels in Cambodia. However, Global Witness is perhaps best known for its work on conflict diamonds, for which it was co-nominated for the Nobel Peace Prize in 2003.*

diamonds and on the government side, primarily by oil. The De Beers cartel was buying 80 per cent of the world's rough diamonds at that time. They freely admitted in their annual reports that they were buying from Angola, yet the diamond fields were under the control of UNITA. This was clearly a problem!

Angola was not the only place with this kind of situation but, in campaign terms, you have to deliver a message that people can read and understand. In 1998, we produced a report, 'Rough Trade', which included extracts from the De Beers report. We concluded that there was an unacceptable open trade in diamonds and noted there was no policy initiative to deal with this.

Our report coincided with the war breaking out once again in Angola. Consequently, journalists covering the war used our report and we were inundated with requests from the media. You usually have to work hard for press coverage, but in this case, it came easily. It hit the right vein in both public and political consciousness.

The term 'conflict diamonds', hitherto unknown, was suddenly on everybody's lips. To give credit, the governments in Britain and the US were already sympathetic to the issue and we had meetings with them and other governments, which led to the creation of the Kimberley Process.

*How have consumers made an impact? Was the 2006 film 'Blood Diamond' helpful?*

I could not say how many consumers we reached in our awareness-raising work, but the industry did get the message fast. In the early days of the campaign, De Beers was terrified that we were planning an anti-fur type approach, i.e. to promote a boycott of diamonds. They were spending around US $200 million a year in advertising and they knew that we could wreck that with just tens of thousands of dollars. But that was never the case. We are not against the diamond trade, only against the trade in conflict diamonds.

'Blood Diamond' was amazingly helpful. Ivory Coast is now the only country where there are still technically any conflict diamonds, but the potential for the conflict diamond trade to continue or return is still there. When the film came out, the industry was trying to tell the world that the problem was solved, which was not the case. In a way that nothing else could, the film was able to bring it up in a way that the public could understand.

Establishing the Kimberley Process was a great success but questions have been raised as to how it can be effectively monitored. It also does not cover other issues such as labour conditions during the production process.

Monitoring is a difficult question. You need verification of the trade chain in the producing countries, and this was one of the challenges from the beginning. That is what certification is all about.

The latest Kimberley Process meeting, held in Brussels in November 2007, started to look at trading centres, not just production. Momentum is growing. That is the kind of progress we have to make and NGOs are pushing for it to happen quicker.

Production conditions are not really an issue for the Kimberley Process, which was never meant to be a panacea for all the ills of the diamond trade. Of course, labour conditions in the extraction process are a concern. Other actions, such as the Diamond Development Initiative, are looking at that. There are also environmental issues: alluvial diamond mining is very destructive, for example. Global Witness has not looked at these issues, not because we do not think they are important, but because we have our hands full with the Kimberley Process.

*Would it be appropriate to have a Kimberley Process equivalent for other gemstones or natural resources?*

The Kimberley Process was the first time natural resources had gained prominence in that way. It captured the public and political imagination because diamonds are sexy. Therefore, the agreement was made.

In hindsight, there are several things wrong with it. For example, the definition of conflict diamonds is flawed under the Kimberley Process: it talks about diamonds from 'rebel-held areas'. That would not apply to conflict diamonds traded by even the most brutal dictator in the world.

There has been a knee-jerk reaction from many policy-makers who would be in favour of replicating the Kimberley Process success story for other resources. There simply would not be the appetite for that. The Kimberley Process resulted in a lot of meetings around the world involving hundreds of people, which would not happen for every resource.

We need to look at what worked for the Kimberley Process and find something that is a catchall for all those resources. Let's not get distracted by just one. We also need a much better understanding of what a conflict resource is. Until we have that, there will never be a coherent response to it.

*What impact can transparency initiatives such as 'Publish What You Pay' make? Have governments been willing to cooperate?*

This also grew out of our work in Angola. As I said previously, the war was funded on the government side by oil and the rebel side by diamonds. We thought we could not just address one side of the problem because it would make it a partisan issue.

Shortly after we produced our first work on diamonds, we came out with a report on oil. A country has a sovereign right to sell its oil. The question was how the government was spending the revenues. Angola was amazingly opaque on this issue. Our best estimates, and those of the IMF, were that around a quarter of the US $4 billion oil revenues was going missing.

While the war effort was being funded, health and education systems were at a standstill. People need to know what their governments are earning to be able to call them to account. Nobody could question the Angolan government because nobody knew what the revenues were. Since they refused to publish what they received, we asked the oil companies to publish what they pay.

That is the campaign we launched in 1999. We became a co-founder of the Publish What You Pay coalition. It was essentially about revenue transparency. That has grown into a very effective coalition of over 300 NGOs. It has also led to the creation of the Extractive Industries Transparency Initiative (EITI), which is the major mechanism to deal with revenue transparency.

*How does China's demand for resources affect the situation in Africa?*

I have an African friend who says that people do not care who buys the resources; what they want is the revenue to go to the right places. Having said that, transparency initiatives such as EITI and Publish What You Pay are put at risk because China's financial support has no political strings attached. Any attempt at exerting pressure on African countries – regarding corruption, transparency, or human rights – is undermined if they can get what they want from China.

In countries where too much GDP is based on primary commodity exports, it can lead directly to what is known as the 'resource curse'. Governments become less accountable to their people and it breeds instability. In the longer term, it is neither sustainable for those countries, nor for China.

To address the issue, we need to look at how resources are accessed. Revenue transparency is critical, as is how those revenues are used. It is very important the international community get together to make that happen. It is not something that can be achieved overnight but that is the direction we need to take.

We should not just single out China. Other countries like Brazil, Russia, and India are also part of the equation. The US has the same attitude with oil-rich states like Equatorial Guinea. The Western consuming powers blazed a trail in unethical acquisition of resources that others have followed.

*How can communities and national governments negotiate good deals with strong, multinational companies that often have an annual turnover that dwarfs the country's GDP?*

The international community needs to help nations that are economically vulnerable or in a post-conflict situation. If I use the latter case as an example, there can be an interim period of two-to-four years between a peace deal being signed and a democratically elected government being installed. In these cases, a caretaker government is often put in place with the support of the international community.

In Liberia, for example, a transitional government signed a 25-year iron ore deal worth only US $900 million with Mittal Steel. Under the terms of the contract, the company controlled every stage of the revenue flow because neither the price nor the method of setting the price was fixed. It even effectively created a state within a state. An unelected transitional government, which at the time only had six months left before elections, should not have had the right to sign such a deal. Fortunately, in this case, when the new government was elected it had a lot of public and political support and a few philanthropists, such as George Soros, came in and helped President Johnson-Sirleaf negotiate a better deal.

The international community must find a cohesive position on post-conflict development. Natural resources must be a major part of any post-conflict process because they are probably a country's best route to economic prosperity.

It is not just about post-conflict situations. Even if the new Liberian government had negotiated the first deal, they would not have had access to the same level of corporate legal advice as Mittal Steel. Countries are terrified of frightening off investors and sometimes do not realise the strong position they are in. They need top legal help to negotiate good deals and to get wise in a cut-throat corporate world.

*Your role involves not only partnership with NGOs, but also with governments and international organisations. What difficulties arise?*

We know that to change policy you have to deal with the policy-makers. We have always tried to be an NGO that is hard-hitting and does not pull its punches, but also one that has the credibility to talk with people at the conference table. That relies on not only being critical but also having a potential solution and being prepared to work towards it.

Vested interests are a difficulty: for example, when we were trying to get sanctions on Liberian timber through the UN, the two countries that initially objected were France and China who also happened to be the biggest buyers of Liberian timber. When Charles Taylor was causing the situation in the Ivory Coast to degenerate, France changed its view because its interests suddenly changed.

Bureaucracy is a major issue, whether dealing with the UN or the EU. And the size of the EU is a difficulty. The timber issue passed through several directorates and the result was a watered down process that was much longer than necessary. The simple thing would have been to pass a law.

The donor community, including the World Bank, condemn corruption in many countries as a major barrier to development. Very often aid provision has been supposedly conditional on eradicating corruption. But when push comes to shove, they do not do anything about it. Corrupt dictators can freely come to our shores to do their shopping and conditions that are imposed on aid are not enforced. This does not only fail to solve the problem, it exacerbates it.

# WATEX: A NEW APPROACH TO PREVENTING WATER BASED CONFLICTS

## Introduction

In March 2004, the UN Office for the Coordination of Humanitarian Affairs (UNOCHA) faced a severe challenge in providing assistance to 110,000 refugees from Sudan in Chad, which grew to 200,000 a few months later.

The United Nations High Commissioner for Refugees (UNHCR) requested urgently the services of Radar Technologies France (RTF) to use the WATEX© process in order to detect and map the water potential of Eastern Ouaddaï in Chad to support existing camps, identify new buried aquifers and support future refugee camps throughout the region and avoid costly water trucking.

In just four months, RTF recorded amazing results applying the WATEX©-based methodology[1] to map the water potential of a region nearly 100,000 km² in size. The humanitarian dimension of the project demanded timely and efficient identification of sustainable aquifers producing sufficient volumes of clean water to support existing and future refugee operations.

This RTF operation in 2004-2005 in eastern Chad led in the following months[2] to the identification of four major campsites able to host some 200,000 new refugees. It also led to the transfer of the first group of 15,000 refugees to the newly identified Gaga Campsite, 65 km east of Abéché and to the increase of drilling success rate from 33 per cent before WATEX© to 89 per cent using the WATEX© methodology.

In December 2005, the US State Department invited me to apply the WATEX© process throughout Darfur in Sudan, over an area of 135,000 km², for 2.5 million internally displaced persons (IDPs), under the supervision of Dr Saud Amer from the US Geological Survey (USGS).[3]

This project, accomplished in six months, revealed that there is enough groundwater in Darfur for several million people – enough to sustain the peace process and the reconstruction through agricultural development.[4] These results were forwarded at the request of the US Agency for International Development (USAID) to 40 NGOs in October 2006 in Khartoum. The *Darfur Drilling Handbook*,[5] based on WATEX© results, was distributed to all the organisations attending the training seminar supported by USAID and UNESCO (Chair in Water Resources, Sudan).

Since October 2006, the NGOs led by UNICEF have achieved a success rate of 100 per cent in drilling 300 wells, whenever applying the drilling handbook recommendations on identified sites:

- at the camps of North Darfur near El Fasher: Abu Shouk, Shagra, Mellit;
- around the camps of South Darfur near Nyala and Kas; and
- around the camps of West Darfur: El Geneina, Riyad, Ardamata, Murnei, Zalingei, Dereisa, Nyertete and Foto Burunga.

## How does WATEX© work?

This paper describes how the geospatial WATEX© process was utilised by RTF to assess the water potential of Eastern Chad and Darfur in Sudan without requiring time-consuming field surveys on ground calibrations for the remote sensing portion of the project. Field surveys in Sudan were completed with ground penetrating radar equipment.

As demonstrated in Chad with the case study of Gaga Camp, the project enabled the UNHCR to, in a very short time, identify new campsites in eastern Chad capable of

*Dr Alain Gachet is the CEO of Radar Technologies, France. As a radar expert he has advised a number of international bodies, such as UNESCO, the UN, UNICEF and the OECD. He spent 20 years in the oil industry working as a Senior Explorationist and Economist negociator in Russia, Kazakhstan, the Middle East and Africa. Currently he is involved in remote sensing interpretation and the exploration of natural resources (groundwater, base metals, minerals and hydrocarbons) and for the monitoring surveillance and environment.*

1 Dr Alain Gachet (July 2004). *Chad–Phase I–Water Exploration in Eastern Ouaddaï–Ground Survey*. Edited by Geneva. Radar Technologies France: UNHCR.
2 Dr Alain Gachet (2005). *Tchad–Phase II–Synthèse des études hydro géologiques par télédetection radar du Ouaddaï Oriental*. Edited by Geneva. Radar Technologies France: UNHCR, pp. 52-4, 83.
3 Dr Saud Amer PhD, 'Water Resources and Remote Sensing Specialist', International Water Resources Branch, USGS, 12201 Sunrise Valley Drive, MS 420, Reston, VA, 20192, USA.
4 Dr Alain Gachet (2006). *Water exploration in Darfur–Sudan* Edited for USGS, UCSB and USAID, 30 May 2006 (89 pp.).
5 Dr Alain Gachet (2006). *Darfur Drilling Handbook in Sudan* Edited for USGS, UCSB and USAID, 30 May 2006 (123 pp.).

supporting tens of thousands of Sudanese refugees.

In Sudan, the study has, in six months, revealed vast stretches of land in central Darfur hosting enough groundwater reserves to sustain 33 million people year round with the Sphere Humanitarian Charter Standards of 15 litres of water per day.

The study has also identified 27 micro-dam sites suitable for aquifers sustainability and agriculture. These aquifers are renewable and easily accessible within a depth ranging from sub-surface to 50 m in unconsolidated sediments, which are easy to drill.

### Challenge and opportunity

The response agencies needed to maintain operations over a region of 300,000 $km^2$. Not only was this region undeveloped and largely inaccessible, it was also within a zone of conflict that affected the security of both refugees and humanitarian relief workers. Facing a refugee population that quickly approached 200,000 in Chad and 2.5 million IDPs in Sudan, the authorities needed to discover, develop and deliver massive water reserves able to sustain water distribution for several years without depleting the natural resources of local communities.

This challenge was further complicated by the extreme urgency imposed by the escalation of the refugee crisis, the limited resources with which to assess hydrological potential and the poor understanding of re-gional geological phenomena. Basic analysis confirmed that the 'Basement Complex' of Darfur degrades groundwater storage potential, except within alluvial sediments, which are unfortunately prone to rapid evapotranspiration if not thick enough. Long-term programs to deliver water by tankers to the refugee camps were not sustainable because of long distances and unreliable tracks, lack of security and deficient bridge infrastructure.

Recognising the severity of these challenges and the inadequacy of utilising traditional water exploration drilling methods and in order to meet the above challenges, UNHCR and USAID decided to employ RTF's WATEX© proprietary remote sensing technology. It guided water drilling operations and optimised the location of refugee camps in minimum time.

It was developed by RTF to support water exploration in arid and semi-arid areas and exploits the increasing data stream from civilian geospatial technologies to analyse large, heterogeneous climatic and geologic regions for water potential.

Several recent trends have made the use of such technology possible:

1. The availability of synthetic aperture radar (SAR) earth observation satellite imagery, which provides highly sensitive geological and hydrological intelligence not discernable through optical imagery.

2. The 2003 release of the Shuttle Radar Topographic Mission (SRTM) global terrain model, which provides slope and elevation data of unprecedented quality compared with other topographic information of the region.

3. The relaxing of the selective availability of global positioning system (GPS) signals, enabling civilian access to precise location information almost anywhere on the surface of the earth.

4. The widely appreciated 'digital revolution', which is now affordable even to small firms without access to high-powered computing, user-friendly analysis software and rich data archives accessible via the internet.

### The WATEX© process

UNHCR, together with USAID, recognised an opportunity to apply geospatial technologies in responding to the Darfur crisis, creating an excellent example of the positive role the private sector can play in humanitarian assistance and sustainable development.

The WATEX© process is a groundwater exploration package used to locate renewable groundwater reserves in arid and semi-arid environments. This process dramatically improves the ability of humanitarian and development organisations to identify areas suitable for (temporary and permanent) settlement, agriculture and sustainable development.

The process is economical, rapid and highly effective for water and soils potential mapping even over heterogeneous areas several hundred thousand square kilometres in size.

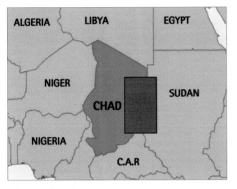

*Figure 1: Location diagrams*

## Process

The radar and optic data acquired by satellite are processed to achieve the project's overarching goal – to detect large renewable water reserves capable of supporting refugee settlements of 20,000 per camp, for up to 200,000 Sudanese refugees, in accordance with the UNHCR's target provision rate of 15 litres per day per person. This automatically precluded water exploration of small or non-renewable reserves, and limited analysis to areas of sizeable, renewable water potential.

## General mapping

After interpreting Landsat 7 to determine lithology, weathering processes, vegetation cover, agriculture, settlements, roads/tracks, the SRTM model was used to delineate watersheds, slopes and river profiles, and to estimate energy level of transportation along *wadi* (i.e. riverbed) courses.

Radar images were processed using WATEX© to map fractures, uplifts and subsidence, which control river direction and affect groundwater circulation, aquifer thickness and storage by reservoir accretion or erosion.

WATEX© was also applied to enhance the soil volumetric moisture effects of near-surface stratum. The penetration and soil moisture sensitivity of SAR imagery has been

well established,[6] and known to be optimal in fine, dry sand with minimum volumetric water content. However, even under ideal conditions, the penetration of microwave signals is restricted to near-surface moisture detection, and therefore RTF focused upon the assessment of alluvial water potential along existing wadis and nearby fractures and faults. (Deeper reservoirs can still be detectable if capillary moisture flow or saturated zone reaches near-surface strata).

## Large-scale groundwater reserve assessment

After the region of interest had been sufficiently mapped, RTF began an assessment of the following five key hydrologic parameters in order to establish an overall rank of each 'water potential anomaly':

1. *Dimension of the radar anomaly,* which is an indicator of the potential of a buried aquifer within a *wadi*. As previously indicated, an aquifer with a renewable capability to produce 90,000 m³ per year is able to support a camp of 20,000 refugees. Assuming an average rock porosity of 10 per cent, this implies the need to find a buried aquifer with an overall production of nearly 1 million m³ per year. This is equivalent to a *wadi* reservoir of about 2 km long and 60 m wide, assuming a reservoir thickness of 7.5 m at an average depth of 10-15 m. Accordingly, only radar anomalies

6 T. Ulaby, R. K. Moore and A. K. Fung, *Microwave Remote Sensing: Active and passive.*
Dedham, MA: Artech House, 1986, vol. 3, *From Theory to Applications.*

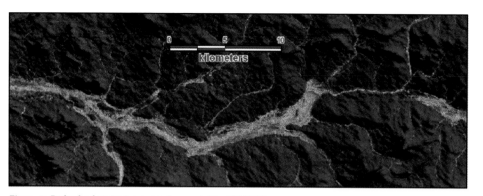

*Figure 2: Radar backscattering anomaly revealed by WATEX©,*
*indicating existence of buried aquifer within the wadi course (© RTF 2004)*

covering a minimum surface of 12 hectares (2 km x 60 m) were considered by RTF in order to meet the above project goal. At this stage, it is not possible to know if the anomaly is due to a buried aquifer or surface moisture linked to clay or silt deposits. More analysis of the short-listed anomalies is required.

2. *Amount of upstream watershed drainage,* since each potentially suitable target must also be fed by an upstream watershed capable of supplying at least 1 million m³ per year of water to the reservoir. (The watershed surface area and average annual rainfall were used by RTF to estimate total yearly catchment, which was then corrected for estimated losses due to evaporation, erratic run-off, etc.)

3. *Quality of aquifer gravels,* since the origin and nature of the gravels which supply the aquifer determine its ability to reliably absorb and store sufficient water volumes. WATEX© discriminates between 'reservoir feeders' and 'reservoir poisoners'. For example, basaltic rock types create excessive silt and reduce reservoir porosity and permeability. Alternatively, 'reservoir feeders' such as quartzite and sandstone can produce high-quality gravels.

4. *Major fault,* since the ideal scenario is an old, well-framed river bed with a reliable and unchanging watercourse, downstream from a high-quality reservoir feeder. A reliable, linear river system controlled by graben-like structures is more likely to contain thick, multi-layered reservoirs, particularly if it sits downstream from a source of gravel or water-storing material.

5. *Slope of upstream wadi* course, since the optimum riverbed slope needs to be be-

tween 0.1 and 0.4 per cent, in order to ensure sufficient vertical recharge of reservoirs within wadi courses. Too shallow a slope, and the reservoir can be prone to excessive silt accumulation, compromising its ability to store sufficient water reserves. Too steep a slope, and the reservoir can be prone to the erosion of the gravel bed that must recharge during the rainy season.

## Overall suitability assessment

The completion of steps 1-5 allows RTF to identify areas of high water potential. In order for these areas to be suitable for refugee inhabitation, RTF also considered the implications of refugee resettlement near areas of existing cattle ranching, crop farming, indigenous settlement, etc. In addition to UNHCR-mandated restrictions in Chad on resettlement within 50 km of the Sudan border or other areas of insecurity, RTF favoured potential camp locations that were close to roads and wood fuel sources. Reservoirs/aquifers with high suitability were then examined to ensure close proximity to a suitable camp platform, located above the seasonal flood plain. (This should be less than 500 m, as recommended by the SPHERE Humanitarian Charter Minimum Water Standards).[7]

## Development of drilling strategy

The final step in the project was to identify drilling locations that were away from the central aquifer and towards the edge of the containment fracture. The construction

7  *The Sphere Project Humanitarian Charter and Minimum Standards in Disaster Response Handbook* (Revised Edition), Chapter 2. Geneva. From www.sphereproject.org, last accessed 15 July 2005.

of well platforms directly in the path of peak *wadi* flow can be catastrophic. By considering the fault structure immediately adjacent to an aquifer but away from the *wadi* channel, well damage from flood-induced erosion can be prevented.

## Results

The project demonstrated that the WATEX© process, merging geospatial analysis with geological and hydrological exploration methods, was capable of improving significantly the ability to predict water potential with limited need for costly, time-consuming field survey.

### Results in Chad

Thanks to the existing database of approximately 540 drilling sites throughout Ouaddaï, it is possible to say that RTF's WATEX© process has improved drilling success rates from 33 per cent to nearly 90 per cent — results based on a review of the water-drilling results of the Chad Hydrological Survey (and various NGOs) through the years in the region compared with more recent success using WATEX©-derived data.

### Identification of the new campsite of Gaga

Key evidence of the efficiency of the WATEX© process is UNHCR's decision to settle a major refugee camp along the Wadi Dalal, based on the analysis provided by RTF.[8]

The Wadi Dalal settlement of Gaga Camp is about 65 km east of Abéché, and was recommend by RTF because of its exceptional combination of hydrogeologic characteristics respecting the aforementioned five key hydrologic parameters.

In February 2005, prior to UNHCR's decision to begin construction of the new refugee camp, RTF estimated that at least 20,000 people could be situated on a platform adjacent to the potential aquifer, based on estimated water reserves. In May 2005 UNHCR announced that the site had the capacity to shelter up to 30,000 refugees to the area.

---

Application of the five hydrologic parameters

1. **Size of the radar anomaly:** Medium to high amplitude, very big size, indicates important aquifer.

2. **Amount of upstream watershed drainage:** an exceptionally high yield of 230 million m³/year minimum coming from the Azum watershed in Sudan (after removing runoff and evaporation).

3. **Quality of the aquifer gravels:** migmatites, granites, quartzites and schists provide high quality grains for the aquifers. Good conductivity is expected from future wells.

4. **Major faults:** this system is well structured by old fractures: alluvial sequences must be thick all along the Bahr Azum alluvial deposits (Lebotigue wells produce more than 30 m³ per hour throughout the year from 9 to 45 m).

5. **Slopes upstream *wadi* course:** with an average of 0.689/100 m the slope is small but due to the water quantities flowing every year, the energy of transportation remains high enough to clear the silts, leading to a favourable vertical recharge.

**Conclusion: Bahr Azoum is most likely the most productive site of Eastern Ouaddaï, with sustainable reserves and soils to feed several hundred thousand people.**

---

8  Gachet (2005), op. cit., see p. 83 on Wadi Dalal.

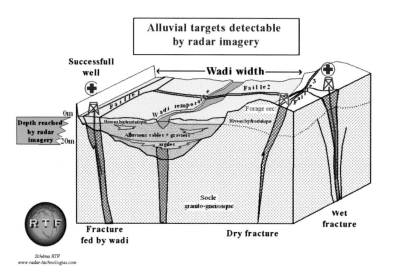

Figure 3: Block diagram illustrates that radar imagery does not penetrate deeper than 18-20 m and that the WATEX© process deals exclusively with near sub-surface aquifers

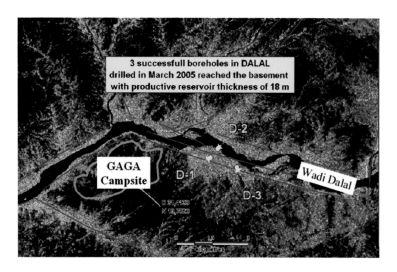

Figure 4: WATEX© image showing three successful exploration wells drilled in March 2005 by UNHCR's drilling contractor (OXFAM), which confirmed RTF's expectation

## Sustainable development potential on the Bahr Azum alluvial aquifer

The Bahr Azum site, which is located 33 km south of Goz Beida in the Dar Syla province south of Eastern Ouaddaï in Chad, is fed upstream by the Azum watershed in Sudan, which drains 230 million m³ per year flowing along 100,000 hectares of alluvial terraces (red colours on *Figure 5*).

This is the most prolific site of Eastern Ouaddaï. It offers a unique combination of groundwater potential and soils which can be the base of the future reconstruction of the economy of Eastern Chad for the benefit of the local population and for the refugees from Sudan.

### Results in Darfur—Sudan

During the US National Groundwater Association symposium in Albuquerque, New Mexico, USA, in May 2007, the results of the WATEX© study in Darfur were presented by Dr Saud Amer PhD and Dr Verne Schneider PhD, from the USGS in the 'Remote Sensing Technique in Groundwater Exploration in Developing Countries' seminar:[9]

Identification of aquifer potential in Central Darfur over an area of 135,000 km² has been achieved by Radar Technologies France, USGS, UCSB and UNESCO in six months.

9  Dr Alain Gachet, Radar Technology France, Dr Saud Amer, and Dr Verne Schneider, US Geological Survey – National Groundwater Association Summit: Remote Sensing Technique in Groundwater Exploration in Sudan, Wednesday, 2 May 2007.

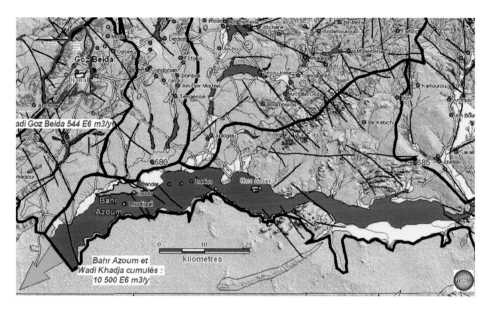

*Figure 5: Interpreted WATEX© image of the Bahr Azum alluvial system flowing from Sudan*

Potential water drilling site maps and drilling manuals have been produced and transferred to 40 NGOs operating in Darfur, under the supervision of UNESCO and UNICEF. Since October 2006, some 300 wells have been drilled thanks to UNICEF with 100 per cent success under the recommendations of RTF's *Darfur Drilling Handbook* near the camps of:

- North Darfur near El Fasher: IDP camps of Abu Shouk, Shagra and Mellit;
- South Darfur around IDP camps of Nyala and Kas; and
- West Darfur near El Geneina, on the IDP camps of Riyad, Kereinik, Um Tagouk, Ardamata, and near the camps of Murnei, Zalingei, Dereisa, Habilah, Ararah, Nyertete and Foto Burunga.

The study was funded by USAID-OFDA over an area hosting 2.5 million people, where security is a major concern.

Such identification was made possible using the WATEX© process based on new radar remote sensing technologies developed and patented by RTF.

This process combined with optical remote sensing, geology, geomorphologic features and climatic data, revealed over 200,000 km² of buried aquifers not visible from the surface.

The study has also revealed vast stretches of land in central Darfur hosting enough groundwater reserves to sustain 33 million people year round with 15 litres of water per day.

These aquifers are sustainable and easily accessible within a depth ranging from subsurface to 50 m in unconsolidated sediments, which are easy to drill.

Ground Penetrating Radar (GPR) was operated by RTF over some calibration points, confirming the depth and structure of aquifers down to 40 m deep. Drilling results collected in Sudan have confirmed the validity of the results with a success rate of 95 per cent on 740 wells and boreholes.

The most important yields of 30 m³ per hour have been recorded within shallow buried aquifers around 30 m deep and the drilling efficiency expressed in cubic metres per metres drilled is 20 times higher inside the recommended WATEX©-mapped areas than outside.

An important drilling success was recorded at greater depths down to 200 m for the UN peacekeeping forces on Shagra wells, in the Nubian sandstones West of El Fasher, as recommended in the *Darfur Drilling Handbook*.

All these results have been monitored and validated by UNESCO (CWR) in Khartoum-Sudan.

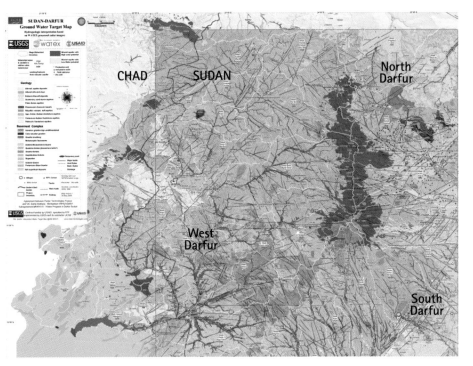

Figure 6: The Groundwater Target Map of Darfur – June 2006.
The most prolific alluvial systems are coded in red

Figure 7: Dr Alain Gachet leading a Ground Penetrating Team in Sudan. October 2006

## Conclusions

WATEX© is an innovative, holistic approach to hydrology, involving a fusion of geological exploration science and geospatial analysis that would not have been possible even just a few years ago and with very limited ground verification only 10 months ago. It has significantly increased the drilling success rate from 33 per cent to more than 95 per cent on new sustainable aquifers which have been discovered after scanning vast stretches of land (over 300,000 km²) between Chad and Sudan.

There is always, of course, some level of exploration risk, but in conditions of humanitarian urgency, timely response, scarce resources, security concerns, and inaccessible and massive areas of interest, this system has demonstrated the ability to identify suitable areas for resettlement and meet international standards for water access.

In Chad, key evidence of the efficiency of the WATEX© process is UNHCR's decision to settle a new refugee campsite of Gaga, based on the analysis provided by RTF. UNHCR announced in May 2005 that this site had the capacity to shelter up to 30,000 refugees.

RTF's identification of the most prolific site along the Bahr Azum watershed in Eastern Ouaddaï, with a unique combination of groundwater and soils, offers the base of future reconstruction of Eastern Chad for the benefit of the local population and for the refugees of Sudan.

In Sudan, the WATEX© process revealed in June 2006 that there is enough groundwater in Darfur for several million people, enough to sustain the peace process and reconstruction through agricultural development.[10]

Future projects include micro-dam construction to increase aquifer replenishments, soil identification and qualifications, irrigation planning and mineral exploration. This is symbiotic with the methodology employed, emphasizing the provision of a sound water resource management plan in order to avoid groundwater resource unsustainability, which could lead to a bigger crisis.

## Acknowledgements

*The author expresses his deep gratitude to UNHCR for funding the Chad project in 2004-2005 and to USAID/OFDA for funding the Sudan project in 2006.*

*RTF joins many others in expressing deep thanks to NASA and the USGS for facilitating collection, processing and distribution of the SRTM mission data, which provided crucial topographic intelligence ingested by the WATEX© hydrologic model.*

*Similar appreciation is extended to the governments of Chad, Japan and the United States for providing the aforementioned data used in the project.*

*Finally, RTF wishes to recognise the vision and courageous support of Dr Saud Amer and Dr Verne Schneider from the USGS (Reston, Virginia), Suzain Tokar from USAID, and Dr John Harrald[11] and Dr Firoz Verjee[12] from ICDRM-GWU.*

10  Dr Alain Gachet (2006). *Water exploration in Darfur–Sudan.* Edited for USGS, UCSB and USAID, 30 May 2006 (89 pp.)

11  Dr John Harrald, Director, Institute for Crisis, Disaster and Risk Management and Professor of Engineering Management, The George Washington University (see jharrald@gwu.edu)

12  Dr Firoz Verjee, DSc, Research Associate Institute for Crisis, Disaster and Risk Management, School of Engineering and Applied Science, The Georges Washington University, 1776 G. Street, NW, Room 109, Washington, D.C. 20052.

# SHORT-SIGHTED VISIONARIES: ASKING FOR DISASTER

A man jumps from a skyscraper and as he passes each floor says to himself: 'so far so good!' This sums up our short-sighted way of thinking. Our daily lack of concern, let alone action, regarding depletion of natural resources, increasing poverty and poor spatial planning, is a recipe for disaster. We behave carelessly and then we are surprised when things go wrong.

Most disasters are not random events without underlying causes. They are the sudden manifestation of slow but continuous degradation processes. Risks multiply through lack of concern or our failure to find alternatives. For example, we cannot put all the blame for the death of 2,750 Haitians on Hurricane Jeanne. The long process of deforestation that preceded it was greeted by deafening media silence. Only after the disaster did *USA Today* write: 'The torrents of water that raged down onto this city, killing hundreds of people, are testimony to a man-made ecological disaster. Poverty has transformed Haiti's once verdant hills into a moonscape of bedrock ravaged by ravines'. Would any of the mainstream media have written about Haiti's 98 per cent deforestation rate before Jeanne struck?

Why does slow degradation go unnoticed? Why are we blinded by footage of one disaster flickering across the screen until the next tragedy takes its place? Our relationship with the media resembles that of a scavenger. The higher the death-toll the bigger the audience. Politicians travel to the scene of a disaster and express their concern for families, but once the tragedy is forgotten what happens to the measures needed to prevent the next disaster?

The explosion at the Chernobyl nuclear power station shocked the whole world. But with privatisation of the electrical sector we read more about cutting costs than improving the safety of nuclear reactors. The media reported every detail of the wreck of the *Kursk* submarine and the loss of 118 sailors. But they say nothing of the dozens of Russian nuclear submarines slowly rusting in the Barents Sea. Much has been written about the crude oil escaping from the wrecks of *Prestige* and *Erika*. Yet every day petrol tankers are voluntarily degassing to cut down on cleaning costs, while media and politicians remain largely indifferent. Double-hulls are still not compulsory. Nor is tank cleaning. Over-fishing affects 72 per cent of our oceans but no regulations are being drafted for international waters, despite the fact that simple measures — the introduction of nets with a bigger mesh and a ban on bottom trawling — would help to prevent depletion of fish reserves. These are just a few examples of slow degradation of environmental and social systems by humans that may ultimately lead to disaster.

The world's environment ministers made a very clear statement with the UNEP Malmo Ministerial Declaration in May 2000: 'Environmental threats resulting from the accelerating trends of urbanisation and the development of mega-cities, the tremendous risk of climate change, the freshwater crisis and its consequences for food security and the environment, the unsustainable exploitation and depletion of biological resources, drought and desertification, and uncontrolled deforestation, increasing environmental emergencies, the risk to human health and the environment from hazardous chemicals, and land-based sources of pollution, are all issues that need to be addressed'.

Common sense dictates that we treat these issues as a top priority. But only sudden events catch our attention. Our societies seem to be led by short-sighted visionaries. There are several reasons for this affliction.

We prefer to avoid trouble. Nobody can be accused of causing tropical cyclones, but it is relatively simple to identify the culprits behind continuous environmental destruction. Government leaders and the senior management of large companies are

*Pascal Peduzzi is head of the Early Warning Unit at the United Nations Environment Program (UNEP/GRID-Europe) in Geneva. Trained as an environmental scientist, he leads a small team to assess effects of environmental degradations (deforestation, climate change) on human populations and ecosystems using satellite imagery, GIS modelling and terrain observations. Recent studies include glacier retreat detection (Peru), contribution to the UNEP atlas, One Planet Many People and the generation of the Disaster Risk Index published by UNDP. He is the author of various scientific and general public publications.*

Published in *Environment & Poverty Times*, No. 3, p.6.
Special Edition for the World Conference on Disaster Reduction, 18-22 January, 2005, Kobe, Japan.
UNEP/GRID-Arendal http://www.environmenttimes.net/ http://www.grid.unep.ch/

directly responsible for contamination of rivers by mining, erosion following unsustainable timber exploitation or soil pollution by industry. But to make such accusations against influential people is tricky. Putting the emphasis on natural hazards is a much safer attitude.

We are fascinated with speed, which makes it difficult to make the headlines with continuous degradation. Although the long-term impact may be much worse, the media just will not make a week-long issue of the underlying causes of thousands of people dying of starvation. It is an uphill struggle keeping readers' and viewers' attention. The media need rapidly changing events to avoid boring their audience.

With our blinkered vision, security and the fight against terror have monopolised the global debate. Climate change threatens millions of people with more frequent heatwaves, rising sea levels, landslides and more severe storms, among others. But combating it will never attract the same amount of funds.

Our perspective is strictly short-term. To stand a chance of being re-elected politicians must focus on what can be achieved in a four to five-year mandate. Long-term issues tend to be sidelined. Our political and economic reflexes prefer quick benefits, leaving the mess to be cleared up later.

We are obsessed with visibility. The media will focus on aid following disasters and government rescue operations. But preventive measures are not attractive enough to make the headlines.

Lastly, we imagine natural resources are infinite, so their price does not reflect the cost of producing such resources. For example, there is no such thing as a petrol producer. Bacteria produce petrol. It takes them 200 million years to transform 24.5 tonnes of fern into one litre of crude oil! If we restricted oil consumption to the quantity produced the previous year its price would be stupendous. We can apply the same reasoning to many natural resources.

As long as our main concern is economic growth, we forget that our planet is a finite space in which continuous growth is impossible. We cannot catch more fish than the numbers that hatch each year. The same is true of the trees we cut down. Such unsustainable practices could soon lead to the collapse of entire systems on which a large proportion of the population depends.

We can no longer wait for the next disaster to happen. We urgently need to reduce the impact of our mismanagement on communities and the environment as a whole. It is a huge task but the goal can be achieved. We must stop ongoing degradation of society and the environment by helping all communities to live on sustainable resources. Priority must be given to renewable energy sources and resources, to supporting development, and promoting family planning and education. Only then we will see a significant reduction in risks. Our economy will certainly benefit from this. We cannot afford to postpone investments in our future. Otherwise the bill will just be too high.

# Is climate change increasing the frequency of hazardous events?

With growing populations and infrastructures the world's exposure to natural hazards is inevitably increasing. This is particularly true as the strongest population growth is located in coastal areas (with greater exposure to floods, cyclones and tidal waves). To make matters worse any land remaining available for urban growth is generally risk-prone, for instance flood plains or steep slopes subject to landslides. Studies of this reveal an exponential increase in disasters. This raises several questions: is the increase due to a significant improvement in access to information? What part does population growth and infrastructure development play? Finally, is climate change behind the increasing frequency of natural hazards?

As it seems less likely for tectonic hazards (such as earthquakes, volcanoes) to be influenced by climate trends we may take them as a benchmark. If we look at data from EM-Dat1, the only publicly available global database on the impact of hazards on humans, we can see that the occurrence of reported earthquakes is increasing along similar lines to other hazards. The increase is certainly exponential but mainly due to a significant improvement in access to information worldwide. How, the reader may ask, do we know that?

The number of earthquakes (of sufficient magnitude to register on a seismograph) that hit populated areas has not increased; rather it is steady. But EM-DAT only reported some of them. In the 1970s only 11 per cent of earthquakes affecting human settlements were reported. The figure for the 1980-1992 period increased sharply reaching 25 per cent. It carried on rising, to 31 per cent between 1993-2003. Demographic factors cannot explain the sudden increase in reporting. The most logical explanation is the tremendous improvement in information technology. By the end of the 1970s the media had achieved global coverage. For the first time television channels broadcast live coverage of a war (in Vietnam). Before 1980 only places with a powerful information network supplied data on events involving natural hazards and only major disasters were likely to be reported.

The second sharp increase appears in the mid-1990s (circa 1995). The emergence of the internet as a global means of information access immediately springs to mind.

But we cannot rule out the impact of climate change on the frequency of hazardous events. Although the number of reported earthquakes is very steady (with an annual range of 20-40 events), the number of reported floods and cyclones increases dramatically over time (a correlation of $R2 = 0.81$ and $0.64$, respectively, compared with $0.25$ for earthquakes). If the flow of information was increasing the number of reported earthquakes would be increasing too. But if tectonic events are steady and climatic events on the increase, there is cause for serious concern about the impacts of climate change on the frequency of associated hazards.

If the scientists can demonstrate that global warming is causing higher casualty rates then countries facing higher risks may decide to sue the largest $CO_2$ producers to cover the extra cost of adaptation. It is equally possible that families of the victims of tropical cyclones may sue them for gross negligence. The failure to introduce measures to combat global warming may rebound, with victims sending in the bill much as they did in the United States when they took the tobacco industry to court.

*Pascal Peduzzi is head of the Early Warning Unit at the United Nations Environment Program (UNEP/GRID-Europe) in Geneva. Trained as an environmental scientist, he leads a small team to assess effects of environmental degradations (deforestation, climate change) on human populations and ecosystems using satellite imagery, GIS modelling and terrain observations. Recent studies include glacier retreat detection (Peru), contribution to the UNEP atlas, One Planet Many People and the generation of the Disaster Risk Index published by UNDP. He is the author of various scientific and general public publications.*

Published in *Environment & Poverty Times*, No. 3, p.7.
Special Edition for the World Conference on Disaster Reduction, 18-22 January 2005, Kobe, Japan.
UNEP/GRID-Arendal http://www.environmenttimes.net/

# Early warning and early impact analysis: WFP Preparedness in action —
# A case study: tropical Cyclone Sidr in Bangladesh

### Introduction: WFP and preparedness

Increasingly the World Food Programme (WFP) is being called on to respond to hunger in the context of a wide range of emergencies, from natural disasters like the tsunami tragedy in Asia to manmade crises such as the ongoing civil conflict in Darfur, Sudan. In 2006, WFP emergency operations provided food aid for 63.4 million people caught up in the ever-widening net of humanitarian disasters. To respond successfully to emergencies entailing food shortages WFP must be able to mobilise its response quickly and efficiently, making preparedness a critical component of any emergency operation.

In recent years, WFP has developed and adopted methodologies and tools for emergency preparedness including a dedicated preparedness unit at its headquarters, establishing a global Early Warning Monitoring Service, mainstreaming the practice of Contingency Planning in its country offices, and creating internal and external web-based information platforms to share key preparedness documents, maps and data. WFP also maintains an active role in promoting preparedness, early warning and 'early action', through co-chairing the UN humanitarian Inter-Agency Standing Committee (IASC) sub-working group on Contingency Planning and Preparedness.

A key challenge still facing WFP is how to link its preparedness systems with decision-making and how to encourage anticipatory action and preparedness at all levels in a timely way. This year, through several pilot projects with leading academic and technical institutions, WFP has taken the opportunity to enhance its capacity to anticipate food security crises and launch rapid needs assessments, especially in natural disasters, using advanced Geographical Information Systems (GIS), high resolution satellite imagery and other forms of remote sensing.

### Early warning and early impact analysis

WFP is building its capacity to anticipate and respond to sudden-onset natural disasters, including any brought on by extreme weather patterns, possibly linked to global climate change. In 2007, WFP started to develop a network of partnerships with academic research institutions, governments and UN agencies working in applied technology (remote sensing, GIS). Particularly notable is a partnership between WFP, the Polytechnic University of Turin (Politecnico di Torino) and the Higher Institute on Innovation Territorial Systems (SiTI). This joint project called ITHACA (Information Technology for Humanitarian Assistance Cooperation and Action) is establishing historical data patterns, developing forecasting mod-

els and applying satellite imagery to rapidly determine and monitor where hurricanes or flooding may occur and assess the damage to both population and infrastructure.

This type of tailored information, if delivered in a timely fashion, can be an invaluable asset in planning and prioritising locations for needs assessments, not to mention providing huge cost and time savings. For example, obtaining initial impact assessments in a natural disaster by conducting a visual survey from a helicopter costs an organisation many thousands of dollars. Helicopters alone rent for approximately US $6,000 each per hour. The current use of remote sensing and GIS, carries virtually no cost to WFP, and has provided extremely valuable information during a time when there is normally an information vacuum. WFP has recently tested this technology in West Africa, and found that it was extremely useful in supporting decisions about where to undertake needs assessments. The mapping outputs have also been used in several cases for operational planning, especially with regard to pre-positioning food stocks where needs are anticipated, and establishing logistics corridors based on information about damage to infrastructure.

When an early warning alert is issued about significant flooding or a hurricane,

*World Food Programme (WFP) is the United Nations front-line agency against global hunger. Over the past four decades, WFP operations have grown to make it the world's largest humanitarian organisation, providing food assistance last year to 88 million people —mostly women and children — in 78 of the world's poorest countries. Its mission is to combat hunger, promote economic and social development and provide speedy relief assistance in emergencies throughout the world. More than 90 per cent of its 10,000 staff is deployed in the field.*

specialised analysts are mobilised within hours through the ITHACA partnership to analyse the satellite images. The analysis and mapping products produced by the ITHACA team are developed at no cost, specifically for WFP's operational needs. The analytical process requires new, timely image acquisitions, although historical data is also needed to detect changes. To acquire, process and analyse the satellite images and disseminate the mapping outputs quickly for WFP staff on the ground, the Remote Sensing partners have established a network between image providers, analysts and users. The main source of the images are satellites owned by governmental space agencies, which publicly disseminate images or provide ad hoc acquisitions at no cost to WFP through bilateral and multilateral agreements.

## Case study of preparedness in action: Cyclone Sidr in Bangladesh

The above tools and methodologies have been piloted for floods during 2007 in Pakistan, Mozambique and, most recently, in West and East Africa, where the mapping has supported WFP emergency assessments and was shared with governments and inter-agency partners. The essential elements of the approach are timeliness, continuing optimisation of information and outputs according to user needs, and the close coordination of internal and external actors.

The recent case of Cyclone Sidr, which hit Bangladesh in mid-November 2007, illustrates WFP's coordination of analytical and mapping functions and dissemination of practical early warning information and early impact analysis for the operational response. The timeline below looks at WFP's early warning and early impact activities during the days leading up to the storm making landfall, as well as the first 48 hours post-impact. While WFP's early warning early-impact activities were just a component of a wider preparedness and response framework involving a broad range of UN, government and NGO actors, the agency's experience piloting remote sensing and GIS technologies in this case further indicates the great potential value obtained from using these forms of applied sciences in humanitarian emergencies. In the case of Sidr, WFP's activities both pre- and immediately post-impact also established a network of actors that continued the critical situational awareness and mapping support to operations, including ongoing mapping updates on road damage in the affected areas.

## Cyclone Sidr timeline
### 12 November 2007

WFP's Early Warning global service issued an alert based on information from the Bangladesh Disaster Management Information Centre, Tropical Storm Risk and other weather and news sources that tropical storm Sidr had formed over the Bay of Bengal south-west of the Andaman Islands and was moving north-westwards. Sidr was forecast to strengthen to a Category-2 Storm by 14 November and was expected to affect Bangladesh, India and possibly Burma/ Myanmar. The alert was posted on WFP's Emergency Preparedness and Response intranet, EPWeb, and disseminated via email to its list of email subscribers.

### 14 November 2007

WFP Early Warning picked up additional reports noting that tropical cyclone Sidr was due to make landfall as a Category-4 Storm on 15 November around 20:00 hours GMT close to the India-Bangladesh border between West Bengal and Khulna. Reports were confirmed at field level. According to the WFP office in Dhaka, the cyclone's impact was potentially devastating, especially in the south-west of the country because of extensive flooding from exceptional rainfall. Early Warning indicated that analysts feared the cyclone would cause severe damage along coastal areas of Bangladesh, eastern India and Myanmar.

WFP Bangladesh GIS and the Remote Sensing focal point in the country office were contacted by the preparedness unit in HQ to discuss the best analysis. The CO suggested priority areas, based on field experience and additional data, thereby guiding the focus of the remote-sensing analysis.

At 10:00 hours, the GIS team at WFP HQ produced the first maps of potentially affected areas based on the forecast typhoon path, including the number of people living in the cyclone corridor who would be affected by high wind speeds. This map was sent to the country office. At 13:00 hours, the team produced another map giving hazard level, mortality and economic risk indicators from historical records.

Also, on the day before impact, the ITHACA team ran a simulation model to identify flood-prone areas and produced a map. (N.B.: this modelling methodology is a prototype and is being refined). The Bangladesh case modelling was shared with the country office for preliminary validation.

Acquiring images quickly was a major concern before the storm actually hit. WFP requested the triggering of the International Charter Space and Major Disasters based on information received from the Bangladesh office, with technical backup from ITHACA. However, the Space Charter refused to book the satellite before the flood as only post-shock activations are currently allowed. To obtain imagery before the event, WFP reached a bilateral agreement with the Italian Space Agency (ISA), which agreed to acquire images for WFP through their COSMO Skymed satellite and transfer the images to ITHACA for analysis.

Additionally, WFP together with UNOSAT requested and endorsed the assistance of the European Space Agency (ESA) and the GMES RESPOND project. The ENVISAT satellite was booked for the time during which flooding was expected to peak (Friday-Saturday). It was agreed that the processed data would be provided to ITHACA, which

would then perform additional analysis as per WFP/ITHACA procedures.

15 November 2007

The storm hit the coast of Bangladesh as a Category 4 (5 being the highest) and was downgraded to Category 2 on moving towards the centre of the country.

After discussing with the country office the previous day's outputs, WFP's preparedness unit agreed that the simulation model was oversimplified and might not yield reliable information. Feedback was sent to ITHACA, which produced a revised model for flood-prone areas.

Two additional maps, giving updates on potentially affected areas, were produced by the preparedness unit and disseminated.

16 November 2007

The preparedness unit support shifted from primarily forecasting to providing information to WFP operations. ITHACA issued a map at 10:00 hours Rome time, indicating potentially flooded areas based on the revised modelling methodology. At 12:00 hours, the information management team activated a Crisis Monitoring page dedicated to the situation, so that WFP staff could access all the maps, along with the key operational data and documents related to the emergency.

Meanwhile the country office, now well into its early response phase, issued a situation update, which showed early warning and preparedness systems in place. The continuing support from HQ dealt mainly with obtaining images through the International Space Charter as well as bilateral agreements with national space agencies. Data from satellites started to arrive on 18 November and the next day the first analyses were shared with the field. These were also used during conference calls between HQ, the regional bureau and country office.

Five WFP assessment teams left Jessore field office at 07:45 hours when the all-clear signal was given. The first WFP convoy set out at 13:00 hours with 20 Metric tonnes (MT) of biscuits to feed 100,000 people. Follow-up convoys were prepared for the afternoon and the following day to provide an additional 300,000 people with 80 MT of biscuits. An additional 100 MT was made available from the Bangladesh country program.

Conclusion

The forward-looking alerts, coupled with the data and analysis obtained through remote sensing translated into practical maps that served the needs of the country office in establishing early on priorities for undertaking needs assessments and operational decision-making. From the pre-positioning of food, to establishing where needs assessments should be undertaken, to providing essential information about damaged infrastructure to our logistics staff on the ground — the use of Remote Sensing and GIS holds the potential to greatly improve WFP's effectiveness in responding to crises.

Additionally, this case and other recent experiences underscore the importance of having an active network of technical partners for the timely acquisition and analysis of the satellite images. Whereas the Charter activation suited delivery of images post-event, WFP also relied on its bilateral relationship with the Italian Space Agency in order to obtain images pre-event for forecasting purposes.

Although the procedures and actual early warning and early impact outputs should undergo further refinement, the experience in the case of Cyclone Sidr further indicates the value of this type of informational support in saving time and money in humanitarian response. WFP will continue to refine its Global Early Warning system and outputs and, through its partnerships with technical institutions such as ITHACA, strengthen its capacity to anticipate and respond to emergencies using the latest technology.

# 'ENVIRONMENTAL NEEDS IN POST-CRISIS ASSESSEMENTS AND RECOVERY'

INTERVIEW WITH DAVID JENSEN

*What do we know about the environmental dimensions of conflicts and disasters?*

UNEP has been conducting detailed assessments on the environmental impacts of conflicts since 1999 and disasters since 2005. To date we've operated in 25 crisis-affected countries and mobilised US $75 million towards environmental assessment and recovery. UNEP's role is to use science and technology to determine the environmental damage caused by conflicts and disasters and to assess the impact this damage may have on humans. UNEP can then provide assistance to address the environmental damage – either in terms of site clean up or restoration or through capacity-building of environmental authorities.

In the last eight years of our post-crisis operations, we have learned two critical lessons that are relevant for today's discussions. First, conflict and disasters always cause environmental damage; while the types and magnitude of damage differ, there are always impacts. Second, this damage affects humans in three specific ways: it threatens health, it threatens human livelihoods and it threatens human security.

*In which way do you mean that conflict causes environmental damage?*

Go back to 1999 – the Kosovo conflict. What do you see? Most will recall the streams of refugees fleeing Kosovo – 500,000 in total, but some might also recall the bomb-ing of the factories and industrial sites that NATO referred to as "strategic targets". To cite one example, the Pancevo industrial site was hit 12 separate times during the conflict. Some 80,000 tonnes of burning oil were released into the environment. Black rain fell onto neighbouring towns and villages.

If you need a way to visualize what 80,000 tonnes of oil looks like, consider that one oil tanker truck holds 20 tonnes. We are therefore talking about 4,000 oil tankers spilled during the war in one single site alone. In addition, a toxic soup of compounds and substances leaked into the air, soil and water around Pancevo, including 2,100 tonnes of ethylene dichloride (a substance causing kidney, liver and adrenal damage), 8 tonnes of metallic mercury (known to cause severe birth defects and brain damage), 460 tonnes of vinyl chloride monomer (a known human carcinogen and a source of dioxins when burned) and finally 250 tonnes of liquid ammonia (which can cause blindness, lung disease and death). In total, another 140 tankers of chemicals. Remember that this is only a single site among more than 50 industrial sites that were hit.

*How was this environmental disaster tackled?*

Imagine if this happened next to where you live. What would you feel? You would most probably be wondering if the air safe to breathe. If the water is safe to drink. If the food is safe to eat. You would ask: what are the risks to my health and the health of my family? You'd demand to know, and so did the local communities across Serbia. People and politicians began calling it an environmental catastrophe. Neighbouring countries, namely Bulgaria and Romania, expressed their deep concern about the possible toxic sludge in the Danube and trans-boundary air pollution. Meanwhile, NATO argued that the environmental damage was minimized by the use of sophisticated weapons and selective targeting.

So, what was the truth? This is where UNEP came in – using environmental experts, mobile labs and satellite images, we pieced together the risks and the environmental legacy. Even though the first casuality of war is truth, the samples of air, soil, and water do not lie. UNEP's first report concluded that the damage was not as bad as people first thought. High concentrations of chemicals were identified at four main hotspots, but the overall situation could not be called a catastrophe. However, a clean up at the four hotspots was needed to protect health and the environment from further risks. The clean-up was considered an urgent humanitarian priority.

This example makes the link between environmental damage and human health clear. Since Kosovo, we've done similar work in Iraq, looking at the risks posed by the 50 oil fires during 2003, as well as at some

*David Jensen heads the Policy and Planning Team of the UN Environment Programme's Post-Conflict and Disaster Management Branch in Geneva, Switzerland. Since 2000, he has worked on ten post-conflict operations either as a technical contributor or as a project coordinator. He has extensive experience particulary with the Balkans, Afghanistan, Iraq, and more recently with the Democratic Republic of Congo. Jensen is now leading UNEP's efforts to provide technical expertise on environment and conflict to the Peacebuilding Commission and the United Nations Development Group.*
*He holds a Master of Science in Biology from the University of Oxford and an undergraduate degree in geography from the University Victoria.*

of the industrial sites that were bombed or looted. In one former arms manufacturing site, called Al Qadissiya, UNEP teams found nearly 100 tonnes of toxic abandoned chemicals including sodium cyanide and hexavalent chromium. Again, five oil tanker trucks worth. You may know that adding water to sodium cyanide creates hydrogen cyanide – the lethal substance used in a gas chamber. Meanwhile, those that have watched the American film 'Erin Brockovich' will know that hexavalent chromium is highly toxic causing mutations in DNA and making your teeth turn yellow and fall out. The fact that both substances were found in the open is not only a health risk, but also a major security risk if they had fallen into the wrong hands.

So the environment and health analysis makes sense when you have a short-duration war in highly industrialized locations using sophisticated weapons.

*What about the environmental impact in other conflicts and civil wars? I am thinking now about situations such as Afghanistan, Liberia, Sudan and DR Congo where the infrastructure is not as advanced as in the Balkans.*

Take Afghanistan as an example. Afghanistan was the first time UNEP dealt with the linkage between environmental damage and livelihoods. In Afghanistan, there was virtually no heavy infrastructure. There was nothing to be bombed and no specific sites to be assessed. But 23 years of conflict had a much deeper and more fundamental

impact. What do I mean? I led a team looking at the conditions of forests in Afghanistan. In some areas, we found that up to 95% of the landscape had been deforested during the conflict. It was cut for fuel, it was bombed to remove cover and it was removed to grow crops and for grazing. Many people say to me: "well that's sad but at the end of the day who really cares?" How about the people that use the forest for fuel wood for heating and cooking? How about the people that need timber for shelter? How about the people that used to collect nuts and seeds to sell at the market? In fact, what we found was that many livelihoods were fundamentally dependant on these forests. Without them, and without alternatives, they were being displaced to cities or engaging in other forms of income generation such as poppy production for the drug trade.

But Afghanistan taught us something much more important about the impact of conflict – at the end of the day what caused the deforestation was survival combined with a complete breakdown in governance. This breakdown not only affected forest management, which I can assure you did exist prior to 1979, but also local systems for water, wildlife and land management – all destroyed leading to a free for all situation and major environmental damage across the country.

Following Afghanistan, we had a new understanding and approach. Environmental damage can affect livelihoods, cause displacement, and fundamentally undermine stability and peacebuilding.

*What about the link between environmental damage and security? How do you see the risk of conflicts rising out of the ashes of natural disasters?*

Most people don't realize that natural resources can act as buffers against natural hazards, thereby reducing their impact. For example, coastal mangroves forests, sea grasses, and coral reefs absorb some of the energy of coastal hazards thereby reducing overall impacts. As we saw in the wake of the December 2004 Indian Ocean tsunami in Sri Lanka, Indonesia, and Thailand, the loss of these coastal resources makes coastal villages more vulnerable to natural hazards. New Orleans also learned this lesson all too well. A similar lesson was also learned in Pakistan. Removing forest cover from steep slopes can have a catastrophic impact during an earthquake, as unstable soils can slide right off the mountainside. So, in a post-crisis situation, we also need to assess if key resources were damaged and if this damage could somehow increase vulnerability to disasters.

On the other side, we need to understand if access to critical resources such as land and water or high-value resources such as timber and minerals was changed in such a way that could cause conflict. For example, one could point to DR Congo – which I have recently returned from – where high-value natural resources in the east are now again fuelling conflict. They are controlled by various militias who fight with each other, with local communities and with the government over control. Therefore, the resources themselves have become security threats. In this regard, immediate management of these resources is fundamental to peacebuilding and stability.

*What does UNEP do to aid in these issues?*

In addition to assessing environmental damage, UNEP also evaluates the capacity of affected governments at the local and national levels to actually respond to identified impacts and needs. What we've found is that in most post-conflict situations, environmental institutions are either non-existent or non-functional, and therefore incapable of putting environmental needs on the political agenda. In post-disaster situations, they are likewise often weak and struggle for a political voice and influence. UNEP has therefore played a key role in assessing their capacity, strengthening their hand, and providing technical and political backstopping in the weeks and months following a crisis.

*What can be done to improve the global response to environmental disasters and security threats?*

In terms of assessing and addressing environmental damage, the Post-Conflict Needs Assessment (PCNA) has emerged as a critical tool in post-conflict countries. UNEP has been involved in all six PCNAs so far and has tried to identify key environmental risks and needs. By integrating these issues in the PCNA, UNEP's aim is to fully integrate environment within the recovery and peacebuilding process. But the key lesson in the PCNA is that the environment should be treated

both as a cross-cutting issue and as a sector. If it is only cross-cutting it tends to be lost. If it is only a sector, the other sectors tend to neglect it. Therefore, a twin approach as we saw in Haiti or Somalia is needed.

We expect the Post-Disaster Needs Assessment (PDNA) to perform a similar role, and UNEP is currently taking the lead for developing the environmental assessment module within the Cluster Working Group on Early Recovery (CWGER). However, as we use this opportunity to critically reflect on the PCNA and PDNA processes, UNEP can say that both tools must begin to look beyond environmental damage caused by the conflict or disaster in order to take a sustainable approach to recovery planning.

*Isn't there also a risk that the relief operations themselves result in an environmental impact?*

In terms of relief operations, I'm just back from DR Congo where recent fighting in North Kivu has lead to the displacement of around 60,000 people into five camps for internally displaced persons (IDP) near the boarder of Virunga National Park. Virunga Park is one of the last two places on earth where mountain gorillas can still be found. In the camps, we have a typical situation where food, water, and shelter are considered essential needs and are being provided by relief agencies. But when it comes to energy for heating and cooking, the IDPs are left to fend for themselves. Of course, the supply comes primarily from the park. Now, I am not saying that conservation needs should

be more important than human survival, but only that these impacts could easily be avoided by the use of energy efficient stoves coupled with sustainably produced wood from woodlots for example. If one of the key humanitarian principles is "do no harm", this should equally apply to the environment. Another recent example comes from Darfur where groundwater aquifers are being pumped above sustainable levels to meet urgent needs. While this may be a short-term solution, what are the medium term implications for local communities that also rely on the groundwater? Wouldn't loss of those aquifers lead to another crisis or potential conflict. Is this smart? Can't we do better?

Now, when it comes to the recovery process itself, we face similar challenges. The post-conflict period represents a massive injection of capital and a flurry of rebuilding activity. About 6 to 20 times more aid per capita is received following a disaster or conflict. As a result, the natural resources that are normally consumed for example over a 5 to 10 year period are consumed in a year in a post-crisis setting. We call this hyper-development and while it is not yet fully quantified, it is possible that more environmental damage actually happens during the reconstruction process than in the conflict or disaster itself. The reason is simple: in the rush to rebuild infrastructure and restore economies, there often isn't time for planning, environmental safeguards, and wise decisions on the sustainable use of resources. Political pressure dictates immediate and visible progress. This is precisely why an early recovery approach is so critical. Early recovery thinking must already begin in a humanitarian setting – if it happens only when recovery starts, it is already too late. The PDNA is a critical tool for defining environmental needs from an early recovery perspective. As I have mentioned, UNEP is currently working with UNDP to develop and test an environmental module. At the end of the day the PDNA process and the early recovery plan should help to re-orient the country towards more sustainable forms of development and to reduce underlying risks of all forms. Of course, we are not saying not to use the resources, only to ensure they are used in sustainable ways – in ways that help to build back better rather than doing more harm and increasing vulnerability.

*Has this already been done? Can you mention some examples?*

I can think of many positive examples coming from the tsunami-affected countries where environmental needs were seriously considered in the recovery process. In Sri Lanka, the NGO Practical Action is helping to commercialise a new bio-gas scheme to provide alternative forms of energy. The government is also in the process of identifying environmentally sound locations for landfills. In the Maldives, the Safe Islands Programme was developed as part of the rebuilding process. This has involved assessing risks from sea level rise and ensuring re-building does not take place in vulnerable areas. The Clinton Initiative also tried to catalyse major investments in alternative

energy for the Maldives. And finally, in Banda Aceh, Indonesia, efforts are being undertaken to prevent groundwater contamination from household sewage by installing septic tanks and leach fields. Another example from Banda Aceh is that a significant portion of the debris waste was recycled – the timber was transformed into furniture and the concrete became road foundation. Unfortunately, for every positive case, I can probably list nine where new environmental risks and impacts are being created due to poor planning. For example, back in Aceh, there was a massive flurry to replant mangroves in order to provide protection from future hazards. In total, 30 million seedlings have been planted. However, 95 per cent were the same species – making the new forests a monoculture and highly vulnerable to disease. Also, incredibly, earthquake standards were not used in rebuilding thousands of new homes: they had to be retrofitted after this critical lapse was discovered. What makes this even more appalling is that Indonesia has earthquake standards that were not followed. This is a good example of not understanding local context, laws, and risks coupled with low institutional capacity for legal enforcement.

Moving on to the Maldives, they tried to take the right approach in terms of crushing and recycling debris waste into building materials for new homes. The only problem is that they did not realize the previous roofing was asbestos. The asbestos was crushed releasing carcinogen fibres into the air and then embedding within the walls of future

homes. All of these risks could have been prevented with better planning and on-the-ground technical advice.

In my final example, I'd like to highlight the importance of understanding the regional dimension in recovery. Rwanda's 2006 policy decision to ban charcoal production provides an important lesson. While the policy may have been effectively implemented in Rwanda, charcoal production and supply shifted to neighbouring DR Congo thereby further increasing extractive pressures, including on the Virunga National Park and World Heritage Site.

So, I've talked about using the early recovery process as an opportunity to look ahead and re-orient countries towards more sustainable forms of development. At the same time, we must also look to the past to understand how environmental degradation actually contributed to the conflict or disaster in the first place.

*What needs to be done for the future in order to ensure more successes like these?*

In my mind, one of the issues that the international community has not yet successfully addressed relates to the underlying root causes of disasters and conflicts. This goes to the heart of the prevention issue. In this regard, there is a fundamental link between environmental management and vulnerability to conflicts and disasters. I've already mentioned the tsunami, New Orleans and Pakistan disasters, but I want to firmly and clearly emphasize that better management of natural resources would have actually reduced the overall damage that was sustained from the hazards.

On the conflict side, since 1990 there have been 17 major conflicts that have centred on the exploitation of natural resources – nine of these were in Africa. Paul Collier's recent book, 'The Bottom Billion' looks at 40 years of instability and concludes that high-value natural resources have been a critical destabilizing factor – acting as more of a curse than a blessing. Natural resources can be both a trigger and a source for funding wars and war economies. In this regard, the EC has played a fundamental role through the Kimberly Process to stem the flow of conflict diamonds, for example. More is needed for timber and other minerals. Further strengthening of the Kimberly Process is also needed, as Global Witness reports that conflict diamonds funds the current instability in the Ivory Coast.

UNEP's recent post-conflict assessment in Sudan also points out that the scarcity of natural resources, particularly land and water, is a critical factor in the Darfur conflict. So we know there is a fundamental connection between natural resources and conflict. What we haven't yet done very well is focus resources on building capacity to govern these resources in fragile states. At the same time, we have not done enough to prepare countries for the recovery process following a conflict or disaster. And what we need to start thinking about more than ever is the impact that climate change could have on natural resources and climatic hazards. In particular, how will the distribution of water change? Which regions will dry out, which regions will be completely flooded, and what is the potential for conflict? What do the predicted increases in the frequency and intensity of storms and weather-related hazards mean for disasters? How should we be planning to take this into account? Where are the hotspots and what do they need to prepare and adapt?

*What are UNEP's priorities for the future in addressing the environmental dimension of conflicts and disasters?*

Our vision first begins with prevention and risk reduction. We need to start identifying on a more systematic basis countries that are vulnerable to conflicts and disasters from poor natural resource management. In particular, fragile states where we can build natural resources management capacity and crisis preparedness. We also need to see things from a climate change perspective, understanding which regions will be affected, how, and what the implications for disaster and conflict risk will be. We do not currently have this capacity and need to build it.

Secondly, if a conflict or disaster does occur, then UNEP will conduct its response assessment in two phases using existing capacities. In phase one, UNEP and OCHA will conduct a rapid environmental assessment of critical threats to human life and health from the release of hazardous substances in a conflict or disaster. Basically, things that can kill you today or tomorrow. What this means is a more systematic deployment of environmental experts on UN Disaster Assessment and Coordination (UNDAC) teams and clear mechanisms in place to provide emergency clean-up assistance.

In phase two, we will do more detailed environmental assessments integrated within the PCNA / PDNA process which look at environmental damage and risks to heath, livelihoods, and security. The assessments should also look ahead at building back better, as well as behind in terms of understanding the root causes of the event. Cross-cutting the analysis would be governance capacity at the national and local levels. All agencies that collect relevant environmental data would feed it into a single shared database. UNEP would be systematically included in each assessment or delegate the roll to a sister UN agency that is better suited for a specific situation. Within the assessments and early recovery plans, it would be essential to build in environmental indicators and monitoring metrics so that progress can be objectively monitored and that all actors can be held accountable. UNEP could also be involved down the road in terms of monitoring and evaluating the environmental performance of the recovery process itself.

Thirdly, following the PCNA / PDNA, UNEP needs to develop capacity to ensure that environmental technical assistance is available to agencies struggling with environmental issues. What specific environmental technologies can be used and what is best practice. What are the key risks that should be considered? UNEP would maintain a trained roster of experts and deploy specialists on an as needed basis. The specialists would collect lessons learned and feed them into a global database on best and worst practices.

Fourthly, in some post-crisis situations, UNEP will need to establish an in-country project to provide targeted capacity building assistance to national environmental authorities. For example, like we have done in Afghanistan, Liberia, Iraq, Sudan, and Sri Lanka. We provide training and technical assistance in terms of developing and implementing laws and policies.

The fifth priority is for UNEP to build further capacity in using shared natural resources as platforms for peacebuilding and conflict prevention. In the European Region, UNEP has been piloting activities with UNDP, NATO, and OSCE called the Environmental Security Initiative. Good lessons have been learnt at the regional level, and it is now time to scale up the services, in particular to Africa. UNEP plans to expand these efforts to the global level, starting with post-conflict countries in Africa.

I would like to add that UNEP is going through a long overdue major internal reform process. The reforms will focus our work into five core areas, instil a results-based management approach, and make us more relevant at the national level. Within the discussions, addressing the environmental dimensions of conflicts and disasters is being proposed by our senior management team as one of the core topics. This would

allow us to achieve the vision I have set out above. However, UNEP cannot and should not act alone. We need partners. Political partners technical partners, national partners and financial partners.

In this regard, we are already working with the International Strategy for Disaster Reduction (ISDR) and the World Bank to include environmental management tools in risk reduction and to identify global risks from natural hazards. We are seconding an expert to the Peacebuilding Commission Support Office to provide expertise and best practice on natural resources management in post-conflict countries. We are working within the UN country teams and UNDP to implement environmental recovery programmes in Afghanistan, Sudan, Sri Lanka, DR Congo, Indonesia, Rwanda, and Nepal. We are partnering with the International Institute for Sustainable Development, the Woodrow Wilson Center, the Universities of Maryland, Duke, and California and Global Witness in developing analytical tools on environment and conflict for the PCNA and the Peacebuilding Commission. We are working with Environmental Law Institute and the International Union for Conservation of Nature and Natural Resources (IUCN) to identify best practice on natural resource management in post-conflict countries. We are providing advice to the Capstone Policy of the Department of Peacekeeping Operations (DPKO). We are a member of the International Recovery Platform and the Cluster Working Group on Early Recovery and are

developing the environmental module for the PDNA. We are also planning to work with Care International to mainstream environment in humanitarian relief and across the cluster approach. Most of these partnerships are in the embryonic stage and need to be expanded and matured. The one missing element in this list is the private sector. There is a fundamental need to engage them in this discussion, with a possible entry-point through the Extractive Industries Transparency Initiative (EITI).

*What role do you see EU having in the work on addressing the environmental dimension of conflicts and disasters?*

The EU's Stability Instrument and Peacebuilding Partnership present a major opportunity to address the issues I have just outlined. UNEP sees the European Commission as a major partner in implementing the vision through a combination of political leverage, technical expertise, and financial resources.

We have the facts, we have the experts, we have the momentum: now is the time to truly integrate environmental issues within the overall meaning of stability and sustainable development. This is not something we can achieve alone, which is why I would encourage cooperation with UNEP to develop a common vision and achieve a shared set of goals. It is like the old African proverb that says a lot about partnerships: "If you want to go fast, go alone. If you want to go far, go together."

[ Part 4: Trans-regional threats, intelligible warnings ]
and intelligent intelligence

[   Denis Dailleux   ]

# Portraits of Cairo, Egypt

In the Egyptian capital, which does not stop expanding, millions of inhabitants do not have any other place to sleep but the roofs of buildings. Up there, a whole world — invisible from the streets — lives in precarious hamlets under the open air.

A city of refugees, where they are born, get married, work and die, as in a real city on top of the city.

The rooftops of buildings in Cairo's entire city centre have been occupied by a deprived population — reflections of a 'bursting' demography and a rural exodus, which are suffocating the capital, bastion of 17 million inhabitants.

Today, everything reflects on Cairo's terraces: the religious disorganisation, the lack of interest from the state in shelter for the poorest in society, the misery.

It is the Egypt of political intrigues, of religious hypocrisy (Copt or Muslim/Moor), of suppressed and clandestine homosexuality, of adultery, of police torture, of radical Islamism...[1]

The image of an Egypt eroded by social inequalities, political repression and the fear all of this raises.

DENIS DAILLEUX

---

1   The photographer is referring to the description of Egypt as portrayed in the book the 'The Yacoubian Building', by the Egyptian author Alaa Al Aswany.

*The roofs of the buildings in the centre of Cairo are occupied by a destitute population. It is the result of a massive population growth and a rural exodus which suffocate the city of 17 million inhabitants.*

© Denis Dailleux / Agence VU / Cairo, Egypt

*District of Boulaq. In the Egyptian capital, the only place to live for thousands of inhabitants is the top of the buildings. A whole world invisible from the streets, lives in tiny makeshift villages, in the open.*

*In the Egyptian capital, the only place
to live for thousands of inhabitants is the top
of the buildings. A whole world invisible from
the streets, lives in tiny makeshift villages,
in the open.*
© Denis Dailleux / Agence VU / Cairo, Egypt

*The rooftop inhabitants sleep out in the open to fight off the infernal heat of the summer nights, just like this family in the district of Boulaq — one of the working class districts of Cairo.*

*Fatma, whose parents came from Nubia, rents*
*a four-room flat in a building of Garden City.*
*Without telling the owners, she built walls isola*
*her from the hundreds of other residents.*

*This old woman had a heart operation.*
*She doesn't leave her refuge on the top of a*
*building in Tallat Harb Street anymore. The street*
*is used for the president Moubarak cortège's, on*
*his way to his palace in Heliopolis. When used,*
*policemen take position on the top of the buildings*
*and lock up the rooftop inhabitants in their homes.*

© Denis Dailleux / Agence VU / Cairo, Egypt

*People live on the rooftops, pray there, and before the avian flu, they used to breed chickens and pigeons there. The roof (here, in Talaat Harb) has become a tiny village with its unspoken rules, tragedies and joys.*

© Denis Dailleux / Agence VU / Cairo, Egypt

*District of Boulaq*
*In the Egyptian capital, the only place to live for*
*thousands of inhabitants is the top of the buildings.*
*A whole world invisible from the streets; living in*
*tiny makeshift villages out in the open.*
*Like a city put on top of the city.*
© Denis Dailleux / Agence VU / Cairo, Egypt

*Ibrahim by the tanners.*

© Denis Dailleux / Agence VU / Cairo, Egypt

*In the city of the dead, the huge cemetery of Cairo,*
*people live in mausoleums or tumbledown houses*
*built between the graves and on the roofs.*
© Denis Dailleux / Agence VU / Cairo, Egypt

*In the city of the dead, the huge cemetery of Cairo,*
*people live in mausoleums or tumbledown houses*
*built between the graves and on the roofs, where*

*The inhabitants of the roofs rarely meet the ones of the buildings. They must take the service stairs, as in this building in Garden City. It gives witness to two worlds who live together without mixing.*

© Denis Dailleux / Agence VU / Cairo, Egypt

*Policeman in the district of Bolac.*

© Denis Dailleux / Agence VU / Cairo, Egypt

*Woman in Ibn Tulun.*
© Denis Dailleux / Agence VU / Cairo, Egypt

*Portrait, Red Sea.*

© Denis Dailleux / Agence VU / A El Quseir, Egypt

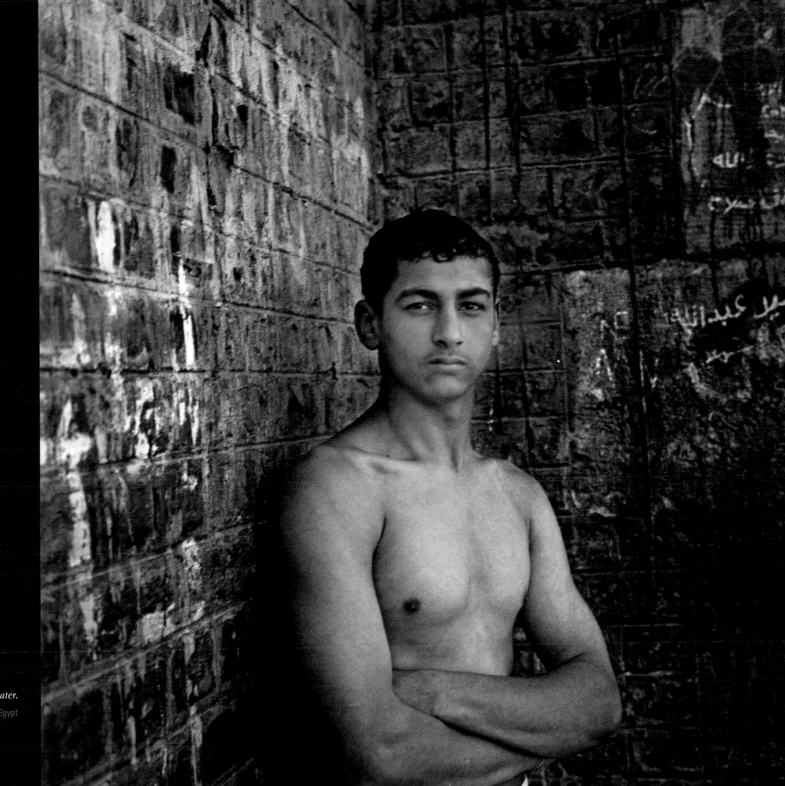

*Young man near the Nile in Anater.*
© Denis Dailleux / Agence VU / Cairo, Egypt

*Teenage boy .*

© Denis Dailleux / Agence VU / Cairo, Egypt

*Amr Ibrahim dressed as a fellah (Egyptian farmer)*
*(30 km north of Cairo).*

© Denis Dailleux / Agence VU / Sin de Bis, Egypt

*Amir's mother in her castle in Sin de Bis,*
*30 km north of Cairo*

© Denis Dailleux / Agence VU / Cairo, Egypt

*Ismail in Amr Sinedebis' castle.*

© Denis Dailleux / Agence VU / Louxor, Egypt

*Photography studio in Bolac district.*

© Denis Dailleux / Agence VU / Cairo, Egypt

# Developing an Early Warning System for Crises

## Introduction

The international community's growing concern with security has generated a renewed and obvious interest in systems to provide warnings and forecasts of crises and conflicts. These can no longer be understood in terms of the relatively simple paradigm of the Cold War. These are jointly known as 'early warning systems', able to improve the action capabilities, in particular for preventative action, of both the international community and its member states.

In a world increasingly seen as a globalized, it has become more difficult to ignore the effects of wars or disasters even though in some cases they are unfolding thousands of kilometres away. The collapse of a state, or a civil war, can destroy past efforts in terms of economic development, can destabilize an entire region, reduce business markets and sources of supply and destroy their industrial investments. It can also significantly disturb raw material and energy markets. It can involve floods of refugees creating, in turn, immigration problems and generate a favourable breeding ground for hostile thinking, which may then be reflected in terrorist acts in far-off lands, thus enlarging the theatre of war to cover the entire world. In addition, there are purely altruistic concerns, which may also motivate members of the international community.[1]

These altruistic concerns led to a number of interventions, usually made once the crisis had begun, aimed at minimising its direct and indirect effects. Such actions, however, are not only inadequate but also extremely burdensome, whereas, in view of the risk, taking no action may not always be an option. Besides, Jack Straw, former British Foreign Secretary, stressed that the intervention in Bosnia-Herzegovina, although it was not able to prevent the civil war or the ethnic massacres, cost the British taxpayer at least £1.5 billion, whereas the cost of preventative action in Macedonia only amounted to £14 million.[2] The aid to Rwanda during the three years following the genocide amounted to over US$2 billion, whereas a preventative intervention would certainly have made it possible to avoid this human tragedy at a cost approximately a third of that amount.[3]

We should therefore make the shift from a reactive strategy to a preventative one, including identification of the signs of crises and, therefore, sufficiently early anticipation[4] – i.e. an operational early warning system – to make it possible to set off an alarm, to provide a detailed diagnosis following the alert, a decision to intervene, planning, and implementation of the response.

However, there is another pitfall. Interventions, even preventative ones, are sometimes ineffective or, worse yet, counterproductive. For example, not only is the preventative nature of the war in Iraq conducted by the coalition subject to question, but so are its effects, particularly in terms of destruction of the machinery of the State contributing to the civil war. Prevention and early warning systems therefore need to be based on an understanding of the mechanisms giving rise to the situations that one is attempting to prevent.

I will first of all give an introduction to the prevention process as a whole, thus locating early warning systems within their

Dr Hélène Lavoix currently works as an independent researcher and consultant, specialising in strategic early warning, conflict prevention, genocide and Eastern Asia. She carries out studies and contributes to seminars, workshops, mainly for state actors (especially the French government), quasi-state actors and with research centres, such as CERI-Sciences Po and Ifri. She has contributed to international conferences, such as the 2007 Canadian Association for Security and Intelligence Studies (CASIS) and a series of seminars like 'Strategic Foresight and Warning – Emerging Threats in the 21st Century', organised by the Centre for Security Studies, Zurich (ETH/CSS). She has published on strategic early warning, indicators, fragile states and genocide. Prior to this, she served as an analyst in international relations for the European Commission and created and headed the Cambodian branch of a development NGO during and after the UN peacebuilding mission (1992-1994).

---

1 With regard to "mixed" motivations, both altruistic and otherwise, that give rise to certain actions, reference may be made, in the case of wars, to Michael Walzer, *Guerres justes et injustes : argumentation morale avec exemples historiques*, Paris, Gallimard, 2006.

2 Speech by Jack Straw, British Foreign Secretary, at the Foreign Policy Centre, 25 March 2002.

3 Carnegie Commission on Preventing Deadly Conflict, December 1997, <www.carnegie.org/sub/research/> quoting *Rebuilding Post-War Rwanda, The International Response to Conflict and Genocide: Lessons from the Rwanda Experience*, Study 4, Copenhagen: Steering Committee of the Joint Evaluation of Emergency Assistance to Rwanda, March 1996, p. 32, and Michael E. Brown and Richard N. Rosecrance (eds), *The Cost-Effectiveness of Conflict Prevention*, Lanham, MD, Rowman & Littlefield, 1998.

4 General Jacques Bonningues, office of the High Representative for Security and Conflict Prevention, "non-paper", 15 May 2006.

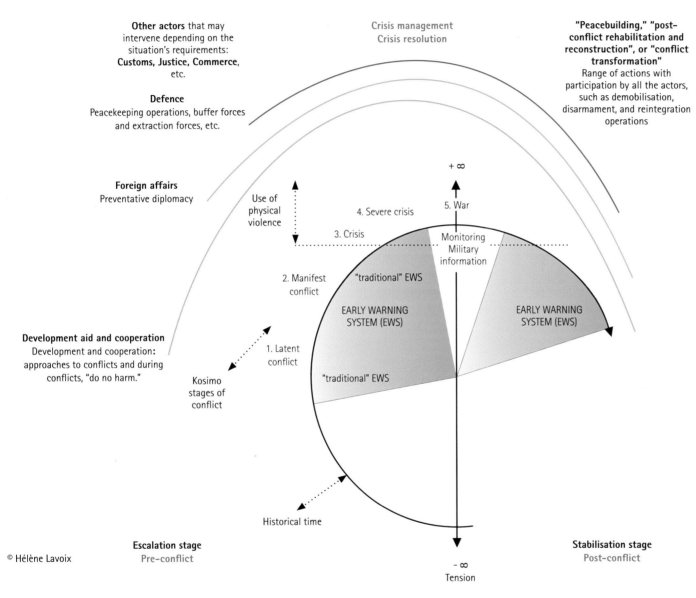

**Other actors** that may intervene depending on the situation's requirements: **Customs, Justice, Commerce,** etc.

Crisis management
Crisis resolution

**"Peacebuilding," "post-conflict rehabilitation and reconstruction", or "conflict transformation"** Range of actions with participation by all the actors, such as demobilisation, disarmament, and reintegration operations

**Defence**
Peacekeeping operations, buffer forces and extraction forces, etc.

**Foreign affairs**
Preventative diplomacy

$+ \infty$

Use of physical violence

4. Severe crisis

5. War

3. Crisis

Monitoring
Military
information

2. Manifest conflict

"traditional" EWS

EARLY WARNING SYSTEM (EWS)

EARLY WARNING SYSTEM (EWS)

**Development aid and cooperation**
Development and cooperation: approaches to conflicts and during conflicts, "do no harm."

1. Latent conflict

"traditional" EWS

Kosimo stages of conflict

Historical time

© Hélène Lavoix

**Escalation stage**
Pre-conflict

**Stabilisation stage**
Post-conflict

$- \infty$
Tension

context. I will then attempt to refute some of the major objections generally raised regarding conflict prevention in general and early warning systems in particular, using them as findings of difficulties that need to be resolved. Finally, taking into account the needs identified earlier, using the experience gained from several early warning systems such as those already existing in Germany, Switzerland, the United States, the United Kingdom and Sweden,[5] I will deal with the various stages which, in our view, should be priorities in the development of an operational and effective early warning system should a country such as France wish to equip itself with such a system.

## The prevention process: several actors, various operations

I will give a brief outline here of the context of which the early warning system forms a part, namely the prevention process as a whole, in the case of a conflict, highlighting the main actor types and the operations implemented. As we will see later, prevention and thus the warning system may also cover other subject matter, such as instability.

At the centre of the process, therefore, is the situation to be prevented: the conflict. This is depicted on an arc, showing escalation towards a conflict as a succession of continuous and contiguous stages. The definition I have selected for these stages, as some early

5 For a description and evaluation of the various existing systems, see Hélène Lavoix, "*Indicateurs et méthodologies de prévision des crises et conflits : Evaluation*", Paris, AFD, 2005b, <www.cedoc.defense. gouv.fr/article.php3?id_article=790>.

## Table 1. Types of crisis and conflict in terms of intensity

| State of violence | Intensity group | Intensity level | Name | Definition |
|---|---|---|---|---|
| Non-violent | low | 1 | Latent conflict | A positional difference on definable values of national meaning is considered to be a latent conflict if respective demands are articulated by one of the parties and perceived by the other as such. |
| | | 2 | Manifest conflict | A manifest conflict includes the use of measures that are located in the preliminary stage to violent force. This includes for example verbal pressure, explicitly threatening violence, or the imposition of economic sanctions. |
| Violent | medium | 3 | Crisis | A crisis is a tense situation in which at least one of the parties uses violent force in sporadic incidents. |
| | high | 4 | Severe crisis | A conflict is considered to be a severe crisis if violent force is repeatedly used in an organised way. |
| | | 5 | War | A war is a type of violent conflict in which violent force is used with a certain continuity in an organised and systematic way. The conflict parties exercise extensive measures, depending on the situation. The extent of destruction is massive and of long duration. |

Source: HIIK, Conflict-Barometer 2005.

warning system practitioners have done, is that laid down by the University of Heidelberg in its Kosimo programme:[6]

In addition to these stages of escalation there are also the stages corresponding to de-escalation or stabilisation, which coincide with a return to peace.

Various actions and actors are involved in these various stages of conflict. During non-violent stages, and this is a relatively new development, development actors are of fundamental importance. They carry out long-term action through development and cooperation aid programmes which, at the very least, attempt to have no detrimental or accelerating effect on the possibilities of conflict. This is the approach known as 'do no harm'. During these stages, diplomatic and military personnel generally focus on their traditional roles, although they may also be involved in cooperation programmes. In addition, their function, in relation to stages of conflict, tends to be connected with observation, collecting information and analysis.

As tensions increase, usually in stage 3, actions known as 'preventative diplomacy' begin. These cover a whole range of negotiations with the aim of resolving disputes, preventing the outbreak of war or reaching a peace agreement once war has broken out. Until recently, preventative diplomacy was the main means for preventing conflicts.

With the use of organised violent force, namely at stages 4 and 5, 'peacekeeping', 'crisis management' or even 'crisis resolution' operations begin. The military play a large

6 Heidelberg Institute on International Conflict Research, *Conflict Barometer 2005, Crises; Wars; Coups d'État; Negotiations; Mediations; Peace Settlements*; 14th Annual Conflict Analysis, revised edition, Department of political science, University of Heidelberg, December 2005, <www.hiik.de/en/index_e.htm>

part in these actions, but they also incorporate, and increasingly so, a civil component. Their aim is to keep in check and monitor the escalation or de-escalation of tension.[7]

Once a peace agreement has been signed, the de-escalation or stabilisation stages commence. All actors participate in these stages and the actions are multi-dimensional. These operations are known as 'peacebuilding'.

The actors involved are both states and international governmental organisations (IGOs) or non-governmental organisations (NGOs). With regard to crises, the latter now have an established role, although on some occasions this is controversial for some types of action[8] and may therefore need to be reconsidered. In addition, the international community's efforts to take action on the funding sources of the various parties involved in a war, such as in the case of conflict diamonds, suggest that private actors as well as commercial and industrial companies also have a role to play in terms of prevention.[9]

The relationship between the conflict on the ground and the actors wishing to prevent, manage or resolve the conflict or reconstruct peace is managed through information structured in a relevant manner, so as to enable an understanding of the situation. Since the action must be prepared, planned, and implemented, the information must be supplied as a forecast, as early as possible. These forecasting procedures, jointly known as 'early warning systems', therefore aim to identify as early as possible a risk or a situation that we desire to prevent, so that the necessary prevention means may be implemented. The specific act of giving a warning on the risks or situations identified – in other words the alert – is only one step in this process.

Originally, 'classical' early warning systems tended to start at stage 3, in an attempt to forecast stages 4 and 5. With the international community's growing interest in preventing conflicts in the long term, this perspective has become inadequate. Early warning systems must now also make it possible to forecast stages 1 and 2.

Early warning systems must be operational not only during stages of escalation but also during stages of stabilisation, when it is more likely that conflict will break out again, since it is a fact that in the ten years following a war the risks of it restarting are especially high.[10] I have, therefore, given a brief definition of early warning systems and set them in their context, thus describing, to a certain extent, the ideal type.

## Questions about early warning systems: identifying constraints and difficulties

When speaking about early warning systems, several points of opposition, resistance and doubts/questions of three types arise.[11] It is vital to respond to these criticisms, not only to convince those who voice them who, very often, will, to a greater or lesser extent, have to take part in the early warning system, but also because the obstacles mentioned often have a solid basis in fact and must therefore be overcome to ensure that forecasting can work properly.

The first type of perceptual constraint is not limited, in fact, to early warning systems but questions the justification for prevention itself; the second poses questions regarding the validity, usefulness, and significance of an early warning system for crises and conflicts; the third, finally, has to do with the

7 Emma Stewart, "Conflict Prevention: Consensus or Confusion?", *Peace, Conflict and Development*, No 3, Dept of Peace Studies, University of Bradford, 06/2003, <www.peacestudiesjournal.org.uk/>.

8 B. R. Rubin, "Afghanistan: la souveraineté comme condition de sécurité", *Critique Internationale*, No 28, July-September 2005, p. 169-183.

9 See, for example, Jean-Marc Châtaignier and François Gaulme, "Agir en faveur des acteurs et des sociétés fragiles : Pour une vision renouvelée des enjeux de l'aide au développement dans la prévention et la gestion de crises", working document, No 5, AFD, September 2005, p. 7-8; Jean-Marc Châtaignier, L'ONU dans la crise en Sierra Leone. Les méandres d'une négociation, Paris, CEAN-Karthala, 2005; International Institute of Security Studies, "Diamonds and conflicts", Strategic Comments, Vol. 6 No 4, 2000

10 PMSU – PCRI - *Investing in Prevention*, 2005, p. 45, quoting Walter, B. "Does Conflict Beget Conflict? Explaining Recurring Civil War", *Journal of Peace Research*, 41:3 (2004) and Paul Collier & Anke Hoeffler, "Greed and grievance in Civil War, Processed Paper", Development Research Group, World Bank, 2002.

11 These reservations were expressed by some participants in the seminar on early warning, but can also be found among the wider public.

posited impossibility of translating the warning into a response.

## Does the need for certain crises invalidate prevention?

The argument whereby a conflict may be positive poses the tricky question of the validity of preventative action. The need for these crises is, in fact, widely acknowledged.[12]

With regard to prevention, however, it is not precisely a question of preventing any crisis or conflict from occurring but, on the contrary, of attempting to mitigate its most negative and destructive effects that are destabilising for the region and possible for the world. The issue is therefore not making a choice between saving lives, which would be put at risk during a violent conflict, while allowing an unsuccessful system to survive, or allowing human beings to die, which is in fact in breach of the current emphasis placed on human rights, on the grounds that once the crisis has been resolved the survivors would benefit from a better system. Instead, it is a question of having a good understanding of the dynamics underlying the crisis that is underway or about to take place to allow the advent of a better situation with as little violence and national and international disturbance as possible[13].

## Is an early warning system and a reflection on its significance necessary? Country risk analysis and the early warning system

The existence of 'country risk' analytical tools already in place may possibly constitute an obstacle to the introduction of a specific early warning system. The aim of the 'country risk' practice is to analyse the economic and financial risks faced by a country and thus potential investors, whether public or private. Examples of this type of measure are the Coface system or those of the US company *World Markets Research Center* (WMRC) or the British company *The Economist Intelligence Unit*.[14]

Although they do not aim to forecast instability or conflicts, these methods nonetheless incorporate a certain measure of political risk, but this is given less weight, in terms of the calculations, than economic and financial risk. Nevertheless, politics is a crucial factor here since, in general, any situation of war or major political instability gives rise to a classification in a very high-risk category, linked in particular to default on payments.

With such a classification, which is relatively broad, it is not possible to distinguish developments in the situation within a coun-

try in crisis, which might be of interest for the various stakeholders. For example, there are the difficulties in the peacebuilding operations such as those currently taking place in Afghanistan. With regard to the political dimension, the 'country risk' approach is therefore inadequate. Some companies, such as the Eurasia group, have positioned themselves on the specific market of political risk forecasting. Thus, together with Deutsche Bank, Eurasia has created the DESIX index of political stability.[15] However, the aim of this approach, namely to evaluate the 'impact of politics on the markets', is again different from that of an early warning system.[16]

Taking into account the disparity in aims and thus in results of these different forecasting tools ought to enable us, in an enriching and constructive manner, to seek the complementary aspects of these methods, including crisis early warning systems, with a view to optimising their usefulness.

## Is an early warning system useful?

With regard to the very relevance of a forecasting system, critics point firstly to the intuition of practitioners and specialists from the countries and regions under analysis, who need no additional tool to know exactly what is happening in their

12 For example, Michi Ebata, *From the discourse to the ground: UNDP activities in conflict prevention*, New York: UNDP Bureau for Crisis Prevention and Recovery, May 2003; Barrington Moore, *Injustice: Social bases of Obedience and Revolt*, London: Macmillan, 1978.

13 It should be noted here that some commentators, such as Edward Luttwak, emphasise that only a full victory can resolve a crisis, "Give War a Chance", Foreign Affairs, July-August 1999.

14 For Coface, see <www.trading-safely.com/sitecwp/cefr.nsf>; WRMC is part of the Global Insight Inc. group <www.wm rc.com/>; for The Economic Intelligence Unit, see <www.eiu.com/>.

15 www.eurasiagroup.net/si/

16 Ian Bremmer, "Managing Risk in an Unstable World" HBR Spotlight, Harvard Business Review, Onpoint article product 1126, 2005.

field of expertise. While not wishing to cast doubt upon the value of this knowledge, the representatives of some institutions with an operational early warning system stress, in response, that on occasion it can be seen that even the best specialists or practitioners, precisely because they are used to the country on which they are working, and in which they live, are sometimes incapable of perceiving an escalation towards a conflict sufficiently early. Being able to put events and changes in them into perspective and summarising them in order to compare them to other situations is often vital for forecasting work, but it is not always easy or possible when one is immersed in the day-to-day life of a country.

Very often, escalation towards conflict and its varying causes are only clear once the conflict has broken out. A famous example, although it has to do with response, is the appeasement policy adopted by Chamberlain and Daladier towards Hitler, which demonstrates how far the situation was misjudged at the time. More recently, it is useful to consider the crisis in the Ivory Coast and to enquire who forecast it and when. According to the testimony of an expert in early warning systems, it does happen that a country expert, confronted with an alert produced by an operational system,

at first denies that a conflict is imminent, and then, having re-examined the various indicators, ends up recognising their relevance, shortly before the outbreak of the conflict.[17] In this sense, intuition, knowledge of a country and experience are necessary but insufficient to enable the symptoms of escalation to be identified precisely enough to ensure that forecasting and warning occur in good time.

It is, in fact, also necessary to know the mechanisms governing the outbreak of conflicts and crises or instability. Some may argue that each conflict or crisis is specific and unique, which is a view emphasised by institutions such as the UNDP or the Department for International Development (DFID) which, as a result, are abandoning warning systems and prioritising analytical methods.[18] It should, firstly, be noted that the use of a single analytical method actually stresses the similarities between conflicts. Secondly, while the manifestations of crises and conflicts do in fact differ, this does not negate either the existence of similar dynamics underlying conflicts or the identification of causes that may give rise to the same effects everywhere, even though they have different outward appearances. Therefore, a scientific approach is needed, which must be sufficiently abstract

to enable it to be applied in varying times and cultural and geographic spaces. For example, we know that a change of regime is a source of instability for a country and that such a period is therefore fragile.[19] If we remained at a lower level of abstraction we would only identify a series of changes, from democracy to more autocratic systems or vice versa, and would see an increase in the probability of conflicts, but we would be unable to draw any conclusion other than one based on the specificity of the crises.

The examples quoted above also cast doubt upon the argument that it is easy to forecast conflicts and that early warning systems already exist. As for the first point, a survey of the research carried out on conflicts and their dynamics reveals how complex the subject is, and that it is not at all obvious,[20] how knowledge can be 'forgotten' and how some results can be counter-intuitive. With regard to the loss of knowledge, it is worth asking how it was possible for the importance of the proper operation of the State, with its monopoly on legitimate means of violence, the theory of which was set out by writers such as Hobbes in the 17th century and Weber in the early 20th century[21] and which has been long practised, to be forgotten to such

17 Interview conducted by the author, spring 2006.
18 Hélène Lavoix, *Indicateurs et méthodologies de prévision des crises et conflits: Evaluation*, Paris, AFD, 2005b, <www.cedoc.defense.gouv.fr/article.php3?id_article=790>
19 E Mansfield & J. Snyder, "Democratization and War" Foreign Affairs, Vol. 74, No 3, p. 79-97, May-June 1995.
20 Alice Ackermann, "The Idea and Practice of Conflict Prevention" *Journal of Peace Research*, vol. 40, No 3, 2003, p. 339-347.
21 Max Weber, *Le savant et le politique*, Paris, 10/18, 1963, originally published in German as "Wissenschaft als Beruf " & "Politik als Beruf" 1919.

an extent, whether we think of the current situation in Iraq, the negative political consequences of the macro-economic reforms of the 1980s or, again, the current emphasis placed on fragile states, all of which is evidence of the rediscovery of the importance of the state.[22]

With regard to the danger of false intuition, we might remember, for example, that poverty, usually measured in GDP per capita, is often considered to be a condition that makes conflicts more likely. Now, theoretical work as well as empirical data, such as the case of the former Yugoslavia as compared with many much poorer countries where war has not broken out, show that this supposition is false, and that it is in fact feelings of injustice and relative deprivation which increase the likelihood of conflict.[23] This last example emphasises, additionally, the importance of early warning systems for crises and conflicts that can be applied universally, including to wealthy countries, because it is no longer elsewhere that crises can break out, affecting them in a knock-on manner, but they can also break out directly in wealthy countries, since 'development' and 'wealth' are no longer guarantees of peace.

With regard to the second point, while it is certain that such early warning systems ought already to exist and to form an integral part of the various institutions of the State focusing on foreign or domestic affairs since one of the State's duties is to ensure external security and domestic peace,[24] the first task will be to verify the effectiveness and relevance of these systems, the extent to which they are geared to the modern world, and how far new knowledge acquired through research and experience has been incorporated. The second task will be to produce an amalgamation of the warnings produced in this way, especially if they come from different departments, agencies or ministries, in order to make them consistent with each other. This confirms the importance of an actively managed early warning system and once again suggests that a federating structure is needed.

This need to bring together and compare existing different warning systems, in order to synthesise their results, emphasises a difficulty which confronts those interested in forecasting, namely the over-abundance of information and reports usually emanating from the experts and practitioners mentioned above, and information, in the form of open or secret sources. This over-abundance of information can overload the information systems and can be more harmful than a lack of information because it gives the illusion of knowledge. It is vital, in fact, that the data available is verified, classified, identified and organised so that it can lead to an understanding. This approach, once again, is that proposed by science and therefore needs to be based on a system which makes it possible to select relevant information, so that through analysis and incorporation into the warning system it is possible for the best forecast to be made, which may possibly lead to additional data being sought out, if it is not available in the current large mass of data.

## Do response difficulties invalidate early warning systems?

With regard to an inability to translate a warning into a response,[25] there are three arguments put forward.

1. The warning would not make it possible to define a programme for action.

2. When the warning is submitted to politicians, it only receives, at best, a limited attention if not ignored. The lack of interest by politicians is said to be due, on the one hand, to the mismatch in time frames between election dates and preventative

22 See the joint work to be published on this subject by the Ministry of Foreign Affairs and the French Development Agency.
23 Nicholas Sambanis, "Using Case Studies to Expand the Theory of Civil War" *CPR Working Papers*, World Bank, Social Development Department Environmentally and Socially Sustainable Development Network, Paper No 5, May 2003; Moore, *op. cit.*
24 Moore, *op. cit.*
25 Cf. In general the majority of works dealing with forecasting and prevention of conflicts; for example, for a good summary, Hugh Miall, Oliver Ramsbotham and Tom Woodhouse, *Contemporary Conflict Resolution*, Cambridge, Polity Press, 1999; or Ackermann, op. cit., on the problem of knowledge and action. In the specific case of genocides, problems connected with forecasting and response are set out by Jacques Sémelin, Purifier et détruire : *usages politiques des massacres et génocides*, Paris, Seuil, 2005.

actions and, on the other hand, to the absence of a suggestion for action accompanying the warning. These two first criticisms are therefore partially connected.

3. In some cases, the difficult situation is said to be well known, and forecast for a long time, but no response is really given.

At each stage in prevention, namely:
1. Forecasting;
2. Warning and dissemination of the warning;
3. Diagnosis;
4. Planning of the response, and finally
5. Response implementation.

Decisions will be necessary and will, on each occasion, give rise to specific difficulties.

The fact that a stage, whatever it may be, may present an obstacle does not mean that the whole process should be abandoned. On the contrary, efforts need to be made to resolve each problem.

The first stumbling block, which is the need to define a programme for action, may only be a stumbling block at first view. We have seen that the early warning system should be based on an understanding of the instability or conflicts and their dynamics, of a scientific nature. Thus, if such a system makes it possible to forecast a situation and to set off a warning, it can only do so because the measures arising from some of the indicators or mechanisms that form it have been identified

as increasing the likelihood of conflict or instability. It follows that the 'crisis-generating' areas are known.

Although, as a precautionary measure, practitioners of early warning emphasize the fact that they can only reveal problems and not propose solutions, it seems that we actually have here, at the least, a preliminary identification of factors in crises. If an additional more detailed diagnostic stage, possibly having recourse to country experts, is incorporated as a final stage in the warning system, then the broad outlines of action programmes can be presented to the politicians or to those taking decisions when the warning is made public. Thus, two of the objections raised above have been dealt with.

The second criticism is more serious and more difficult. It stresses the difficulties encountered by contemporary democracies, which are often prisoner to the media, and by complex machinery of State, in adapting to the modern world. In the long term, it seems unlikely that political systems will be able to last if they cannot take decisions and act on the basis of political-historical time, which is a long period. We are therefore faced with an obstacle that goes beyond the subject of early warning and is an integral part of a major challenge confronting many countries. Overcoming it will probably require numerous adjustments and some time. However, the fact that we need to resolve this problem, which is broader than the one concerning us here, is no reason to do nothing, since any

attempt to improve even a very small part of a system contributes to the collective efforts required to improve the whole.

Finally, with regard to the lack of response despite a well-known diagnosis, as in the case of Darfur, such a verdict would firstly require a detailed analysis including knowing when the exact situation became known – in other words, at what stage in the conflict was a warning given? In addition, developing an early warning system does not imply intervention in all situations. It is a question of obtaining an as clear a picture as possible of possible developments in the current situation, so that informed choices can be made based on the objectives and available resources. Thus, in view of the specific goals of an actor and its resources, or those of the international community, if the warning is given at too late a stage in escalation, it may become impossible to provide an appropriate response.

So, having examined several major objections to prevention in general, and to early warning systems in particular, we have seen that they may be dealt with if the difficulties that they emphasise are taken into account. An early warning system must thus make it possible to select and organise a large variety of information derived from various sources, while being based on an understanding of instability or the dynamics of conflicts and crises, and of a scientific nature and regularly verified and updated. It may use the results of other warning or risk analysis systems and present, as a minimum, outlines for action proposals when communicated to politicians. These first results must be included in the introduction of an early warning system for which we are now going to see in more detail how and in what stages it may be developed.

### Implementing an early warning system
#### The structure responsible
#### for the warning

We saw in the introduction that by positioning them at state level, for early warning systems and for prevention more generally, three main areas of intervention were involved: development and cooperation aid – the actors being, in addition, involved earlier and for longer in the prevention of the crisis – foreign affairs and defence. An early warning system should be able to meet the expectations of the three actors involved and facilitate joint action by them. In view of these imperatives and those concerned with coordination, joint work is required.

Besides, in view of the diverse interests, actions and perceptions of the various actors, the experience of some officials in charge of early warning systems appears to indicate that it is necessary to make use of a federating body, or even to create one. These three types of actor and the information services would participate in the body. This structure could go beyond individual needs and merge them together. It could also arrange for ac-

tion by other actors, depending on circumstances, such as justice, commerce, customs, etc. As forcefully confirmed by an official with experience in early warning systems and forecasting systems within state institutions, it is therefore vital for the body to be given sufficient authority, within the framework of its duties, and the requisite staff and resources.

It is not a case of depriving traditional bodies of their various early warning capacities, nor of interfering with their tasks, but, on the contrary, of structuring in the best way possible these different areas of expertise within a coherent whole.

In cases linked to an emergency, in particular, and thus to traditional type early warning systems, an overarching structure could also promote inter-ministry or inter-institutional dialogue, to discuss the results of the warning and the diagnoses and to contribute to the planning of a coordinated response. Although having benefits in terms of cost, the most flexible solution, consisting solely of inter-ministry or interdepartmental meetings, even if these are regular, seems in fact unable to function, precisely because of the lack of an authority responsible for synthesising and acting as a referee, as well as monitoring and forecasting system management issues, in the event of a change in personnel. However, there is a risk that the federating structure could turn into an 'extra' institu-

tion, and thus that its authority would be diluted and its effectiveness diminished. Thus, the positioning of this body in the general establishment plan of the state concerned will be a crucial decision, as will the readiness to cooperate of the participating ministries or agencies and the investment and motivation of the staff leading it.

#### Objectives and priorities

The aim of an early warning system, as defined by a high-ranking official in charge of such a system, is to obtain sufficient details on the world situation sufficiently early to enable the authority in place to establish a policy, whether this is in terms of total prevention or mitigation of potential adverse consequences, and this is to be achieved in line with overall political objectives.

The smooth operation of an early warning system thus requires some effort with regard to the definition of the general objectives of the actor involved. For example, the main security objective could be to protect a country from terrorist threats or from any kind of threat. This may be combined with an energy supply objective, with purely geopolitical considerations, with a wish to increase political influence or strengthen historical links, a wish to protect its nationals, etc. Since it will lead to the definition of priorities, this prior highlighting exercise will also be crucial once the stage of planning a response is reached.[26]

---

26 For an outline of the importance of priorities, Général Bonningues, *art. cit.*

## What phenomenon should the warning relate to?

Depending on the objectives defined, the early warning system will attempt to identify the main elements and dynamics leading to the risk or situation to be prevented.

Thus, the warning may relate to instability, if it has been judged to be the main cause of the threats that need to be forecast. It may also relate to conflicts, if identifying and preventing them makes it possible to achieve the objectives already defined.

## Creating the warning system
### Understanding, consistency and modelling

Once the objectives and the object of the warning have been defined, as the experience of those in charge of operational early warning systems teaches us, we need to create a system that can successfully identify and forecast the phenomenon to which the warning relates. This, as we have seen, requires a scientific approach. It will therefore be necessary to attempt, initially using the results of existing research, as some

state bodies have done when they decided to equip themselves with an early warning system, to understand the mechanisms and dynamics underlying the problem in question. A synthesis of the various theoretical approaches will be required, together with transformation of social science research that is not always designed to be applied.

The main types of method used for forecasting can be placed along an axis ranging from purely qualitative, where there is a detailed analysis by one or more experts, including a varying number of cases, to quantitative, usually based on a statistical approach seeking to correlate various variables and the result sought, such as the ACTOR system of the US Center for Army Analysis, or some work done by the University of Maryland.[27] The quantitative perspective also includes the collection of varying sizes of indicators, measurable and measured, such as those of the Country Indicators for Foreign Policy (CIFP) in Canada, which offer its users an exceptional database.[28] However, if no link between these indicators is provided, it is then imperative that the whole be

contextualised by analysts.[29] In addition, aggregating measures together, while remaining difficult, only makes it possible to give an index at the macro level.[30]

While the quantitative approach permits the necessary comparison and systematisation, its main problem is an inability to highlight chains of causation and dynamics.[31] The traditional qualitative approach, for its part, requires the use of many experts, which makes systematisation and comparison difficult, although they are vital for forecasting and warning. However, the qualitative method may be systematised by the use of indicators of the 'key questions' type, measured in a binary or logical manner (yes/no).[32] Similarly, the automatic approach of the quantitative method can incorporate measures of qualitative analysis and consideration of causation chains (if these have previously been identified), for example through event data analysis.[33]

Briefly, by coding each element of a phrase (who, what, to whom, where, when), this method makes it possible to calculate

27 The data on ACTOR, FORECITE and FOREWARN come from MORS Workshop: "The Global War on Terrorism: Analytic Support, Tools and Metrics of Assessment" 30 November-2 December 2004, Naval War College, Newport, Rhode Island, Phalanx online *The Bulletin of Military Operations Research* – Vol. 38 No 1 2005, and from Chris Yiu and Nick Mabey, "Countries at Risk of Instability: Practical Risk Assessment, Early Warning and Knowledge Management" Risk Assessment; PMSU Background Paper, February 2005, p. 40 & 43, quoted in Lavoix, Op. Cit. 2005b, for a brief outline of the US system ACTOR, p. 141-142 and the databases of the CIDCM programme of the University of Maryland, p. 143.

28 <www.carleton.ca/cifp/>. For an introduction and analysis of these indicators, see Lavoix, op. cit., 2005b, p. 31-61 and 118-121.

29 Carment, David, "Assessing Country Risk: Creating an Index of Severity" Background Discussion Paper prepared for CIFP Risk Assessment Template, CIFP, May 2001

30 *Ibid.*

31 MORS, *art. cit.*

32 Angelika Spelten, "An Indicator Model for Use as an Additional Instrument for Planning and analysis in Development Co-operation" *Crisis Analysis in Development Co-operation*, (Bonn: BMZ, August 1998) and *Early Warning Indicators of Armed Conflict*, BMZ, 2003.

33 For example, Bond, Doug, Bond, Joe, Oh, Churl, Jenkins, J. Craig, Taylor Charles Lewis, "Integrated Data for Events Analysis (IDEA): An Event Typology for Automated Events Data Development" *Journal of Peace Research*, vol. 40, No 6, 2003, p. 733-745. For a summary of this method and its use, see Lavoix, *op. cit.*, 2005b, p. 128-138 and p. 142. The work on " traitements automatisés des données discursives" carried out by Céditec of the University of Paris 12, working together with other research centres, could be analysed with a view to applying them to early warning.

the occurrence of events such as those specifically defined by the user. In the sphere of prevention of an ethnic war, for example, one could thus know how many times, in a country X, a group of actors (to be defined) has threatened another group (also to be defined). A marked increase in such an indicator could suggest that the transition towards violence is underway. This method is used by the Virtual Research Associate company (VRA) created by Harvard researchers; by SwissPeace Foundation's early warning system, FAST, in combination with pure qualitative analysis focused on networks of actors; and by the FORECITE (using open sources) and FOREWARN (using restricted sources) systems of the US Center for Army Analysis.[34]

Before adopting any method and being able to assess its relevance, it therefore seems necessary to understand the object of the warning as well as possible. If the warning relates to conflicts, then first of all we must define what a conflict is. An effort will be made to understand its dynamics by including, for example, the Kosimo stages of escalation, as shown in Table 1 above. In view of developments in the understanding of the object of the warning, secondary objectives may also be added, seeking, for instance, to identify increasing fragility of states, this being considered to be a cause

of conflict, as has seemed to be the case since early 2005.[35]

If the objective is to prevent instability, then after having defined the concept, efforts will be made to find the processes that underlie instability. One could, for instance, use the following as analytical categories connected to instability: the collapse of states, humanitarian emergencies, large-scale conflicts, violent regime changes, or the existence of areas outside the law within the country. It will then be possible to make use of statistical quantitative methods. However, with these tools it is not possible to take processes into account. It would thus be necessary, for each of these categories, to understand their dynamics, as well as the interactions between various categories that may increase the risks. For example, a humanitarian emergency is not destabilising in itself, but needs to be understood within its context and development. The famine linked to the desertification of the Sahel or the tragic living conditions in certain parts of Bangladesh during the floods are humanitarian emergencies. However, the consequences in terms of instability may be neither direct nor immediate. It would probably be necessary to introduce a special approach for these kinds of risk which, along the lines of early warning systems linked to natural risks, might be categorised as 'slow and erosive'.[36]

The approach chosen may consist of a narrower and more specific definition of risks, which therefore attempts to create as many early warning systems as there are risks. At this stage in creating the system, it may turn out that these risks are all generated by the same types of cause or are governed by the same dynamics, such as instability or civil wars, and therefore that an early warning system that takes a broader approach to the principal cause may be more successful and less onerous. It will then be necessary to carry out the process again for the new subject of the warning.

Once these theoretical foundations have been defined, a synthesis or selection of the methods that seem to be the most successful with regard to the object must be carried out. Next, the task will be to translate these theories into an operational system that make forecasting and warning possible.

With regard to conflicts, specific 'indicators/questions' can be created, based on the precise assumptions connected with the understanding that has been developed, making it possible to take into account the history and values of the countries involved with the aim of collecting and ordering information.[37] The questions may be grouped by subject, with each category being then given a different weight for final

---

34 *Ibid.* For VRA see <vranet.com/>; for FAST, <www.swisspeace.org/fast/>, for FOREWARN and FORECITE, see note 16.
35 See note [15].
36 Glantz, Michael H., *Usable Science 8 - Early Warning Systems: Do's and Don'ts*, Shanghai: Report of the Workshop on Early Warning Systems, 20-23 October 2003; 6 February 2004, p. 12-13.
37 As an example, we have the BMZ system of indicators, created by Angelika Spelten, *art. cit.* and *op. cit.*

aggregation, in line with its significance with regard to the outbreak of a conflict. For instance, structural factors may be assessed as having less weight than those measuring escalation towards violence. This method can be described as belonging to the systematic qualitative type.

Faced with a great diversity of explanations and tools and attempting to retain the best of them, a synthesis appears impossible and the choice may be to select some quantitative methods, and then to try to identify the countries with the same 'profiles'. These countries will then be grouped according to their similarities. The first disadvantage of this method is that it is not based on an understanding of the dynamics and therefore it seems that it will not allow a warning focusing on a small period of time, whereas this is one of its main objectives. In addition, it would tend to aggregate variables without seeking the links between them. The risk is therefore that of being left with an inoperative warning system or of generating unjustified warnings as far as it mixes issues together without placing them in order.

Another way of tackling the diversity of methods, and this choice has been made by some of institutions, is to add expert analysis to the statistical quantitative approaches and event data analysis based on an identification of the dynamics of conflicts or instability. More than just an early warning system, such as system then becomes a process.

The time period under consideration for forecasting and warning may range from six months to five years, as we will see in the section dealing with results. It is vital for this to be linked in a consistent way with the system developed.

### What entities will the warning deal with?

When the system is being created, and as a logical connection to the model developed, the 'population' which will be the subject of a potential warning must be defined. In view of the objectives of the warning, this population is usually made up of the member states of the international community. The basis may thus be the 192 member states of the United Nations, an approach chosen by some States.

However, as confirmed by some creators of early warning systems, depending on the original objectives of the actor implementing the warning system, this may be reduced, for instance, by only taking into account certain countries that fall within a traditional area of influence. It will be necessary, however, to check that such an a priori selection is consistent with the original objectives previously defined.

It might also be imagined that, for various reasons connected with the subject of the warning, a classification using member states is not the most relevant. Thus, geographical regions that combine several states might in some cases be chosen, such as the Great Lakes region in Africa, or parts of states, as in the CEWARN early warning system of the Intergovernmental Authority on Development (IGAD),[38] provided that they are then subdivided into states again, these being the main actors on the international stage.

Similarly, a warning system that seeks to forecast specific threats from non-state actors defined in terms of their ideological affiliations, for instance, could validly choose these groups of actors as its population. They might later be combined with other criteria with a view to monitoring the emergence of new groups. For this forecasting method, it might then be useful to include analysis of networks of actors.[39] The states could combine such a system with a more traditional approach, and a synthesis would then again be required to obtain a coherent whole.

38 The member states of IGAD are: the Republic of Djibouti, Éritrea, the Federal Democratic Republic of Ethiopia, the Republic of Kenya, the Republic of Somalia, the Republic of Sudan and the Republic of Uganda. CEWARN site: <www.cewarn.org/>. For a brief introduction, see Lavoix, op. cit., 2005b, and p. 133-134.
39 For an example of an early warning system that incorporates an analysis of actors' networks, see the FAST system, August Hämmerli, Regula Gattiker, Reto Weyermann, "Conflict and Cooperation in an Actors' Network of Chechnya Based on Event Data", Journal of Conflict Resolution, Vol. 50 No 2, April 2006, p. 159-175.

At all levels of designing the system, it is therefore crucial to develop a dynamic understanding of the subject and to abide by the logical links between the various stages, which will ensure that the system created actually does direct the forecasting and the warning towards the situation to be prevented.

## Using the early warning system: organisation, information and results

Once the modelling of the warning system has been developed, it needs to be activated and managed, which requires an organisation and an input of data, in order to obtain the results to which the warning will, in the end, relate.

### Organisation

The experience of users of early warning systems shows that the whole warning process is conducted in general about once or twice a year. At the same time, units that are the subject of an extremely urgent warning may be monitored regularly.

When the warning system is made up of a single mode, composed for instance of key questions, use can be made of an external centre of experts, or personnel working on the ground may be asked, after receiving brief training, if necessary, to complete the questionnaire. It is vital that the questionnaire be made up of simple questions and that it can be completed in one or two hours per country.

One person or a team, working cooperatively and in such a way that the members can compare the results obtained, will then be responsible for collecting the information, analysing the responses and carrying out the calculation. If the results are very different from those obtained previously, the analyst must verify with the person who filled in the form the reasons for this change in order to reduce the likelihood of disparities that might be the result of bias in perception. For each country, the initial questionnaire may be summarised in one or two pages, stressing developments as compared with the previous analysis and giving a graphic depiction of the curves for the various indicators.

When the warning system is made up of a mixture of various tools, the first stage will be to obtain the results derived from the different methods. With regard to the use of analysts at the beginning of the process, it seems sensible to make use of as broad a range of experts as possible, combining knowledge that is external and internal to the actor for whom the warning is being carried out. The results will then be compared. Where they converge, the countries involved will be placed in the corresponding category. Where they diverge, the structure with responsibility for the early warning will contact the various experts involved and try to analyse the reasons for this divergence. A decision to place a country in a particular warning category will, in the end, be the responsibility of the structure in charge of the warning system.

After this first classification, which is particularly useful in removing from the 'population' to be analysed those countries with only a very slight degree of risk, those remaining on the list may be grouped by geographical regions. A second stage of classification may then begin, using, for instance, detailed interviews with specialists, as well as a specific questionnaire connected with the subject of the warning. A particular concern at this stage will be to emphasise the dynamics of conflict or instability that exist for each of the countries examined. This diagnosis will then make it possible to prepare possible response options.

Then, analysts from the early warning unit may meet and examine, one by one, the results obtained for each country. They will thus locate each country within its category, either on the curve of conflicts or in relation to the risks of instability.

Whatever form of organisation is chosen, it is important to combine two ingredients: the use of human analysis and one or more of the most systematic, comparative, and objective methods that exist. As well as meeting the criteria seen above, a quantitative approach makes it possible to correct or minimise any bias linked to human perception or, in the case of meetings, to group dynamics; a qualitative approach adds back in, within a designed framework, intuition, analytical and synthetic capacities, emotional elements and complexity of thought.

Finally, the organisation must include knowledge management and self-assessment, which will enable it to include the results of new research and also to learn from any errors that may be made. Each error detected must be the subject of a diagnosis to identify its origin and correct the system appropriately. This process must be planned over the long term so that very remote warnings can be taken into account.

## Information

Information may come from open or restricted access sources. As we saw previously, it is not so much the availability of information as its relevance that poses a problem. With regard to a state, in fact, a lot of data is put forward, without reference to any particular situation, because of the existence of information services and networks of diplomatic bodies and other agencies covering the various political, military, economic, and social milieus. Comprehensive access to the media and the use of networks of external experts may be added to this arrangement.

The problem of selecting relevant information is directly related to the design of the warning system and should therefore be resolved during the design process. In particular, the model created must make it possible to combat involuntary cognitive closures (obedience to methods, unconscious choices, selective screening caused by emotion, prejudice, etc.).[40] It must also ensure that information from sub-national sources, depending on the circumstances, can be passed on. Whatever the warning system, the main concern when it is being used will be to assess the validity of the raw information, then to restrict any bias linked to the perceptions of the analyst.

With regard to raw information, the double assessment system using the source, on the one hand, and vectored information, on the other hand, has proven itself in particular within the information services or more recently in the system introduced by FAST. It should, however, be noted that rumours, partially true news and narration may be useful, in that they reveal the beliefs and aims, concerns and anxieties of the actors under consideration.[41]

In addition to reducing them through the use of a systematic model, the perceptual bias of the analyst will be easier to correct by comparing analyses over time and with other countries, as well as through a check on the internal consistency and logic of the argument set out.

## The results

The final result will display a distribution of the units covered by the warning system, which are usually countries, classified with regard to the subject of the warning.

As existing early warning systems show, if the subject is conflict, then the countries may be classified depending on their position on the curve of stages of conflict. If the subject is instability, then the countries may be grouped in line with various time horizons of instability, such as six months, two years, and five years. This second form of classification, although more traditional and easier to manage in terms of planning a response, is also less certain. In fact, it imposes a measuring scale, namely time, as an extrinsic absolute, whereas historical time is really variable in terms of the actors' interactions.[42] To overcome this difficulty, it would be necessary to explain the mechanisms and dynamics connected with instability, as has been done for conflicts.

On the other hand, the locating of a result on the curve of conflicts, which is more faithful to reality and therefore gives more reliable results, will possibly be difficult to translate into a response, especially due to the habitual practices of planning. Additional 'translation' work will therefore need to be carried out to convert from time measured in

---

40 For an example of closure and opening of cognitive filters in crisis situations, Hélène Lavoix, 'Nationalism' and 'Genocide': the construction of nation-ness, authority and opposition — The case of Cambodia (1861-1979), PhD Thesis, SOAS — University of London, 2005a.
41 See, for example, the work of the philosophers Wittgenstein and Quine or the neurobiologists Maturana and Varela. For an example of application to specific cases, Lavoix, op. cit., 2005a.
42 See Lavoix, op. cit., 2005b, p. 26-28.

tension to time measured in the traditional form of months and years.

The number of countries, classified by categories and appearing on the final list, will in fact depend on the reality of the situation. It is impossible to set in advance the number of countries that are unstable or at the risk of a conflict. If we imagine, for example, that a new world war is on the horizon, then a very large number of countries will be in a state of advanced escalation. It would be impossible and even dangerous to arbitrarily decide that only some of these should be marked out as the subject of a warning. The indices that make it possible to detect global danger would not be perceived, and a suitable diagnosis would not be performed nor would the requisite responses be planned. It is therefore not possible to restrict in advance the final result of the early warning system.

## Correlating the results from the early warning system with objectives and resources

The resulting list of countries, appropriately classified, may, or rather must be correlated with the objectives defined initially and the resources available. From this point, a new list of, for instance, between 20 and 60 countries, may be selected for intervention or response.

## Launching the warning: decision and proposals for action

As we saw in the second section, it would seem that a warning in itself is not enough to attract the attention of politicians. They also need solutions to be put forward to them.

Therefore, a detailed diagnosis needs to be attached to the warning, with assessments of possible preventative actions and their consequences, and finally proposals for a response, the latter being put forward together with the result of the warning.

Early warning systems thus allow a relatively broad first analysis, at the least, of the problems facing the countries being monitored. Next, an expert or group of experts should be consulted, for each country, to draw up a precise diagnosis of risk, instability or conflict situation for each country. The skills that will be required at this level must include not only knowledge of the country but also an understanding of the dynamics underlying the phenomena that are to be prevented. The team in charge of the early warning system must then review these detailed analyses. It might be advisable to employ the scenarios method at this stage. Possibly, further coordination with the results obtained by the specific early warning 'sub-systems' of other institutions may then take place.

Next, with the involvement of the various relevant ministries, departments or agencies, these scenarios would be transformed into potential short intervention programmes or response planning, setting out the broad strategic approach for an action that would be as effective as possible, and then all the responses would be reviewed and assessed in terms of the objectives and available resources, thus defining some priorities.[43]

This process would make it possible not only to examine the multi-dimensional effects of an action, but also to select the best time to act. Only a correlation of the potential actions and the dynamic dimension of the processes to which the warning relates can produce such a picture in the long term.

It is this list of countries, categorised and accompanied by possible responses, which can finally be used to launch the warning, and thus be submitted to the final decision-makers. At the same time, a decision may be taken to systematically monitor the countries with the highest level of risk, as is currently the case, so that developments in the situation can be monitored continuously. An internal warning may also be issued within various institutions, including diplomatic bodies, offices and agencies on

43 For an outline of the importance of priorities, Général Bonningues, art. cit.

the ground, so that all the actions taken in respect of these countries are redefined and coordinated to take into account the forecast situation.

### The early warning system and the international system: alignment

At this stage, relying on its knowledge of the international situation generated by the early warning system and with a clear vision of its objectives and the resources to be implemented to achieve them, the actor will be able to meet other states and multilateral bodies so that a coordinated international response, which is satisfactory to it, can be put in place. As this process lies outside the field of this study, I will restrict myself here to examining the difficulties and benefits that may result from the use of various early warning systems by the various international actors. This diversity is a result of the anarchic nature of the international system, albeit one governed by rules. In contrast to the case within a country, it is impossible for a single warning system to be selected as the authoritative one.

However, as the diversity of warnings may give rise to doubts and prolong the time taken for consideration and decision-making, some may suggest that one country and therefore one warning system be adopted as a reference point. Such an approach would run counter to the principle of the independence and sovereignty of states and might have dangerous consequences in terms of hegemony. In a world where responses must be coordinated for reasons of effectiveness, cost, and legitimacy, how is diversity to be managed without it resulting in inaction? A managed diversity may represent one form of response.

Within the early warning process, an additional stage of communication with the other actors in the international community can be inserted. Thus, the results of warning systems, before being correlated with the resources and objectives of each state, could be exchanged, according to the wish of the actors. The differences between the results would then be compared, using a technical approach, and without forgetting that the initial objectives of the actors will have governed the creation of the early warning systems. This would require efforts in terms of transparency, but would also make it possible perhaps to improve forecasting tools and to disseminate knowledge, while reducing reasons for a lack of understanding.

At this stage, the consequences of too wide a communication of the results of the early warning systems should be taken into account, particularly for the countries or groups affected. These potential effects will have to be assessed and incorporated into the general strategy.

Lastly, there will still be negotiations connected with the diverging objectives of the international actors, which also guarantee a certain degree of freedom.

### Conclusion

First of all, I defined what an early warning system should be, while setting out the overall prevention process of which it forms a part.

Next, based on the resistance and opposition generated by the use of early warning systems, I pointed out several difficulties and constraints that should be taken into account when the procedure is being designed.

Lastly, I suggested that a federating structure within a state body would be best able to successfully manage this warning system, because of the needs for synthesis and management of differing time horizons required. I then analysed seven major stages in the implementation of an early warning system, from the definition of the state's objectives and overall strategies to the system's design, use and finally the difficulties relating to the need for a coordinated response prepared within the inescapable diversity of the international world.

Challenging the inevitability in the preventative approach, that would say that only failure can be detected, early warning systems, by helping to incorporate responses into an overall strategy and helping to measure their effects regularly, contribute to creating the confidence upon which, in the end, the reduction of uncertainty and insecurity is based.

## Bibliography

Ackermann, Alice, "The Idea and Practice of Conflict Prevention", *Journal of Peace Research*, vol. 40, No 3, 2003, p. 339-347.

Bond, Doug, Bond, Joe, Oh, Churl, Jenkins, J. Craig, Taylor Charles Lewis, "Integrated Data for Events Analysis (IDEA): An Event Typology for Automated Events Data Development", *Journal of Peace Research*, vol. 40, No 6, 2003, p. 733-745.

Bonningues, Jacques, Général, Bureau du Haut Représentant pour la Sécurité et la Prévention des Conflits, "non-paper", 15 May 2006.

Bremmer, Ian "Managing Risk in an Unstable World", HBR Spotlight, *Harvard Business Review*, Onpoint article product 1126, 2005.

Briand, Aristide, Sénat, 25 March 1930, quoted on the monument "À Aristide Briand – Pax", placed in front of the Ministry of Foreign Affairs, Paris.

Brown, Michael E. and Rosecrance, Richard N., eds., *The Cost-Effectiveness of Conflict Prevention*, Lanham, MD, Rowman & Littlefield, 1998.

Carment, David, "Assessing Country Risk: Creating an Index of Severity" *Background Discussion Paper prepared for CIFP Risk Assessment Template*, CIFP, May 2001.

*Carnegie Commission on Preventing Deadly Conflict*, December 1997, <www.carnegie.org/sub/research/>.

Châtaignier, Jean-Marc et Gaulme, François, "Agir en faveur des acteurs et des sociétés fragiles : Pour une vision renouvelée des enjeux de l'aide au développement dans la prévention et la gestion de crises", *Document de travail*, No 5, AFD, September 2005.

Châtaignier, Jean-Marc, *L'ONU dans la crise en Sierra Leone. Les méandres d'une négociation*, Paris, CEAN-Karthala, 2005.

Collier, Paul & Anke Hoeffler, "Greed and grievance in Civil War" *Processed Paper*, Development Research Group, World Bank, 2002.

Ebata, Michi, *From the discourse to the ground: UNDP activities in conflict prevention*, New York, UNDP Bureau for Crisis Prevention and Recovery, May 2003.

Glantz, Michael H., *Usable Science 8 - Early Warning Systems: Do's and Don'ts*, Shanghai: Report of the Workshop on Early Warning Systems, 20-23 October 2003; 6 February 2004.

Hämmerli, August, Gattiker, Regula, Weyermann, Reto, "Conflict and Cooperation in an Actors' Network of Chechnya Based on Event Data", *Journal of Conflict Resolution*, Vol. 50 No 2, April 2006, p. 159-175

Heidelberg Institute on International Conflict Research (HIIK), *Conflict Barometer 2005, Crises; Wars; Coups d'État; Negotiations; Mediations; Peace Settlements*; 14th Annual Conflict Analysis, revised edition, Department of Political Science, University of Heidelberg, December 2005; <www.hiik.de/en/index_e.htm>.

International Institute of Security Studies, "Diamonds and conflicts", *Strategic Comments*, Vol. 6 No 4, 2000.

Lavoix, Hélène, *"Nationalism" and "Genocide": the construction of nation-ness, authority and opposition – The case of Cambodia (1861-1979)*; PhD Thesis, SOAS – University of London, 2005.

Lavoix, Hélène, *Indicateurs et méthodologies de prévision des crises et conflits: Evaluation*, Paris, AFD, 2005, <www.cedoc.defense.gouv.fr/article.php3?id_article=790>

Luttwak, Edward "Give War a Chance", *Foreign Affairs*, July-August, 1999.

Mansfield, E, & Snyder, J., "Democratization and War" *Foreign Affairs*, Vol. 74, No 3, p. 79-97, May-June1995.

Miall, Hugh Oliver Ramsbotham and Tom Woodhouse, *Contemporary Conflict Resolution*, Cambridge, Polity Press, 1999.

Moore, Barrington, *Injustice: Social bases of Obedience and Revolt*, London, Macmillan, 1978.

*MORS Workshop*: "The Global War on Terrorism: Analytic Support, Tools and Metrics of Assessment" 30 November – 2 December 2004, Naval War College, Newport, Rhode Island, Phalanx online, The bulletin of Military Operations Research – Vol. 38 No 1 2005.

PMSU–PCRI - *Investing in Prevention*, 2005.

Rubin, B. R., « Afghanistan: la souveraineté comme condition de sécurité » *Critique internationale*, No 28, July-September 2005, p. 169-183.

Sambanis, Nicholas "Using Case Studies to Expand the Theory of Civil War" *CPR Working Papers*, World Bank, Social Development Department Environmentally and Socially Sustainable Development Network, Paper No 5, May 2003.

Sémelin, Jacques, *Purifier et détruire : usages politiques des massacres et génocides*, Paris, Seuil, 2005.

Spelten, Angelika, "An Indicator Model for Use as an Additional Instrument for Planning and Analysis in Development Co-operation" *Crisis Analysis in Development Co-operation*, Bonn, BMZ, August 1998.

Spelten, Angelika, *Early Warning Indicators of Armed Conflict*, Bonn, BMZ, 2003.

Steering Committee of the Joint Evaluation of Emergency Assistance to Rwanda, *Rebuilding Post-War Rwanda*, The International Response to Conflict and Genocide: Lessons from the Rwanda Experience, Study 4, Copenhagen: March 1996.

Straw, Jack, Speech given at the Foreign Policy Centre, 25 March 2002.

Walter, B. "Does Conflict Beget Conflict? Explaining Recurring Civil War", *Journal of Peace Research*, 41:3, 2004.

Walzer, Michael, *Guerres justes et injustes : argumentation morale avec exemples historiques*, Paris, Gallimard, 2006.

Weber, Max, *Le savant et le politique*, Paris, 10/18, 1963, originally published in German as « Wissenschaft als Beruf » & « Politik als Beruf » 1919.

Yiu, Chris and Mabey, Nick, "Countries at Risk of Instability: Practical Risk Assessment, Early Warning and Knowledge Management;" Risk Assessment; *PMSU Background Paper*, February 2005.

Internet Sites:
Carnegie Commission, <www.carnegie.org/sub/research/>
Centre de documentation de l'École militaire (CEDOC),
CEWARN,
CIFP, <www.carleton.ca/cifp/>
Coface, <www.trading-safely.com/sitecwp/cefr.nsf>
FAST, <www.swisspeace.org/fast/>
Groupe Eurasia, <www.eurasiagroup.net/si/>
HIIK, <www.hiik.de/en/index_e.htm>
The Economic Intelligence Unit,
VRA,
WRMC,

# ON THE INDICATORS OF POTENTIAL CONFLICT

## Introduction

This article will focus on the main factors that contribute to the dangers of violent armed internal conflict erupting, or re-igniting after a peace has been concluded in an erstwhile conflict zone. I have argued that for either of the two forces that have been identified in the literature to cause conflict – greed or grievance – to take the form of large-scale violence there must be other factors at work, specifically a weakening of the 'social contract'.[1] Such a viable social contract can be sufficient to restrain, if not eliminate, opportunistic behaviour such as large-scale theft of resource rents, and the violent expression of grievance. The social contract, therefore, refers to the mechanisms and institutions of peaceful conflict resolution.

What causes these mechanisms underlying a social contract to degenerate? I argue that the term 'failed state' is inappropriate, as very few states actually fail totally; there is degeneration rather than the total breakdown of the social contract. So what factors lead to the breakdown of the social contract within a nation-state? What circumstances create incentives for groups within societies to choose war rather than resolve disputes peacefully?

## Redistributive mechanisms

Within nation-states, the fiscal system will secure a workable social contract if the allocation of public expenditures and the apportionment of taxes are judged to be fair, or at least not so unfair that some groups judge taking resources by force the better option.

There are many examples of conflicts emerging out of fiscal disputes. Côte d'Ivoire, for instance, became unstable with the collapse of the social contract engineered by the late president Houphouët-Boigny, in which he allocated public spending across the regions to successfully buy the loyalty of the country's ethnic groups. Disputes over the apportionment of revenues from natural resources are especially common and, as in Indonesia and Nigeria, these take on ethnic and regional dimensions.

Contemporary civil wars are more often related to the breakdown of explicit or implicit arrangements to share resources or revenues, rather than the absence of an agreement to share resources or rents. One reason that a contract to share revenues encounters difficulties is the imperfect credibility with which the side that controls the 'pot' honours its commitment. Indeed, the presence or discovery of oil or gas may promote secessionist tendencies among groups who do not wish to share it with the rest of the nation.[2]

## Democratic transitions

Political science research points out that the risk of conflict is lower in both well-established democracies and autocracies. It suggests that conflict risk is at its highest during transitions to and away from democracy when state capacity is weak, and also in fledgling and imperfect democracies (anocracies). There is more violent expression of grievances during early democratic phases as the aggrieved feel suddenly empowered. Most developing countries are imperfect democracies, or at any early stage of the democratic transition. In the interim between full-blown forms of either autocracy or democracy (anocracy) countries may have electoral processes which characterise democracy, co-existing with weak or non-existent separation of powers between the executive and the judiciary in particular. This not only prevents them from functioning like true democracies, but impairs governance, especially the rule of law. Another problem is the widespread electoral violence in anocracies. Finally, there is the risk that new democracies can periodically slide back

*Syed Mansoob Murshed of the Institute of Social Studies in the Netherlands is also Professor of International Economics at Birmingham Business School, University of Birmingham, UK. He was the first holder of the rotating Prince Claus Chair in Development and Equity in 2003. He was a Research Fellow at UNU/WIDER in Helsinki where he ran projects on 'Globalisation and Vulnerable Economies' and 'Why Some Countries Avoid Conflict, While Others Fail'. He also ran a project on' The Two Economies of Ireland', financed by the International Fund for Ireland at the Northern Ireland Economic Research Centre (NIERC), Belfast, UK. He is the author of five books and more than 75 book chapters and journal articles. His research interests are in the economics of conflict, aid conditionality, political economy, macroeconomics and international economics.*

1 See Syed Mansoob Murshed and Zulfan Tadjoeddin (2007). 'Reappraising the Greed and Grievance Explanations for Conflict', MICROCON Research Working Paper no 2, see http://www.microconflict.eu/
2 See Michael L. Ross (2003). 'Oil, Drugs and Diamonds: The Varying Role of Natural Resources in Civil Wars', in Karen Ballentine and Jake Sherman (eds), *The Political Economy of Armed Conflict: Beyond Greed and Grievance. Boulder* CO: Lynne Rienner: pp. 47–70.

to autocracy engendering a vicious cycle of democracy to autocracy, back to democracy and so on.

Given the imperfect nature of democracies and good governance in most developing countries we need to be cognizant of the motivation and incentives of their rulers. With regard to incentives faced by rulers in developing countries, it has to be remembered that until the end of the Cold War most developing countries were ruled by strong men. In other words, they were autocracies. Some promoted development, others did not. Compare Mobutu's Zaire (1965-97) to Suharto's Indonesia (1965-98). In Indonesia and Zaire resource flows were volatile. In one case the dictator (Suharto) chose diversification and growth-enhancing strategies, as well as policies aimed at equalisation and poverty reduction to contain political opposition. Development in Indonesia was impressive, and may have led, at least partially, to endogenous demands for democracy. In the other case (Zaire, now DRC), Mobutu did not, because he felt that diversification and investment in infrastructure would loosen his grip on power and strengthen political opposition to him based on ethnicity. Zaire, or the DRC, has perhaps the poorest post-1960 growth record on the planet. Perhaps, in East Asia greater fears of communism strengthened benevolence in dictators (South Korea, Taiwan, Singapore and Indonesia), whereas in Africa a certain type of factionalism dominated policies and politics, retarding growth enhancing economic diversification and infrastructural development.

## The lack of economic progress

The most robust indicator that predicts the risk of conflict is the lack of economic growth and development in low-income countries. In fact, at a higher income people have a lot more to lose from violent means of conflict resolution.[3] The lack of growth also increases vulnerability to economic shocks. Furthermore, the absence of economic growth retards institutional development (democracy and governance), contributing to the risk of armed conflict. It is no surprise that most rich countries are peaceful democracies. Also, the state's capacity to either assuage (through transfers) or suppress (by armed force) malcontents is weaker the poorer the country in question. By the same token, post-conflict economic recovery must be inclusive and broad-based to prevent a new outbreak of grievances.

## Synthesis

To get an empirical feel for some of these channels, a descriptive look at the data may be in order. *Table I*[4] gives us 17 countries with the highest conflict incidence since 1960, along with their average annual long-term growth rates of per-capita income, accompanied by the typology of the economy and the most frequent regime type. In *Table I*, we compare growth rates, the combined democracy and autocracy score known as polity,[5] endowment type and conflict intensity or incidence in selected developing countries during the period 1965-2000. The polity score is an imperfect proxy for institutional capacity and governance, but we have good time series data on these. This is coded 1 for autocracies (those with an autocracy score below –4), 3 for democracies (for democracy scores above 4) and 2 for anocracies that have both democratic and autocratic characteristics (with scores of between –4 and 4). The endowment typology is based upon a country's principal exports,[6] and is subject to change. Note that countries can have more than one year of civil war in any given calendar year if there are several conflicts taking place within the nation simultaneously (e.g. Burma/Myanmar, India, etc.).

3 Seymour Lipset (1960). *Political Man: The Social Bases of Politics*, New York: Doubleday.

4 S. Mansoob Murshed (2006). 'Turning Swords into Ploughshares and Little Acorns to Tall Trees: The Conflict Growth Nexus and the Poverty of Nations', background paper for the UN Department for Economic and Social Affairs World Economic Survey, 2006, at http://www.un.org/esa/policy/wess/

5 These scores range from –10 to 0 for autocracy and 0 to 10 for democracies, making –10 the greatest autocracy score and 10 the highest democracy score; see Murshed (2006) op. cit. for further details.

6 This is based on a country's principal exports, which are described as Point (mineral or fuel), Coffee/Cocoa, Diffuse (other agricultural) or Manufacturing, where arguably dependence on mineral or fuel exports ex ante enhances the risk of conflict.

## Table I: Conflict years, growth, polity and economic typology in selected countries

| Country | Conflict incidence in years, 1960-2000 | Most frequent regime type | Annual average per capita income growth rate, 1965-99 | Economic typology |
|---|---|---|---|---|
| Burma/Myanmar | 177 | 1 | 1.5% | Diffuse, Point |
| India | 104 | 3 | 2.4% | Manufacturing |
| Ethiopia | 81 | 1 | -0.3% | Coffee/Cocoa |
| The Philippines | 59 | 1; 2; 3 | 0.9% | Diffuse, Manufacturing |
| Iraq | 57 | 1 | -3.5% | Point |
| Angola | 43 | 1 | -2.1% | Point |
| Iran | 41 | 1; 2 | -1.0% | Point |
| Algeria | 37 | 1; 2 | 1.0% | Point |
| Chad | 36 | 1 | -0.6% | Point |
| Colombia | 35 | 3 | 2.1% | Coffee/Cocoa |
| Indonesia | 32 | 1 | 4.8% | Point, Manufacturing |
| Guatemala | 31 | 1; 2 | 0.7% | Coffee/Cocoa |
| Sudan | 31 | 1; 2; 3 | 0.5% | Diffuse, Point |
| South Africa | 31 | 2 | 0% | Point |
| Mozambique | 27 | 1 | 1.3% | Diffuse |
| Uganda | 23 | 1; 2 | 2.5% | Coffee/Cocoa |
| Sri Lanka | 22 | 3 | 3.0% | Diffuse, Manufacturing |

Source: Murshed (2006), op. cit, table 4

(a) Only five of these high-conflict incidence nations reported in Table 1 have a per-capita income growth rate in excess of 2 per cent per annum in the long-term: Indonesia, India, Sri Lanka, Colombia and Uganda. Generally speaking, poor growth performers have more conflict years in Table 1. Furthermore, only three point-sourced countries and four coffee/cocoa economies did not descend into some form of civil war.

Diffuse economies also have conflict; examples of the high incidence of civil wars occurring in diffuse economies are in South Asia – the Philippines and Burma/Myanmar – as well as Mozambique and Zimbabwe in Africa. In total, 8 out of 30 diffuse economies have avoided civil war, a record that is better than for point-sourced and coffee/cocoa-based economies. Manufacturing exporters are least likely to experience outright civil war. Perhaps this is because they have the best growth rates and institutional quality. They are also more diversified economies, and are able to withstand the commodity price and national income fluctuations that make growth failure more likely. Growth also needs to be pro-poor, which ultimately means less inequality, so as to minimise the effects of group inequalities and polarisation.

(b) It is discernable that India, Sri Lanka and Colombia are the stable democracies in the post-1960 era that have had civil wars, including high-intensity conflict. Many of the transitions in regime type from autocracy to anocracy to democracy (during 1960-2000) are described in Murshed (2006) op. cit. Multiple switches in all directions are possible, and not just from autocracy to democracy. Nevertheless, only 5 out of the 17 nations with a high conflict incidence have ever been democracies with a democracy score over 4. Democracy, even stable democracy, does not guarantee the absence of armed conflict, both of the secessionist and rebel varieties, as the examples of India, Colombia, Sri Lanka, the Philippines and others indicate. Autocracies also fall into conflict; nevertheless, stable autocracies such as China and Singapore have avoided civil war, as did Taiwan and South Korea, which became democracies recently. Despite prominent outliers such as India, Colombia and Saudi Arabia, most conflict prone countries are neither stable democracies nor autocracies, lending support to the finding that conflict risk is greatest when regime types are in transition, for example from autocracy to democracy.

In summary, problems associated with the democratic transition, the degeneration of redistributive mechanisms and the lack of economic growth contribute to long-term conflict risk. Their short-term manifestations take the form of the inability to cope with economic shocks (associated with falling export prices or natural calamities), or violent political instability. Either way, there are plenty of indicators of both for observers and policy-makers to see; in many cases they will benefit from exchanging information. Decision-makers in developed countries like those in the EU then need to decide when, where and how to intervene – the extent of their reaction is something that is ultimately related to their own political incentives and imperatives.

# IMPROVING EARLY WARNING AND RESPONSE SYSTEMS:
# LEARNING FROM HUMAN SECURITY, PREPARING FOR CLIMATE CHANGE

## Introduction

Effective early warning and response (EW&R) systems would be able to prevent a great deal of human suffering and far-reaching instability caused by manmade and non-manmade violence and harm. An effective EW&R system can be compared to a relay race. All members of the relay team have to work closely together, well attuned to each other and give their best in reach the goals set at the beginning to the race. If the result was less successful than expected, lessons must be learned to improve chances to perform better during the next race. The EW&R system works in a similar, cyclical fashion (*see Figure 1*). Unfortunately, in EW&R systems individual team members do not know each other well, do not understand each other well and are poorly coordinated in reaching their joint goals. Much can be done to improve this situation. As will be argued in this article, many such EW&R systems understand their goal only poorly: threats are pre-defined and pre-selected without much relevance to the affected populations, with early warning systems monitoring trends leading towards or away from those pre-defined threats. For most early warning systems the focus is on the likelihood of political, armed violence. In summary, EW&R systems often suffer, among other technical difficulties, from three main conceptual flaws: they are focused on the

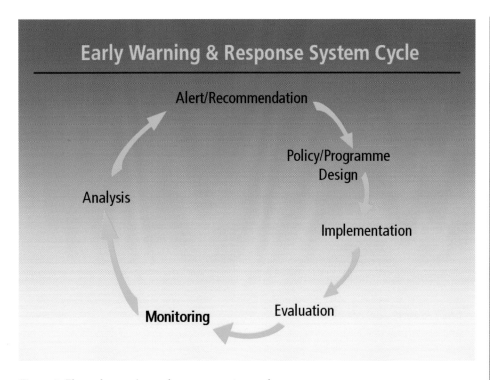

Figure 1: The early warning and response system cycle

wrong threat; their various – ideally integral – parts do not work well together; and thus much timely warning does not lead to timely, relevant and effective action.

In the following text we will look at these challenges by reflecting on some of swisspeace's experience and lessons learned in early warning and response activities. A new focus will be suggested: threat analyses should take the place of conventional conflict analyses when devising and running EW&R systems. Together with improvements in more effective joint efforts when moving from the definition of threats to their monitoring, analysis, warning, policy influence and implementation, working on key threats will likely make the greatest contribution to assuring peace, security and stability. Moreover, as will be argued, success

*Albrecht Schnabel: is the director of the research programme on human security (HUSEC) and coordinator of the early warning programme FAST International at swisspeace, the Swiss Peace Foundation in Bern, Switzerland. He is also a lecturer in International Organisations and Conflict Management at the Institute of Political Science at the University of Bern. Before joining swisspeace in 2003, he served as Academic Officer in the Peace and Governance Programme of the United Nations University, Tokyo, Japan (1998-2003). He has taught at Queen's University (1994), the American University in Bulgaria (1995-1996), Central European University (1996-1998), and Aoyama Gakuin University (2002-2003). In 1997 he was a visiting research fellow at the Institute for Peace Research and Security Policy at the University of Hamburg and participated in OSCE election monitoring missions in Bosnia-Herzegovina. Since 1999 he has served as a trainer for the UN System Staff College course on Early Warning and Early Response and, in 2001-2002, as President of the International Association of Peacekeeping Training Centres.*

in future EW&R efforts is not only desirable but crucially important in the face of one of the most important future threats: climate-induced environmental disasters and their multiple, negative consequences.

## Fine-tuning early warning and response: experience and lessons learned

The work of swisspeace on early warning and early response (see www.swisspeace.org) includes both methodological development as well as practical operationalisation of early warning tools as policy and decision-support aids. More specifically, this work is based on three activities: an early warning programme (FAST), the development of a global crisis prevention mechanism (GCPM) and a human security-focused analysis and monitoring system (OPHUSEC).

## FAST – early analysis of tensions and fact-finding

The political early warning system – FAST – was developed in 1998 to assist development cooperation agencies in their longer-term work on structural prevention. With the help of country teams in each of the 20 to 25 countries monitored by the system, FAST collects cooperative and conflictive event data on both national and sub-national levels. The data serves as the foundation for quantitative as well as qualitative event data and trend analyses. FAST's quantitative research team has developed a tool that allows quantitative forecasting of stability and instability trends (*see Figure 2*). Coun-

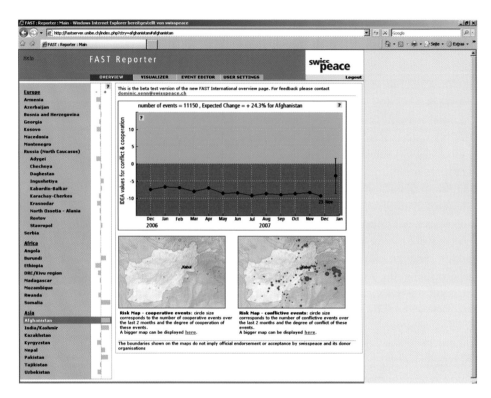

*Figure 2: The FAST early warning system – FAST Reporter*

try desk officers in Bern cooperate with the relevant country teams and international experts in writing bi-monthly qualitative reports on trends in conflict and cooperation. The early warning system monitors events that are relevant to an assessment of an increase – or decrease – of the likelihood of armed conflict.

## GCPM – Global Crisis Prevention Mechanism

For the past two years swisspeace and the Alliance for Peacebuilding (AfP) have been working towards the creation of a global mechanism for initiating effective direct action to address the causes of mass violence in countries at risk (*see Figure 3*). By combining current early warning information with additional data collection and linking this pooled assessment system with an efficient mechanism for effective response, GCPM has so far resulted in the creation of an international network of conflict analysis, warning and response mechanisms and institutions, with a pilot project in Guinea-Bissau. Elements of this system are already

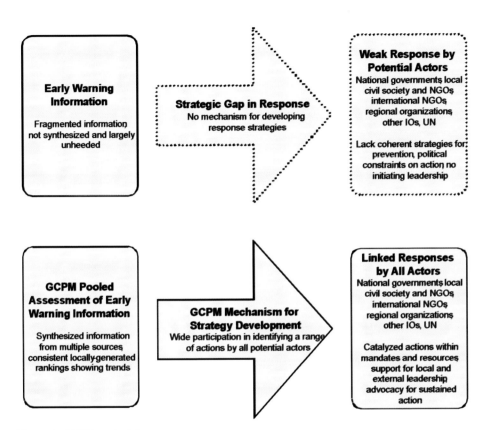

*Figure 3: GCPM methodology*

(direct and structural violence) to the existence and survival of populations. The aim is to identify key threats in a given context and to develop threat and context specific response measures, mechanisms and implementation strategies. The project claims that threat analyses are more effective than conflict analyses in detecting – and consequently managing – threats that are relevant to specific populations in specific contexts. The methodology designed for this project has so far been integrated in early warning trainings and briefings for the African Union and several African regional economic communities.

### Lessons and experiences

In the context of these experiences, a number of lessons emerged. These will guide our future activities in operationalising early warning and response mechanisms and may also prove useful for other, similar, activities:

- first, systematic fact-finding and analysis are essential requirements for producing reliable risk analyses. However, this does require a presence in the country or region to be covered. Regardless of the type of information collected (such as event data or statistical information), it needs to be gathered and analysed at least partly from sources accessible only from within the country. Moreover, when collecting information, the focus should not only be on 'bad news'; that is, evidence for tensions or otherwise

underway, including an actively engaged provisional governing board, a steering committee for West Africa information, a list of resource organisations in West Africa, the pilot in Guinea-Bissau, and considerable funds committed to this process.

### OPHUSEC – operationalising human security

Also for the past two years, the Research Programme on Human Security (HUSEC) has been working on a population- and context-focused threat and response analysis, monitoring and warning system, entitled 'Operationalizing Human Security', or OPHUSEC (*see Figure 4*). The focus is currently on pilot case studies in Ethiopia, Kyrgyzstan and Caracas (the latter as a distinctly urban context). Local research teams and multi-stakeholder groups take a human security focus in identifying key threats from a multitude of traditional and non-traditional threats

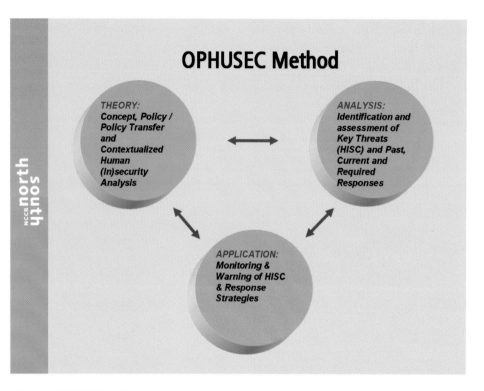

*Figure 4: OPHUSEC methodology*

deteriorating conditions. 'Good news', such as cooperative trends and general information that points to overall improvements are necessary in creating reliable reflections of the various political, economic or social forces characterising the degree of stability experienced by a particular country;

- second, early warning efforts often suffer from expectations that are too high: very specific events such as the outbreak of a crisis tend to be reported after the fact, not right before. Early warn-

ing is not about reading the crystal ball. However, 'trends' of conflict and cooperation, of instability and stability, can be predicted quite reliably. Based on those trends, scenarios can be developed about what will likely happen if preventive measures are taken or not;

- third, in many situations the focus of early warning neglect the real threats and challenges at stake: information is collected on the likelihood of political crises while people suffer and die in much greater numbers of many other,

often unrelated yet foreseeable and preventable threats. Thus, unless specifically tasked to address a very specific threat, early warning systems should not automatically focus on a pre-selected threat (such as armed conflict or environmental disasters) without a careful analysis of actual threats, causes and actors. Otherwise responses do not match threats, and resources and opportunities are lost. Additionally, different threat situations and early warning systems require different data and analysis methods. For example, the analysis of event data (or opinion polls or structural data) might work for one threat, but not for others;

- in this context, and as a fourth point, it proved helpful to take a population-centred human security approach. The advantage is that such an approach takes into account both 'traditional' direct violence and 'non-traditional' structural violence. It therefore helps addressing also those longer-term threats that are key to sustainable peace and security even after international actors have left a conflict or post-conflict theatre. Moreover, this approach highlights one important issue: if at all possible it is important to mitigate and resolve existing stress factors before and while preventing additional ones. Often doing the first will be a crucial contribution to the latter. However, with limited resources and limited possibilities of being involved in all and every potential crisis situation, it is important to pay special attention to fragile populations that do not have the coping capacities to absorb new stress factors. Thus, it will for instance be important to analyse and determine the degree to which different societies will or will not be able to cope with the negative fall-out of climate change, as climate change-induced disasters might, for instance, trigger natural resource conflicts much faster in a fragile society than in a stable society featuring a range of coping capacities. This issue will be discussed in more detail below;

• a fifth, but not at all new lesson points, to the often frustrating recognition that much greater emphasis has to be put on assuring effective responses and implementation. As stated previously, an early warning and response system mirrors a relay, in which objectives will not be met unless all parts work together efficiently and effectively. An early warning system without an effective link to the implementation of response measures has little value unless information is transferred and addressed with some degree of responsibility and concern about its utilisation. Here again, context-driven analyses of threats and responses may be able to provide information that is more relevant, that

is thus more eagerly awaited and used, and might thus lead to more effective responses. Manageable, feasible, multi-actor responses to the most relevant threats and root causes will add legitimacy to a politically sensitive process. Reaching the right target audience at the right time, with information that is needed (and desired!) is as important as it is difficult to accomplish unless continuous information and feedback loops are in place;

• as a sixth and final point, it is crucial to assure joint local, national and international expertise and collaboration from analysis to warning to response. What works best, is a multi-stakeholder approach: only in this way shared ownership is supported from the analysis to the response. In an interdependent system of different actors perform different tasks, but as in a 'relay run', all parts of the team have to work harmoniously together. Only then can the monitoring and analysis of situations lead to their eventual improvement and the prevention of crisis escalation. Also needed is less duplication and competition. Instead there need to be efforts to pool ideas, experiences and resources to generate information and policy advice that is timely, relevant and legitimate. With some persuasion and, not least, with the

financial pressure exerted by the donor community, collaborative efforts can be achieved, by enticing the many scattered efforts in researching, developing and implementing better early warning and response methodologies into cooperating more closely. In addition, such networks of excellence should receive support that is solid enough to allow them to refocus their work to joint efforts in meeting some of the key challenges in early warning and response initiatives. The Conflict Prevention Network, supported by the European Commission, is an example for such an approach.

In the following sections we will address one of the key challenges of the coming decades: the negative consequences of climate change. As will be shown, heeding the lessons discussed above will offer opportunities to create workable and efficient preventive and remedial measures to address climate change-induced crises and suffering.

### Sailing the 'Perfect Storm'[1] – tackling climate change with a human security-based EW&R system

Climate change is primarily a result of human activities, particularly the burning of fossil fuels and deforestation. Rising carbon dioxide levels lead to global warming, which in turn contributes among others to global ice melting, thermal expansion of the oceans and

---

1 The phrase 'perfect storm' refers to the simultaneous occurrence of events which, taken individually, would be far less powerful than the result of their chance combination. Such occurrences are rare by their very nature, so that even a slight change in any one event contributing to the perfect storm would lessen its overall impact. (Source of definition: *Wikipedia*.)

rising sea levels, shifting wind patterns and distribution of rainfall, heat waves, drying out of currently fertile regions, melting permafrost regions (which will further release $CO_2$ emissions into the atmosphere) and a large range of resulting environmental disasters. According to IPCC findings, global temperatures have been rising by 0.74˚C over the past 100 years, with an expected further increase of 1.1˚C to 6.4˚C by the end of the 21st century. This could cause a rise in sea levels by 18 to 59 cm, and much higher levels if the Greenland ice sheet or Antarctica continues to melt.[2]

Climate change-induced environmental disasters will likely cause great human suffering and pose great risks to economic development and social and political stability. Those risks are real and already felt.[3] The results of climate change will cause natural disasters, food shortages and displacement of peoples. In addition, the impact of climate change will significantly intensify already existing threats to the point where they could trigger instability and violent conflict.[4] Yet, climate change can be managed through an effective early warning and response system.

Despite current international efforts to mitigate greenhouse gas emissions, climate change will likely continue largely unhampered for some time to come. We will have to adapt to new climate patterns and climatic conditions. However, there is wide variation in countries' ability to cope with and adapt to the negative impact of climate change. Countries with surplus wealth will develop coping mechanisms. Although costly, those measures will move populations away from danger zones, adapt agriculture and industry, and generate other means to minimise the inconveniences caused by climate change to society, economy and the political system. Early preparedness and response will allow those societies to absorb the negative fallout of climate change.

Countries that are already affected by multiple-stress factors, including poverty, social and political instability, will be much more susceptible to the negative consequences of climate change for at least two reasons: On the one hand, they possess only limited means to prepare for countering climate change impacts and, on the other hand, they are already suffering from a variety of threats that will only be amplified by the latter. For example, single-crop economies will be more susceptible to rising temperatures, and poverty-stricken populations will have no means of developing coping strategies to deal with changing climate patterns, to resist rising water levels in costal regions or migrate into higher-lying areas. Inadequate health services will not be able to cope with mounting cases of old and new diseases. Achievements towards reaching the Millennium Development Goals will be reversed – poverty and disease will increase, as will migration pressures and social and political tensions. This will exacerbate tensions within already fragile societies in the South – all the while the North is possibly less likely to divert resources to the South as increasing efforts are required to secure their own well-being. Global institutions like the UN and regional institutions like the EU might be unable to impress upon the North the need and moral responsibility to share the burden of helping the South adapt to climate change. Until the latter's failure to do so will trigger explosions of violence, instability and population movements strong enough to pose severe threats to the stability and well-being of the North.

Thus, the global community will need to assess realistically the unavoidable threats posed by climate change and explore means and ways to limit its negative impact. Finding the right balance between self-preservation and incentives to actively support other nations in their quest to adapt to and avert climate change is a tremendous challenge.

2  Jean-Pascal van Ypersele, 'Climate change and cities: The IPCC case for action'. Keynote speech at the C40 Large Cities Climate summit, New York, 15 May 2007, p. 2. See also: http://www.un.org/climatechange/bg.shtml. See also the IPCC working group reports at: http://www.un.org/climatechange/ipcc.shtml

3  P. Hoyois, J.-M. Scheuren, R. Below and D. Guha-Sapir, Annual Disaster Statistical Review: Numbers and trends 2006, Brussels: Centre for Research on the Epidemiology of Disasters (CRED), School of Public Health, Catholic University of Louvain, May 2007, p. 13. See Intergovernmental Panel on Climate Change (IPCC), Fourth Assessment Report, 2007.

4  Please note: for the purpose of this article the author focuses exclusively on the negative impact of climate change.

Violent conflict and its impact on stable and instable nations and regions alike is of great concern to international organisations who are called upon prevent the escalation of climate change-induced stress to social and political tensions, crises and armed violence. The exact impact of climate change on political stability can at best be assumed. The Oxford Research Group speaks of 'a global catastrophe costing millions of lives in wars and natural disasters' and 'resulting persistent food shortages and even famines [that] would lead to increased suffering, greater social unrest and the pressure of greatly increased migration.'[5] While the IPCC reports that conflicts are among multiple stresses affecting exposure, sensitivity and adaptation capacity among populations confronted with the impact of climate change, it does not specifically outline the impact of climate change on the likelihood of new climate change-induced conflicts. Such a link cannot be determined. Research has shown that there is no mono-causal, direct link between environmental degradation or climate change and the outbreak of violent conflict.[6] Negative impacts of climate change cannot be understood or mitigated outside the larger political, economic and social conditions and threats characterising an affected society. However, it is safe to expect that the higher the level of instability and fragility due to other threats, the greater will be the impact of climate change.

### Proper preparation through a human security focus: early analysis, monitoring, warning and response

Climate change has the potential of greatly affecting human security levels among affected populations. The operationalisation of human security, a concept that focuses on the survival and well-being of individuals and populations — with marked positive effects on state security and stability — can serve as the foundation for effective adaptation and mitigation policies.

The human security approach asserts that the frustration of and threats to the basic human needs of individuals and communities leads to human suffering, social and communal deterioration, and therefore to violence in its many direct and structural manifestations. This is a cyclical relationship. On the other hand, however, if individuals and communities feel secure and protected from the existential threats that emanate from social, political and economic injustice, military violence, environmental disruptions or natural disasters — that is, if their basic human security is guaranteed — human suffering on an individual level and conflict and violence on communal, regional and international levels can be significantly reduced.

It is important to note that the concept of human security focuses not only on military conflict and its consequences for civilians but also on many non-traditional security threats, including disease, economic or environmental threats. As will be noted below, depending on the context of analysis, the costs of non-traditional security threats can be more devastating for human beings than those of traditional security threats, while carrying the potential to escalate into violence and war.

### Innovation 'human security'

What are the key characteristics of the human security concept? These include:

- the focus on the individual and the population as the referent objects of security (a unique characteristic of the human security approach);
- the recognition that the focus on the security of individuals and the population is at least as important as security of states/national;
- the recognition that investments in national military security (by maintaining armies to ward off potential external enemies) seem misplaced when most people are killed through environmental disasters (drought, floods, earthquakes, etc.) and disease;
- the recognition that the security infrastructure must go beyond national actors to include sub-national, regional and global efforts to respond to local, cross-border and global threats that affect individuals and communities;

---

5 Oxford Research Group, *Global Responses to Global Threats: Sustainable security for the 21st century*, Briefing Paper, June 2006, pp. 6–7.
6 Simon Mason, Albrecht Schnabel, Adrian Muller, Rina Alluri and Christian Schmid, *Linking Environment and Conflict Prevention — The role of the United Nations*. Zürich and Bern: Center for Security Studies, ETH Zürich and swisspeace, forthcoming.

- the parallel focus on the alleviation of threats and efforts to strengthen affected populations' coping capacities to adapt to ongoing human insecurity.

## Giving more attention to non-traditional risks to peoples' life and security

We need to re-think security by moving from analysing 'conflicts' to analysing 'threats.' An Oxford Research Group study has recently noted that '[t]he Cold War way of thinking focused on security as "defense". This paradigm has continued to dominate attitudes to international security, even though the global trend in major armed conflict and interstate wars has continued to decrease in the post-Cold War era and new challenges have emerged to threaten peace and security. What is needed [...] is a system of 'sustainable security' that addresses the security concerns of all peoples and tackles both old and new threats.'[7] They argue that 'current security policies are self-defeating in the long-term, and so a new approach is needed'. Moreover, commenting on the current focus on transnational terrorist threats, the Oxford Research Group argues that, 'international terrorism is actually a relatively minor threat when compared to other more serious

global trends, and [...] current responses to those trends are likely to increase, rather than decrease, the risks of future terrorist attacks'.[8] The group identified four root causes of conflict and insecurity in today's world: climate change, competition over resources, marginalisation of the majority of the world and global militarisation. The interdependence between these four factors seems apparent: negative consequences of climate change will intensify competition over increasingly scarce and fought-over resources, which will further add to the growing marginalisation and deprivation of the poorest, while continuing investments in traditional military defence and security assets will divert resources away from addressing the most pressing human security threats. In other words, resources urgently required to address the threats at hand are diverted to prepare for traditional, familiar, but often much less significant threats given the magnitude of socio-economic and environmental threats compounded by climate change.

To put this argument into perspective, a recent study undertaken for the SIPRI Yearbook 2007 argues, '[i]f the ultimate objective of security is to save human beings from preventable premature death and disability,

then the appropriate security policy would focus on prevention instruments and risk reduction strategies for their causes'. Thus, '[w]hile collective violence causes a great many premature deaths and disabilities, other types of injury cause an even greater number'.[9]

According to statistics prepared by the World Health Organisation, in 2005 (the most current year for which data was available), 17 million people worldwide died of communicable diseases, among them 2.8 million of HIV/AIDS; 1.7 million of diarrhoea-related sicknesses; 900,000 of malaria; 3.7 million of respiratory infection; and 2.4 million of perinatal conditions. Non-communicable diseases were responsible for the deaths of 35.3 million people, among them 17.5 million from cardiovascular diseases and 7.5 million from cancers. In comparison, 5.4 million people died of injuries — 3.7 million of unintentional violence (including 1.3 million road accidents); and 1.7 million of intentional violence, of which 912,000 were self-inflicted (suicide), 600,000 due to interpersonal violence (homicide), and 184,000 as a result of collective violence.[10]

This further strengthens the argument emanating from human security thinking that investments in national military security

---

7 Oxford Research Group, Global Responses to *Global Threats*, op. cit., p. 6. At the very threshold of the post-Cold War era this subject was discussed in the Swiss context — also with reference to climate change as a non-traditional security threat — in Heinz Krummenacher, 'Was hat die Klimakatastrophe mit Dissuasion zu tun? Überlegungen zur Weiterentwicklung der schweizerischen Sicherheitspolitik', in *Sicherheitspolitik und Friedenspolitik: Gegensatz oder notwendige Ergänzung?* Lenzburger Protokolle 1/89, Bern: Swiss Peace Foundation, 1989.

8 Oxford Research Group, op. cit., p. 4.

9 Elisabeth Sköns, 'Analysing risks to human lives', in SIPRI Yearbook 2007: *Armaments, disarmament and international security.* Stockholm: Stockholm International Peace Research Institute and Oxford: Oxford University Press, 2007: p. 243.

10 Sköns (2007), op. cit., p. 250.

must be re-thought – and possibly re-allocated – when by far most people are killed by preventable diseases compounded by poverty and environmental impediments.

## Climate change as a 'hyper threat': a powerful amplifier of existing threats

Climate change-induced environmental disasters have the potential of bringing major catastrophes upon countries already weakened by fragile political, economic, social or environmental conditions. They are likely to create problems that will, in combination with other factors, generate human suffering, economic decline and political instability. The negative consequences of climate change serve as powerful 'amplifiers' of already existing problems and threats to human and state security. In the absence of such threats, the impact of climate change is less severe and enough resources might be available to invest in averting its most serious consequences. If a country is already stable, prosperous and without significant social tensions, resources can be targeted at the negative fallout of climate change. In this case adaptation is possible without risking social, political, economic and security breakdown.

In countries with already existing threats and low social, political, economic and military stability, the impact of the same consequences of climate change will be much more severe. It will more rapidly amplify existing cleavages and instability, trigger escalation to further tension, while little capacity and resources exist to mitigate the onslaught of climate change-induced threats. Thus, if we assume that climate change will continue, that its negative consequences will affect all countries worldwide, and that its impact feeds on and increases threats already affecting a society, then the most severe consequences of climate change can be effectively resolved by addressing already prevalent threats, particularly those that are most susceptible to climate change-induced impact. The following section will offer an approach that will help in pinpointing those exact threats.

## Towards a context-relevant analysis of human security threats and responses

Five issues are key to effective human insecurity mitigation:

1. Context-specific threat identification and analysis;
2. Threat, context and actor-specific designs of preventive measures and countermeasures;
3. Targeted prevention of state-based and non-state-based violence through multi-actor strategies;
4. Monitoring and assessment of threat levels and of the implementation of mitigation and adaptation measures; and
5. Measurable reduction of human suffering and improved stability.

Designing of effective responses to human insecurity and undesired follow-on effects such as the outbreak of armed violence depends on careful, context-focused analyses of threats and mitigation measures.

The first step consists of a thorough threat analysis, followed in the second step by a careful analysis and assessment of past, ongoing and required responses for each threat. What are the main threats in a given context? How are they best addressed and how are they or will they be affected by climate change?[11]

The third step consists of the selection and examination of the most severe threats in a selected context, as well as opportunities for timely, effective and feasible responses. This involves making difficult and strategic choices, based on available means and resources. The focus should be on the most severe threats where the combination of hazard and vulnerability turns a threat into a 'life-threatening' and existential one; and on strategies to address causes (not only symptoms) that allow for cooperative measures by

11 The methodological approach towards human security analysis, monitoring, warning and response described in this article is informed in large part by the project 'Operationalizing Human Security for Livelihood Protection: Analysis, Monitoring and Mitigation of Existential Threats by and for Local Communitie', jointly sponsored by swisspeace (HUSEC) and the National Center of Competence in Research (NCCR) North–South: Research Partnerships for Mitigating Syndromes of Global Change. The project is directed by the author of this article. For further background on this project, see www.swisspeace.org

both state and non-state actors. Particular attention must be paid to the role of climate change in causing and triggering direct and structural violence. We need to ask:

- is climate change-induced impact felt locally, nationally, and/or across borders?
- what are the results of climate change for each threat experienced in a particular geographic context?
- how does climate change affect those threats (worsen, improve or mutate already existing threats)?
- how are existing threats intensified (in scope, severity and duration), how are responses obstructed (or in some cases aided)?
- which additional efforts are required to manage the impact of climate change on existing threats and their management?

At this point indicators to measure trends in the escalation and de-escalation of threats as well as sources and techniques for the collection of relevant data are chosen, and monitoring, warning and response mechanisms are put in place. Using this framework as the basis for identifying human security threats will help identify priority threats and entry points for effective counter measures. The response side of this equation will remain a challenge; however, as the following section argues, not an elusive one.

### Human-security based early warning and response system

Returning to the cyclical EW&R system cycle mentioned at the beginning of this article, a human security-based early warning and response system would consist of the following six components:

1. The threat analysis and identification of key threats that require continuous monitoring; followed by continuous monitoring (collection of data and information);

2. The analysis and assessment of collected information (structural data, statistics, event data, etc.), focusing among others on the following points:
   - type and extent of the threat;
   - extent of the risk (who is being threatened by whom, when, where and with which impact; which gaps exist in adaptation and mitigation?);
   - scenarios of escalation and de-escalation;
   - assessment of existing and new preventive and counter-measures;
   - development of specific actor-related measures;
   - development of implementation strategies for the required measures;
   - feedback to and correction of the threat analysis (step 1).

3. Early warning along with policy recommendations requires knowledge about relevant target groups and implementation actors, including their capacities, needs and opportunities for action.

4. Influence of policy and programme priorities of targeted local, national, regional and international governmental and non-governmental actors (in foreign, security, human rights, economic or development policy). Contact with these actors and a thorough understanding of their needs and opportunities for action are critically important throughout the entire process.

5. Implementation of envisioned measures as short, medium and long-term activities; either within existing or creation of new policies and programmes.

6. Evaluation of measures taken: evaluation results are to be incorporated into continuous monitoring.

### Conclusion

It is undoubtedly crucial that the causes for climate change must be addressed. Over time, this may halt and possibly reverse climate change and its destructive impact. However, how feasible is this approach, given continuing global demographic, economic and energy demand growth? How feasible is the approach, given the capacity of the top (and possibly middle) third of the world's population to adapt to climate change impacts while the bottom third suffers the most but is also least able to improve its resilience? Clearly, key contributors (polluters) to climate change must agree to effective measures (such as the Kyoto Protocol and its successor) to halt and reverse greenhouse emissions before new polluters can be expected to join. Still, the costs of action are likely to be much lower than the costs of inaction (according to one estimate 0.12 per cent reduction of average annual GDP growth rate)?[12]

### Focus on adaptation

Even if climate change can be halted and reversed in the long run, some impacts of global warming are irreversible, and consequences will be felt — and need to be responded to — for some time:

- adaptation mechanisms will have to be put in place to allow populations to survive and cope with climate change-induced or intensified socio-economic threats;
- the resilience and coping capacity of those affected (particularly those most vulnerable) to the impacts of climate change must be strengthened;
- existing factors of vulnerability (other threats and their causes) must be addressed to release the social, economic and political capital necessary to manage new threats created by climate change; and
- it would be wise to expect and prepare for severe repercussions of climate change for existing problems and threats.

Responses must be taken immediately and, separately and jointly, at local, national and regional/international levels — by individuals, households, civil society actors, state governments, regional organisations (such as the EU) and the UN.

### Early warning and response

Climate change and its devastating consequences for the most affected and vulnerable countries calls for the need to revisit efforts taken during the past years in improving early warning and response ideas, initiatives and actions. EW&R systems are necessary and, if properly designed, they will be capable of alleviating some of the harshest consequences of climate change. It will be important to move beyond a single focus on violent conflict or armed violence and consider the entire range of threats that pose lethal risks to affected populations. Conducting systematic analyses and generating effective ideas for response will improve the chances that information will lead to better understanding, more specific and informed warning, and timely and effective mitigation.

### Challenges in information exchange

Especially in an age of information overflow, exchanges between actors involved in stabilising peace and preventing instability ('peace partners') are crucial: While there is an overflow of information, much of it is irrelevant, repetitive, duplicated, scattered — a great amount of information that does not add up to much if it is not integrated. This makes it all the more important to systematically collect, consult, share and analyse information. Everyone's time and resources are limited. It is therefore important to have the best, most accurate and relevant information

at hand — and at the right time. There are advantages and risks associated with information exchange. Depending on the focus of information collection, political sensitivity varies, and therefore the difficulties for those collecting and sharing information vary. It also depends on the type of information: collecting sensitive (and even less sensitive) information in a closed political system and society for external political actors can be a dangerous task.

Civil society organisations, both local and external, can be subject to threats if they are perceived to pursue activities that undermine the interests of the political authorities. Therefore, there is a limit to the degree to which civil society actors can pursue roles that are too sensitive to pursue by international actors — especially if they do not protect them. Collecting such information in an open political system and society is of course less problematic. In those cases, civil society actors are closer to the ground than international actors, closer to society and its dynamics, and in a better position to judge the relevance of a certain event or development for its impact on stability or instability.

### Role of the EU and international donors

The EU can serve as a force of collaborative, integrated action between various peace partners involved in one or more stages of the

12 van Ypersele, 'Climate change and cities: the IPCC case for action', p. 4.

early warning cycle: threat analysis, monitoring and data gathering, information analysis, policy recommendations, or in implementation. The new Instrument for Stability — and particularly the Peace-building Partnership — can serve as vehicles for such exchange and improved, effective collaboration in achieving the goals set out in this article.

The anticipated catastrophes caused by climate change should serve as an opportunity to re-visit the important debates and efforts of the past decade in developing early warning and response methodologies and mechanisms. It should also be an opportunity to improve them in the light of lessons learned thus far and utilise them in an efficient manner to avoid the major human catastrophes (with impacts reaching far beyond the initially affected populations) that will otherwise unravel in the years to come.

# MAKING SENSE OF THE TURMOIL IN THE MUSLIM WORLD

## Introduction

The shocking events of Tuesday 11 September 2001 once again threw the spotlight on a corner of the vast territory, large demography and rather unstable political geography of what we call the Muslim world. The Muslim world, comprising some 50 sovereign states and large minorities in many other countries, is a well-integrated and integral part of the modern world of states. It does, however, also contain a complex and intricate web of relations and forces which it periodically unleashes on the rest of the international system.

As we have witnessed, at times the points of contact have been surprisingly violent and dramatic. But on the whole, much of the energies of the Muslim world are either taken up with matters internal to that community or else used up by the individual Muslim states in their efforts to make way in today's globalised socio-economic and cultural system. In this mode, I am often struck by how defensive the Muslim states are and how difficult they seem to find the struggle to defend their own interests. Little room is left for forging a concerted effort to defend what are regarded to be legitimate Muslim interests. It is in this relative vacuum that the radical Islamic forces find a role.

## Learning from history

If we were to adopt a slightly longer-term view of the evolution of the Muslim world

in the modern era, which indeed we must do if we are bent on making sense of the current crisis, then we can find many signs from pages of history which point to the deep structural flaws in the way in which the Muslim states emerged onto the international scene. It is my view that since the turn of the 20th century the Muslim world has been saddled by two fundamental problems.

First, the collapse of the Ottoman Empire in the early 1920s, at one of the most important turning points in modern times, left it voiceless at the top table of international players. Without the shelter of that Islamic empire, which was not regarded as a perfect model by many Muslims outside Anatolia, the Muslim world found itself exposed and exploited by the bigger European powers such as Britain and France. This was after the humiliations which had followed Napoleon Bonaparte's invasion of Egypt in 1798 and the systematic weakening of the Persian and Ottoman empires in the face of European encroachments in the 19th century. European colonialism in the region was often brutal and has had a profound legacy in terms of both political institutions and culture.

The Muslim world has probably never recovered, or been given the chance to recover, from these traumatic encounters with the West. But their sensibilities were further

tested with the creation of the State of Israel in 1948 in the heart of Muslim lands and the slow removal of Palestine as a political and cultural entity. Israel's foundation, its location and Zionist ideology, have been considered by countless people in the Muslim world as a national and religious challenge, and the systematic subjugation of the Palestinian people by Israel as a conspiracy to deprive the Palestinians of their rightful homeland and the occupation of all of Holy Jerusalem by Jews.

The second problem was associated with the very nature of the state in the Arab and the wider Muslim worlds. The modern state in many parts of the Muslim world is not only largely a European creation, where even its boundaries are often those defined by the colonial powers, but one which is overwhelmingly reliant on a highly centralised state machinery and a patriarchal infrastructure. While the former has impregnated these states with a serious legitimacy problem, which was severely tested in the Kuwait crisis of 1990-1991 for example, the latter has made the elites of these countries more impervious to the calls of their citizens for a bigger share of the economic and political pie.

The deepening political and economic problems at home, brought about partly by corruption, nepotism and bad management,

*Anoushivaran Ehteshami is professor of international relations and head of the School of Government and International Affairs at Durham University. He has published several books on the political situation in the Middle East. His current research revolves around five over-arching themes: the Asian balance of power in the post-Cold War era; the 'Asianisation' of the international system; foreign and security policies of Middle East states since the end of the Cold War; the impact of globalisation on the Middle East; and good governance and democratisation efforts in the Middle East.*

and partly by the ill-defined goals of economic liberalisation and IMF-style structural adjustment, have enabled the radical Islamic forces — who have been able to flourish as other (more secular) political forces were marginalised or exterminated by the ruling elites — to step into the breach and challenge the rulers in the Muslim states. Their challenge is felt from Indonesia to Pakistan and Turkey, in the key Arab countries of Saudi Arabia, Jordan, Syria and Egypt, as well as in the North African Muslim states of Algeria, Tunisia, Morocco and Libya. Their slogan is a simple one: 'Islam is the Solution'.

While for the most part the radical groups remained locked in a struggle with their own ruling regimes, with their quarrels largely confined to the territory of the country concerned, the Islamists are now increasingly finding themselves battling much greater outside forces. The infiltration of outside forces they view as beachheads for the 'Americanisation' of the Muslim way of life, as a bombardment of alien and corrupting values and influences. This, they believe, requires an international response, which partly explains the existence of international networks of Islamist groups.

Indeed, as the forces of globalisation — from the realm of commerce to those of television, food, clothes and the entertainment media — prize open the doors of traditional Muslim societies and challenge the norms and value systems of the local populations, so do they encourage the Islamist forces to

act as defenders and protectors of the greater Muslim rights: to become the Muslim community's latter-day cultural nationalists. In the face of the Islamists' uncompromising claims to righteousness and protectors of the divine right, the rulers find themselves impotent to act and open to sharp criticism from their opponents for bowing to Western pressure or for harbouring pro-Western sentiments. They are, in short, accused of being 'Westoxicated' — a difficult label to shrug off if they are seen to be aiding the West in search of its own interests.

Sadly, as in today's world the mediating power for the expression of frustration is nothing more articulate than the faceless force of globalisation itself, little chance of a genuine dialogue emerging between the parties seems likely. This much is depressingly clear in the aftermath of the US Embassy bombings in Kenya and Tanzania in August 1998 and Washington's response to the bombings. The statement of the 'Islamic International Front for Fighting Jews and Crusaders', issued soon after the US missile attacks on Sudan and Afghanistan, sounded ominous: 'Holy struggle operations will continue until American forces withdraw from the land of Muslims'.

The world has indeed entered a new age since the ascendancy of the neo-conservative global vision in the United States in the new millennium. In this new world order, the 'neo-cons' find themselves lined up against the neo-fundamentalist forces of political

Islam who look to the 'golden age of Islam' for reserve and inspiration. The two sides, adopting the crude tools of old missionaries, seem to relish the confrontation. In practice, the broad American neo-conservative agenda for global change has galvanised its opponents, from France and China to political Islam, into action.

As a consequence, so long as the forces of radical Islam interpret every American act as hostile and an attack on Islam they will rally against it, inevitably plotting a violent response. The cycle of violence deepens the more intensive the interactions become between the Muslim world and the political and commercial forces of the West. The image of the United States as the New Rome merely makes it easier for the radical Islamists to justify their own violent acts on the basis of the enemy's threatening grand design.

In sum, it is reasonable to suggest that radical Islam has failed to gain state power, has failed in its main mission of 'liberating' Muslim lands from Western influence, and convince the Muslim masses of the virtues of its brand of jihad. But this is not the same as concluding that political Islam has lost the capacity to act, to remain militant, to undertake sophisticated military-style operations, or to generally pose a serious security challenge to Western interests worldwide.

As the West is now revisiting another corner of the Muslim world it is perhaps time to reflect on how the same forces of globalisation have inadvertently invited into the arena actors who refuse to play by the established rules and are bent on breaking the norms. This is less a 'clash of civilisations' and more an encounter between forces which are resistant to the other's 'rules of the game'.

# LESSONS FROM THE STRUGGLE AGAINST AL QAEDA — OUTLINING A HOLISTIC MULTI-PRONGED EU RESPONSE

## Introduction

It would be a gross exaggeration to claim that the terrorism planned and carried out by the Al Qaeda network is the greatest threat to global and transregional security. In the longer, or perhaps even the medium term, threats to global environmental security are far more serious. Nor should we loose sight of the dangers of major inter-state wars escalating and leading to the use of nuclear weapons. Arms control and non-proliferation agreements have so far failed to prevent the emergence of new nuclear weapon states, for example, India and Pakistan, and the International Atomic Energy Agency (IAEA) has warned that there are now 40 states with sufficient civil nuclear technology to produce a nuclear weapon in a matter of months. Many observers are convinced that the Iranian regime's nuclear enrichment programme is aimed at creating a nuclear weapon capability, despite Tehran's repeated denials. It should hardly be necessary to point out that nuclear weapon proliferation, both vertical and horizontal, in such conflict-prone regions as the South and Southwest Asia and the Middle East poses a major threat to transregional and global security.

Unlike the bipolar confrontation that characterised the Cold War, the opening decades of the 21st century have been marked by a number of only partially suppressed tensions between nuclear armed neighbours with a long history of mutual mistrust (e.g. India and Pakistan, China and the United States over Taiwan).

Nor should we overlook the dangers of inter-state conflicts using chemical or biological weaponry. The materials and the methods to weaponise them are very accessible and cheap to acquire.

The current strategic environment also remains vulnerable to the threat of major conventional wars between non-nuclear states. The ending of the Cold War, far from extinguishing ethnic, religious and religio-political conflicts and bitter power rivalries over resources and territory has given way to multi-polar conflicts, many of which could develop into major conventional wars. Moreover, the proliferation of conventional weapons has been allowed to proceed without any effective controls/restraints by the UN or other international organisations.

It is also the case that the trend towards US unilateralism and George W. Bush's doctrine of preventative war have, sadly, made it more difficult to dissuade states from seeking to acquire nuclear weapons. It has made it far harder to bring constructive diplomacy of conflict prevention and conflict resolution to bear in time to prevent hostilities and to halt the rapid escalation of conflict (e.g. the 2006 war between Israel and Hezbollah, which has set back the Lebanese economy by more than 20 years).

## The concepts of war, terrorism and 'terror wars'

War and terrorism are conceptually distinct, and historically the weapon of terrorism has often been used without any wider guerrilla or conventional war taking place.

Terrorism is the use or threat of extreme violence to create a climate of fear among the wider audience than the immediate victims of the violence. It involves random and symbolic targets, including civilians. War can be briefly defined as armed conflict between two or more parties, nations or states. (The days when the term 'war' could be restricted purely to conflicts between states are long past).

However, since the late 20th century we have seen an increasing number of conflicts in which the weapon of terror is employed as an auxiliary weapon by one or more parties involved in war. In these 'terror wars', as they have been termed, there are, typically, no front lines; attacks on civilians become the norm, particularly savage violence is used in 'ethnic cleansing' of whole

*Paul Wilkinson is Emeritus Professor of International Relations and Chairman of the Centre for the Study of Terrorism and Political Violence, University of St Andrews, UK. He has authored and edited a dozen books on terrorism and problems of democratic response, including 'Terrorism and the Liberal State' (second edition, 1986) and 'Aviation Terrorism and Security' (co-edited with Brian Jenkins, 1998). His recent publications include 'Terrorism Versus Democracy: the Liberal State Response' (second edition, 2006) and (as editor) 'Homeland Security in the UK' (2007). He was adviser to Lord Lloyd of Berwick's Inquiry into Legislation Against Terrorism and wrote volume 2, the research report of the inquiry.*

communities, and often they are massacres, mass rape and torture. There are major violations of the Geneva Convention, often by all sides, and there are no easy exits from such conflicts because they are characterised by intense ethnic or religious hatred because both sides see themselves as fighting a total war. Terror wars can go on for decades, apparently unresponsive to UN or other efforts to broker ceasefires or to promote peace processes. Chauvinistic leaders and ideologues are in many cases capable of mobilising large numbers of their fellow nationals to support war (e.g. Milošević and Tudjman in the bitter civil war in the former Yugoslavia). These terror wars can lead to massive fatalities among civilians (e.g. Iraq since 2003). Our progress in science and technology has evidently not been accompanied by any reduction in the barbarisation of warfare.

However, while 'terror wars' may be an accurate description for conflicts such as that being waged in parts of Iraq, there are considerable problems involved in the use of the phrase 'war on terror' adopted by President George W. Bush after 9/11 as the umbrella label for the global response to terrorism. The term is far too wide to be useful and, as in the phrase 'war on crime', appears to be more of a slogan or a rallying cry. Moreover, the term 'war' arouses expectations among the public that the predominant response to the Al Qaeda's terrorist campaign should be military and that military action will suffice to defeat the terrorists. In reality the Al

Qaeda network's declared 'global jihad' is being waged in many countries without any accompaniment of a wider war. It is effective intelligence, police and judicial cooperation between many countries that is needed if Al Qaeda's terrorists, based in more than 60 countries, are to be ultimately suppressed or neutralised. The military certainly has a valuable contribution to make in countering some aspects of Al Qaeda's global campaign, but it is unfair and unrealistic to expect them to bear the burden of suppressing a global movement of extremists well hidden among the civilian population in dozens of cities. Last but not least, the term 'war on terror' provides an unintended gift to Al Qaeda propagandists, implying that they have the status of legitimate freedom fighters on behalf of a 'victimised' world of Islam. My own view is that 'the struggle against Al Qaeda', a phrase favoured by the EU, is far more accurate and useful.

In order to succeed this struggle must be both multilateral and multi-pronged. In spite of its status as the world's only superpower and its huge economic and military resources, the United States is unable to suppress the globally dispersed Al Qaeda network single-handedly. It desperately needs the full support and cooperation of all its allies in the Coalition Against Terrorism established in the aftermath of 9/11. A winning strategy to suppress or at least marginalise Al Qaeda has got to be multi-pronged with international intelligence, police and judicial cooperation of the highest possible quality

and professionalism and determined efforts to suppress terrorist finances and supplies of weapons and explosives. Additionally, there need to be measures to prevent proliferation of WMD materials and technology to terrorists, an intensive 'hearts and minds' campaign to prevent young Muslims both in the Islamic world and among the Muslim diaspora communities, from being recruited into extremist groups and groomed and indoctrinated in preparation to carry out suicide bombings and other kinds of terrorist attacks. If we fail to win the battle for hearts and minds the world will face future generations of suicide bombers filled with hatred and a fanatical commitment to waging 'global jihad'.

## Assessment of the results of the struggle against Al Qaeda as of 11 November 2007

There have been numerous claims from journalists and self-styled 'experts' on Al Qaeda, who have claimed that the movement is no more than a label or 'brand name' and that the core leadership no longer has any real influence. I believe that these attempts to write the obituary of Al Qaeda are, to say the least, premature. The movement has always been rather different from traditional terrorist groups. It is a globally dispersed network of cells and affiliates who look to Al Qaeda's leaders for ideological leadership and inspiration and strategic direction. The ideological and propaganda task of the leadership is now largely provided through the internet and through information of the kind provided in the *Encyclopaedia of the Jihad*. They can also train militant activists in some of the key techniques of bomb-making, etc. and although they were forced to vacate their training camps in Afghanistan after the fall of the Taliban regime in 2001, they still operate training camps in Pakistan and elsewhere. All the evidence from recent police investigations and trials of jihad conspiracies in Europe and elsewhere proves beyond doubt that Al Qaeda is still very much in business. It is the worst terrorist threat to international security because:

- it is explicitly committed to mass fatality attacks;
- it uses coordinated no-warning suicide attacks, the most difficult type of terrorism to prevent in an 'open' democratic society;
- it has 'global reach';
- it is 'incorrigible', i.e. it shows no sign of any change to greater pragmatism or modification of its absolutist ideology or its utterly ruthless methodology;
- it is ideologically committed to waging a terrorist campaign against not only the United States and Israel, but also all the countries in the Coalition Against Terrorism and all the Muslim countries that cooperate with Western countries, which they condemn as 'Apostate' countries.

In short, Al Qaeda is the most dangerous non-state perpetrator of terror to have emerged in modern history. It is clearly a prime duty of the EU to struggle to suppress it because it not only poses a major threat to the most basic of all human rights, the right to life: it is also a threat to global and transregional peace and security because, as has already been shown, it is capable of acting as a precipitating factor in triggering and exacerbating wider internal and international conflicts.

## Failures of the struggle against Al Qaeda

- failure to capture Bin Laden and his depute Zawahiri;
- failure to follow through in Afghanistan with adequate security and economic assistance to President Karzai's government, thus enabling Taliban and Al Qaeda to re-infiltrate the country;
- the strategic blunder of diverting large-scale military and financial resources to a war to topple Saddam, thus handing Al Qaeda a valuable propaganda weapon and hundreds of coalition targets (military and civilian) in Iraq;
- failure to stop Al Qaeda using other means to move funds across borders to include organised crime;
- overall neglect of the important tasks of winning 'hearts and minds' in the Muslim world and in the Muslim diaspora;
- failure to maintain solidarity and maximum level of cooperation among members of the Coalition Against Terrorism.

## Achievements of the struggle against the Al Qaeda network

- formation of Coalition Against Terrorism, including Russia, China and Pakistan;
- removal of Taliban regime;
- capture/killing of some key members of Al Qaeda's top echelon and large numbers of militants including al-Zarqawi, the Head of Al Qaeda in Iraq;
- blocking of millions of dollars of Al Qaeda cash in the international banking system;
- valuable initiatives by the UN in persuading Member States to take firm action to suppress the Al Qaeda network, denying them finances and weaponry, and sustaining a wide range of measures to prevent terrorism;
- big improvements in intelligence sharing among members of the Coalition Against Terrorism;
- strengthened national legislation and other measures by many governments in response to a perceived heightened threat to their own security (e.g. the United States, the UK and other NATO allies, and 'front-line' Muslim countries, such as Saudi Arabia, Jordan, Pakistan and Indonesia.

## Outline of a winning EU holistic multi-pronged, multilateral strategy to suppress the Al Qaeda network
Maximise:

- political will, industry will and public support and cooperation;
- high-quality intelligence;
- international intelligence co-operation and overall counter-terrorism cooperation;
- long-term efforts to win battle of ideas with leaders/mentors of new terrorism;

- adoption of biometric forgery-proof passports and tighter border controls;
- comprehensive and rigorous counter-proliferation measures to prevent acquisition of chemical, biological, radiological or nuclear (CBRN) weapons materials by terrorists.

### Priority EU tasks in the light of the current situation

Enhanced EU intelligence gathering, analysis and sharing are key requirements for a more effective response. The greatest need is still for high-quality human intelligence (HUMINT) on Al Qaeda network intentions and plans. The large number of foiled and disrupted Al Qaeda-linked attacks shows that intelligence has improved greatly over the past seven years and enabled more conspiracies to be prevented from reaching fruition. However, there are still many gaps and counterproductive barriers to the exchange of operational counter-terrorism intelligence within the EU.

The situation in Afghanistan, where the Taliban and its Al Qaeda allies are making a very determined effort to seize control of large areas, is far more serious than the majority of the public and even EU governments appear to understand. Currently there are simply not enough troops on the ground to attain the level of security and stability needed for reconstruction and economic development so desperately required if the democratically elected government headed by President Karzai is to survive. More EU countries should come aboard to help the hard-pressed troops in the front-line against the Taliban.

### The role of the military in helping the 'front-line' countries against Al Qaeda

Military forces are ideal for certain counter-terrorist tasks, but it is a huge mistake to assume they are a panacea. Sophisticated modern terrorists of the Al Qaeda network know how to hide and operate covertly in cities around the world and how to melt into their surroundings and to keep their communications secret. Over dependence on military operations and heavy-handed use of firepower in civilian areas, which is likely to cause heavy casualties among innocent civilians, is a huge strategic blunder, fuelling support and recruitment for terrorist groups.

### Protecting the EU homeland

Attacks and attempted attacks in Spain, Germany, the UK, Italy and other EU countries underline the importance of strengthening our homeland security.

To prevent radicalisation and recruitment to terrorism we need to work for an EU-wide partnership with moderate Muslim leaders to help ensure that Al Qaeda's claim to be 'true Islam' is totally discredited. (This effort will be helped by Al Qaeda's ruthless and deadly terrorist attacks in which hundreds of fellow Muslims have been killed – a huge strategic blunder by Al Qaeda). Let us ensure that our own preparedness for dealing with the emergency of mass-casualty terrorist attack is greatly improved. The Al Qaeda network is capable of using tactics such as suicide vehicle bombs and suicide airline attacks, but also could potentially use some types of CBRN materials (e.g. for using 'dirty bombs' or RDDs). It would be foolish to discount 'worse case' scenarios. Our police and emergency services require the best possible equipment, training and real-time exercises to prepare for such contingencies.

# FORMALISING THE INFORMAL WHILE NEGLECTING TRADE TRANSPARENCY: ISSUES IN THE REGULATION OF *HAWALA* AND FINANCIAL CONTROLS AGAINST TERRORISM

## Introduction

*Hawala* means 'transfer' in Arabic and refers to a traditional, informal and efficient funds transfer method used by millions of expatriates to send remittances to their families around the world. Several studies emphasize *hawala*'s economic and humanitarian significance. In the midst of calls to shut down all potential means used by militants to finance their terror, the First International Conference on *Hawala*, held in 2002 in Abu Dhabi, was successful in offering an opportunity to examine *hawala* beyond media sensationalism and rushed policy responses.

Nevertheless, any optimism that the conference would lead to appropriate and effective regulatory arrangements was soon frustrated by hurried approaches at both the national and international levels that seem to be more fitting for formal institutions than informal networks. Indeed, some of the measures introduced in recent years have caused serious damage to ethnic communities dependent on their relatives' remittances.

The argument of this chapter develops through the following main points:

- *hawala* serves honest people as well as serious criminals;
- financial controls of terrorism are critical but no panacea;
- there has been a counterproductive over-emphasis on *hawala* as uniquely vulnerable to abuse;
- current regulatory arrangements fail to meet stated objectives, and
- careful consideration of sound empirical evidence and genuine dialogue with the sector are indispensable.

These points will be addressed as we examine the appeal of *hawala* – the regulatory objectives, challenges and risks. We conclude with implications for a sensible and evidence-based policy.

## The appeal of Hawala

*Hawala* originated in the Indian subcontinent and constitutes one of numerous informal value transfer systems operating globally (El Qorchi, Maimbo and Wilson, 2003; Passas, 1999). Deliveries are made in cash quickly, cheaply, and conveniently in places where banking services are unavailable, expensive, or unreliable.

Two main aspects can be distinguished in the *hawala* business: the sending and receiving of money (the relationships between a *hawaladar* [*hawala* operator] and his or her clients, and the settlement process (relationships among intermediaries).

The first part is relatively straightforward. Clients hand in their cash and request an equivalent amount to be delivered in local or, more rarely, another specified currency. *Hawaladars* and those acting as their agents accept cash in their premises – usually some other business, such as a corner store, a delicatessen, a music or electronics business, a travel agency – or may go to their clients' workplace or home for a cash pickup. In most cases, no fees are discussed. Rather, the transaction cost is factored into the quoted exchange rate or the amount that will be delivered overseas in local currency for their US dollars, pounds, dirhams, riyals, etc.

At the end of each day, *hawaladars* consolidate all deals into ledgers for each agent and counterpart they do business with, including a running balance. The funds transfer requests are organised into payment instruction sheets – containing the amounts and the name, address and telephone number of the recipient – and faxed to counterparts in other parts of the world. The serial number of a rupee or other note in the hands of the intended recipient is also faxed: it is often used for identification. Some communications may also be done by e-mail or telephone. *Hawaladars* maintain such records at least until accounts are settled; in labour-importing countries (e.g. USA, Europe or the UAE) ledgers are often kept for several years.

*Nikos Passas is Professor of Criminal Justice at Northeastern University, Boston, USA. He specialises in the study of corruption, terrorism, money laundering, regulation of remittance channels and trade, organised crime and international criminal law. He has published a number of books on corruption, organised and trans-border crime. He regularly serves as an expert witness in court cases and as a consultant to financial institutions, law firms, consulting companies, academic and policy institutions, the UN, World Bank, IMF, and government agencies in numerous countries. He is also the editor of the international journal, 'Crime, Law and Social Change'.*

The delivery takes from a few minutes to 48 hours, depending on the urgency and the destination of the funds. Cash may be handed over at the recipients' premises or taken to their doorstep. Each *hawaladar* keeps a pool of cash, which enables payments as soon as instructions arrive. Thus, local cash is typically used for payments on behalf of overseas clients. In this way, actual fund transfers are minimised (for more details, see Passas, 2003b, 2003c, 2004b, 2006, 2006b).

*Hawala* serves millions of immigrants from South Asia, Africa, the Middle East and elsewhere whose remittances are often desperately needed as a means for survival. The funds also provide important support for economic development (Ratha, 2003). Formal financial institutions have recently made strong efforts to increase their share of the remittance market by lowering fees, widening their networks and using better technology. The law enforcement and regulatory attention drawn by *hawala* has also increased operating costs in the informal sector. Nevertheless, *hawala* continues to be the best option for most immigrants and the only one for those coming from regions devastated by civil conflict and disasters.

Data updated in November 2004 from the United Arab Emirates illustrate the competitiveness of *hawala*. Table 1 contrasts the cost of sending about US $100 from the UAE to South Asia, including exchange rates, charges for telegraphic transfers or drafts by banks and exchange houses, and Western Union fees. In short, *hawala* offers much better exchange rates and no fees at all.

The financial benefits to remitters' families become clearer in Table 2, which uses Pakistan as an example and compares the amounts received by beneficiaries in local currency for about US $100 sent from Dubai. *Hawala* beats all the competition by far. The amount received in cash is higher than all other options. Moreover, all formal methods involve charges and fees requiring the remitters to add US $1.32 to US $27.22 to the cost. In short, better rates and lower costs make *hawala* the best option financially. Other advantages include having convenient home delivery or pickup, interacting with people speaking the same language and from the same region, avoiding bureaucratic procedures and paperwork, preserving confidentiality, and achieving fast delivery even in the remotest villages. The relationship of trust and the mutual in-

### Table 1: Comparative cost of sending US $100 to South Asia from Dubai

| Institution | Charges (US $) | | Rate of AED/US $ |
|---|---|---|---|
| | Draft | Telegraphic transfer | |
| Exchange house | 1.36–2.722 | 9.52–16.33 | 3.6735–3.68 |
| Bank | 2.722–6.80 | 12.25–27.22 | 3.678–3.693 |
| Western Union | 9.52 | – | 3.7 |
| *Hawala* | 0 | – | 3.673–3.6736 |

Source: N. Passas' own research

### Table 2: Comparative amounts received in Pakistan for remittance of US $100 from Dubai, UAE

| Method of remittance | Charges | Total paid | PK rupees received |
|---|---|---|---|
| Draft (exchange house) | 1.36–2.722 | 101.36–102.722 | 5901–5910 |
| Draft (bank) | 2.722–6.80 | 102.722–106.80 | 5890 |
| TT (exchange house) | 9.52–16.33 | 109.52–116.33 | 5901–5910 |
| TT (bank) | 12.25–27.22 | 112.25–127.22 | 5890 |
| Western Union | 9.52 | 109.52 | 5858 |
| *Hawala* | 0 | 100 | 5920 |

Source: N. Passas' own research

terests of *hawaladars* and their clients support the efficient global *hawala* networks. Finally, 'cultural inertia' and the forces of old habits add to the hurdles faced by formal institutions seeking to capture a larger share of the multibillion-dollar (US dollars) global remittance market.

## Need for regulation

At the same time, research clearly shows that *hawala* is vulnerable to criminal abuse, just like all other financial institutions. We know that *hawala* clients include money launderers, militants, corrupt politicians, fraudsters and tax evaders (Carroll, 1999; Howlett, 2001; Passas, 1999, 2003 a, b, c, 2004 b, c; FATF, 2001, 2003). Legitimate clients and funds are occasionally commingled with illicit ones. As *hawaladars* use local cash pools to pay for overseas remittances, the father of someone sending honestly earned funds from the United States or UAE could actually receive the cash a corrupt official or smuggler wishes to launder or secretly take out of the country.

Most vulnerable to abuse, however, is the process of settlement among *hawaladars*. The cash pools on which they draw for payments are always asymmetrical, as each operator transfers funds to and from multiple locations every day. Apart from compensatory payments, other ways of balancing accounts include formal transfers (check, wire, bank-to-bank, etc.), the use of couriers and payments in kind, as well as through commercial transactions, falsified invoices and third parties. Not being subject to the same rules as formal institutions and operating frequently in parallel economies through not always known third parties make the whole process susceptible to illegal uses. Commercial and financial transactions are integral components to the settlement process. Unfortunately, there is little to no transparency and verification of transactions in the import/export business (Passas, 2004d, 2006c). The problem is not merely theoretical; there is evidence that money derived from drug trafficking, illegal arms sales, body part trade, corruption, tax evasion, and all kinds of fraud have indeed moved through *hawala* and trading networks.

In this light, leaving *hawala* completely unregulated, as was the case in many parts of the world before 9/11, is no longer realistic. The question is how to regulate it (Maimbo et al., 2005; Passas, 2003a, 2003b, 2003c, 2006a). One important point to consider is that trust is a defining element of *hawala*, which makes the system not only more efficient, but also reliable. Informal dispute-resolution mechanisms most often resolve issues among *hawaladars*, and individual remitters have seldom lost their money even after law enforcement actions, accidents or bankruptcy (Maimbo, 2003; Passas, 2004a, 2004b, 2004c, 2006a, 2006b). Hence, a consumer protection type of regulation is not as necessary as many a Westerner might think.

### Regulatory objectives and challenges

The main task is to reconcile two sets of public policy priorities. On the one hand, we must counter terrorist financing, money laundering and other financial crime. Labour exporting countries are also concerned about the economic or other damage caused by *hawala* in local economies thirsty for foreign currency.[1] On the other hand, we need to reduce the hurdles faced by labourers remitting funds to their homeland and to avoid unnecessary disruptions of capital flows and commerce, both of which are vital to economic development.

More specifically, the crime-control objectives are to (a) achieve more transparency by identifying operators and clients and by enhancing the traceability of transactions, (b) provide a measure of deterrence and prevent abuses of funds transfer networks, (c) prevent the financing of terrorist operations, and (d) collect intelligence and monitor the activities of criminal groups and extremists.

The economic aims are to (a) lower the cost of remittances, (b) widen the range and increase the speed of remittance options, (c) ensure compliance, (d) protect the consumer, and (e) ensure a level playing field for the various competitors in the remittance market.

---

1 Because *hawala* draws on local cash pools for making remittance payments, it is feared that *hawala* deprives the country of valuable foreign exchange.

The synchronisation of these objectives is complicated by the dilemmas of undocumented immigrants, who may be earning legitimate funds without authorisation to work, which means that they could not use formal institutions for remittances or other business. Another serious challenge is the harmonisation of controls internationally and regionally, as the contexts vary dramatically and render some rules unenforceable or unrealistic.

Challenges specific to *hawala* networks include the following:

- there is often no uninterrupted transparent audit trail;
- it may be hard or impossible to interpret idiosyncratic *hawala* records;
- the fusion of *hawala* with other businesses makes it difficult to disentangle transactions and may easily hide illicit activities;
- the interface with grey/black markets makes it harder to supervise *hawala* and offers opportunities to obscure transactions;
- fine-tuning regulations and law enforcement targets to avoid harm to innocent actors is particularly difficult and requires study and appreciation of ethnic, cultural, political and socio-economic specificities;
- ensuring a balanced approach and proper regulation of the formal sector requires the conception and implementation of rules appropriate for very different actors, modus operandi and traditions;

- finally, assessing and measuring the effects of measures and policies relative to *hawala* are hard, given the availability of a wide range of other informal methods that could be used by those determined to evade regulation. Thus, reduced illegal *hawala* activity may not necessarily be a positive development, to the extent that activities get displaced to less transparent and less understood informal value transfer methods (Passas, 2003c).

## Shortcomings of current arrangements

No thorough and systematic effort has been attempted to assess the effect of policies that were introduced very shortly after the 9/11 attacks. There are strong indications, however, that most of the policies — both national and international — are not producing the desired effects and may indeed be counterproductive.

In South Asia and other labour-exporting countries, for example, *hawala* has been and remains either criminalised or outlawed. This means that certain large parts of the *hawala* networks are by definition illegal, forcing operators and clients to keep a low profile and hide their business as much as they can. Some European countries, such as France and Spain, allow no informal funds transfer (IFT) operations. Others require costly and burdensome procedures for de facto licensing, pushing a number of *hawala* operators underground.

The same applies to the United States, where federal efforts to increase compli-

ance and transparency through registration are completely undermined by an uncoordinated patchwork of state regulations. Most US states mandate licensing. In some of them, however, the capitalisation or bond requirements amount to hundreds of thousands of US dollars. If a *hawaladar* has clients in more than one jurisdiction, he would need to comply with the rules of all states (see Passas, 2006a). This is an unaffordable and non-pragmatic arrangement that effectively seeks to formalise the informal. Attempting to apply to *hawala* rules that are appropriate to formal financial institutions and corporations is unwise and unworkable. *Hawaladars* are left with three options: to introduce or substantially raise fees and charges to customers, to stop offering the funds transfer service to their ethnic communities, or to operating without a license. However, operating without a required state license has become a federal offence. This has effectively pushed many *hawaladars* out of business or underground. Judging by reports of arrests and charges for this offence, *hawala* has been largely criminalised in the United States.

Even in the liberal environment of the UAE, where *hawala* is legal and compliance is affordable (simple registration), *hawaladars* shun the limelight and would not come forward, even to attend *hawala* conference.

Many countries are eager to heed calls by the Financial Action Task Force and others to apply anti-money laundering and terrorist finance recommendations and rules. However, interviews with officials suggest that despite formal compliance with such international standards, enforcement is problematic and impractical. Attempts to formalise the informal equal efforts to alter the age-old traditional networks, which successfully resisted prohibitions and authoritarian regimes in the past. The chances of succeeding are slim, particularly if the informal sector is not consulted.

### The risks of unsuccessful regulation

Financial controls are essential and necessary. They deter and prevent serious crimes, offer investigative leads to detect and arrest offenders, reduce the harm of planned or committed crimes, and generate opportunities for intelligence collection. However, if our aspirations get lofty, there is the danger of causing more problems than we solve. All of the objectives set out above risk being frustrated, and we can expect the following responses:

- a reduction of the positive economic effects of labour remittances;
- fewer, more expensive remittance options available to expatriates;
- unnecessary criminalisation of legitimate actors;
- higher human costs to the families of immigrants;
- alienation of large segments of the population who would be helpful in counter-terror coalitions;

- shifts to less well-known informal value transfer methods and thus less transparency and traceability of transactions.

Contrary to popular perception, there were no *hawala* transactions in the 9/11 terrorist operations. Myths about huge amounts raised and made available to Al Qaeda and associated groups have been dispelled (National Commission on Terrorist Attacks upon the United States, 2004). Terrorism is inexpensive and financed through a wide range of methods. *Hawala* has certainly been used to transfer militants' funds, but it is not the most important vehicle. Assumptions about a centrally and rationally organised Al Qaeda have also been rejected, as evidence points to loose networks unified by ideas and beliefs rather than structures. Militants tend to raise their operational funds locally and through ordinary crime, such as robbery, kidnapping, blackmail, fraud or commodity smuggling.

Furthermore, because of the strong emphasis on naming, shaming, freezing and seizing the assets of suspected supporters of terrorist groups, we may expect groups to use funds transfer methods and infrastructures akin to money laundering. Thus, instead of hiding the illegal source of money, people would now want to hide themselves as the source of funds given to extremist groups.

### Conclusion: the way forward

As we try to avoid 'collateral damage' and undermine our own objectives, the fight against transnational crime could turn out to be a very useful counter-terrorism approach. Infrastructures set up for one kind of secret finance and smuggling can be employed by militants as well. Some of them may also team up temporarily with criminal groups. Hot spots of financial crime, which abound in all continents, must be investigated. Anti-crime and counter-terrorism policies ought not to be regarded as conflicting or competing, but as complementary and mutually supportive.

The most promising approach to *hawala* regulation, and an efficient separator of users from abusers, is through a dialogue and outreach to all stakeholders of this significant economic sector. By taking the views of *hawaladars* into account and by building a consensus, future compliance and transparency, or traceability of transactions, is far more likely. Encouraging further cost reductions and more convenient and accessible formal remittance avenues would ensure the continuation of vital services to needy communities.

At the domestic level, countries would be wise to harmonise their federal, state, and local rules and responses on the basis of evidence, appreciation, and understanding of the networks they seek to supervise and control. Internationally, it may be useful to establish specific policy goals and urge countries to meet them in their own way, consistent with local traditions, culture, and socio-economic conditions. In that way, we would promote a legal harmonisation while allowing for the necessary diversity and flexibility.

Regulation will be most effective to the extent it becomes truly cross-agency and international. It must be emphasized, however, that financial control will never work while trade remains non-transparent. Gigantic sections of the world economy currently operate 'under the radar' and constitute an enormous risk for proliferation of crime, terrorism and WMD. Precious stones and metals have received some attention, but it is all trade that needs to be better regulated (Passas, 2004d). Once trade transactions are transparent, they must also be connected with financial transactions. This is the only way genuine transparency and accountability may be achieved.

Given the lack of trade transparency and threats it poses, the recent emphasis on risk-based approaches led by good evidence and sound analysis, a long-term study focused on the mapping of illicit networks is essential. Criminals rarely specialise in one kind of crime. When we look into the acts of serious offenders, we see that they usually commit multiple offences that transcend the jurisdictional arrangements we have for investigations and prosecutions internationally and domestically. Investigators and prosecutors may be overwhelmed with the tasks involved in identifying corrupt assets, tracing them to different countries, chasing witnesses and suspects, identifying all co-conspirators and facilitators, filing mutual legal assistance requests, etc. The cost of these operations is often daunting. Additional hurdles are raised by:

- 'facts by repetition' on security, terrorism, organised crime and corruption cases, when intelligence and open-source information is distorted, inaccurate or misinterpreted;
- jurisdictional firewalls of information and knowledge slowing down the process and impeding investigations;
- the focus on particular offences may lead to a neglect of ways in which a variety of serious crimes may be committed by or through the same actors and networks;
- open source information is not collected, organised and analysed in a systematic fashion. There may be data available through courts, media, scholarly publications, and think-tank, government or other reports. If they are scattered and not readily accessible, under-resourced anti-corruption actors cannot avail of them. In addition, in cases where the suspects are fugitive or the cases are settled without trial, the data on what they did how and with whom, will not make it to any common knowledge base. Those who directly worked in these cases move to the next job while the valuable information is shelved or destroyed.

A project designed to map illicit and corrupt networks will address all of these problems and make inroads into effective crime control, anti-corruption action and accountability. This project would look in depth into the division of labour, geographic location, methods of operation of corrupt actors, nexus with other serious crimes,

changes over time, interface with legitimate actors, etc.

We will be able to know what sets of offences are committed by what networks of offenders using what types of methods and routes. The relationships can be classified or coded by intensity/volume, duration, frequency and significance (whether they represent the only resource of other offenders or offenders are able and willing to diversify and reduce their dependence).

Mapping such illicit landscapes will help strategically, operationally and preventively. The users of such knowledge are legion and include the following:

- *investigators* and prosecutors looking for suspects or likely *modus operandi* or jurisdiction through which cases were committed or assets may have crossed – cutting down on usual suspects or likely *modus operandi* and jurisdictions to look at of mutual legal assistance requests or other formal and informal cooperation;
- asset recovery, especially in grand corruption cases, where sophisticated methods and professionals in multiple jurisdictions are often involved;
- strategic planning: enabling the analysis of systemic or other vulnerabilities and threat/risk assessments for both private and public organisations and actors;
- understanding how legal and illegal actors interface (not only for antithetical interests, but also when their relationship may be symbiotic. This is important when

seeking to anticipated consequences of law enforcement actions or reform, planning for functional alternatives and support for conventional actors, reducing market and demand for illicit enterprises; see Passas, 2003, for typology as one possible organising conceptual framework);

- technical assistance providers and implementers of international standards or evaluators of implementation and compliance progress;
- development agencies seeking to make the best use of their resources and providing effective aid;
- good governance policy makers in private and public sectors;
- operational support: knowing where the critical nodes of certain networks are is important when the aim is to take out/destroy an illicit network; knowing what other relationships/activities will be undermined when given actors or entities are removed is necessary in order to prepare for collateral effects or other consequences we may thus anticipate;
- victim support: knowing visible and invisible victimisation of serious crime and corruption helps construct and implement safety nets and relief programmes for support, reparation of damages, enhancing victim collaboration with authorities or NGOs, and better/more accurate reporting of misconduct;
- criminal intelligence gathering: knowing where the information-rich nodes are in a given network;
- anticipatory analysis: in the light of previous adjustments and plans for immediate/future action against illicit actors, what are likely future shifts one could predict in a given environment?
- causal analysis and remedial action planning: insights will be offered on the factors producing demand for illegal enterprises (goods and services) and the factors that knowingly or systemically bring together conventional and criminal actors. Having an up-to-date view of the big picture of transnational serious crime assists in developing policy and well-targeted responses.

Finally, a demand-side approach to counter-terrorism must supplement the supply-side, law enforcement and military approaches. Terrorism is also a socio-economic and political issue reflecting both local and global problems. Our policies must pay attention to new recruits and sympathisers, who could use their illegal or legal businesses to facilitate fund raising and transfers 'for the cause'. Our long-term success will be founded on long-term policies that address the fundamental problems underlying extremism of all kinds.

## Bibliography

Carroll, L. (1999). 'Alternative remittance systems', FOPAC Bulletin: 20.

El Qorchi, M., S. M. Maimbo and J. F. Wilson (2003). *Informal Funds Transfer Systems: An analysis of the informal hawala system*, IMF Occasional Paper No. 222. Washington, D.C.: International Monetary Fund.

FATF (Financial Action Task Force) (2001). *2000-2001 Report on Money Laundering Typologies*. Paris: Financial Action Task Force, OECD.

- (2003). *Combating the Abuse of Alternative Remittance Systems: International Best Practices*. Paris: Financial Action Task Force, OECD.

Howlett, C. (2001). *Investigation and Control of Money Laundering via Alternative Remittance and Underground Banking Systems*. Sydney: Churchill Fellowship.

Maimbo, S. M. (2003). *The Money Exchange Dealers of Kabul: A Study of the Informal Funds Transfer Market in Afghanistan*. Washington, D.C.: The World Bank.

Maimbo, S. M., R. Adams, R. Aggarwal and N. Passas (2005). *Migrant Labor Remittances in the South Asia Region*. Washington, DC: The World Bank.

Maimbo, S. M. and N. Passas (2004). 'The regulation and supervision of informal remittance systems', *Small Enterprise Development*, vol. 15(1): 53-62.

National Commission on Terrorist Attacks upon the United States (2004). *Monograph on Terrorist Financing (Staff Report to the Commission)*. Washington D.C.: National Commission on Terrorist Attacks upon the United States.

Passas, N. (1999). *Informal Value Transfer Systems and Criminal Organizations: A study into so-called underground banking networks*. The Hague: Netherlands Ministry of Justice.

- (2003). Cross-border Crime and the Interface Between Legal and Illegal Actors. *Security Journal*, 16(1), pp. 19-37.

- (2003a). 'Financial Controls of Terrorism and Informal Value Transfer Methods', in *Transnational Organized Crime. Current developments*, H. van de Bunt, D. Siegel and D. Zaitch (eds). Dordrecht: Kluwer.

- (2003b). '*Hawala* and other informal value transfer systems: how to regulate them?' *Journal of Risk Management*, pp. 39-49.

- (2003c). *Informal Value Transfer Systems, Money Laundering and Terrorism*. Washington D.C.: National Institute of Justice and Financial Crimes Enforcement Network (http://www.ncjrs.org/pdffiles1/nij/grants/208301.pdf)

- (2004a). 'Indicators of *hawala* operations and criminal abuse', *Journal of Money Laundering Control*, vol. 8(2): 168-72.

- (2004b). *Informal Value Transfer Systems and Criminal Activities*. The Hague: WODC, Netherlands Ministry of Justice.

- (2004c). 'Law enforcement challenges in *hawala*-related investigations', *Journal of Financial Crime*, vol. 12(2): 112-19.

- (2004d). *The Trade in Diamonds: Vulnerabilities for financial crime and terrorist finance*. Vienna, Virginia: FinCEN, US Treasury Department.

- (2006). Terrorist Finance and the Nexus with Transnational Organized Crime: Commodities Trade. Washington D.C.: Report to the National Institute of Justice (NIJ).

- (2006a). 'Fighting terror with error: the counter-productive regulation of informal value transfers', *Crime, Law and Social Change*, 45(4-5): 315-36.

- (2006b). 'Demystifying *hawala*: a look into its social organisation and mechanics', *Journal of Scandinavian Studies in Criminology and Crime Prevention*, 7 (Suppl. 1): 46-62.

- (2006c). 'Setting global CFT standards: a critique and suggestions', *Journal of Money Laundering Control*, 9(3): 281-92.

Ratha, D. (2003). 'Workers' remittances: an important and stable source of external development finance', in *Global Development Finance*. Washington D.C.: The World Bank.

# TRANSFORMING THE EU'S APPROACH TO OUTREACH AND TECHNICAL ASSISTANCE IN THE AREA OF EXPORTS CONTROLS

## Introduction

Suspicions about an illicit nuclear programme in Iran, clandestine support for North Korea's nuclear weapon programme, and the discovery of the international nuclear trafficking ring coordinated by Abdul Qader Khan – the senior scientific adviser to the government of Pakistan on nuclear matters – have moved export controls up on the international political agenda and underlined that more effective export controls are needed around the globe. The goal of export control is twofold: to facilitate legitimate trade and to prevent illicit trafficking and use of weapons and dangerous related materials. It is an essential dimension of national security and, in today's world, a global issue that transcends national sovereignty and policies. Today what exactly falls within a single government's – and its industry's – scope of responsibility is far from clear-cut. As the line between civil and military technology is increasingly difficult to police, preventing dual-use goods and technologies from reaching illegal Weapons of Mass Destruction (WMD) programmes, military end-users in embargoed destinations and terrorists, has become both increasingly challenging and important.

While there is justifiably emphasis on the transfer of nuclear and space technologies the problem spans the full spectrum of military equipment. An arms embargo does not inhibit China from using reverse engineering techniques to amongst other things develop military vehicles incorporating European technology. With the International Atomic Energy Agency (IAEA) identifying a persistent problem with the illicit trafficking in nuclear and other radioactive material Europe's security against the threat of nuclear terrorism is equally dependant on the competence of customs and border officials in regions such as the Caucasus's and Central Asia. States and companies need to accept and ensure responsibility for controls along the whole supply chain, which requires looking beyond the traditional focus on national territory to include consideration of many other relevant factors including licensed production, the role of multinational companies and subsidiaries, and cooperation with and assistance to third countries.

Export control assistance emerged in the post-Cold War context of the 1990s. The United States initially focused export control assistance on the Soviet Union and its successor states, but now has a worldwide operating programme (Export Control and Related Border Security Assistance – EXBS) with a budget of some US $40 million per year. As part of the process of developing an EU contribution, Member States strengthened and intensified cooperation. While there was

also an element of expanded contact with other states, this did not amount to an EU assistance programme, as much of it was bilateral, uncoordinated and lacking any sustained funding. Member State outreach has included participation in EXBS activities and export control regime outreach, the raising of export control issues in political dialogue, and some bilateral activities in particular with accession countries.

*Importantly, improving other countries' export controls is not an unselfish act of generosity, but rather, in the security and economic interest of the EU.* States cannot achieve their export control objectives by themselves since their own policies could be undermined if economic cooperation partners and recipients lack the legal, administrative and physical capability to prevent diversion of goods to unauthorised end-users or end-uses, or to control re-exports.

In the European Union this message was explicitly acknowledged in 2003, when the political context changed and a range of measures to strengthen its approach to security in general and the proliferation of WMD in particular were introduced. These included the adoption of the EU Strategy against the Proliferation of Weapons of Mass Destruction (EU WMD Strategy), which states the EU's commitment to 'strengthen export

*Dr Sibylle Bauer is head of the Export Control Programme at the Stockholm International Peace Research Institute (SIPRI). Since joining SIPRI's Non-proliferation and Export Control Project in 2003, she has conducted research and implemented technical assistance programmes in the area of dual-use export controls in a number of countries, in particular South-East Europe. Prior to this, she was with the Institute for European Studies (ULB) in Brussels. She has published widely on European export control, armaments, and security issues.*

*John Mattiussi is a career civil servant with the UK Ministry of Defence with a wide experience of security policy having worked in the EU, NATO and the USA. Between June 2003 and May 2007 he was seconded to the European Commission working on EU policy for non-proliferation and counter terrorism. This work included helping to set up the European Commission's programme for third country assistance in the area of dual-use export control. The views expressed in this article are his own.*

control policies and practices within its borders and beyond, in coordination with partners'. UN Security Council Resolution (UNSCR) 1540 of 2004 subsequently created an obligation to put effective export controls in place and a mandate for assistance.

Export control is one area where a contribution from the Community's first pillar budget can support the implementation of the EU WMD Strategy. That is why three Pilot Projects, funded under a European Parliament initiative, have focused on export controls. The first (led by the Stockholm International Peace Research Institute – SIPRI) amongst other things was designed to prove the Commission's ability to deliver effective export control assistance in view of the potential funding for a long-term programme, the second and third (led by BAFA) were dedicated to expanding and developing this work. BAFA is also implementing a Commission programme of export control assistance with the Russian Federation.

The establishment of the Instrument for Stability (IfS) in 2006 with its focus on capacity building, including for effective export control of dual-use goods, has provided the European Commission with the financial resources to support an EU assistance programme over the period 2007-2013.

This paper examines the progress of the EU export control assistance programme, some of the challenges it faces and explores the potential for its future development.

## Strategy

The European Security Strategy (ESS) of December 2003 identifies the proliferation of WMD as potentially the greatest threat to Europe's Security. It notes that export control has had a beneficial effect in slowing the spread of WMD. The EU WMD Strategy sets out the detailed framework for EU action on export controls. There are three inter-linked elements, reinforcing export control in an enlarged Europe, a programme of third country assistance and strengthening export control policies in coordination with partners in the multilateral export control regimes.

The development of the export control assistance programme has had some linkage with the other two elements referred to in the strategy. Notably the dual-use regulation is in the process of revision inter alia to better reflect international requirements, such as UNSCR 1540. Internal EU best practice and delivering a coherent and credible message in the context of assistance programmes are clearly mutually reinforcing. To date this strong internal/external interdependence has not been systematically exploited: for fully effective assistance programme it needs to be e.g. third-country assistance has exposed inconsistencies and weaknesses in EU dual-use export controls, which need to inform and impel internal EU capacity-building.

## Lessons learned from the Pilot Project 2004

Identifying the challenges and limitations of EU action was an important aspect of the first Pilot Project. This project had three elements: first, a wide ranging scoping study to investigate how Community funding under the IfS could be best used to implement the EU's WMD strategy. Papers on a range of issue areas were produced including chemical weapons destruction, bio-security, nuclear security and export control assistance. Each examined the state of play, and where and how the EU could add value through an assistance programme. Second, an international conference was held in Brussels in December 2005 to discuss the findings and recommendations. Third, a Field Validation Exercise intended to investigate the potential for future development of Community actions was conducted during 2005-2006. It aimed to test the findings for one of the issue areas, export control assistance, in one specific region, South-East Europe. The purpose was twofold: first, to help set up dual-use export control systems in important neighbouring countries, Bosnia-Herzegovina, Croatia, Serbia and Montenegro; second, to test specific approaches to export control assistance to help draw up a comprehensive EU export control assistance programme.

The Field Validation Exercise focused on four areas, which were determined in co-operation with the partner countries: licensing, industry outreach, the role of customs in export control and investigating and prosecuting export control violations. In each of the three countries (four following Montenegro's independence) a regional approach was combined with country-specific events.

The range of activities included needs assessment visits, in-country and regional seminars and workshops, specialised seminars in EU Member States, study visits to EU Member States, training courses and sponsorship of participation in related EU and third-party activities.

The main conclusions of the pilot programme were as follows:

- to be credible, the EU needs to deliver a consistent and coherent message and this requires consistent and sustainable engagement, a prerequisite for which is a secure funding base;
- a successful programme needs the effective combination of outreach and assistance to make them mutually reinforcing. Outreach can be considered as an instrument to persuade either states or exporters of the need to conform to the highest international standards and ensures political buy-in from the top. Assistance helps translate the political commitment into a functioning export control system through strengthening the legal framework and technical/institutional capacity. The required balance between the two depends on the stage of development of a country's export control system (i.e. is it a question of political will or capacity or both?);
- to be effective, an EU programme must be capable of assessing a country's export control system and of conducting the outreach and delivering the specific type of assistance required in key areas: legisla-

tive and regulatory framework, licensing, enforcement, in particular customs, investigation and prosecution and industry outreach;

- regional and country-specific approaches were clearly mutually reinforcing;
- the Pilot Project highlighted the importance of the peer approach that has characterised EU engagement, and of trust, confidence-building measures and relationship building, which in turn require sustained engagement;
- the need for systemic and structured coordination and cooperation with other actors was apparent, but requires mechanisms and procedures to support it. Many donors are engaged in areas relevant to export controls: different EU institutions (and different sections within the institutions), EU Member States, the United States (in other regions, Japan and Australia), the UN, specialised international organisations, international foundations. Cooperation with these donors is not only essential but mutually beneficial. The same cooperation is also a prerequisite within the EU: between Member States, between Member States and the Commission, and between the different parts of the Commission. This involves systematic information exchange about past and future activities;
- a comprehensive database and forward-looking calendar of EU outreach and assistance efforts needs to be established, which would include a description of the type of activity and the institutional context;

- finally, there is a need to expand human resources in the EU. This requires increasing the number of licensing and enforcement officers competent in dual-use export controls to make sure a sufficient number is available for delivering assistance, and making training third countries part of the core tasks, which requires top-level recognition of the value of working with third countries. The number of technical experts on the dual-use control list available for assistance missions also needs to be increased.

### The programme today

The European Commission, working with the Member States, has progressively expanded the geographic scope of activity in the three Pilot Projects. Cooperation is now underway with a range of different partners covering South-East Europe (Albania, Bosnia-Herzegovina, Croatia, Macedonia (FYROM), Montenegro and Serbia), China, Morocco, Ukraine and the United Arab Emirates, and further progressive expansion is planned under the IfS. These programmes focus on legal assistance, training licensing and customs officers, facilitating inter-agency cooperation and conducting industry outreach.

There was agreement early in 2007, on criteria for prioritising beneficiary countries. Decisions on future recipient countries for export control assistance are now based on five factors:

1. Relevance to the non-proliferation of WMD;
2. Relevance to the EU's foreign policy in general (e.g. as a candidate for future enlargement, in the context of the European Neighbourhood Policy, in other policy such as the Barcelona Process or through significance as a trade partner, etc.);
3. The need for technical assistance;
4. Willingness to accept assistance and to cooperate on non-proliferation;
5. Existence of an EU comparative advantage over other donors.

There remains however the risk that the EU will make political commitments on export control assistance that it will not be able to satisfy expeditiously. A list of priorities for the implementation of the WMD Strategy presented by the Office of the Personal Representative of the EU High Representative for the non-proliferation of WMD and endorsed by the GAERC (General Affairs and External Relations Council) in December 2006, identified a number of potential candidate countries for EU export control co-operation, highlighting the 71 Africa, Caribbean and Pacific (ACP) states, Albania, India, Pakistan and, additionally, Belarus, Moldova, Macedonia (FYROM), Kenya, Malaysia and Morocco. Albania, Macedonia (FYROM) and Morocco were subsequently introduced into the programme in 2007 but there are limits to what the programme can take on.

Member States' provision of licensing and enforcement experts is the crucial determining factor. The existing pool appears reasonable with about 60 experts 'available' from 18 Member States. However, their availability is not guaranteed and accessing the appropriate experts for assistance missions remains far from straightforward. This is currently the primary limiting factor on the potential for future expansion. Developing a strategy to both expand the expert base (in particular for technical and enforcement experts) and also to access expertise more effectively is clearly critical to the programme's health.

One fundamental problem is the reluctance of many Member States to mainstream export control assistance into their core work and the result is a lack of capacity. The Commission has been exploring possible ways to support increased capacity in Member States but these ideas need further development. There exists the possibility of using 'contractors' but there are obvious difficulties with such an approach including the potential to dilute quality. Up-to-date, hands-on knowledge of the issues and access to official networks are also crucial.

Also important to the programme is the availability of sufficient dedicated capacity in the EU institutions and in the implementing agent. There needs to be a high degree of continuity, given the importance of an institutional memory and of the time that goes into confidence-building in both donor coordination and relations with the beneficiary country. Given the complexity of launching and running an export control assistance programme, requiring coordination within the EU institutions, amongst Member States, with other donors/international actors as well as the recipient governments, a professional and sophisticated organisation is required.

Unfortunately, there is no staff entirely dedicated to export control assistance in the European Commission. There will be a role for the WMD Centre in the Council Secretariat in helping frame policy and pursue outreach – a natural role for the Personal Representative (and the relationship with the Council Secretariat must deepen in view of the new EU treaty and the consequential institutional changes foreseen). It will be important that the programme is managed by Commission staff in coherence with other Commission activities as well as the Council. There are a range of useful Community instruments and a number of interested parties, particularly the staff in DG RELEX (External Relations), DG TRADE (responsible for the EU Dual-Use Regulation) and those responsible for customs (DG TAXUD), justice (DG JLS), enlargement (DG Enlargement) and the resources of the Commission's Joint Research Centre (DG JRC), particularly in the complementary areas of combating nuclear trafficking and border monitoring that need to be coordinated to maximise the effectiveness of the programme. Additionally the Commission's delegations in recipient countries can, if properly prepared, make a valuable contribution to outreach and assistance on the ground. It is difficult to envisage any of this being done optimally without dedicated staff working in support of policy.

The implementing agent has a vital role. It manages the day-to-day work and must put together the appropriate package of assistance and recruit the Member State experts for the target country or region in question. The first Commission Pilot Project was implemented by a small team from SIPRI. The remaining projects are being implemented by Germany's Federal Office of Economics and Export Control (BAFA), with SIPRI's support. BAFA has the right credentials for the role, being the largest export control organisation in Europe. It is a growing player in EU outreach and invests in the necessary infrastructure. They were the only organisation interested in implementing the long-term programme and consequently are in line to receive the first export control assistance contract under the IfS. To date they have done well developing their organisation to accommodate an expanding programme.

While it is too early to make conclusive judgements on progress with beneficiary states some trends are apparent. It is difficult to compare the individual country programmes as they are each tailored to the specific country requirement and range from the creation of an export control system to targeting specific needs. That said, work in South-Eastern Europe has progressed smoothly; the cooperation with Russia and China has gone well, whereas the activity with Ukraine commenced slowly and cooperation with UAE has had difficulties getting started. Many of these problems appear to be related to factors beyond the control of those running the programme, and indicate that the programme has to factor in a preparatory phase for study and analysis to prepare the ground for more substantive work.

More work needs to done on what facilitates good, timely cooperation. Based on initial observations the following factors appear important: a technical rather than political focus (the political framework is important but it really needs to be in place before the real cooperation on the ground can begin); investing equally in laws, institutions and people and engaging with the beneficiary country over the full range of potential institutional partners (all those involved with the export control process, from laws and licensing through to enforcement as well as industry). It is also crucial to connect, at an early stage, with the other active donors and programmes in related areas to exchange information, in particular to identify cooperation partners, conduct an analysis of key actors, share needs assessments and avoid any duplication of effort. Reciprocal participation in events is also helpful.

Given the developing nature of the programme regular evaluation and feedback are necessary to fine tune project activities. A means of assessing the progress of the countries receiving assistance is equally important. Since quantitative indicators such as the number of events or participants are not adequate measures of performance, a set of process-based qualitative indicators needs to be developed, such as the function/role of participants in developing/strengthening a country's export control system. These will need to be adapted to the situation in the beneficiary country and factor in questions such as what external assistance can realistically achieve, and which obstacles need to be addressed internally.

### Future challenges

The requirement for dual-use export control assistance is compelling. What remains to be decided is the scope and comprehensiveness of the EU response. The initial structure put together by the European Commission is fit for its purpose, subject to Member States continued support, and a sound basis on which to build. It is likely that further success will be rewarded with contracts for export control assistance covering the whole of the IfS funding period. It is clear from the experience to date and the model provided by the US EXBS programme that the full potential of this activity is considerable. Strengthening the enforcement components and complementing export control assistance with other anti-trafficking measures such as border control obviously makes sense. The full potential of tools to combat illicit trafficking should be explored in which a variety of actors need to be involved, ranging from regional and international organisations to the different national enforcement agencies. These tools would support and complement ongoing export control assistance programmes. Working more closely with other important international players, such as IAEA, OPCW (Organisation for the Prohibition of Chemical Weapons) and WCO (World Customs Organisation), should be pursued. Achieving the programme's maximum potential through strengthened internal and external coherence should be the objective. Member States' full involvement will be essential for both programme development and successful implementation.

# FOR A CONSISTENT POLICY IN THE STRUGGLE AGAINST PROLIFERATION NETWORKS

## Introduction

Proliferation networks operate like companies.[1] They must be capable of coordinating a series of elementary logistics, financial and technical functions.

Due to the increase in worldwide exchanges, the reinforcement of existing export control tools alone will not be sufficient to face the increase in proliferation flows. Despite widespread reporting in the media, interdiction operations[2] also can only have limited effect on networks, due to their occasional nature, if they are undertaken independently of an approach targeting other functions. It also seems hardly realistic to wish to neutralise a proliferation network only by freezing part of its credits in the framework of a repressive approach.[3]

Setting up an overall policy provides a means of coordinating intelligence actions, repression tools and interdiction means both nationally and internationally, and therefore appears as the only viable solution in the struggle against proliferation networks.

This is a complex task, for it requires the organisation of inter-ministerial (or inter-agency) responsibilities, and in particular it requires an equilibrium between long-term and short-term actions. Finally, it depends on the reinforcement of links between the administrations involved and private participants including service companies, financial institutions and enterprises.

## Intelligence, a central tool in the struggle against networks

The first step in an efficient struggle against proliferation networks is to carry out a mapping operation (network structure and operating modes). This requires intelligence capability in the various fields in which the networks are involved.

The network 'mapping' work depends first on monitoring of flows, individuals and companies so as to detect proliferating activities. For example, monitoring of an identified intermediary in the Khan network provides a means of finding supplier companies, intermediary banks and possibly other agents belonging to the network.[4] Two traps must be avoided in this approach; the temptation to stop an operation before the network has been fully established can be very strong. It has the risk, however, of a major reorganisation and by the disappearance of participants who could have been observed to identify a key node.[5] On the other hand, failing to act before the network has been fully established can allow transactions to be completed with dramatic consequences in terms of dissemination of technologies.

Therefore, an equilibrium has to be found between the need to obtain the most complete and detailed map possible and constraints to take action against a particular transaction or against a participant considered to be sufficiently important so that his or her neutrality will affect network activities in the long term.[6]

In terms of the national intelligence organisation, the three large Western countries (the United States, United Kingdom and

*Guillaume Schlumberger has been the Executive Director of Fondation pour la Recherche Stratégique (FRS) since June 2005. Until that date, he was deputy to the Director of the Policy Branch of the MoD (Délégation aux Affaires Stratégiques – DAS). After graduating from Ecole Polytechnique and Ecole Nationale d'Administration, he was posted to the MoD as a civil servant in 1985. There he served in several senior positions, in the International Affairs Directorate of the Procurement Branch (DGA) from 1985 to 1997, and in the Policy Branch (DAS) from 1998 to 2005.*

*Bruno Gruselle has been a research fellow at FRS since September 2005, where he follows issues related to missile proliferation, counter-proliferation and missile defence. He served in the MoD from 1995 to 2005, where he was sent to Iraq several times as an international inspector (UNSCOM). He graduated from Engineering School in 1995 and received a Master Degree from the University of Poitiers in Detonics. In 2003, he became head of the Industrial Security Branch of the Export Control Bureau of the MoD before joining FRS.*

1 B. Gruselle and G. Schlumberger. 'Proliferation networks: between sopranos and supermarkets', FRS notes, July 2006.
2 The interdiction consists of blocking ongoing transfers and operations. It may be done within a legal framework (seizure in customs, freeze account, sanctions) or militarily (interception of cargo at sea).
3 Repression is intended to neutralise the activity of network agents or to prevent the completion of operations undertaken by them. For example, the objective may be to prevent access of the network to intermediate banks, to stop an intermediary or a priori to prevent the export of goods or transfer of technologies organised for the benefit of the network or one of its clients.
4 http://www.armscontrolwonk.com/1140/urs-tinner
5 The notes for the 'Terrorism Financing and State Responses in Comparative Perspective' conference, Centre for Contemporary Conflict, 4-5 November 2005, are particularly interesting in this question.
6 The example of the dismantlement of the Khan network is based on this equilibrium logic, US intelligence services probably having delayed action against the network so as to be able to act at the greatest possible depth.

France) have relatively similar tools – an internal security service and one or several organisations dedicated to intelligence abroad. This complete assembly can monitor activities of any networks on its own territory and their ramifications outside.

Furthermore, financially the United States has created a structure that is distinctive in that it includes intelligence tools and means of taking action against networks, including international networks.[7] The Office of Terrorism and Financial Intelligence (OTFI) was created within the Treasury Department in 2004, and it has legal powers that enable the US government to target banks acting on behalf of networks,[8] and specific tools designed to monitor international financial flows. In particular, this 'arsenal'[9] appears to include obtaining targeted data originating from the Society for Worldwide Interbank Financial Telecommunication (SWIFT).

Finally, the functional concentration achieved within the Treasury department for financial security activities, enables the OTFI to obtain assistance from all services that might be concerned, including those originating from intelligence or financial repression activities.

In order to improve the efficiency of the intelligence function, it appears necessary to improve *dialogue between services and small sensitive companies.* These are an attractive target particularly for networks, due to their economic vulnerability. The first step would consist of drawing up an exhaustive list of companies that might be concerned, and keeping it up to date. It would then be necessary to define the nature of exchanges between companies and intelligence services. For example, the US Treasury Department performs an information mission before financial institutions in addition to advertising actions about cases for which repressive measures have been taken. Similarly, the TRACFIN unit receives declarations of suspicions but also in principle sends feedback to the declarer.[10]

## How to neutralise networks?
## Towards setting legal bases

Since Resolution 1540 was adopted by the UN Security Council in April 2004, efforts in the struggle against proliferation networks are backed up by a formal framework that fixes key measures to be taken by members of the organisation in terms of:

1. *Interdiction of illegal intermediation activities* for weapons, vectors and related

elements. In particular this is the purpose of item c) in article 3 that imposes that measures shall be taken to detect, dissuade, prevent and fight intermediation.

2. *Control of end users:* point d) in article 3 applies essentially to control of transit and transfers, but it also obliges states to set up means of controlling the nature of the end user.

3. *Control of services and funds:* related to export operations; this particular point also obliges states to check 'the supply of funds or services – for example financing or transport – related to export or transfer operations that contribute to proliferation'.

However, it is regrettable that in terms of checking the service industry (transport, freighting, banks), Resolution 1540 only recommends monitoring of activities related to exports *stricto sensu.* Furthermore, as a first reading, it is limited to criminalising the proliferation of unconventional weapons carried out by non-state players.[11] Consequently, and even if the text is intentionally ambiguous concerning proliferation of WMD by states, its extension to this case would appear politically improbable; some

7 'Prepared Remarks by Stuart Levey, Under-Secretary for Terrorism and Financial Intelligence before the American Enterprise Institute', 8 September 2006.
8 This applies to Executive Order 13382, 28 June 2005, 'Blocking Property of Weapons of Mass Destruction Proliferators and their Supporters', enables the departments of Justice, the Treasury and the State Department to prevent any transaction between the United States and persons or companies participating in proliferation activities. Section 5 authorises the Treasury department to use these powers without prior notification to the persons concerned. It also applies to Section 311 in the 2001 Patriot Act, which enables the Secretary of the Treasury to cut a foreign institution designated as being 'of primary money laundering concern' from the US economic system.
9 'Prepared Remarks by Stuart Levey ...' ibid.
10 In two forms: information about processing of a specific declaration and information, training and targeted or untargeted awareness actions.
11 See articles 1 and 2. Note that the application field is interpreted differently in different states.

countries legally pursue their activities for the development of nuclear weapons and a *fortiori* missiles.

Resolution 1718, 14 October 2006,[12] voted following the North Korean test on 9 October 2006, could become a reference in the struggle against proliferation networks to the extent that it is complementary to provisions of Resolution 1540. Apart from giving UN members the right to freeze North Korean assets abroad, article 8.d states that states must prevent their nationals and persons operating within their frontiers from providing financial assistance to any person or entity involved in North Korean missile or nuclear programmes. Article 8.f also decrees that all cargo entering or leaving the territory shall be searched. Application of this resolution, apart from its utility as an example for future or existing proliferation affairs, could help to improve methods used by some service companies who support operation of networks and possibly reinforce the dialogue between the private sector and services and agencies responsible for the struggle against proliferation.

Similarly, Security Council Resolution 1737 imposing targeted sanctions on Iran[13] applies measures of the same nature to Teheran's nuclear programme, targeting activities of institutions and intermediaries acting for the acquisition network. By setting up a committee responsible for its application, it opens up the possibility of modifying this list that takes account of the network's financial activities.

## Widening the action field against proliferation networks

Economic globalisation makes it necessary to coordinate policies of states creating technologies and countries sheltering service activities[14] that could be used by organisations involved in the trade of weapons of mass destruction. Progress has undoubtedly been made since 2003 following the launch of the *Container Security Initiative* and the *Proliferation Security Initiative* in terms of cooperation on flow control. In particular, they have made it possible to set up systems for checking exports or goods in transit in some states that acted as relays for network activities.

But genuine problems arise with the creation and the use by states of lists of goods and technologies for which export and transit are generally subject to prior authorisations. Complete systems and their main components are usually relatively well controlled because their end use is not questionable. On the other hand, the creation and updating of lists of dual-use goods can prove difficult considering constant changes of technologies.[15] For a country with limited administrative resources,[16] the volume of work involved in the management of export or transit applications (including transport documents)[17] for dual-use goods may become such that it introduces dysfunctions in their processing: delays, superficial analyses, errors, etc. Similarly, ill-informed or uninformed companies tend to submit incomplete or misleading demands to export control administrations.

However, a number of improvements could be considered:

- *setting up of 'catch-all' clauses*. The purpose is not to make a judgement about the intrinsic sensitivity of a product, but rather the intrinsic sensitivity of the end user and the possible use he might make of it.[18] 'Catch-all' clauses also oblige exporters to inform control authorities about any suspicions they have about the end-use of the goods or the nature of the end user, thus contributing to making companies more responsible[19] (like the control over financial flows);

12 Voted under chapter VII.
13 http://www.mideastweb.org/1737.htm
14 Financing, transport/freight, transfer, intermediation.
15 All that is necessary to be convinced of this is to look at the lists of goods produced by the Wassenaar arrangement.
16 Precisely those for which vigilance is particularly desirable in terms of control to the extent that they are the main targets of networks.
17 Cargo manifests in particular.
18 Irina Albrecht, 'Catch-all controls', paper prepared for the International Control Conference, London, 2004.
19 Ibid. An example suspect declaration can be seen at: http://www.bis.doc.gov/ forms/eeleadsntips.html

- *the possibility of producing lists of suspect final destinations must be considered and generalised.* Such documents, despite the political difficulties that may surround their creation, have a genuine use in the context of the struggle against proliferation networks, provided that prior intelligence work has made it possible to map their structure. This is particularly true because production of this type of document may be envisaged within multinational groups,[20] so as to better coordinate efforts made by a group of countries;
- *reinforcement of the required precision for transport documents should be envisaged* to prevent suspect and unusable declarations.

### Struggle against financing of networks

Even if its action is now concentrated on money laundering and financing of terrorism, the adoption of Resolution 1540 *provides a basis for extending the scope of the international Financial Action Task Force (FATF)[21] to include the struggle against financing of proliferation.*

FATF recommendations apply essentially to the need for states to have a legal framework for tracking persons and legal entities involved in laundering activities and freezing their credits. Furthermore, the FATF proposes several ways of reinforcing the role of financing institutions in their struggle against laundering and financing of terrorism that could be interesting in terms of financing of proliferation.

### Have legal tools to supervise the intermediary business

*The generalisation of provisions aimed at supervising the activities of brokers is becoming urgent.* Intermediaries play an important role in the operation of networks by acting as the main relays for acquisition attempts in other countries.[22] Apart from the United States, which introduced provisions in 1996 related to brokers in the law on control of weapon exports,[23] few countries have any legal instruments that they can use against brokers.[24] However, there are some countries including France that have set up such tools. The European Union Council adopted a common position in 2003 on the control of armament intermediaries.[25] In both cases, the objective is to:

- list brokers operating on the territory concerned. It is sometimes envisaged to set up an activity authorisation system, as a better means of controlling operators;
- oblige intermediaries to obtain prior authorisation for each operation in which they make a commitment;
- set up a legal system punishing unauthorised intermediation activities.

### Building a consistent inter-ministerial and international structure

The question of overall consistency must inevitably arise as new tools of different natures are added to the range of means designed to struggle against proliferation networks. The struggle against proliferation networks cannot depend on a logic of isolated and independent operations, it must form part of a coordinated international approach targeting all network functions.

There is no doubt that there is no organisation or forum that has the task of precisely coordinating interception actions, possible financial operations and intelligence. The PSI provides an attractive framework for the creation of such an organisation, because it already coordinates interception activities. However, its operational and informal nature does not make it suitable for such a function. Therefore, it could be more useful to consider creation of an organisation that would have the role of managing the use of all available tools to neutralise a specific network that would

---

20  For example, for supplier groups: MTCR, NSG.

21  The FATF was created in 1989 by the G 7, and now includes 33 member countries, this core being extended by observer countries and the existence of regional forums — for example an Asia-Pacific group to which China belongs — and the participation of international agencies or organisations.

22  B. Gruselle and G. Schlumberger (July 2006), op. cit.

23  Loretta Bondy, 'The US law on arms brokering in 11 questions and answers', presentation to UN workshop in preparation of consultations on illegal brokering, May 2005.

24  Note that US law makes authorisation of brokering compulsory for all citizens of the United States, regardless of their country of residence.

25  EU Council, 'Position on the control of intermediaries in armament', 2003/468/CFSP, 23 June 2003

include the various administrations concerned, including treasury, customs, defence and intelligence services. The extent to which such an initiative could significantly improve the level and quality of intelligence exchanges essential for its operation remains to be seen.

Finally, it is important to bear in mind that whatever measures and actions are taken to improve the struggle against proliferation networks, their economic impact on legitimate activities must be taken into account. In particular, it appears to be essential to find a balance between the need for security and constraints related to international development of private players, at the risk of making measures that might be taken inoperative.

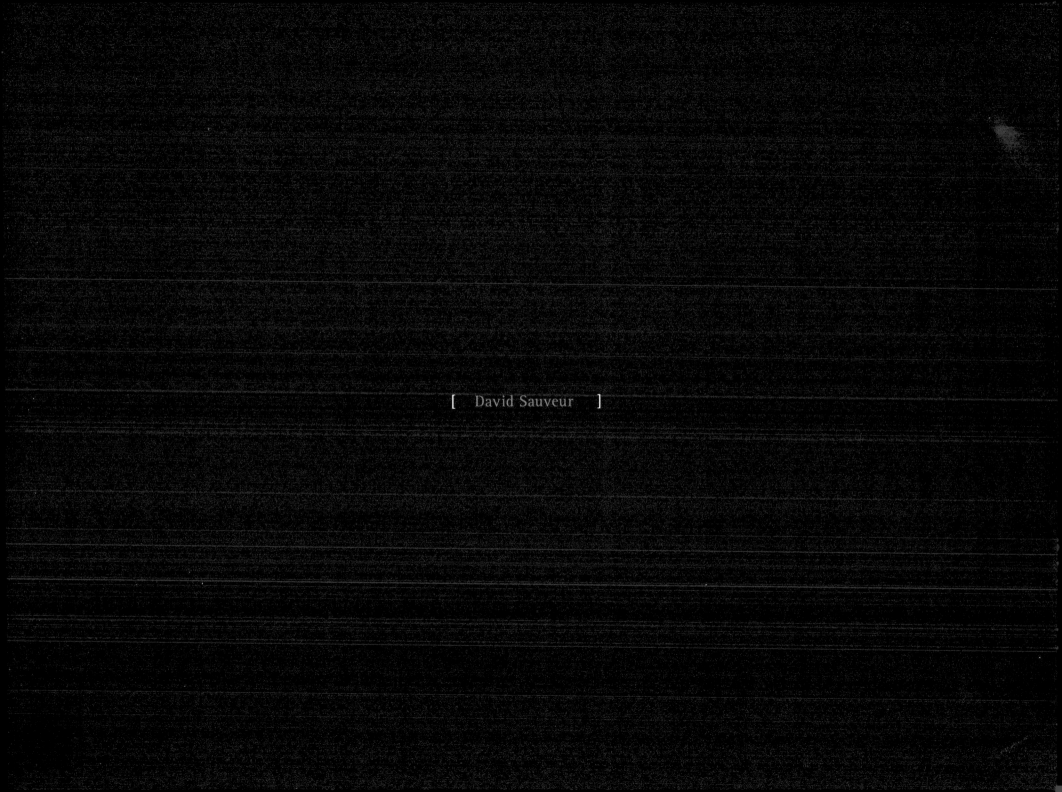

[   David Sauveur   ]

# Afghanistan – the time of the Hazaras

This land is indeed far away from where the little GIs are getting lost in the sand waging their 'war on terrorism', just like the soldiers of Britain's Glorious Majesty did before them in the days of Kipling's 'Big Game'.

Far away in space and in time. Afghanistan is a country of borders, at the crossroads of several worlds, and a place where more than one invader has lost his way.

The Hazaras we see in these images are themselves descendants of one of the nomadic peoples absorbed into Afghanistan. A little different from the other Afghans: Tajiks, Uzbeks and Pashtuns, who come from Central Asia.

As for their religion, they look towards Persia: they are Shia Muslims. They came in the wake of Genghis Khan's hordes and settled in villages of fortified farms, where the high mountains impose their law and where every drop of water and every fruit that grows matters.

The trip across the mountains is an ordeal in space and in time: your breath gets shorter and your steps more sluggish, the slopes are dangerous. When the first rains come, the sand saturates and holds back the traveller's car; it wears out both horses and men. You must not hurry. Afghanistan is still a stranger to speed. You can not impose your will on the mountain just like that.

In this country, blighted by 30 years of war, every scar on the ground, on the walls and on peoples' faces are traces of an era: nomadic invasions, empires that came and fell and civil wars. Afghanistan still lives in an age of strongholds, warlords and soldiers of fortune. The Hazaras know this well; they have often been victims of civil wars and Pashtun invasions. Seen as 'heretics' for their Shia faith, they are despised by other Afghans, who are Sunnis. Very devout, they seem close to a 'quietist' philosophy of Shia Islam: their life belongs to God and religion does not mix with politics ... One day the Mahdi will return to impose a righteous order on earth. This life of today is ephemeral and paradise awaits the good and the meek.

In Kabul, where they live in the grubby suburbs, the rhythm is no longer the same as in the mountains. Time accelerates: we are much more in the present. From year to year the city expands in the most anarchic way. Down there the Hazaras are the 'small hands' of the city: porters, water-carriers, workmen, vendors... They make their livelihoods in the dust of the roads and the brick kilns. Some still prefer to escape the country to Iran or to the small Hazara community in Quetta, Pakistan. The Hazaras are trapped in time – between the secular past as a community attached to the mountains and the present day globalised war, which is catching up on them, before the fall of the next empire...

David Sauveur

*On the road between Band-Al-Amir*
*and Bamyan, a wreck of a Russian tank.*
© David Sauveur / Agence VU /
Province of Day Kundi, Afghanistan

*This area is renown as one of the most*
*beautiful in Afghanistan: the suspension lakes*
*of Band-Al-Amir, formed by natural dams.*
*The legend says that the formation*
*is due to miracles carried out by the Imam Ali,*
*considered as a saint by the Shiite people.*

© David Sauveur / Agence VU /
Band-Al-Amir, Afghanistan

*Wrecks in Kabul bus station.*

*The king's palace destroyed
during the civil war.*

© David Sauveur / Agence VU / Kabul, Afghanistan

*Near the Omar Museum,
a man does his first prayer
in front of a plane wreck.*

© David Sauveur / Agence VU / Kabul, Afghanistan

*Day Kundi Province, at a general*
*store near the cemetery.*
*Background: a mausoleum built*
*around the grave of a saint.*

*Volleyball game
outside a general store.*

© David Sauveur / Agence VU / Jangalak, Afghanistan

*This area is renown as one*
*of the most beautiful in Afghanistan:*
*the suspension lakes of Band-Al-Amir,*
*formed by natural dams.*
*The legend says that the formation*
*is due to miracles carried out*
*by the Imam Ali, considered*
*as a saint by the Shiite people.*

© David Sauveur / Agence VU / Band-Al-Amir, Afghanistan

*In a hamlet on the road between Nili and Yakawlang, at the first winter snowfall. A family clears off the snow of their house cob roof.*
© David Sauveur / Agence VU
Province of Day Kundi, Afghanistan

*Northern Hazaradjat. Afghan people*
*call it the 'City of Murmurs'.*
*Formerly a place for pilgrimage*
*and Buddhist retreat. Bamyan sheltered*
*the giant Buddha which was sculpted*
*in the cliffs and has been destroyed*
*by the Taliban. Along the valley,*
*there are many caves in the cliffs that*
*were built for retreat and meditation*
*during the Buddhist period.*

*Outside the general store.*
© David Sauveur / Agence VU /
Nili, 17th district, Afghanistan

*In the 16th district, near the animal market, on the road to Kandahar. Many Hazara people are gathered in this recently built district. The constructions are anarchically built without infrastructure, electricity, or water. A strong rainstorm flooded many houses that day.*

© David Sauveur / Agence VU / Kabul, Afghanistan

*At the top of the 'TV Hill'.*
© David Sauveur / Agence VU / Kabul, Afghanistan

# AIDING AFGHANISTAN
## INTERVIEW WITH BETTINA MUSCHEIDT

*What relevancy does Afghanistan have for the European Union? With the United States' active engagement in the country, does Afghanistan need to be high up on the EU's agenda?*

Afghanistan has direct relevance for the European as it does for the US – in today's world all countries are interconnected. As opposed to previous times we can no longer afford to "forget" countries, leaving them behind to become failed states. Sooner or later they will "remind" us of their existence: by sending streams of destitute refugees across their borders destabilising neighbouring countries with a domino effect on the wider region, by sending drugs even to other continents because the domestic rule of law is weak.

So, these are just some of the reasons why even a country so far away from the US and Europe matters to us in a very immediate manner. Let me add to this one more aspect: the last few years have brought unprecedented economic growth to many parts of our planet, life expectancy keeps on increasing and there is, albeit slowly, progress in reaching the Millenium Development Goals. So, then tell me how can we reconcile with leaving one country out of this equation? Afghanistan continues to be at the very low end of UN lists classifying countries according to progress made in human development, making reference to very basic parameters. We cannot afford this situation

to continue – Afghanistan's people have a right to development and participation in political life.

*How would you rate the European Union's early warning and early response mechanisms? What lessons in early warning have been learned in recent years in Afghanistan?*

In Afghanistan we are already making use of a financial instrument that responds to the EU's strengthened capacity in early warning and early response mechanisms – the launching phase of the EC justice reform programme is financed from the Stability Instrument. Essentially, it allowed us to quickly react to a need identified in 2006. The EU was challenged to make a substantial contribution to improving the rule of law in Afghanistan. With the ESDP mission and the EU justice programme, implemented in close synergy, we will make a coherent contribution to improving the rule of law sector. Having a new financial instrument, that allows us to react to such challenges made such a timely intervention possible.

*You have recently returned from a trip to Afghanistan. What were your impressions?*

My impression is slightly more optimistic than what you're likely to read in the news. On the ground lots of things are actually happening. Progress in social development and even economic growth has been remark-

able in Afghanistan and that's something that is easily overlooked. Growth has been double digit in the last years, albeit from a very low base and with the understanding that some of it comes from the drugs economy and the spin offs from it.

Social development has probably seen the most remarkable change. Almost 80 per cent of Afghans now have primary healthcare cover. In 2001, only 7 per cent had such access. As a clear result of this, child mortality has dropped by over 25 per cent since 2001. Second, Afghan schoolchildren have access to education again and over three million children are in schools, with well over a third being girls. Sadly, we hear about reports of Taliban targeting individual girls' schools, but that does not take away from the overall advancement in education. Adults who lost so much during the war years are also taking adult literacy classes – for me a very clear sign of Afghan energy, initiative and vision. These people are not willing to give up and want a better future.

*So globally are things getting better or worse?*

On the development agenda, things have been making steady progress after three decades of warfare. The Afghan government started from scratch and it remains weak, but it has set up village councils in the last years and on other parts of the development agenda we are definitely on track. However,

*Bettina Muscheidt is the political desk officer for Afghanistan in the European Commission's External Relations Directorate-General. A German native, she studied agricultural economics in Bonn before graduating with a Master's degree in international relations at the Fletcher School of Law and Diplomacy in Boston. She has spent most of her working life trying to bring economic development to the Middle East. For more than 11 years she has worked on issues related to the Palestinian territories for the European Commission and European Investment Bank.*

we are lagging behind in other areas – like rural development, justice and security – where it took longer for donors and the government to agree a common vision.

*Is the main problem the deteriorating security situation in large swathes of the country?*

One thing that helped us over the first few years was the relatively benign security situation. The insurgency we now see in the south makes any development a major challenge, if not almost impossible. Very closely linked to the security situation is the drugs problem. The latest report from the United Nations Office on Drugs and Crime shows a clear link between the insurgency, criminal networks and drugs.

In some places development is not only stagnating but is being rolled back. We have experienced some nasty surprises, like in the province of Nangahar, where the progress that was made was negative. There is renewed planting of opium poppy and now this province that was relatively stable is again being affected by the insurgency. It is difficult for development to move ahead without security.

*Can the EU do anything about the drugs epidemic?*

We're already doing something that's very comprehensive, but not all over the country. The EU programme is concentrated in the east and north-east and in these regions, particularly with our emphasis on rural livelihood and finding alternatives to the growing of poppy, we've seen quite a lot of progress in the last years. But this is being endangered by the insurgency.

*How can the EU, a non-military organisation, help bring more security to the Afghan people?*

We are, of course, not involved with the Afghan Army. That is not our role and others do that. But we are very strongly involved in other aspects of the security agenda. We've been instrumental in funding the salaries of the police through the law and order trust fund – to the tune of €135 million in 2002-2006 – which is also a vehicle for police reform.

We are also focusing on justice reform because initial steps in this area addressed legal issues, not institutional ones, and we believe a lot needs to be done to make the Afghan judiciary more professional. For that reason, we have deployed a short-term justice mission under the Stability Instrument to reform the justice sector. This consists of sending experts who are embedded within the three key justice institutions – the Ministry of Justice, the Supreme Court and Attorney General's office. By the middle of next year we hope to have a fairly comprehensive plan for the reform of all the justice institutions that would be the basis for a reform programme that we aim to fund.

Everyone agrees that progress in Afghanistan hinges on progress in the rule of law, – which is why we place such emphasis on our rule of law mission in the country. Security is vital, but you also need a professional justice system, so that those who are detained can receive due process. For that reason, our police-training mission and justice reform mission are very closely related to each other, because Afghans have to see that their state delivers justice, is equitable and ensures human rights are upheld.

*Ultimately though, would you agree that there has to be a military solution in Afghanistan – that without the defeat of the Taliban, development cannot take place?*

It has to be a parallel process. Our partners on the ground have no choice but to advance the development agenda while, quite possibly, something very bad is happening in the next village. Over the years we have lost a number of health workers who were bringing better health, survival and quality of life to their Afghan compatriots. Tremendously tragic as it is, this hasn't stopped us from pursuing our development programme.

In Afghanistan you don't find any virgin green field in which you can start building-up villages. This is simply unrealistic. We have to show the Afghan people that now they can improve their lives and get their products to the market and send their kids to school. If we didn't continue with our development efforts in a very hard-nosed way, there would be no alternative to turn to in the face of the onslaught of the insurgents' attacks. We have seen unspeakably horrid suicide attacks but people doggedly continue going about their business.

*Does this emphasis on development differ from the EU's partners?*

Not judging from the evidence in the field. All those who are militarily engaged are also very heavily engaged in development. Our American partners are in first place when it comes to civilian reconstruction – they have set aside some €2 billion over two years – and also paying the salaries of Afghan soldiers. So these are enormous amounts and we mustn't forget the Americans are particularly bent on cumbersome and dangerous tasks like building roads, dams and other essential infrastructure. They have undertaken to build the entire ring road around Afghanistan, and I say this with some emphasis because there are still some provinces that don't even have a centimetre of tarmac. Without better roads you cannot enable people to pursue alternative economic development, which is why we have funded the road from Kabul to Pakistan. We have upgraded the border posts to provide security and ensure the smooth functioning of trade and have similar programmes now on the border with Central Asia.

*The international community is doing a lot for Afghanistan, but is it doing enough?*

The financial needs of Afghanistan will remain very important, not just in terms of building infrastructure, but also in helping the central government stand on its feet, because it is not yet strong enough to do so on its own. Over many years to come the EU will need to continue contributing to trust funds which are essential to help ensure the functioning of the Afghan state to help steady it.

Having said this, a lot of people say the answer to Afghanistan's problems lies in increasing financial assistance. But there are some things that you cannot buy with more money, and which will not go any faster with more funds. If you look at female health or education, if you want to bring services to remote, conservative communities, you will need local females to do this – and it takes time to train them. You will also need to convince their families of the need to do this and make it socially acceptable for them to leave their villages to study. So, there is an issue with absorptive capacity which we have to bear in mind.

*So in summary, are you optimistic that things will get better in Afghanistan?*

Things must get better because in the globalised world we can't allow a country to slip back and fall prey to systems and ideologies that restrict individuals in their social and economical development and take away their human and social rights.

The international community has a duty to stand by the Afghans by showing that there is an alternative – even if progress takes longer than people expected.

# Early warning and the responsibility to prevent conflicts[1]

## Introduction

Developed countries donate a large amount of money for development to under-developed countries around the world. Take Norway, as an example, which is one of the world's most generous donors, donating 0.95 per cent of its GDP to developing countries, most of them in Africa. Yet the tragedy of Africa is that, despite the attention Norway and the rest of the developed world has paid to the region over the decades and the billions of euros in aid that have been channelled there, we seem little closer to removing the scourge of conflict that continues to devastate much of the continent.

You just have to look at the news headlines any day of the week and there will be yet another story of some civil war or coup in Africa. The devastating situation in Darfur continues to get even worse — hard though that it is to believe. Daily clashes are being reported in the oil rich delta region of Nigeria. Weeks of fighting in Somalia's capital, Mogadishu, claimed over 100 lives. Côte d'Ivoire is in the middle of a 4-year civil war. Ethiopia and Eritrea are contemplating going to war with each other again. The murderous Lord's Resistance Army rebel group from northern Uganda is now operating freely in southern Sudan, and has recently crossed into the Congo. And it's not as though the Congo doesn't have enough problems of its own, with some 40,000 people dying each month from conflict related disease and malnutrition.[2]

So, that's the news — and without some context, you could be forgiven for thinking that Africa is beyond assistance, destined forever to be wracked by conflict. But is that really the case?

## A future for Africa?

Some of the answers can be found in an excellent report published in 2005 — the Human Security Report — put together by Andy Mack and his team at the Human Security Centre in Canada, and funded by the Norwegian Royal Ministry of Foreign Affairs, among others. For the first time it pulled together a whole range of statistics on conflicts around the world, with much of the data coming from the International Peace Research Institute in Oslo and Uppsala University.

The report's headline is an encouraging one, and perhaps counterintuitive; namely that there has been a 40 per cent reduction in the number of armed conflicts since the early 1990s.

The picture for Africa was mixed. There has been a big fall in the number of state-based conflicts in Africa over the last 15 years — a reduction by half — but Africa is still home to most of the world's conflicts. The report found that in 2003 Africa was home to 46 of 89 cases of armed conflict and one-sided violence that year, and that of the 29 countries experiencing such violence, 13 of them were in Africa.

Combine this with two statistics from the Oxford academic Paul Collier — that almost half the countries coming out of civil war fall back into conflict within five years, and the average civil war costs a country and its neighbours around US $54 billion dollars in direct costs and lost growth — and you have a pretty stark demonstration of the conflict trap in Africa.

## The challenge of early warning and early response

The title of this article describes an ideal — i.e. a community of nations with systems in place to alert them to the risk of looming conflict, and a willingness and ability to intervene to prevent full scale conflict from breaking out. However, as you are all too aware, the reality is far from the ideal.

*Nick Grono is Vice President for Advocacy and Operations at the International Crisis Group. He has overall responsibility for the operation of all programmes and executive oversight of Crisis Group's operations, research unit, media and IT. He also coordinates Crisis Group's advocacy efforts worldwide, and takes the lead on issues relating to the International Criminal Court. Nick is a lawyer by background and, before working for Crisis Group, was Chief of Staff and National Security Adviser to the Australian Attorney-General. Nick has a law degree from the University of Sydney and a Master's in Public Policy from Princeton University.*

---

1 Re-edited speech given at the conference on Conflict and Good Governance in Africa, Labor Party International Forum, Oslo — 24 April 2006

2 [ed.] These events relates to the current situation at the time the speech was written in April 2006.

Why do we find it so hard to intervene to prevent conflicts? There is no shortage of early warnings out there for those that want to be informed. There is a shortage perhaps of early warning systems – systems that rigorously and systematically track indicators that correlate to increased risk of conflict – but not of early warning itself. You just have to go to the website of the International Crisis Group to find a huge amount of early warning material. The real problem is one of political will. Early warning rarely leads to effective and timely response. And one of the reasons for this is that early warning is largely a technical exercise, while early response is a political exercise. There needs to be political will to intervene, but all too often the will is just not there.

The political obstacles to early action are on full display at the United Nations. The UN Secretariat still does not have a functioning early warning system for conflicts. This has been a longstanding problem at the UN. Thorvald Stoltenberg, who used to be an UN Mediator for the Balkans in the mid-90s, told me about when he was working with David Owen, the EU Representative, and French and German colleagues. Each of these colleagues would receive morning intelligence reports and analysis from their countries' agencies – and he received nothing from the UN – not even a collation of open source information with some minimal analysis. This is clearly an untenable situation if the UN is to play an informed role. The Brahimi report recommended creation of a small body (EISAS – Information and Strategic Analysis Secretariat) to collect and analyse information on possible conflicts, but member states blocked it.

So why is there such an aversion to the creation of effective mechanisms to track and warn about conflict? Leaving aside bureaucratic inertia, there are two main reasons. The first is that many Northern states prefer to keep the UN in a position of dependence on their resources, and hence more effectively control its actions. The second is that many Southern states fear that early warning will lead to early intervention, thus trampling on their sovereignty. So, the result is that the UN Secretariat has to rely on other sources for its early warning – its missions, contributions by member states, and NGOs such as Crisis Group. However, even when it has all the information necessary to enable it to act, it and the international community it represents usually fail to act in time to prevent conflict from spiralling out of control.

## International response to Darfur

What we have seen in Darfur since early 2003 is slow motion ethnic cleansing taking place before the world's eyes. More than 200,000 have died in the conflict, most from conflict-related disease and malnutrition. More than two million have been forced from their homes, and over 200,000 Sudanese are refugees in neighbouring Chad. To put these awful figures into perspective, that is as though half the population of Oslo (540,000) had died because of the conflict, and half the population of Norway (4.6 million) had been driven from their homes.

What makes this all the more tragic is that policy-makers and leaders around the world know exactly what is happening there. They cannot plead ignorance. There was no lack of warning about what is going on as it unfolded.

Thanks to the work of Crisis Group, Human Rights Watch and others such as Nick Kristof of *The New York Times* and Juan Mendez, the UN's Special Adviser on the Prevention of Genocide, these atrocities are all too well documented. Yet, despite all the evidence, the international community has utterly failed in its responsibility to protect the people of Darfur.

## So what action has the international community taken?

In the case of Darfur, the UN Security Council has been appallingly slow to put any real pressure on the Sudanese government. It was some two years after the conflict started, and in the face of repeated provocations from the Sudanese government – including its utter failure to disarm the Janjaweed – that the Security Council belatedly decided to impose sanctions against the Sudanese government (Resolution 1591, 29 March 2005). However, it was still arguing over which individuals are to be subject to those sanctions – some three years after the conflict started, and a year after the resolution was passed.

The Security Council did take more robust action on the legal front, after much lobbying from Crisis Group, Human Rights Watch and others. In March 2005, it referred the situation in Darfur to the International Criminal Court (ICC) for investigation. The ICC opened its investigation into Darfur and is now actively investigating crimes in the region – despite much obstruction from the Sudanese government.

The other key international actor on Darfur has been the African Union. Darfur has been a test case for the fledgling organisation. It has done as much as could be expected with its limited resources and mandate, but now its limitations are being exposed. The African Union established a small monitoring mission in Darfur mid-2004, consisting of some 60 monitors and 300 troops to protect them. Over the following couple of years, the mission gradually expanded to some 7,700 troops and monitors. However, we have seen a large gap between intentions and capabilities. Those 7,700 were expected to patrol an area almost double the size of Norway. Another critical limitation of the AU mission was its mandate. It was largely an observer mission. It did not have a mandate to go out and proactively protect civilians. In fact, it could only protect civilians when they are being attacked before its eyes, and only then, if it felt it had enough forces to intervene.

That leaves the European Union, NATO and the United States as the remaining key international actors. The approach of the

European Union was largely to support the work of the African Union. The EU made it clear that it saw the AU as the lead international player in Darfur, and that the EU's role was primarily to support African solutions to African problems, by funding the AU mission. NATO has been a strategic competitor of the EU in Darfur and has been providing expertise and logistical support to the AU mission. However, NATO currently has no intention of going beyond its limited support and logistical role and actually putting troops on the ground in any significant numbers.

Then there is the United States, which has a mixed record on Darfur. In its rhetoric, the US has been at the forefront of international action. Both Colin Powell and George Bush called events in Darfur a 'genocide'. In addition, both Powell and Condoleezza Rice have been to Darfur. The US has been generous in its aid contributions, supplying well over half the food supplies to the displaced Darfurians. And in perhaps its most significant move, the US abstained from the Security Council vote on the ICC referral, allowing the referral to go through – a very significant step for an administration that had made opposition to the ICC a leading plank of its foreign policy until then.

Nevertheless, while the US has called events in Darfur a 'genocide', and has yet to put real pressure on the Sudanese regime, there is a tragic irony about the US response to Darfur when compared with its response to Rwanda some 12 years ago. Then, the ad

ministration did everything it could to avoid calling events in Rwanda a 'genocide' – using all sorts of word play to avoid making that judgement, fearing that if it did it would have to take far stronger action that it was prepared to. This time around there has been little hesitation in calling the situation a genocide, in the light of far more ambivalent evidence – with the apparent conclusion that doing so did not impose any commensurate obligation to act.

## The Regional Impact

All conflicts in Africa have impacts beyond the borders of the country suffering from the conflict. We have seen that most starkly in Chad where the government was nearly overthrown in March 2006 by rebels who advanced to the outskirts of the capital N'djamena, and were only just turned back – but they have by no means been defeated.

This was simply the latest phase in a regional conflict in which the actors are the Chadian and Sudanese governments, and the Chadian and Sudanese armed groups operating in the Darfur region. There are two main rebel alliances and a plethora of smaller armed groups now fighting in Chad. One recruits predominantly among the Tama tribal group and is directly sponsored by the Sudanese government (the Front for Unity and Change (FUC), and its core group the Rally for Democracy and Liberty (RDL)). The other is led by defectors from the Chad army (The rally of Democratic Forces (RaFD-SCUD dissolved itself into RaFD in early 2006). Although they are members of Chadian President Idriss Deby's own clan of the Zaghawa people, these defectors are opposed to him because they do not think he has done enough to protect members of his tribe, the Zaghawa, in Darfur, where they are being killed and driven off their lands by the Sudan government's Janjaweed militias. They also oppose him running for a third term, after amending the constitution in 2005. Theirs is therefore a revolt that seeks to preserve their hold on power, while the FUC's aim is to challenge the control of the Zaghawa elites of the government.

Deby himself is supporting one of the rebel groups in Darfur (SLA-Minawi), and has cut off diplomatic relations with Sudan. He threatened to drive the 200,000 Sudanese refugees now in eastern Chad back into Darfur, though he has since backed away from that threat.

Therefore, a situation that looked to be as hopeless as it could be, now threatens to get considerably worse. However, none of this is surprising. Crisis Group has been warning for the last 18 months that the Darfur conflict was destabilizing Chad. We have publicly predicted as of early 2006 that Chad was about to implode with probable drastic consequences for the refugees and Chadian civilians, but our warning has yet to lead to meaningful international engagement to contain the worst of the violence. While prevention at this stage has little material

cost for the international community, the situation would become more intractable with each passing day, causing large scale displacement and ethnically driven purges, and requiring intervention at a much greater cost.

## Why hasn't the world acted?

So why hasn't the international community done more to prevent the atrocities in Darfur, or to stop Chad spiralling into conflict?

The very sad reality is that Darfur just does not matter enough, and Sudan matters too much, for the international community to do more.

Much as governments in Europe and the US are disturbed by what is happening in Darfur – and they genuinely are – almost without exception they are not prepared to commit their troops on the ground in Sudan. Hence, their enthusiastic support for African solutions to African problems. The situation is a difficult one for the US because, in its war on terror, it has a close intelligence relationship with the Sudanese government and in 2005 it flew Salah Gosh, the chief of intelligence and one of the architects of the Darfur atrocities, out to Virginia on a private plane for meetings. As for the UN, it is a creature of its members. So on the Security Council you have China, with large oil imports from Sudan, ready to block any overly intrusive UN measures. In addition, both Russia and China are very wary about UN intervention

in civil conflicts, fearing it may lead one day to intervention in Chechnya or Tibet or Xinjiang.

The Arab League, and most of its member states, is utterly opposed to a Western-led intervention in North Africa, and strongly protective of one of their own. Moreover, the AU is operating in Darfur with the consent of the government of Sudan, and is reluctant to push too hard for fear of being further marginalised. It also desperately wants to prove that it can resolve one of Africa's most destructive conflicts, even when all the evidence now is that it cannot.

And in Chad, the international community has not put any real pressure on the government to resolve the issues that are driving much of the conflict there – issues such as a lack of democratic avenues for political grievances to be resolved; human rights abuses; corruption; and the utter lack of development despite increasing oil wealth. The approach here is very much one of dealing with the devil they know.

These motivations all combine to ensure that the international community shies away from effective intervention. Instead, it focuses its efforts on providing humanitarian assistance – thereby addressing the consequences, but not the causes.

## Responsibility to protect

So how should the world be responding? Simply put, the international community should be fulfilling its responsibility to prevent conflict and protect civilians.

The UN held a World Summit in New York in September 2006 to celebrate the 60th anniversary of the United Nations. It was the largest ever gathering of world leaders. There was hope that the Summit would agree major reforms to the UN and take bold decisions on human rights, security and development. In the end, the Summit was a disappointment, with member states largely failing to take strong action on any of these fronts. However, one significant success was the agreement to acknowledge the doctrine of responsibility to protect as an international responsibility. Specifically the Summit agreed to the following:

Each individual State has the responsibility to protect its populations from genocide, war crimes, ethnic cleansing and crimes against humanity. This responsibility entails the prevention of such crimes, including their incitement, through appropriate and necessary means. We accept that responsibility and will act in accordance with it.

This is an historic step, because until now state sovereignty was formally, if not in practice, sacrosanct. This is perhaps understandable – no state wants to be the object of coercive intervention by others. However, there are situations, such as Rwanda or Kosovo/a, in which such intervention is the only way to stop genocide and other atrocities. Now, for the first time, the UN has explicitly recognised that there are circumstances in which failures by states to protect their own populations gives rise to an obligation by the international community to intervene in that state's sovereign affairs.

Such a responsibility is vested first with the sovereign state itself, but when they are unwilling or unable to ensure such protections, that responsibility must be borne by the broader community of states. However, the responsibility to protect is about much more than intervention. It extends to a whole continuum of obligations from the responsibility to prevent crises, to react to situations of compelling human need, and to rebuild in post-conflict situations, including recovery, reconstruction and reconciliation.

In Chad, this means that Deby's government has primary responsibility to address those issues fuelling the conflict. However, the international community must assist, by uniting to push for a delay in the upcoming third term elections, so that a more inclusive political process can be developed.

As for Darfur, Khartoum has the lead responsibility to prevent the massacre of its own people but, by its active involvement in the slaughter and displacement of civilians in Darfur, it has clearly and wantonly failed in that responsibility. The obligation then shifts to the international community to intervene.

In 2006, the Crisis Group repeatedly argued that the international community needed to pursue three objectives in Darfur.

The **first** was that of civilian protection. The UN must take over from the AU forces in 2006, with a larger force and stronger mandate. The UN has agreed to do so, but the government of Sudan is objecting, and the AU is hesitating. More pressure must be brought to bear to ensure this handover takes place. In the meantime, the UN must approve a stabilisation force to work with the AU mission in protecting civilians and securing the border with Chad.

The **second** objective was to implement accountability in Darfur. This means putting in place the UN sanctions immediately. It also means widening the sanctions to target Sudan's oil industry. And it means supporting the ICC investigation – the AU and member states should provide relevant information on a timely basis to the ICC. Member states should also make sure that the ICC has the resources needed to thoroughly investigate Darfur.

The **third** objective was to build a Darfur peace process. This means that the government of Sudan delegation must represent the new Government of National Unity – i.e. it must include representatives of the southern SPLM playing a substantive role, and not just the hard-line National Congress Party. The international community, which includes Norway as a key player, must apply consistent and united pressure. In addition, more support needs to be provided to the two main rebel movements, the SLA and JEM, to unify their negotiating positions.

The peace process must remain a focus, as in the end the solution to the conflict in Darfur will only be found in a negotiated settlement.

However, as the conflict drags on, we are beginning to see a falling off in moral outrage over Darfur, and international community fatigue. My fear is that we will soon settle for a low intensity conflict in the region, handing over responsibility to the humanitarian agencies – as we have in so many other places in Africa – only to look back in a decade or so and vow "never again", when it was within our means to ensure that it never happened on this scale in the first place.

Darfur is just one, albeit truly horrific, example of what happens when the international community fails to take head of early warning, and act to intervene at an early stage. The failure in Darfur is now destabilizing the whole region, spreading mayhem well beyond the borders of Sudan.

The international community needs to get serious about its commitments to prevent genocides, crimes against humanity and war crimes. Until it does so, conflict in Africa will continue to claim hundreds of thousands of lives each year through disease and malnutrition. Moreover, it will continue to devastate development efforts in that continent, consigning the half of Africa's population that lives on less than US $1-a-day to continued abject poverty.

# CONFLICT EARLY WARNING SYSTEMS AND SUPPORT OF THE COMPREHENSIVE PEACE AGREEMENT IN SUDAN

## Introduction

I will address two issues in this article, the first concerns the re-engagement of Sudan with the Conflict Early Warning and Response Mechanism (CEWARN) in its engagement along the borders of neighbouring countries within the Horn of Africa. Second, I will consider the potential and use of an early warning system to support the peace process in Sudan.[1]

To make the point that the Sudan peace process, both North/South and that regarding Darfur (never mind the East) is going through a difficult patch, is merely a statement of the obvious. In general the peace agreement remains fragile, although it is still on track. A recent report by the International Crises Group starts its executive summary as follows:

More than a year after it was signed, Sudan's Comprehensive Peace Agreement (CPA) is showing signs of strain [...] and continues to lack broader support throughout the country, particularly in the North. The current equation for peace in Sudan is a worrying one: the NCP has the capacity to implement but lacks the political will, whereas the SPLM has the commitment but is weak and disorganised. There is a real risk of renewed conflict down the road.[2]

When it comes to the application of early warning theory to conflict prevention practice, we need to 'mind the gap' – reflected in a 1996 report on early warning:

There appears to be two forms of early warning: one in theory and one in practice. [...] While international organisations frequently articulate an interest in conflict prevention, in practice they are almost solely concerned with the settlement or management of existing disputes.[3]

Different from intelligence systems, which serve a national security purpose where the focus is on high-quality and often secret sources of information, early warning systems typically serve intergovernmental purposes and are based on networks and open sources for their information. Early warning systems originated with the requirement (within humanitarian relief agencies) for a single, reliable source of analysis to serve a coalition of clients rather than a single government. Domestically conflict early warning systems are complex and fraught with all kinds of problems since they are easily perceived to be agents of or hostile to state security interests within the context of an undemocratic or non-responsive state – or, as is the case in Sudan – where state power is contested.

Yet, in the absence of a functioning, legitimate state system across much of Sudan after several decades of war, the establishment of a neutral conflict prevention and early warning capacity dedicated to support the political transition could fill an urgent void – that of the provision of independent information and analysis.

## Some general pointers

Generically, the aim of conflict early warning is to identify critical developments in a timely manner, so that coherent response strategies can be formulated to either prevent violent conflict or limit its destructive effects. Effective early warning involves the collection and analysis of data in a uniform and systematised way and according

*Dr Jakkie Cilliers has B.Mil (BA), BA Hons, MA (cum laude), D.Litt and D.Phil degrees from the universities of Stellenbosch and South Africa. He co-founded the Institute for Defence Policy in 1990, which subsequently became the Institute for Security Studies (ISS). Since 1993 Dr Cilliers has served as executive director of the ISS. He has been awarded the Bronze Medal from the South African Society for the Advancement of Science. He has also been awarded the H Bradlow Research Bursary for his work. Dr Cilliers regularly lectures on security issues and has published, edited and contributed to a large number of journals, books and other publications, as well as served on a number of boards and committees.*

---

1 The background paper refers to the fact that: 'The ultimate objective of the conference is to facilitate a debate led by Sudanese on the appropriateness and the specifications of an Early Warning System for Conflict Prevention in Sudan'. Furthermore, 'The signing of the Comprehensive Peace Agreement on January 9th 2005 is ... a unique opportunity to revive the Sudan engagement to CEWARN, to explore other conflict areas to be included in an adapted EWS for the Sudan, and to increase the capacity of the government and international community to monitor, prevent and respond to local conflicts'.

2 'Sudan's Comprehensive Peace Agreement: the long road ahead', Africa Report No. 106, 31 March 2006, p. i.

3 Netherlands Institute of International Relations, *Conflict Prevention and Early Warning in the Political Practice of International Organizations*, January 1996, p. 71.

to a commonly shared methodology. It requires the formulation and communication of analysis and policy options to relevant end-users – information towards action.

In a basic form, conflict early warning needs to tackle:

- which issues (manifestations, precipitating, proximate and root causes) underpin and drive the conflict?

- which factors put a brake on conflict and serve as the basis for peace?

- who are the main stakeholders in the conflict?

- what are the practical options available to policy-makers who wish to affect the emerging conflict, avoid human suffering in the short term and move toward a sustainable settlement in the longer term?

- the timely communication and engagement with policy-makers – to close the loop from analysis to action.

These are all highly political and partisan questions within Sudan and within the region and considerable thought would have to go into designing a system and in the choice of partners in such a system. These relationships are depicted in the schematic diagram presented in *Figure 1*.

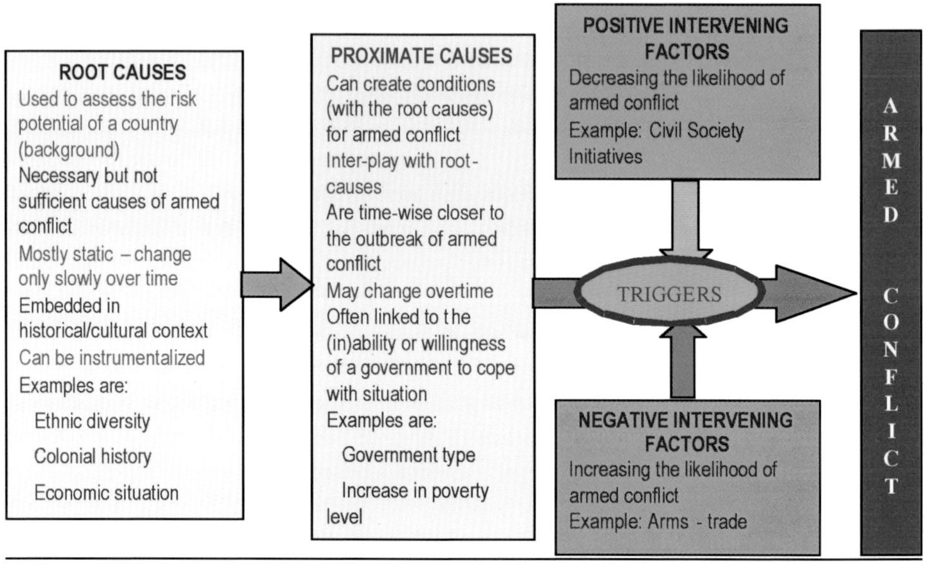

**ROOT CAUSES**
Used to assess the risk potential of a country (background)
Necessary but not sufficient causes of armed conflict
Mostly static – change only slowly over time
Embedded in historical/cultural context
Can be instrumentalized
Examples are:
  Ethnic diversity
  Colonial history
  Economic situation

**PROXIMATE CAUSES**
Can create conditions (with the root causes) for armed conflict
Inter-play with root-causes
Are time-wise closer to the outbreak of armed conflict
May change overtime
Often linked to the (in)ability or willingness of a government to cope with situation
Examples are:
  Government type
  Increase in poverty level

**POSITIVE INTERVENING FACTORS**
Decreasing the likelihood of armed conflict
Example: Civil Society Initiatives

TRIGGERS

**NEGATIVE INTERVENING FACTORS**
Increasing the likelihood of armed conflict
Example: Arms - trade

ARMED CONFLICT

*Figure 1: Schematic display of a conflict EWS [4]*

### CEWARN in the Horn of Africa

The African Union's (AU) CEWS at continental level and regional systems including that of CEWARN in the Horn were established to avoid inter-state conflict and secondly to stop national problems from becoming regional headaches. CEWARN is, however, more specific and focused than that found elsewhere in Africa. Article 5 on the functions of CEWARN reads, in part, as follows:

1. The functions of CEWARN cover both early warning and response and shall include the following:

a) Promote the exchange of information and collaboration among member states on early warning and response on the basis of the following principles:

   i)   timeliness
   ii)  transparency
   iii) cooperation
   iv)  free flow of information

b) Gather, verify, process and analyse information about conflicts in the region according to the guidelines provided in the Annex.

4 This is taken from CEWARN, but is generic to a number of systems.

c) Communicate all such information and analysis to decision-makers of InterGovernmental Authority on Development (IGAD) policy organs and the national governments of member states.

The Annex to the CEWARN Protocol that sets out the 'Operating Guidelines for CEWARN', reads, in part, as follows:

Part I: mandate

1. CEWARN is mandated to:

a) receive and share information concerning potentially violent conflicts as well as their outbreak and escalation in the IGAD region;
b) undertake and share analyses of that information;
c) develop case scenarios and formulate options for response;
d) share and communicate information, analyses and response options;
e) carry out studies on specific types and areas of conflict in the IGAD region.

Currently CEWARN is primarily aimed at providing early warning to national response mechanisms located within an appropriate government ministry, such as the Department of Foreign Affairs (in the case of Ethiopia) and the Office of the President, Provincial Administration and Internal Security (in the case of Kenya). It does so in respect of the following matters in the Annex to the CEWARN protocol:

Part II: information

1. CEWARN shall rely for its operations on information that is collected from the public domain, particularly in the following areas:

a) livestock rustling;
b) conflicts over grazing and water points;
c) smuggling and illegal trade;
d) nomadic movements;
e) refugees;
f) landmines;
g) banditry.

At the moment, CEWARN focuses on the increasingly violent pastoral conflict along border areas that is fuelled by the availability and presence of small arms. This followed a detailed analysis of the enduring nature of the various cross-border problems and the debilitating impact that armed cattle theft has in the region. The signature of the CEWARN protocol was followed by a series of expert workshops and consultancies that eventually provided the substantive theoretical basis for the subsequent system.[5]

CEWARN is in many ways unique. On the one hand it exists as part of the IGAD. On the other it draws heavily on civil society participation. This hybrid is arguably possible since national agencies and civil society organisations from one country naturally coalesce and mobilise in support of common national interests. This has allowed for the uncontested integration of the national components of CEWARN, the CEWERU's,[6] into state structures in countries such as Ethiopia and Kenya where they are seen to complement existing state security and delivery structures.

In simple terms, CEWARN-appointed field monitors provide incident and weekly reports through a dedicated National Research Institute[7] to the CEWERU within the country concerned. The CEWERU reports to the CEWARN unit in Addis Ababa where the data is codified and where quality control is performed. Based on a sophisticated analysis and reporting tool, CEWARN puts out monthly and alert reports.[8]

---

5  The 'Khartoum Declaration' in Khartoum, 2000, preceded the signature of the CEWARN Protocol in January 2002. The first Meeting of the CPS was in Entebbe, Uganda, May 2002. A workshop on the Identification of Indicators in November 2002 was followed by various workshops to engender the CEWARN Mechanism (2003). The company VRA undertook the development of the CEWARN Reporter. A second meeting of the CPS was held in Khartoum, March 2003, followed by missions to the Karamoja and Somali Clusters. The selection of NRIs and Training of CCs and FMs followed and the Official opening of the CEWARN Office occurred on 30 June 2003. The CEWARN Protocol entered into force in August 2003 and the TCEW was operationalised in June 2004.
6  National conflict early warning and response mechanisms.
7  InterAfrica in Ethiopia, Africa Peace Forum in Ethiopia, Centre for Basic Research in Uganda. Probably, the Peace Research Institute at the University of Khartoum for Sudan.
8  During the conference participants were briefed about the two alert reports that have been issued thus far, namely one on 27 July 2005 about the conflict between Dassenech and Rukana fisherman about fishing activity on Lake Turkana that involved Kenyan security forces and that could have invited reciprocal intervention from the Ethiopian security forces. A second alert was issued on 9 September 2005 about conflict between two Ethiopian pastoral communities, the Nyangatom and Dassenech, during which ten persons were killed and 220 cattle were stolen.

*Figure 2: Current CEWARN areas of engagement*

Currently CEWARN is active in two clusters (as pilot projects), namely the Karamoja (Uganda, Kenya, Sudan, Ethiopia border) and Somali (Ethiopia, Kenya, Somali) clusters. Apparently a welcome expansion into the Sudan/Uganda border area is being considered.

The Institute for Security Studies (ISS) concluded a 2005 paper on the CEWS[9] by remarking that:

The ECOWAS system is at an early stage of development but represents the most comprehensive and logically integrated system for conflict prevention and management on the continent [...] The conceptual maturity of the regional system also reflects a commitment by West African leaders to engage with the extensive regional conflict systems in the region. They have institutionalised (on paper if not always in practice) the linkage between good governance and conflict prevention through the adoption of a supplementary protocol on democracy and good governance.

Whereas West Africa has the most politically developed and mature system, IGAD/CEWARN is potentially the most sophisticated available amongst the RECs, if still limited in geographical scope.

Beyond the technical and conceptual challenges associated with early warning and response, the single biggest challenge faced by all early warning and response systems is linking good analysis with timely action. The linkage to timely action means clarity, proximity and engagement with those institutions responsible for action. In the case of the AU the key users for the CEWS are: the Peace and Security Council, the office of the Chairperson of the Commission and that of the Commissioner for Peace and Security, other departments within the AU and various components of the PSC system such as the Panel of the Wise. In the case of CEWARN there is a complicated and some-what distant relationship between the system and its response mechanism (national governments, the IGAD secretariat and its political masters) that still has to prove itself in practice. Hence the conclusion in an earlier ISS report:

Technically, the CEWARN system is complex and authoritative but has not yet closed the gap between analysis, options and actions. It is difficult to see how this will be possible in the longer term without the co-location of CEWARN (in Addis Ababa) and IGAD (in Djibouti) and the development of an integrated conflict prevention, management and response system similar to that working in West Africa and under development in Southern Africa. Without the mechanisms to harness and focus political will to action by IGAD Member States, the danger is that CEWARN may not be able to operationalise its conflict prevention ambitions at the regional level.'[10]

Admittedly this conclusion does not give credit to the second and potentially fruitful focus of CEWARN, namely to initiate and support local conflict prevention working with and through local structures.

Early warning systems are necessarily tailored to their particular function and client(s). Each end-user (such as the Peace

---

9  Jakkie Cilliers, 'Towards a Continental Early Warning System for Africa', Institute for Security Studies Paper, No. 102, April 2005.
10  Other conclusions related to costs, the utility of the CEWARN methodology at the regional as apposed to the local level and the requirements for relatively transparency open sources and civil society involvement. Jakkie Cilliers, op. cit., p 14

and Security Council of the AU) necessarily needs a system to meet its particular needs, resources, organisational culture and response mechanisms. CEWARN in the Horn is a particularly distinct and carefully designed system to meet particular and specific requirements. But equally the early warning system for the ECOWAS Mediation and Security Council differs from that being developed for SADC and its Organ on Politics, Defence and Security Cooperation.

This view leads to two obvious conclusions. On the one hand a degree of practical scepticism appears to be warranted on the idea that Africa would be able to develop an integrated CEWS system. It is more likely that the AU and each regional economic community (REC) would develop an own system tailored to the specific requirements and usage of each organisation within a loose cooperative relationship between systems. More relevant to this paper, it probably rules out the option of expanding the CEWARN (dedicated to pastoral conflict across common borders) system for use in the Sudan (i.e. at national level) without considerable adaptation.

### An early warning system for Sudan

The fact that CEWARN may not be appropriate for use in support of the transition process in Sudan should not detract from the requirement for a system of conflict early warning to:

- provide independent information on the state of (in)security/the implementation of the peace process in an objective and non-partisan manner to the government of National Unity in Khartoum, the government of South Sudan in Juba, participating State governments, the UN system, donors/partners and critically, ordinary Sudanese;
- initiate local conflict prevention action (for example, through links with tribal leaders) or inform prevention action at the state or national level.

Given the limited information flows in Sudan, any system would have to rely on field monitors in each participating state for the provision of event data. Each participatory state could probably be 'covered' by an average of five field monitors – costing less than US $1,000 per month per state. These monitors would have to be trained and have access to appropriate communication means with one of the two coordination unit, one in Khartoum (for the GNU) and the other in Juba (for the GSS)[11] and it would have to build-in appropriate accountability and consultative mechanisms through which all key stakeholders are brought to the table. Each of the two coordination units would require an office, computers, a minimum of three staff

with guaranteed power supply and internet access. Additional provision would have to be made for dissemination, liaison functions, a briefing room replete with maps and graphs, as well as additional experts to feed and add in the analysis that is generated by various other components within the UN and other systems. In contrast to the cautious approach adopted by CEWARN, a public dissemination strategy in the interests of its primary beneficiaries – ordinary Sudanese – is a key success factor for such a system. Once quality assurance and information dissemination/ outreach systems have been put in place the only outstanding item would be the development of geographical information presentation tools.

The practical phases in the establishment of this system are relatively straightforward and consist of: the choice and customisation of an established system, baseline research, implementation (deployment and training) and maintenance.

#### Choice

Time and cost considerations would favour the choice of an established and mature system such as the Integrated Data for Event Analysis (IDEA) that has, amongst others, been adopted by FAST International and customised for pastoral conflict by CEWARN. Fully fledged IDEA systems have a wide focus and include more

---

11   Both coordination units would feed into a single database so that all the components of system for Sudan would be available at both units.

than 200 different event types that would require limited additional input for application in the Sudan. System costs are difficult to estimate but could range from, say, US $30,000 (including customisation) to several hundred thousand dollars if developed commercially.

Base-line study

All conflict response systems start off with a base-line assessment on the level of insecurity and threats to human security – and such an assessment is absolutely critical in Sudan to build sustainable peace. Sudan does not have sufficient or appropriate data upon which to plan much of the post-conflict reconstruction and development projects that are unfolding at the moment and that will do so in the years that lie ahead. Perhaps the most pressing of these examples relate to the information requirements upon which to plan the various security sector reform projects that are needed. Various mechanisms exist that could assist in this regard, including crime victimisation studies and the like. A number of applied research survey techniques and related efforts could help fill the information gap that will inevitably constrain and limit response strategies.[12]

Implementation

The most important aspect of implementation would be the choice of the hosting institution, oversight and political/domestic ownership considerations. The associated processes would imply a series of participatory workshops with political and civil society actors, various training activities and the identification of the parameters of the system (e.g. the decision on which states would be covered), definition of the types of events, etc..

Maintenance

Refresher training, ongoing quality assurance, IT and other ongoing support, including support from the software system supplier. Given the intensity that will be required from a Sudan human security early warning system output would be high – probably requiring weekly rather than monthly reports.

It would be crucial for a Sudan conflict early warning system to be able to feed off the extensive applied research that is being done for the multitude of agencies engaged with the transition process. To this end the establishment of the system discussed in these pages should be complemented by a

research and analysis capacity that can access and digest these results.

Conclusion

In an ideal world there would be little impediment for the various negotiating parties in Sudan to agree on the establishment of a neutral and separate system that tracks conflict or security concerns in the country.[13] In the real world, control of information flows is deeply political and security is not a neutral, value-free concept. The political independence and integrity of a conflict early warning system for the Sudan and the choices regarding the organisations/institutions with which it is formally affiliated and of its key staff are critical matters if such a system is to survive and traverse the turbulent domestic politics of Sudan – in many ways more important than the challenges presented by the diverse ethnic, religious and linguistic diversity, and limited infrastructure, that will inevitably complicate implementation.

While this article did not discuss the re-engagement of Sudan within the current operations of CEWARN, this is an obvious requirement if the region is to move towards a regional conflict response mechanism. Having Sudan commit fully and unequivocally to the

---

12 Admittedly, some efforts are already underway to map Sudan's insecurity. For example, a Human Security Baseline Assessment in Sudan is [at the time of writing] one week into its first household surveys of small arms demand and effects. The largest (500-1000) of the undertaking concerns Rumbek and its immediate environs. A second, smaller initiative concerns the Juba area (250-500 households). The deteriorating security situation in and around Yei made an effort to conduct a survey there too chancy to proceed but discussions on conducting surveys in Wau, Malakal and Kapoeta have occurred. The project plans to conduct similar surveys in the East and in the West over the next 12 months. Elsewhere a system to track and monitor returnees to Southern Sudan already works towards a Joint Operations Centre.

13 For legal and practical considerations it would not be possible to simply extend CEWARN to cover Sudan. CEWARN is established within the framework of IGAD and at the behest of member states and such a decision would require changes to the legal protocol that governs CEWARN as well as the legal agreement of the negotiating parties to the Government of National Unity of Sudan. Second, the CEWARN system would have to be reconfigured to allow for a wider system of event data than its current format optimised for pastoral conflict.

commitments reflected in the CEWARN protocol would be good for Sudan, the region and for IGAD. The Horn of Africa faces many challenges of which armed-resource competition across borders is a key ingredient. With peace in Sudan the opportunities and demands that will be placed on CEWARN to extend its operations along the complex and divisive boundaries in the South (in particular) present numerous challenges, as would Darfur and the situation in the East. Once CEWARN has expanded to cover these additional border areas the major challenge for IGAD remains the development of a comprehensive response system at the national and regional level similar to that under development in other regions such as ECOWAS.

Nothing written in this article can detract from the ultimate responsibility for domestic security that must lie with the government of Sudan and its various agencies. Any measures in support of the transition in Sudan should therefore have, as its ultimate purpose, the building of state systems and act in support of legitimate post-transition national institutions. A conflict early warning system for Sudan can, therefore, only be of a transitory nature. The challenge for Sudan is the absence of legitimate national systems in the interim and the vagrancies of the transitional period that lie ahead that will severely degrade the capacity of national security agencies and institutions. The development of a dedicated system to track conflict trends related to (in)security in support of the Sudan peace process should therefore be seen for what it is — a temporary arrangement that should, in time, become part of the state system or fade away.

Yet at the current stage of the peace process a conflict early warning system could go a long way to removing the provision of key conflict information from contested political control. Ideally, such a system should be developed with the full cooperation and support of the parties to the CPA, the parties to the talks on Darfur and elsewhere. This 'best' solution may, however, not be practically achievable within reasonable time. While is theoretically possible for the UN to establish an independent mechanism to monitor and track violence in Sudan, or for donors to fund various Sudanese partners to perform such a function, the option to appoint an independent neutral agent to implement (but not staff) an early warning system or to create an entirely new unit for this purpose in the Sudan may be less desirable but inevitable.

[    Alvaro Ybarra Zavala    ]

# The children of sorrow

'The children of sorrow' is designed so that the people directly affected by crises in societies and ignored by the international community can have a voice and be heard. It is an appeal that makes us stop and think, recalling real-life situations that once made headlines around the world but have now sunk into oblivion, to widespread indifference. This oblivion means that a second generation is now the victim of problems we have forgotten but which unfortunately, are still there and still killing people. The war in Chechnya, conflict in Colombia, ethnic cleansing in Darfur and violence in Uganda are just a few examples of armed conflict that seemed to have been submerged by the all-embracing wave of the 'war against terrorism'.

Endemic issues such as the exploitation of children and the HIV/AIDS epidemic no longer make headlines, and yet there are more and more victims of these scourges, as can be seen with the annual statistics published by international organisations. Other issues such as cancer in third world countries, the effect of an end to the agreement on generics drugs, and the lack of concern for the plight of native communities in Latin America are all real situations that attract no interest as they only affect third world countries.

'Children of sorrow' endeavours to show that in all these very real but forgotten situations, a new generation of victims is now growing up – to the general indifference of the broader community. The following photos taken in Darfur are a reminder of the plight faced daily by children in so many parts of the world.

Alvaro Ybarra Zavala

> *All the refugee camps set up in Chad are full of war orphans.*
© Alvaro Ybarra Zavala / Agence VU / Chad

< *A boy running away from the genocide in Darfur. He survived a storm in the middle of the desert.*
© Alvaro Ybarra Zavala / Agence VU / Sudan

<
*A group of Internally Displaced People*
*are fleeing the genocide in Darfur.*
© Alvaro Ybarra Zavala / Agence VU /
Near Kutum, Sudan

>
*A refugee convoy will take all*
*these people to the Bahai refugee camp.*
© Alvaro Ybarra Zavala / Agence VU / Chad

<

*Child soldier members of the SLA,*
*one of the rebel groups against*
*the government in Khartoum.*
© Alvaro Ybarra Zavala / Agence VU /
Near Kutum, Sudan

>

*Members of the SLA,*
*one of the rebel groups against*
*the government in Khartoum.*
© Alvaro Ybarra Zavala / Agence VU /
Near Kutum, Sudan

> *Member of the SLA.*
© Alvaro Ybarra Zavala / Agence VU /
Near Kutum, Sudan

< 
*Members of the SLA,*
*one of the rebel groups against*
*the government in Khartoum.*
© Alvaro Ybarra Zavala / Agence VU /
Near Kutum Sudan

*Child soldier members of the SLA, one of the rebel groups against the government in Khartoum.*

# [ Part 5: Annex ]

# Regulation (EC) no 1717/2006 of the European Parliament and the Council of 15 November 2006 establishing an instrument for Stability

THE EUROPEAN PARLIAMENT AND THE COUNCIL
OF THE EUROPEAN UNION,

Having regard to the Treaty establishing the European Community, and in particular Articles 179(1) and 181a thereof,

Having regard to the proposal from the Commission,

Acting in accordance with the procedure referred to in Article 251 of the Treaty[1],

Whereas:

1. The Community is a major provider of economic, financial, technical, humanitarian and macroeconomic assistance to third countries. The promotion of stable conditions for human and economic development and the promotion of human rights, democracy and fundamental freedoms remains one of the prime objectives of European Union (hereinafter referred to as "the EU") external action to which Community instruments for external assistance contribute. The Council and the Representatives of the Governments of the Member States meeting within the Council, in their November 2004 Conclusions on the effectiveness of EU External Action, concluded that "peace, security and stability as well as human rights, democracy and good governance, are essential elements for sustainable economic growth and poverty eradication".

2. The EU Programme for the Prevention of Violent Conflicts, endorsed by the European Council, underlines the EU's "political commitment to pursue conflict prevention as one of the main objectives of the EU's external relations" and states that Community development cooperation instruments can contribute to this goal and to the development of the EU as a global player.

3. Measures taken under this Regulation in pursuit of the objectives of Articles 177 and 181a of the Treaty establishing the European Community (hereinafter referred to as "the EC Treaty") may be complementary to and should be consistent with measures adopted by the EU in pursuit of Common Foreign and Security Policy objectives within the framework of Title V and measures adopted within the framework of Title VI of the Treaty on European Union (hereinafter referred to as "the EU Treaty"). The Council and the Commission should cooperate to ensure such consistency, each in accordance with their respective powers.

4. The European Consensus on Development, adopted by the Council and the Representatives of the Governments of the Member States meeting within the Council, the European Parliament and the Commission on 22 November 2005 and welcomed by the European Council on 15 and 16 December 2005, states that the Community, within the respective competences of its institutions, will develop a comprehensive prevention approach to State fragility, conflict, natural disasters and other types of crises, to which goal this Regulation should contribute.

5. The European Council approved the European Security Strategy on 12 December 2003.

---

1 Opinion of the European Parliament delivered on 6 July 2006 (not yet published in the Official Journal) and Council Decision of 7 November 2006.

6. The European Council Declaration on Combating Terrorism of 25 March 2004 called for counter-terrorist objectives to be integrated into external assistance programmes. Moreover, the EU Millennium Strategy on the prevention and control of organised crime, adopted by the Council on 27 March 2000, calls for closer cooperation with third countries.

7. Post-crisis stabilisation requires a sustained and flexible engagement from the international community, in particular in the first years after a crisis, on the basis of integrated transition strategies.

8. Implementation of programmes of assistance in times of crisis and political instability requires specific measures to ensure flexibility in decision-making and budget allocation, as well as enhanced measures to ensure coherence with bilateral aid and mechanisms for the pooling of donor funds, including the delegation of public authority tasks through indirect centralised management.

9. The Resolutions of the European Parliament and the Conclusions of the Council following the Commission Communications on the Linking of Relief, Rehabilitation and Development emphasise the need to ensure effective bridging between operations financed from different Community financing instruments in the context of crisis.

10. In order to address the above issues in an effective and timely manner specific financial resources and financing instruments are required that can work in a manner complementary to humanitarian aid and long-term cooperation instruments. Humanitarian aid should continue to be delivered under Council Regulation (EC) No 1257/96 of 20 June 1996 concerning humanitarian aid[2].

11. In addition to the measures agreed with partner countries in the context of the policy framework for cooperation established under the related Community instruments for external assistance, the Community must be able to provide assistance which addresses major global and transnational issues having a potentially destabilising effect.

12. The 2001 "Guidelines for strengthening operational coordination between the Community, represented by the Commission, and the Member States in the field of external assistance" emphasise the need for enhanced coordination of EU external assistance.

13. This Regulation establishes for the period 2007 to 2013 a financial envelope which constitutes the prime reference amount for the budgetary authority according to point 37 of the Interinstitutional Agreement of 17 May 2006 between the European Parliament, the Council and the Commission on budgetary discipline and sound financial management[3].

14. The measures necessary for the implementation of this Regulation should be adopted in accordance with Council Decision 1999/468/ EC of 28 June 1999 laying down the procedures for the exercise of implementing powers conferred on the Commission[4].

15. This Regulation aims at covering the scope of and replacing a number of existing Regulations concerning Community external assistance; those Regulations should therefore be repealed.

16. Since the objectives of this Regulation cannot be sufficiently achieved by the Member States, because of the need for concerted multilateral response in the areas defined in this Regulation, and can therefore be better achieved at Community level, taking ac-

2 OJ L 163, 2.7.1996, p. 1. Regulation as amended by Regulation (EC) No 1882/2003 of the European Parliament and of the Council (OJ L 284, 31.10.2003, p. 1).
3 OJ C 139, 14.6.2006, p. 1.
4 OJ L 184, 17.7.1999, p. 23. Decision as amended by Decision 2006/512/EC (OJ L 200, 22.7.2006, p. 11).

count of the scale and global effects of the measures provided for herein, the Community may adopt measures, in accordance with the principle of subsidiarity as set out in Article 5 of the EC Treaty. In accordance with the principle of proportionality, as set out in that Article, this Regulation does not go beyond what is necessary in order to achieve these objectives,

HAVE ADOPTED THIS REGULATION:

## Title I
## OBJECTIVES AND SCOPE

### Article 1
Objectives

1. The Community shall undertake development cooperation measures, as well as financial, economic and technical cooperation measures with third countries under the conditions set out in this Regulation.

2. In accordance with the objectives of such cooperation and within the limits as laid down in the EC Treaty, the specific aims of this Regulation shall be:

   (a) In a situation of crisis or emerging crisis, to contribute to stability by providing an effective response to help preserve, establish or re-establish the conditions essential to the proper implementation of the Community's development and cooperation policies;

   (b) in the context of stable conditions for the implementation of Community cooperation policies in third countries, to help build capacity both to address specific global and transregional threats having a destabilising effect and to ensure preparedness to address pre- and post-crisis situations.

3. Measures taken under this Regulation may be complementary to, and shall be consistent with, and without prejudice to, measures adopted under Title V and Title VI of the EU Treaty.

### Article 2
Complementarity of Community assistance

1. Community assistance under this Regulation shall be complementary to that provided for under related Community instruments for external assistance. It shall be provided only to the extent that an adequate and effective response cannot be provided under those instruments.

2. The Commission shall ensure that measures adopted under this Regulation are consistent with the Community's overall strategic policy framework for the partner country, and in particular with the objectives of the instruments referred to in paragraph 1, as well as with other relevant Community measures.

3. In order to enhance the effectiveness and consistency of Community and national assistance measures, the Commission shall promote close coordination between its own activities and those of the Member States, both at decision-making level and on the ground. To that end, the Member States and the Commission shall operate a system for exchange of information.

### Article 3
Assistance in response to situations of crisis or emerging crisis

1. Community technical and financial assistance in pursuit of the specific aims set out in point (a) of Article 1(2) may be undertaken in response to a situation of urgency, crisis or emerging crisis, a situation posing a threat to democracy, law and order, the protection of human rights and fundamental freedoms, or the security and safety of individuals, or a situation threatening to escalate into armed conflict or severely to destabilise the third country or countries concerned. Such measures may also address situations where the Community has invoked the essential elements clauses of international Agreements in order to suspend, partially or totally, cooperation with third countries.

2. Technical and financial assistance referred to in paragraph 1 shall cover the following areas:

(a) support, through the provision of technical and logistical assistance, for the efforts undertaken by international and regional organisations, state and non-state actors in promoting confidence-building, mediation, dialogue and reconciliation;

(b) support for the establishment and the functioning of interim administrations mandated in accordance with international law;

(c) support for the development of democratic, pluralistic state institutions, including measures to enhance the role of women in such institutions, effective civilian administration and related legal frameworks at national and local level, an independent judiciary, good governance and law and order, including non-military technical cooperation to strengthen overall civilian control, and oversight over the security system and measures to strengthen the capacity of law enforcement and judicial authorities involved in the fight against the illicit trafficking of people, drugs, firearms and explosive materials;

(d) support for international criminal tribunals and ad hoc national tribunals, truth and reconciliation commissions, and mechanisms for the legal settlement of human rights claims and the assertion and adjudication of property rights, established in accordance with international human rights and rule of law standards;

(e) support for measures necessary to start the rehabilitation and reconstruction of key infrastructure, housing, public buildings and economic assets, as well as essential productive capacity, and for the re-starting of economic activity and the generation of employment and the establishment of the minimum conditions necessary for sustainable social development;

(f) support for civilian measures related to the demobilisation and reintegration of former combatants into civil society, and where appropriate their repatriation, as well as measures to address the situation of child soldiers and female combatants;

(g) support for measures to mitigate the social effects of restructuring of the armed forces;

(h) support for measures to address, within the framework of Community cooperation policies and their objectives, the socio-economic impact on the civilian population of anti-personnel landmines, unexploded ordnance or explosive remnants of war; activities financed under this Regulation shall cover risk education, victim assistance, mine detection and clearance and, in conjunction therewith, stockpile destruction;

(i) support for measures to address, within the framework of Community cooperation policies and their objectives, the impact on the civilian population of the illicit use of and access to firearms; such support shall be limited to survey activities, victim assistance, raising public awareness and the development of legal and administrative expertise and good practice.

Assistance shall be provided only to the extent necessary to re-establish the conditions for social and economic development of the populations concerned, in a situation of crisis or emerging crisis as referred to in paragraph 1. It shall not include support for measures to combat the proliferation of arms;

(j) support for measures to ensure that the specific needs of women and children in crisis and conflict situations, including their exposure to gender-based violence, are adequately met;

(k) support for the rehabilitation and reintegration of the victims of armed conflict, including measures to address the specific needs of women and children;

(l) support for measures to promote and defend respect for human rights and fundamental freedoms, democracy and the rule of law, and the related international instruments;

(m) support for socio-economic measures to promote equitable access to and transparent management of natural resources in a situation of crisis or emerging crisis;

(n) support for socio-economic measures to address the impact of sudden population movements, including measures addressing the needs of host communities in a situation of crisis or emerging crisis;

(o) support for measures to support the development and organisation of civil society and its participation in the political process, including measures to enhance the role of women in such processes and measures to promote independent, pluralist and professional media;

(p) support for measures in response to natural or man-made disasters and threats to public health in the absence of, or to complement, Community humanitarian assistance.

3. In the exceptional and unforeseen situations referred to in paragraph 1, the Community may also provide technical and financial assistance not expressly covered by the specific areas of assistance set out in paragraph 2. Such assistance shall be limited to Exceptional Assistance Measures as referred to in Article 6(2), which:

— fall within the general scope and specific aims set out in Article 1(a), and

— are limited in duration to the period laid down in Article 6(2), and

— would normally be eligible under the other Community instruments for external assistance, but which, in accordance with Article 2, should be addressed through this Regulation because of the need to respond rapidly to a situation of crisis or emerging crisis.

## Article 4
### Assistance in the context of stable conditions for cooperation
The community shall provide technical and financial assistance in pursuit of the specific aims set out in Article 2(b) in the following areas:

1. Threats to law and order, to the security and safety of individuals, to critical infrastructure and to public health;

Assistance shall cover:

(a) strengthening the capacity of law enforcement and judicial and civil authorities involved in the fight against terrorism and organised crime, including illicit trafficking of people, drugs, firearms and explosive materials and in the effective control of illegal trade and transit.

Priority shall be given to trans-regional cooperation involving third countries which have demonstrated a clear political will to address these problems. Measures in this area shall place particular emphasis on good governance and shall be in accordance with international law, in particular human rights law and international humanitarian law.

With regard to assistance to authorities involved in the fight against terrorism, priority shall be given to supporting measures concerning the development and strengthening of counter-terrorism legislation, the implementation and practice of financial law, of customs law and of immigration law and the development of international procedures for law enforcement.

With regard to assistance relating to the problem of drugs, due attention shall be given to international cooperation aimed at promoting best practices relating to the reduction of demand, production and harm;

(b) support for measures to address threats to international transport, energy operations and critical infrastructure, including passenger and freight traffic and energy distribution.

Measures adopted in this area shall place particular emphasis on trans-regional cooperation and the implementation of international standards in the fields of risk awareness, vulnerability analysis, emergency preparedness, alert and consequence management;

(c) contributing to ensuring an adequate response to sudden major threats to public health, such as epidemics with a potential trans-national impact.

Particular emphasis shall be placed on emergency-planning, management of vaccine and pharmaceutical stockpiles, international cooperation, early warning and alert systems;

2. Risk mitigation and preparedness relating to chemical, biological, radiological and nuclear materials or agents;

Assistance shall cover:

(a) the promotion of civilian research activities as an alternative to defence-related research, and support for the retraining and alternative employment of scientists and engineers formerly employed in weapons-related areas;

(b) support for measures to enhance safety practices related to civilian facilities where sensitive chemical, biological, radiological and nuclear materials or agents are stored, or are handled in the context of civilian research programmes;

(c) support, within the framework of Community cooperation policies and their objectives, for the establishment of civil infrastructure and relevant civilian studies necessary for the dismantlement, remediation or conversion of weapons-related facilities and sites where these are declared as no longer belonging to a defence programme;

(d) strengthening the capacity of the competent civilian authorities involved in the development and enforcement of effective control of illicit trafficking in chemical, biological, radiological and nuclear materials or agents (including the equipment for their production or delivery), including through the installation of modern logistical evaluation and control equipment;

(e) the development of the legal framework and institutional capacities for the establishment and enforcement of effective export controls on dual-use goods, including regional cooperation measures;

(f) the development of effective civilian disaster-preparedness, emergency-planning, crisis response, and capabilities for clean-up measures in relation to possible major environmental incidents in this field;

as regards the measures covered by points (b) and (d), particular emphasis shall be placed on assistance to those regions or countries where stockpiles of materials or agents referred to in points (b) and (d) still exist and where there is a risk of proliferation of such materials or agents.

3. Pre- and post-crisis capacity building

Support for long-term measures aimed at building and strengthening the capacity of international, regional and sib-regional organizations, state and non-state actors in relation to their efforts in:

(a) promoting early warning, confidence-building, mediation and reconciliation, and addressing emerging inter-community tensions;

(b) improving post-conflict and post-disaster recovery.

Measures under this point shall include know-how transfer, the exchange of information, risk/threat assessment, research and analysis, early warning systems and training. Measures may also include, where appropriate, financial and technical assistance for the implementation of those Recommendations made by the UN Peacebuilding Commission falling within the objectives of Community cooperation policy.

## Title II
# IMPLEMENTATION

### Article 5
#### General framework for implementation
Community assistance under this Regulation shall be implemented through the following measures:

(a) Exceptional Assistance Measures and Interim Response Programmes;

(b) Multi-country Strategy papers, Thematic Strategy Papers and Multi-annual Indicative Programmes;

(c) Annual Action Programmes;

(d) Special Measures.

### Article 6
#### Exceptional Assistance Measures
#### and Interim Response Programmes

1. Community assistance under Article 3 shall be carried out through Exceptional Assistance Measures and through Interim Response Programmes.

2. The Commission may adopt Exceptional Assistance Measures in a situation of crisis as referred to in Article 3(1), as well as in exceptional and unforeseen situations as referred to in Article 3(3), where the effectiveness of the measures is dependent on rapid or flexible implementation. Such measures may have a duration of up to 18 months. Individual measures may be extended in duration by a further six months in the case of objective and unforeseen obstacles to their implementation, provided that the financial amount of the measure does not increase.

3. Where an Exceptional Assistance Measure is costing more than EUR 20,000,000, that measure shall be adopted in accordance with the procedure referred to in Article 22(2).

4. The Commission may adopt Interim Response Programmes with a view to establishing or re-establishing the essential conditions necessary for the effective implementation of the Community's external cooperation policies. Interim Response Programmes shall build on Exceptional Assistance Measures. They shall be adopted in accordance with the procedure referred to in Article 22(2).

5. The Commission shall keep the Council regularly informed about its planning of Community assistance under Article 3. Before adopting or renewing any Exceptional Assistance Measures costing up to EUR 20,000,000, the Commission shall inform the Council of their nature, objectives and the financial amounts envisaged. It shall take account of the relevant policy approach of the Council both in its planning and subsequent implementation of such measures, in the interests of the coherence of EU external action. The Commission shall likewise inform the Council before

making significant substantive changes to Exceptional Assistance Measures already adopted.

6. At as early a stage as possible, following the adoption of Exceptional Assistance Measures, and in any case within seven months of doing so, the Commission shall report to the European Parliament and the Council by giving an overview of the existing and planned Community response, including the contribution to be made from other Community financing instruments, the status of existing Country and Multi-Country Strategy Papers, and the Community's role within the broader international and multilateral response. This report shall also indicate whether and, if so, for how long the Commission intends to continue the Exceptional Assistance Measures.

## Article 7
### Multi-country Strategy Papers, Thematic Strategy Papers and Multi-annual Indicative Programmes

1. Multi-country and Thematic Strategy Papers shall constitute the general basis for the implementation of assistance under Article 4.

2. Multi-country and Thematic Strategy Papers shall set out the Community's strategy for the countries or themes concerned, having regard to the needs of the countries concerned, the Community's priorities, the international situation and the activities of the main partners.

3. Multi-country and Thematic Strategy Papers, and any revisions or extensions thereof, shall be adopted in accordance with the procedure referred to in Article 22(2). They shall cover an initial period of no longer than the period of application of this Regulation and shall be reviewed at the mid-point.

4. Strategy Papers shall be consistent with, and avoid duplication of, Country, Multi-country or Thematic Strategy Papers adopted under other Community instruments for external assistance.

Strategy Papers shall, where appropriate, be based on a dialogue with the partner country, countries or region concerned, including with civil society, so as to support national development strategies and to ensure the participation and involvement of the partner country, countries or region. In addition, joint consultations shall be carried out between the Commission, Member States, and other donors where appropriate, in order to ensure that the cooperation activities of the Community are complementary to those of the Member States and other donors. Other stakeholders may be associated where appropriate.

5. Each Multi-country Strategy Paper shall, where appropriate, be accompanied by a Multi-annual Indicative Programme summarising the priority areas selected for Community financing, the specific objectives, the expected results and timeframe of Community support and the indicative financial allocation, overall and for each priority area. The financial allocations may be given in the form of a range where necessary.

6. The Multi-annual Indicative Programmes shall determine the financial allocations for each programme using transparent criteria, based on the needs and performance of the partner countries or regions concerned and taking into account the particular difficulties faced by countries or regions in crisis or conflict.

7. Multi-annual Indicative Programmes, and any revisions or extensions thereof, shall be adopted in accordance with the procedure referred to in Article 22(2). They shall be established, where appropriate, in consultation with the partner countries or regions concerned.

8. The financial amounts of Multi-annual Indicative Programmes may be increased or decreased as a result of reviews, taking into account changes in a country's situation, performance and needs, in accordance with the procedure referred to in paragraph 7.

## Article 8
### Annual Action Programmes

1. Annual Action Programmes shall set out measures to be adopted on the basis of the Multi-country and Thematic Strategy Papers and Multi-annual Indicative Programmes referred to in Article 7.

2. Annual Action Programmes shall specify the objectives pursued, the fields of intervention, the expected results, the management procedures and total amount of financing planned. They shall contain a summary description of the operations to be financed, an indication of the amounts allocated for each operation and an indicative implementation timetable. Where relevant, they should include the results of any lessons learned from previous assistance. Objectives shall be measurable.

3. Annual Action Programmes and any revision or extension thereof shall be adopted in accordance with the procedure referred to in Article 22(2).

## Article 9
### Special Measures

1. Notwithstanding Articles 7 and 8, in the event of unforeseen needs or circumstances, the Commission may adopt Special Measures not provided for in the Multi-country and Thematic Strategy Papers and Multi-annual Indicative Programmes referred to in Article 7 or the Annual Action Programmes referred to in Article 8.

2. Special Measures shall specify the objectives pursued, the areas of activity, the expected results, the management procedures used and the total amount of financing planned. They shall contain a description of the operations to be financed, an indication of the amounts allocated for each operation and an indicative implementation timetable.

3. Special Measures costing more than EUR 5,000,000 shall be adopted in accordance with the procedure referred to in Article 22(2).

4. The Commission shall inform the Committee set up pursuant to Article 22(1) within one month of adopting Special Measures costing up to EUR 5,000,000.

## Title III
## BENEFICIARIES AND FORMS OF FINANCING

## Article 10
### Eligibility

1. The following shall be eligible for funding under this Regulation for the purposes of implementing the Exceptional Assistance Measures and Interim Response programmes referred to in Article 6, the Annual Action Programmes referred to in Article 8 and the Special Measures referred to in Article 9:

(a) partner countries and regions and their institutions;

(b) decentralised bodies in the partner countries, such as regions, departments, provinces and municipalities;

(c) joint bodies set up by the partner countries and regions and the Community;

(d) international organisations, including regional organisations, UN bodies, departments and missions, international financial institutions and development banks, and institutions of international jurisdiction, in so far as they contribute to the objectives of this Regulation;

(e) European agencies;

(f) the following entities and bodies of the Member States; partner countries and regions and any other third country in do far as they contribute to the objectives of this Regulation:

i    public and para-statal bodies, local authorities or administrations and consortia thereof;

ii   companies, firms and other private organisations and businesses;

iii  financial institutions that grant, promote and finance private investment in partner countries and regions;

iv   non-state actors referred to in paragraph 2;

v    natural persons.

2. Non-state actors eligible for financial support under this Regulation shall include: non-governmental organisations, organisations representing indigenous peoples, local citizens' groups and traders' associations, cooperatives, trade unions, organisations representing economic and social interests, local organisations (including networks) involved in decentralised regional cooperation and integration, consumer organisations, women's and youth organisations, teaching, cultural, research and scientific organisations, universities, churches and religious associations and communities, the media and any non-governmental associations and private and public foundations likely to contribute to development or the external dimension of internal policies.

3. Other bodies or actors not listed in paragraphs 1 and 2 may be financed when this is necessary to achieve the objectives of this Regulation.

## Article 11
Types of measures
1. Community financing may take the following forms:

(a) projects and programmes;

(b) sectoral or general budget support, where the partner country's arrangements for managing public funds are sufficiently transparent, reliable and effective, and where proper sectoral or macroeconomic policies have been put in place by the partner country and approved by its main donors, including international financial institutions where applicable. Budgetary support may in general be one of several instruments. It shall be allocated with precise objectives and related benchmarks. Disbursement of budgetary support shall be conditional on satisfactory progress towards achieving the objectives in terms of impact and results;

(c) in exceptional cases, sectoral and general import-support programmes, which may take the form of:

i    sectoral programmes for imports in kind,

ii   sectoral import programmes providing foreign currency to finance imports for the sector in question, or

iii  general import programmes providing foreign currency to finance general imports, covering a wide range of products;

(d) funds made available to financial intermediaries in accordance with Article 20, with a view to providing loans (to support investment and development of the private sector, for example), risk capital (in the form of subordinated or conditional loans) or other temporary minority holdings in business capital, to the extent that the financial risk of the Community is limited to these funds;

(e) grants to fund measures;

(f) grants to cover operating costs;

(g) funding for twinning programmes between public institutions, national public bodies or private-law entities with a public-service mission of a Member State and those of a partner country or region;

(h) contributions to international funds, in particular those managed by international or regional organisations;

(i) contributions to national funds set up by partner countries and regions to attract joint financing from a number of donors, or contributions to funds set up by one or more donors for the purpose of the joint implementation of operations;

(j) human and material resources required for effective administration and supervision of projects and programmes by partner countries and regions.

2. Community financing shall in principle not be used for paying taxes, duties or charges in beneficiary countries.

3. Activities covered by Regulation (EC) No 1257/96 and eligible for funding thereunder may not be funded under this Regulation.

## Article 12
Support measures

1. Community financing may cover expenditure associated with the preparation, follow-up, monitoring, auditing and evaluation activities directly necessary for the implementation of this Regulation and the achievement of its objectives. Community financing shall also cover expenditure on administrative support staff employed at Commission Delegations to manage projects funded under this Regulation.

2. Support may be financed outside the scope of Multi-annual Indicative Programmes. The Commission shall adopt such support measures in accordance with Article 9.

## Article 13
Cofinancing

1. Measures financed under this Regulation are eligible for cofinancing from the following, *inter alia*:

(a) Member States, and in particular their public and para-statal agencies;

(b) other donor countries and in particular their public and para-statal agencies;

(c) international and regional organisations, and in particular international and regional financial institutions;

(d) companies, firms, other private organisations and businesses, and other non-state actors referred to in Article 10(2);

(e) partner countries and regions in receipt of funding, and other bodies eligible for funding as referred to in Article 10.

2. In the case of parallel cofinancing, the project or programme is split into a number of clearly identifiable sub-projects, which are each financed by different partners providing cofinancing in such a way that the end-use of the financing can always be identified. In the case of joint cofinancing, the total cost of the project or programme is shared between the partners providing the cofinancing and resources are pooled in such a way that it is not possible to identify the source of funding for any given activity undertaken as part of the project or programme.

3. In the case of joint cofinancing, the Commission may receive and manage funds on behalf of the bodies referred to in points (a), (b) and (c) of paragraph 1 for the purpose of implementing joint measures. In this case, the Commission shall implement the joint measures centrally, either directly or indirectly, by delegating the task to Community agencies or bodies set up by the Community. Such funds shall be dealt with as assigned revenue in accordance with Article 18 of Council Regulation (EC, Euratom) No 1605/2002 of 25 June 2002 on the Financial Regulation applicable to the general budget of the European Communities[5].

5  OJ L 248, 16.9.2002, p. 1.

## Article 14

### Management procedures

1. The measures financed under this Regulation shall be managed, monitored, evaluated and reported on in accordance with Regulation (EC, Euratom) No 1605/2002.

2. The Commission may decide to entrust tasks of public authority, and in particular budget implementation tasks, to bodies referred to in Article 54(2)(c) of Regulation (EC, Euratom) No 1605/2002 if they are of recognised international standing, comply with internationally recognised systems of management and control, and are supervised by public authority.

3. In the case of decentralised management, the Commission may decide to use the procurement or grant procedures of the beneficiary country or region.

## Article 15

### Budget commitments

1. Budget commitments shall be made on the basis of decisions taken by the Commission in accordance with Articles 6, 8, 9 and 12.

2. The legal forms for Community financing shall include (*inter alia*):

   — financing agreements,

   — grant agreements,

   — procurement contracts,

   — employment contracts.

6 (1) OJ L 312, 23.12.1995, p. 1.

7 OJ L 292, 15.11.1996, p. 2.

8 OJ L 136, 31.5.1999, p. 1.

## Article 16

### Protection of the financial interests of the Community

1. Any agreements resulting from this Regulation shall contain provisions ensuring the protection of the Community's financial interests, in particular with respect to fraud, corruption and any other irregularities in accordance with Council Regulation (EC, Euratom) No 2988/95 of 18 December 1995 on the protection of the European Communities' financial interests[6], Council Regulation (Euratom, EC) No 2185/96 of 11 November 1996 concerning on-the-spot checks and inspections carried out by the Commission in order to protect the European Communities' financial interests against fraud and other irregularities[7] and Regulation (EC) No 1073/1999 of the European Parliament and of the Council of 25 May 1999 concerning investigations conducted by the European Anti-Fraud Office (OLAF)[8].

2. The agreements referred to in paragraph 1 shall expressly entitle the Commission and the Court of Auditors to have the power of audit, on the basis of documents and on the spot, over all contractors and subcontractors who have received Community funds. They shall also expressly authorise the Commission to carry out on-the-spot checks and inspections, as provided for in Regulation (Euratom, EC) No 2185/96.

3. All contracts resulting from the implementation of assistance shall ensure the rights of the Commission and the Court of Auditors, as provided for in paragraph 2, during and after the implementation of contracts.

## Article 17

### Participation and rules of origin

1. Participation in the award of procurement or grant contracts financed under this Regulation shall be open to all natural or legal persons from Member States.

2. Participation in the award of procurement or grant contracts financed under this Regulation shall be open to all natural and legal persons from:

   — any country that is a beneficiary of the Instrument for Pre-Accession Assistance[9],

   — any non-EU Member State of the European Economic Area, and

   — any other third country or territory in cases where reciprocal access to external assistance has been established.

3. In the case of measures taken in any third country considered a Least Developed Country according to the criteria laid down by the OECD, participation in the award of procurement or grant contracts shall be open on a global basis.

4. In the case of Exceptional Assistance Measures and Interim Response Programmes referred to in Article 6, participation in the award of procurement or grant contracts shall be open on a global basis.

5. In the case of measures adopted in pursuit of the objectives referred to in Article 4, participation in the award of procurement or grant contracts shall be open, and rules of origin shall extend, to any natural or legal person of a developing country or of a country in transition, as defined by the OECD, and to natural or legal persons of any other country eligible under the relevant strategy.

6. Participation in the award of procurement or grant contracts financed under this Regulation shall be open to international organisations.

7. Experts proposed in the context of procedures for the award of contracts need not comply with the nationality rules set out in this Article.

8. All supplies and materials purchased under contracts financed under this Regulation shall originate from the Community or a country eligible under paragraphs 2 to 5.

9. Participation by natural and legal persons from third countries or territories with traditional economic, trade or geographical links to the partner country may be authorised on a case-by-case basis. The Commission may, moreover, in duly substantiated cases authorise the participation of natural and legal persons from other countries, or the use of supplies and materials of different origin.

## Article 18
### Prefinancing
Interest generated by prefinancing payments to the beneficiaries shall be deducted from the final payment.

## Article 19
### Grants
In accordance with Article 114 of Regulation (EC, Euratom) No 1605/2002 natural persons may receive grants.

## Article 20
### Funds made available to the European Investment Bank or other financial intermediaries
The funds referred to in Article 11(1)(d) shall be managed by financial intermediaries, the European Investment Bank (hereinafter referred to as "the EIB") or any other bank or organisation capable of managing them. The Commission shall adopt implementing provisions for this Article, on a case-by-case basis to cover risk-sharing, the remuneration of the intermediary entrusted with the task of implementation, the use and recovery of interest on the fund and the closure of the operation.

---

9 Council Regulation (EC) No 1085/2006 of 17 July 2006 establishing an Instrument for Pre-Accession Assistance (IPA) (OJ L 210, 31.7.2006, p. 82).

## Article 21
### Evaluation

The Commission shall regularly evaluate the results and efficiency of policies and programmes and the effectiveness of programming in order to ascertain whether the objectives have been met and enable it to formulate recommendations with a view to improving future operations. The Commission shall send for discussion significant evaluation reports to the Committee set up pursuant to Article 22(1). These results shall feed back into programme design and resource allocation.

## Title IV
# FINAL PROVISIONS

## Article 22
### Committee procedure

1. The Commission shall be assisted by a Committee.

2. Where reference is made to this paragraph, Articles 4 and 7 of Decision 1999/468/EC shall apply.

   The period provided for in Article 4(3) of Decision 1999/468/EC shall be set at 30 days.

3. The Committee shall adopt its Rules of Procedure.

4. An observer from the EIB shall take part in the Committee's proceedings with regard to questions concerning the EIB.

## Article 23
### Report

The Commission shall examine progress achieved in implementing the measures undertaken pursuant to this Regulation and shall submit to the European Parliament and the Council an annual report on the implementation of the assistance. The report shall also be addressed to the European Economic and Social Committee and the Committee of the Regions. The report shall contain information relating to the previous year on the measures financed and information on the results of monitoring and evaluation exercises and the implementation of budget commitments and payments, broken down by country, region and cooperation sector.

## Article 24
### Financial envelope

The financial envelope for implementation of this Regulation over the period 2007 to 2013 is EUR 2,062,000,000. Annual appropriations shall be authorised by the budgetary authority within the limits of the financial framework.

In the period 2007 to 2013:

(a) no more than 7 percentage points of the financial envelope shall be allocated to measures falling under Article 4(1);

(b) no more than 15 percentage points of the financial envelope shall be allocated to measures falling under Article 4(2);

(c) no more than 5 percentage points of the financial envelope shall be allocated to measures falling under Article 4(3).

## Article 25
### Review

The Commission shall submit to the European Parliament and the Council, by 31 December 2010, a report evaluating the implementation of this Regulation in the first three years, if appropriate with a proposal introducing the modifications to the Regulation.

## Article 26
### Repeal

1. As of 1 January 2007 the following Regulations are repealed:

   — Regulation (EC) No 2130/2001 of the European Parliament and of the Council of 29 October 2001 on operations to aid uprooted people in Asian and Latin American developing countries[10],

- Council Regulation (EC) No 1725/2001 of 23 July 2001 concerning action against anti-personnel landmines in third countries other than developing countries[11],

- Regulation (EC) No 1724/2001 of the European Parliament and of the Council of 23 July 2001 concerning action against anti-personnel landmines in developing countries[12],

- Council Regulation (EC) No 381/2001 of 26 February 2001 creating a rapid-reaction mechanism[13],

- Council Regulation (EC) No 1080/2000 of 22 May 2000 on support for the United Nations Interim Mission in Kosovo (UNMIK) and the Office of the High Representative in Bosnia and Herzegovina (OHR)[14], with the exception of Article 1a of that Regulation,

- Council Regulation (EC) No 2046/97 of 13 October 1997 on north-south cooperation in the campaign against drugs and drug addiction[15],

- Council Regulation (EC) No 2258/96 of 22 November 1996 on rehabilitation and reconstruction operations in developing countries[16].

2. The repealed Regulations shall continue to apply for legal acts and commitments implementing the budget years preceding 2007.

## Article 27
### Entry into force

This Regulation shall enter into force on the 20th day following that of its publication in the Official Journal of the European Union.

It shall apply from 1 January 2007 to 31 December 2013.

This Regulation shall be binding in its entirety and directly applicable in all Member States.

Done at Strasbourg, 15 November 2006.

For the European Parliament
*The President*
**J. Borrell Fontelles**

For the Council
*The President*
**P. Lehtomäki**

10 OJ L 287, 31.10.2001, p. 3.
11 OJ L 234, 1.9.2001, p. 6.
12 OJ L 234, 1.9. 2001, p. 1.
13 OJ L 57, 27.2. 2001, p. 5.
15 OJ L 122, 24.5.2000, p. 27.
16 OJ L 287, 21.10. 1997, p. 1.

European Commission

**From early warning to early action?**
**The debate on EU's crisis response continue**

Luxembourg: Office for Official Publications of the European Communities, 2008

2008 — 497 pp. — 29.7 x 21 cm

ISBN 978-92-79-07028-0